Facing the Other

VERITAS

Series Introduction

". . . the truth will set you free." (John 8:32)

In much contemporary discourse, Pilate's question has been taken to mark the absolute boundary of human thought. Beyond this boundary, it is often suggested, is an intellectual hinterland into which we must not venture. This terrain is an agnosticism of thought: because truth cannot be possessed, it must not be spoken. Thus, it is argued that the defenders of "truth" in our day are often traffickers in ideology, merchants of counterfeits, or anti-liberal. They are, because it is somewhat taken for granted that Nietzsche's word is final: truth is the domain of tyranny.

Is this indeed the case, or might another vision of truth offer itself? The ancient Greeks named the love of wisdom as *philia*, or friendship. The one who would become wise, they argued, would be a "friend of truth." For both philosophy and theology might be conceived as schools in the friendship of truth, as a kind of relation. For like friendship, truth is as much discovered as it is made. If truth is then so elusive, if its domain is *terra incognita*, perhaps this is because it arrives to us—unannounced—as gift, as a person, and not some thing.

The aim of the Veritas book series is to publish incisive and original current scholarly work that inhabits "the between" and "the beyond" of theology and philosophy. These volumes will all share a common aspiration to transcend the institutional divorce in which these two disciplines often find themselves, and to engage questions of pressing concern to both philosophers and theologians in such a way as to reinvigorate both disciples with a kind of interdisciplinary desire, often so absent in contemporary academe. In a word, these volumes represent collective efforts in the befriending of truth, doing so beyond the simulacra of pretend tolerance, the violent, yet insipid reasoning of liberalism that asks with Pilate, "What is truth?"—expecting a consensus of non-commitment; one that encourages the commodification of the mind, now sedated by the civil service of career, ministered by the frightened patrons of position.

The series will therefore consist of two "wings": (1) original monographs; and (2) essay collections on a range of topics in theology and philosophy. The latter will principally by the products of the annual conferences of the Centre of Theology and Philosophy (www.theologyphilosophycentre.co.uk).

Conor Cunningham
Eric Austin Lee
Series editors

Facing the Other

John Paul II, Levinas, and the Body

NIGEL ZIMMERMANN

Foreword by
BRICE DE MALHERBE

CASCADE *Books* · Eugene, Oregon

FACING THE OTHER
John Paul II, Levinas, and the Body

Veritas Series 13

Cascade Books
An Imprint of Wipf and Stock Publishers
199 W. 8th Ave., Suite 3
Eugene, OR 97401

www.wipfandstock.com

ISBN 13: 978-1-62564-402-2

Cataloguing-in-Publication Data

Zimmermann, Nigel.

Facing the other : John Paul II, Levinas, and the Body / Nigel Zimmermann
Veritas 13

xvi + 346 p. ; 23 cm. Includes bibliographical references and indexes.

ISBN 13: 978-1-62564-402-2

1. John Paul II, Pope, 1920–2005. 2. Lévinas, Emmanuel. 3. Human body—Religious aspects—Christianity. 4. Human body—Religious aspects—Judaism. I. Series. II. Title.

BX1795.B63 Z56 2015

Manufactured in the U.S.A.   07/24/2015

In memory of Jason Wardley and Michael Purcell

Contents

Foreword

"SHOULD SOMETHING BE REMEMBERED about John Paul II three hundred years from now, it will surely be his anthropology and theology of the body." These were Angelo Scola's words when he taught us in the early nineties at the Pontifical John Paul II Institute for Studies on Marriage and Family in the Lateran University in Rome. The then-bishop of Grossetto, Tuscany (at present Cardinal Archbishop of Milan) spoke in his capacity as a thorough investigator of past and contemporary global culture, following in the steps of Don Luigi Giussani's eagerness to establish a solid dialogue between faith and culture. Both for the latter, founder of *Communione e Liberazione,* and for his disciple, it was clear that a Christian had to confront the manifold expression of human culture as though it was an echoing of the sometimes-unconscious struggle of the human soul with, and thirst for, the mystery of Christ. What was and still is at stake is the authentic self-development of each person within the human community. The risk being for each one or for each society to tread an estranged route leading to violence and even autodestruction, as it had done more than once in the past. The Christian's renewed mission is ever to open minds and hearts to the light that Christ brings, not only concerning humanity's salvation in the world to come, but already guiding us in our search for happiness, love, and peace in the present world.

Central to man's quest for fulfillment is to apprehend his own identity: who he is and how he deals with his relationship to God, to the world, to his fellow men. In the Western world, since the Renaissance, the general tendency has been to try and enhance man's capacities by strengthening his power over nature and enlarging the field of his freedom to the detriment of any kind of social authority and of God's effective presence. This indeed has led to an impressive development of technology and to some political achievements that are potentially beneficial in the long run to many individuals. Alas, it did not prevent—indeed, it rather fostered by its oblivion of

God's wisdom—the spread of different political tyrannies, the indifference to ecological equilibrium, and the excesses of economic systems centered on the success of a happy few.

Having endured the disasters of two tyrannies—that of Stalin and, after that, of Hitler—and because of his Polish origin, considering Poland's historical struggles many a time in history to preserve its culture and its very existence, Karol Wojtyla was well prepared through the sufferings entailed in this "novitiate" to guide his fellow men in the quest for a renewed humanism. In his second encyclical, Saint Jean Paul II revealed his frame of mind as a philosopher. He writes in the opening paragraph of *Dives in Misericordia*, his encyclical written in 1980 on the Almighty Father:

> While the various currents of human thought both in the past and at the present still tend to separate theocentrism and anthropocentrism, and even to set them in opposition to each other, the Church, following Christ, seeks to link them up in human history in a deep and organic way. And this is also one of the basic principles, perhaps the most important one, of the teaching of the last Council.[1]

To link theocentrism and anthropocentrism, then, because the relationship between God and man is a covenant of love and not a permanent negotiation between rivals. And here is where the reflection on the human body becomes fully pertinent. For human flesh concretely bears witness to creation as the first covenant. Otherwise it is purely matter, freely disposed of by man's intelligence and directed toward the benefit of his welfare projects.

The seventeenth-century philosophers invented a connection to the body that bore the imperative of a new relationship to God. The heirs to Bacon and Descartes end up by rooting reality in blind matter of which thought is only but an effect. The body is just an automaton inhabited by a pure mind. God does not exist and faith is the lie of the powerful to justify political oppression.[2] The philosophical response to these theories will come more than two centuries later when phenomenology rehabilitated the body as a crucial element of lived experience and therefore as a condition to any rational process. It is no surprise, then, to see Wojtyla, a reader of Max Scheler, reflecting on the meaning of the human body in order to approach a better perception of the mystery of the human person. He does so by "following Christ," which means that the philosophical effort to express the person's unity, body and soul, is enlightened by faith in the incarnation

---

1. John Paul II, *Dives in Misericordia*, 3.
2. For a thorough investigation see Villemot, *Dieu et la chair au 17ème siècle*.

of the Word: a mystery that indeed seals the reconciliation between God and man.

But it is not only Wojtyla's faith that stimulates his rational research: his entry into phenomenology, welcomed not as a discredit, but rather as a complement to the Aristotelian-Thomistic tradition, helped him to develop an original theological anthropology that, as Scola put it, will still forever reshape the church's theological and pastoral work and hopefully influence the way in which the person is thought of and treated. In so doing, Wojtyla-John Paul II revives a patristic trend. Thomas Aquinas, following Augustine, barely includes the body in the *imago Dei*, as the trace (*vestigium*) of God's image in the human soul.[3] But Tertullian—in some of his writings at least—and Irenaeus, on the contrary, were very affirmative about the body's participation in the *imago Dei* and in humanity's path to salvation.

In *Dives in Misericordia*, quoted above, Saint John Paul II recalls the role of the Second Vatican Council in the reconciliation between theocentrism and anthropocentrism. This council was certainly a landmark in Wojtyla's intellectual quest and spiritual experience. He himself played an important part in the elaboration of the pastoral constitution *Gaudium et Spes* in which a theological anthropology is developed from the mystery of the incarnate Word. The key phrase of the constitution is undoubtedly that which is often quoted by John Paul II himself: "Christ, the final Adam, by the revelation of the mystery of the Father and His love, fully reveals man to man himself and makes his supreme calling clear" (*GS* no. 22). From this starting point, the constitution develops a reflection on man as an individual and as a member of society, where marriage and family are fundamental in helping each one to grow and fulfill themselves within a *communio personarum*. Working on *Gaudium et Spes* surely gave Bishop Wojtyla the opportunity to confirm a solid christological and Trinitarian grounding in which he could develop his theology of the body, implemented thanks to his personal reflections and experience in counseling young students of both sexes and married couples. Thus, the meditation he began with *Love and Responsibility* and *The Jeweler's Shop* continues and flourishes, notably in the great catechesis he developed from 1979 to 1984.

To enable both theologians and philosophers, and more largely anyone wishing to scrutinize the mystery of the human person's nature and destiny, to draw great benefit from Karol Wojtyla–John Paul II's invaluable contribution, Nigel Zimmermann has chosen to prolong the dialogue the Polish philosopher and pope established with Emmanuel Levinas. It is a judicious choice. Both thinkers have endured the disastrous consequences

3. Cf. Aquinas, *S.T.*, Ia, Q. 93.

of ideological madness, both are inscribed in the inheritance of Edmund Husserl, both have rooted their philosophical work within the context of a religious experience lasting throughout a lifetime, both had a deep knowledge of their respective work and shared a mutual esteem. Both, insists Zimmermann, have something to bring to so-called "postmodernity" in their insistence—although with real differences—on the humble respect one should always adopt while "facing the other." For the other is a mystery, the clue of which is hidden in God's heart, albeit this mystery is embedded in a body—or is it just a face?—through which he becomes manifest to us. In postmodernism, the body tends to become idol or object, never an icon, for God is forgotten. For Levinas, and more convincingly so for Wojtyla, the body is a sense-bearer, although in different ways.

Levinas stresses the absolute ethical value born by the presence of the face of the other. Yet, impressed with Heidegger's watchfulness against any conceptual trapping of "being" and situated in a religious tradition emphasizing God's transcendence, he brings this radical ethical call almost to wall up the other in his irreducible otherness. Wojtyla, still welcoming Aquinas' realism and worshipping an incarnate God, reads the body in its sexual difference as an appeal to live all relationships in view of building a *communio personarum* through a form of nuptial mystery. Each individual's existence is structurally oriented towards the other.

Both Wojtyla and Levinas view self-giving as the ethical dynamism that is the foundation of a truly human society, and this begins with the way man and woman live their sexual relationship, mirrored in the erotic dimension of any human relationship. Nevertheless Zimmermann is quite convincing in showing the greater coherence of Wojtyla's teaching. What he calls Levinas' constant "hesitation before incarnate presence" makes it difficult for the Jewish philosopher to fully express and reflect on human experience. Therefore, his ethical claim seems weakened. As Zimmermann writes: "Has anyone truly loved another to the point of sacrifice for the sake of that person's *otherness* alone?" But this again is both a religious and a philosophical question. Must one read the opening of John's gospel in order to fully understand the opening of Genesis? To what extent can the body be apprehended as the person's epiphany?

In this very well-documented publication Nigel Zimmermann has rooted the dialogue between Levinas and Wojtyla in the experience of both authors and in the philosophical and theological dynamics, ancient or modern, nourishing their own thinking. Closely following the main writings of each and advancing with great ease through the unfolding of their thoughts, he puts forward their respective logic with clarity and renders them available to an attentive reader. Thanks to an impressive layout of the secondary literature, whether it be critical or laudatory of the authors analyzed, their intellectual stand is constantly challenged and appears all the more stimulating, although the limits thereof are clearly stated. Special attention is given to the sacramental economy and its repercussion on consideration of the human body. Further developments are suggested, especially through exploring Jean-Luc Marion's work on *eros*. There is no doubt that this work is an important contribution to philosophical and theological research, helping each reader to positively reconsider his way of relating to "the holiness of the other" in his embodied otherness.

Brice de Malherbe
Ordinary Professor, Faculté Notre-Dame, Paris
Co-Director, Department of Research in Bioethics,
Collège des Bernardins, Paris
Consultant to the Pontifical Council for the Family

Acknowledgments

Ad majorem Dei gloriam.

I AM GRATEFUL FOR the wisdom shared by various scholars during the course of writing this book, especially Mike Purcell, Fergus Kerr, Werner Jeanrond, Oliver O'Donovan, and Tracey Rowland.

With gratitude I acknowledge the encouragement of Conor Cunningham to contribute to this book series, and to Robin Parry and his colleagues at Wipf & Stock.

Of friends who warmly benefited this project with their support, I chiefly thank Jason Wardley: charitable, learned, wonderfully eccentric, and immutably loyal, whose sage council continues in perpetuity.

I am indebted to friends and colleagues in the University of Notre Dame Australia, the University of Edinburgh, and various learned societies.

Along the way, Katrin and Hamood, Josh Kaiser, Becky Kaiser, Ian Clausen, Joe Rivera, Byron Smith, Scotty Manor, Richard Davis, Matt Arbo, Ryan Gladwin, Crystal Lubinsky, Simon Podmore, Matthew Tan, Joel Hodge, and Peter Comensoli each contributed friendship that was more crucial than they might realize. *Merci mille fois.*

In the midst of writing, I am constantly recalled by my children to that which is wondrous and mysterious, producing more sleeplessness and more joy than I anticipate. These imperfect words honor the gift of Dominic, Timothy, Perpetua, Alexander, and Matthew.

My heartfelt thanks to Christine: thank you for keeping faith.

Introduction

Therefore I tell you, do not worry about your life, what you will eat or drink; or about your body, what you will wear. Is not life more than food, and the body more than clothes?

Matt 6:25[1]

Arguing for the theological significance of the body

THIS BOOK ADDS TO a litany of works in recent years that argue for a theological significance of the body. It shares the sentiment of Matthew's gospel that the theological meaning of the body exceeds outer apparel, even the language used to describe it or the metaphors with which it is dressed. It is indeed "more than clothes." However, this book resists the temptation to merely propose a carnivalesque or reductionist postmodern account of the human person in which goodness and truth are tied to the pleasures of the body. Rather, the approaches of two notable twentieth-century thinkers are teased out and considered carefully; one a Roman Catholic philosopher and theologian and the other a Jewish philosopher and Talmudic commentator. Something altogether more radical, and paradoxically more traditional, is proffered in the work of these scholars, although their differences are profoundly important. For Karol Wojtyla (Pope John Paul II, 1920–2005) and Emmanuel Levinas (1906–95), the body offers a signification—a language—that concerns questions of anthropology and of God. With Wojtyla's canonization in the Roman Catholic calendar (now commonly known as St. John Paul II), Catholics will be interested to explore the various conversations he conducted with those of other traditions. It will be established that a dialogue had already begun between Wojtyla and Levinas

1. Unless stated otherwise, Scripture references in this book are taken from the English Standard Version (ESV).

1

that has been overlooked in secondary literature, but that further work is needed to develop it fruitfully. It will be seen that their common formation in phenomenological method provides a foray into embodied human experience at both intellectual and historical tangential points. Furthermore, their approaches to God and religion shapes their understanding of the body, but with varying results. Indeed, the key points of divergence between their positions will be critically evaluated in the final chapters. Finally, the body shall be understood in light of what is *desired* in the body (including *eros* and sexuality) and what is *given* in the body, thus opening the way for a theology of embodied alterity.

Background to the question

To date, no substantive comparative study of the relationship between Levinas' and Wojtyla's thought has been published. This book makes a contribution to that endeavor, with particular focus on the topic of the body. Wojtyla encouraged philosophers to read Levinas and, as pope, welcomed him to Castel Gandolfo more than once, alongside other scholars.[2] Along with the French philosopher Paul Ricœur, Levinas became friends with Wojtyla. One incident is worth retelling. It is said that Ricœur was meeting with Wojtyla for one of these gatherings at the time of Levinas' wife's death. Upon travelling back to Paris and meeting Levinas, Ricœur recounted to him a message from Wojtyla to pass on to Levinas his "respect and admiration."[3] Even in a state of immediate mourning, Levinas had the presence of mind to comment, "[I]n the end, a Protestant is needed for a Catholic to speak to a Jew." This short story tells something of the human side to a man who was often in the shadows of other public French intellectuals. In struggling with Levinas' writings (to read Levinas is to wrestle with his overbearing perspicacity about the other) his philosophy can appear humorless and lacking a sense of joy. Its austere focus was for some a turn-off, but for others, such as Ricœur, Jacques Derrida, and Jean-Paul Sartre, a significant contribution that cannot be overlooked. Levinas' radical appropriation of post-Husserlian phenomenology owes much to German and French antecedents, but also relies on insights from his Talmudic tradition. Nevertheless, his thought has not gained a wide theological reception. This might be changing, but theologians have been hesitant to receive his emphasis upon the other.

---

2. Weigel, *Witness to Hope: The Biography of Pope John Paul II*, 466–67.

3. This story is recounted by Ricœur in an interview with Levinas' biographer Salomon Malka. See Malka, *Emmanuel Levinas: His Life and Legacy*, 193–94.

Indeed, an uncritical reception of Levinas would be foolish, but a measure of careful reading provides profound insight into the incarnate reality of ethical living, upon which Levinas' philosophy insists. Wojtyla noticed this and refers to Levinas three times in an interview he published as Bishop of Rome, *Crossing the Threshold of Hope*.[4] Wojtyla encouraged others to read Levinas and his name is mentioned with solemn esteem in contexts such as Wojtyla's first visit to Paris at a delegation of French Jewish intellectuals or during his first visit to the United States of America, when referring to the importance of contemporary Jewish thinkers.[5] For his part, Levinas published early thoughts on Wojtyla's philosophy after his papal election and concurrent threads of interest united the two men for the rest of their lives. Both were concerned with relating any notion of the divine and ethics to the embodied human subject, whose face is both a revelation and concealment. The face is a common, and yet rarely commented upon reference point between Wojtyla and Levinas. Upon reading George Weigel's biography of John Paul II, James Schall comments:

> The pope often spoke of the "face" of Christ, of the face as a philosophical insight. Weigel is amused that Wojtyla may be the only man in the world who read for pleasure the French philosopher, Emmanuel Levinas, whose philosophy is based on the human face.[6]

This indicates the complexity of Levinas' writings; they are neither whimsical nor straightforward. There is no doubt that his texts are an example of that French phenomenological approach, which is both dense and subtle, rich in nuance, and which issues a demand upon its readers.[7] Jokes about Wojtyla's own writing have also abounded. It was said among his clergy in the Archdiocese of Kraków that purgatory would consist of having to read Wojtyla's central phenomenological text, *The Acting Person*.[8] There also is a book that is long and demanding. But in this and other texts, there is present a phenomenological interest in the revelatory nature of the

---

4. See John Paul II, *Crossing the Threshold of Hope*, 35, 36, 210–11.

5. John Paul II, "Address of John Paul II to the Representatives of Jewish Organizations," *Apostolic Journey to the United States of American and Canada*.

6. Schall, "The Greatest of Men."

7. Derrida likens reading Levinas' *Totality and Infinity* to the ocean waves: "It proceeds with the infinite insistence of waves on a beach: return and repetition, always, of the same wave against the same shore, in which, however, as each return recapitulates itself, it also infinitely renews and enriches itself. Because of all these challenges to the commentator and the critic, *Totality and Infinity* is a work of art and not a treatise." From footnote 7, chapter 4, "Violence and Metaphysics," in *Writing and Difference*, 398.

8. Williams, *The Mind of John Paul II*, 196.

human that shares much with Levinas. The face is a central motif in both Wojtyla and Levinas' major works.

The emphasis upon the face in Wojtyla's thought is subtle, but even for a thinker who produced more writings than any other pope in history, he did not make reference to such a theme without an attentive sense of its importance and its hermeneutical value in proclaiming the gospel. Furthermore, the papacy of John Paul II was deeply invested in healing old wounds, especially those between Christians and Jews. For Wojtyla, Levinas was a Jewish thinker who spoke both from *beyond* Christianity, and yet profoundly *to* Christianity, for his thought flowed creatively from within the Hebrew and Talmudic tradition.

Yet Wojtyla is also a controversial figure; a Polish priest, poet, actor, playwright, and philosopher who not only lived, thought, and prayed more publicly than perhaps anyone else in his century, but who died in a profoundly public manner. His elevation to the episcopate, the College of Cardinals, and finally the papacy surprised the world and his church, and with such an extended service at the Barque of Peter, his contribution will have a long-lasting effect upon the Christian world. He has both unwavering supporters and campaigning adversaries, even years after his death. In a life of public service his thought is already of historic interest, and his canonization is not uncontested amongst some Christians. Yet it remains true that his intellectual project, especially as wrought in an early interest in Thomistic metaphysics, Husserlian phenomenology, and mysticism, remains open to new discoveries. Critical attention is needed, especially in those areas of his thought—theological and philosophical—that seem to develop Christian thought in new ways.

This is acutely true of the "theology of the body," which has its detractors and disciples.[9] It was originally produced as a book-length manuscript and was unpublished at the time of Wojtyla's papal election, but was edited and presented in the form of weekly catechesis for the next five years and after some years translated into English directly from the original manuscripts. In a sense, it has not made more than a superficial impression on much of the Catholic world. One commentator, John Cornwell, describes it as lacking in influence: "[t]his work, which constitutes, in the view of some keen papal supporters, John Paul's vital legacy to the world, has been

---

9. All references to this text will be cited first as the numbered presentation in general audience (for example "40") and second its section number within that presentation (for example "1"), hence a reference to the first part of the fortieth general audience presentation on the body is rendered "40:1." See John Paul II, *Man and Woman He Created Them*.

perhaps his least influential."[10] Nevertheless, the ingenuity of Wojtyla's positive appreciation of the human body in describing God's presence is to be welcomed and is worthy of critical attention. Such attention cannot be achieved without consideration of the postmodern context in which it is relevant. The manifestation of the body in attesting to truths of the incarnation has resonances with postmodern thought.

Equally, the influence of Emmanuel Levinas on the complex thought of Wojtyla deserves further critical attention. According to Adriaan Peperzak:

> The pope read him, and I suspect that he probably took him to be the best Jewish thinker. I cannot prove this, and undoubtedly he met with other Jews. But knowing a bit of what the pope wrote, there is no doubt to my mind that Levinas was, for him, the model of a great Jewish thinker.[11]

Wojtyla was indeed familiar with Levinas' thought and influenced by him. Further to their dialogue, the place of the body in their thought will be considered, especially in terms of theological anthropology. Wojtyla's theology of the body places it at a pivotal point both in human experience as well as revelation. Levinas' approach is, however, less equivocal: he denies an incarnational avatar in describing the human person. He insists on an infinite responsibility for the other but lacks a clear commitment to the body in its fullness. This is made problematic in that his use of metaphor and ethical appeal is bound always to language that is theological and embodied.

The place of the body in Wojtyla and Levinas' thought remains an understudied site of interest, especially as it might further develop theological anthropology and dialogue with postmodern thought.

Communio and altérité

In facing each other's work, the approaches given by Wojtyla and Levinas to the body might be described as *communio* and *altérité*, which summarize the primary modes of ethical sociality proffered by each thinker. *Communio* is the Latin derivation of the Greek *koinonia* and refers to the spiritual fellowship shared by Christians. It denotes the unity of difference within the body of Christ and emphasizes love rather than a hierarchical, legal, or formal unity, finding its bearings within the nascent church described in the New Testament. That is, it does not exclude hierarchy or a canonical framework, but situates these things in their correct proportion. On the

10. Cornwell, *The Pontiff in Winter*, 139.

11. Malka, *Emmanuel Levinas*, 209.

other hand, *altérité* is the French term (from the Latin *alter*, meaning the other of two) common to postmodern writers and of central importance in Levinas' philosophy. Its meaning is found in the simple concept of that which is other, or rendered in Levinas primarily as *the* other. Its English equivalent, which will be used hereafter, is alterity. For Wojtyla and Levinas, their philosophy considers the question of the other and of difference in a conflicted and post-Holocaust world. They are not only concerned with the question of otherness, but with alterity as a designation of the otherness of the particular other person, or indeed of the second or third person and of the alternative subject in intersubjectivity. Appraising Wojtyla in terms of *communio* and Levinas in terms of alterity provides an appropriate lens through which to interpret their work and their dialogue.

For Wojtyla, the ultimate objective of the body and embodied person-hood is *communio* in the life of the church and with God. For Levinas, it is in an ethical responsibility that flows nonreciprocally from the experience of alterity. It is for this reason that the human person might be seen as a subject who uniquely exists between the two objectives, critically subvert-ing impositions from without and ethically seeking after the sacramental relationship of the divine Other within. *Communio* is always the lived com-munion of persons, the concrete complexity of intersubjectivity. It means more than a community or a society or even a family, for it relies on what Wojtyla calls the "personalistic norm," in which persons recognize in their human counterparts an irreducible value; one that cannot be taken from them and that affirms their essential freedom to act.[12] Moreover, it relies on the notion that it is Christ who holds the communion of disciples together in the fellowship of his body. *Communio* is therefore a subversive concept, because it counters any cultural imposition that is caught up in the logic of violence, whether it be ideological, political, statist, or even ecclesiastical. This is important, because the ecclesiology of the Second Vatican Council embraced a commitment to *communio* as a principle of the church's unity.[13] It finds its origin and its logic within the Trinity, whose tripersonal com-munion is the preeminent order of self-giving love. For Wojtyla, *communio* is both personal and interpersonal because of its Christian meaning:

12. Wojtyla provides a definition of the "personalistic norm" in these terms, espe-cially the "affirmation of the value of the person," in John Paul II, *Love and Responsibil-ity*, 121–25.

13. The term "*communion*" does not feature extensively in the Council's documents as such, however the theme of communion is strengthened repeatedly. This is noted in the 1985 report of that year's extraordinary synod of bishops from around the world: "The ecclesiology of communion is the central and fundamental idea of the Council's documents." See Catholic Church, *The Final Report of the 1985 Extraordinary Synod*, 2.C.I.

> For Christians in general, the concept of *communio* itself has a primarily *religious and sacral meaning, one connected with the Eucharist*, which is a *sacramentum communionis* between Christ and his disciples—between God and human beings.[14]

It is here argued that Wojtyla's use of *communio* to describe human relationships is his ethical answer to the problem of alterity. Furthermore, his notion of the nuptial mystery serves as his principle paradigm of alterity. As a philosopher whose early interest was in the work of Husserl's student, Max Scheler, and whose doctoral research in theology was on St. John of the Cross, Wojtyla understood the many possible ways of dealing with the challenge of otherness, especially human otherness. His phenomenology was shaped by Husserl's early works, so its methodology conforms to Husserl's phenomenological structure in the *Logical Investigations*, rather than Husserl's later transcendental turn. Wojtyla's priestly years, like his intellectual interests, were constantly attuned to the pastoral dimensions of the various social contexts he was involved in. Under Communist surveillance, the Polish church was undergoing its own dark night of the soul, and Wojtyla wished to minister meaningfully to the young men and women he encountered. Like countless other young pastors, he discovered both the richness of spiritual life present in these young adults, as well as the restless anxiety of a thousand questions concerning social ethics, sexuality, politics, and the body. Relationships were dynamic and emotionally complex and a lingering Manichean tendency throughout much of the church was an obstacle to understanding themselves in the context of the beauty, coherence, and the giftedness of their own human bodies. A tendency in Catholic life to denigrate or undervalue the body was an obstacle to many. Wojtyla could not respond openly on the university campus, so he took his students for walks in one of Wojtyla's favorite destinations, the mountains. There, he could speak openly with these other embodied creatures, without condemnation and with openness to the other. This is the pastoral background to what, years later, would become his theology of the body, originally as a book-length manuscript and then, interrupted by his papal election, via his weekly public catechesis. Wojtyla's early formation in the incarnate moments of face-to-face encounters with the other, and his desire to affirm the gifts of sexuality, marriage, and the body without recourse to the church's historic failings in these regards, found a general pulpit from 1978 onwards. The structure of *communio* between two spouses became Wojtyla's response to the problem of alterity.

---

14. "The Family as a Community of Persons," in John Paul II, *Person and Community*, 320.

Adventurously, Levinas comments that the "bare fact of life is never bare."[15] In the appearing of the other's body, meaning and significance are not naked to one's perception, but must be sought out within what nourishes the body's presence and existence. It is the same with embodied relationships. In Wojtyla's account of the nuptial encounter, two persons are never laid bare in all their signification, although they may offer themselves without actively hiding aspects of themselves. Why is it that after sixty years of marriage two people might still have something new to say to each other? Even after such a length of time—as habits intertwine and sentences are mutually completed, as memories of one become the memories of two, and as the lives of two ever more show themselves publicly as one—there remains something new to be said, some surprise in the appearance of the other. Indeed, the other *remains* the other. Yet, while Wojtyla takes up this mystery and gives his answer in *communio*, the embodied other is problematical for Levinas. For him, no name or category or imposition can be placed upon the other. The other is located at a point of infinite distance from one's own intentionality and may not be enfolded within one's own desires, categories, or impositions. His or her welfare is one's own responsibility and the self is responsible for everyone, all of the time. In this way, the suffering of the other becomes one's own suffering, and in the gleam of the face the measure of glory reveals the immensity of an ethical and nonreciprocal correlation to the other's presence. In Levinas' thought, there remains a disparity between absolute alterity and his account of the body.

On the one hand, the other has no incarnate avatar, for the self has no authority to determine the other. Describing the particular features of one body in opposition to any other body is too prescriptive, determining the other's body in what Levinas calls "the same."[16] This is a difficult *lacuna* in Levinas.

On the other hand, Levinas' language relentlessly recourses to the language of the body; of the face, flesh, blood, tears, heart, hunger, and thirst. His examples of ethical intersubjectivity, such as the tearing of bread from one's mouth to give to the hungry face of the other, concern almost nothing but the body (although, it has to be said, concrete examples are rare in Levinas). This is the problem of alterity in Levinas: his insistence on its absolute infinity limits it from the possibilities of incarnation and embodiment.

---

15. Levinas, *Totality and Infinity*, 112.
16. Ibid., 289.

Names and titles

This book follows standard English writing practice regarding the names of the two chief interlocutors, Wojtyla and Levinas. For both of them, historical circumstances have some bearing upon the meaning of their names.

Karol Józef Wojtyła

Wojtyla was born on May 18th, 1920 in the town of Wadowice, during the Second Polish Republic, at a time when Russian military forces were again engaged in war with Poland. Wojtyla was baptized on June 20th with the names of Karol (Anglicized "Charles"), after Emperor Charles of Austria (whose army Wojtyla's father had served in) and Józef, after the dominating figure of Marshal Józef Piłsudski, who led the Polish Republic.[17] Within two months of his birth, during August 16th–17th, the Red Army invasion of Europe came to an end in what the Polish people came to call the "Miracle on the Vistula," a decisive battle, but not one remembered as a major victory for much of continental Europe.[18] In the face of every expectation to the contrary, and with the diplomatic corps having fled Warsaw (with the exception of the papal representative, Archbishop Achille Ratti), Polish forces issued a surprise attack on the Red Cavalry of General Semën Budën-nyi, successfully turning the Trótsky army away from its Western European objectives. Through these events, Wojtyla's name is forever associated with Polish national identity and its complex Christian, political, and military history. During his early years, Wojtyla used occasional pseudonyms, which are referred to later in this book. Upon his papal election on October 16th 1978, Wojtyla took the title Ioannes Paulus PP. II, the same combined name of his immediate predecessor and in continuity with John XXIII (convenor of the Second Vatican Council) and Paul VI (whose papacy saw the completion of the Council). When Wojtyla took the name John Paul II it became customary to rebrand all his previous publications as authored by John Paul II rather than his baptismal name. In this book, publications are therefore all listed under John Paul II. However, because these texts were written over the course of a lifetime that spans both prepapal and papal time periods, it is appropriate to refer to writings generally as written by, or according to the thought of, Wojtyla. Where specific works were first published after his papal election, authorship will be referred to as John Paul II. Occasional references will be made to Wojtyla/John Paul II, for the sake of emphasizing

17. Emperor Charles of Austria was beatified by John Paul II on 3rd October 2004.
18. Weigel, *Witness to Hope*, 2.

both aspects of his authorship. The standard nonuse of Polish accents in English scholarly works is adhered to.

Emanuelis Levinas

Levinas was born on December 30th, 1905 according to the Julian calendar, which was in use by the Russian Empire at that time (January 12th, 1906 according to the Gregorian calendar) in Kaunas, Lithuania.[19] The city is situated at the meeting of the Neman and Neris rivers at the border of Latvia and Russia, intersecting at the extreme occident and the beginning of the orient, and as biographer Salomon Malka observes, it lies under the shadow of Vilna, once known as the "Jerusalem of the East."[20] Part of a practicing Jewish family and educated early in Hebrew and the Torah, Levinas was raised in a context that experienced German National Socialism and Soviet Communism. Following his adoption of French citizenship and culture, he altered the spelling of his name in accordance with French orthography to "Emmanuel." While his surname was commonly published according to the French "Lévinas," it is standard practice in English texts to use the Anglicized Levinas, which will be used here.

A note on sources: Wojtyla and Levinas

Primary sources in Wojtyla

The primary text for Wojtyla's theology of the body is the collection of his catechesis on the subject, *Man and Woman He Created Them*.[21] The English translation published in 2006 is the first direct translation in any language of the original Polish documents. His reflections on Levinas in *Crossing the Threshold of Hope* and *Memory and Identity* are also relevant.[22] These works were simultaneously published in multiple languages, including English, although it is assumed by biographers that the original texts were handwritten in Polish. Wojtyla's early philosophical works, *Love and Responsibility*, *The Acting Person*, and his essays in *Person and Community* are of direct relevance to his phenomenological analysis of the person in the

---

19. Levinas' hometown of Kaunus (called Kovno at his birth) is approximately 466 miles (750km) from Wojtyla's home town of Wadowice.

20. Malka, *Emmanuel Levinas*, 3.

21. John Paul II, *Man and Woman He Created Them*.

22. John Paul II, *Crossing the Threshold of Hope*; John Paul II, *Memory and Identity*.

field of action.[23] His sermons to the papal household, *Sign of Contradiction*, clarify his theology in addition to his Trinitarian and Marian catechesis, *The Trinity's Embrace: God's Saving Plan* and *Redemptoris Mater*.[24] Of his fourteen encyclicals, the following are of most interest to this book, especially for their clarification on matters related to postmodernity, rationality, Thomism, and matters concerning the body: *Redemptor Hominis*, *Veritatis Splendor*, *Evangelium Vitae*, *Fides et Ratio* and *Ecclesia de Eucharistia*.[25] Of course, other documents also have much to say on the topic of the body, but the present focus has been limited to what relates most directly to the *theology* of the body, and not to other moral or philosophical issues Wojtyla elsewhere addresses.[26]

Primary sources in Levinas

Of Levinas' entire published corpus, his two most influential works are *Totality and Infinity* and *Otherwise than Being*.[27] In the first, he outlines his unique contribution to philosophy, a phenomenological interruption of the Western philosophical tradition of being, with new awareness of alterity and of the other. In the second, he extends his project to thinking comprehensively outside the tradition to describe ethics beyond being. The body is a major reference point in both texts and for this reason a focus will remain on them. However, other texts will be referred to as they are relevant, such as interviews, collected philosophical papers, and his Talmudic commentaries, the two most significant having been collected in English translation as *Beyond the Verse* and *In the Time of the Nations*.[28] French editions have been consulted and, where appropriate, French words and phrases will be

---

23. John Paul II, *Love and Responsibility*; John Paul II, *The Acting Person*; John Paul II, *Person and Community*.

24. John Paul II, *Sign of Contradiction*; John Paul II, *The Trinity's Embrace, God's Saving Plan*; John Paul II, *Redemptoris Mater: On the Blessed Virgin Mary in the Life of the Pilgrim Church*.

25. Encyclicals are referenced according to section number rather than page number. See John Paul II, *Redemptor Hominis: The Redeemer of Man*; John Paul II, *Veritatis Splendor: The Splendor of Truth*; John Paul II, *Evangelium Vitae: The Gospel of Life*; John Paul II, *Fides Et Ratio: Encyclical Letter on the Relationship between Faith and Reason*; John Paul II, *Ecclesia De Eucharistia: Encyclical Letter on the Eucharist in Its Relationship to the Church*.

26. To avoid the controversy concerning the English translation of Wojtyla's *Osoba i Czyn*, the French edition has also been consulted. See: John Paul II, *Personne Et Acte*.

27. Levinas, *Totality and Infinity*; Levinas, *Otherwise Than Being*.

28. Levinas, *Beyond the Verse*; Levinas, *In the Time of the Nations*.

included to clarify Levinas' meaning.[29] There are other texts that have been consulted, such as his final lectures at the Sorbonne, *God, Death, and Time*, and works such as *Discovering Existence with Husserl, Existence and Existents*, and *Of God Who Comes to Mind*.[30]

Scripture, the body, and a point of departure in theological anthropology

In the Hebrew Scriptures, the term *bâsâr* is commonly used for what in English is termed "flesh."[31] It is common to see it in reference to the materiality of human bodies, pertaining especially to the skin and the substance of which bodies are made.[32] However, there is no direct and obvious term consistently used for the English word, "body." Instead, *bâsâr* is used in a cluster of other terms to indicate a body. This is apparent in the Old Testament narratives that deal specifically with the distinctions between human bodies that denote relationship and good order, such as the Genesis accounts of creation (see Gen 1:23, in which the man and the woman are one "flesh"). Yet flesh—*bâsâr*—is altered in relation to human choices as the scriptural narrative unfolds. The original goodness of the shape and form of the flesh (see Gen 1:31) declines after the eating of the fruit of the knowledge of good and evil, resulting in dire consequences. In the time of Noah, it is precisely *bâsâr*, and indeed *all* flesh, which God looks upon and finds corrupt (Gen 6:12).[33] The human body in the Old Testament, in relation always to the

---

29. French editions consulted: Levinas, *Théorie De L'intuition Dans La Phénoménologie De Husserl*; Levinas, *De L'existence Ý L'existant*; Levinas, *Totalité Et Infini; Essai Sur L'extériorité*; Levinas, *Difficile Liberté: Essais Sur Le Judaïsme*; Levinas, *Noms Propres: Agnon, Buber, Celan, Delhomme, Derrida, Jabès, Kierkegaard, Lacroix, Laporte, Picard, Proust, Van Breda, Wahl*; Levinas, *Autrement Qu'etre Ou Au-Dela De L'essence*; Levinas, *Le Temps Et L'autre*; Levinas, *Altérité Et Transcendance*.

30. Levinas, *God, Death and Time*; Levinas, *Discovering Existence with Husserl*; Levinas, *Of God Who Comes to Mind*.

31. The term is used in a variety of contexts such as in Job 19:26, translated in English as: "And after my skin has been thus destroyed, yet in my flesh I shall see God." "Flesh" is translated from "*bâsâr*."

32. The body relies on God as the source of holiness and likewise requires the state of holiness before it can be in proximity to God. See Lipka, "Profaning the Body: תרד and the Concept of Loss of Personal Holiness in H," in *Bodies, Embodiment, and Theology of the Hebrew Bible*, 90.

33. For a detailed account of how the biblical development of the terms flesh and body relate to a renewed philosophical account of bodily ethics and metaphysics see Welton, *The Body*. Welton emphasizes the way the Hebrew Scriptures present the body (of flesh) as caught up in life and death struggles in a profoundly moral way, highlighted by the religious and symbolic connotations of the Old Covenant ritual laws.

flesh, is treated as an integrated whole. There is no absolute distinction between body, mind, soul, and spirit. Where there is reference to the life or
spirit (*nephesh*) of the enfleshed person, it remains a reference to the whole
person and not to one aspect of the person.

As Donn Whelton puts it, "[i]n these texts the whole person is constantly in view and the difference between body and soul is treated like two
variations on a single theme."[34] The emphasis in such texts, at least as far as it
pertains to the body, is upon its action in a moral field, with close attention
to the body's choices in difficult circumstances, or its danger and loss against
the horizons of sin and death. To speak of the spirit or the flesh of the body
in this context as if they are somehow markedly distinct does a disservice
to the texts. A *soft* distinction between spirit and body might be spoken of
in the Old Testament, emphasizing as they do the integrated wholeness of
the human person, even in the midst of travail and moral brokenness, but
certainly not a *hard* distinction.[35]

Distinctions become more important in the New Testament, especially
in the Synoptic Gospels, in which an integrated wholeness is still clear, but
with new emphasis upon features such as the heart, the eye, the ear, and the
hand.[36] Inner conflicts become more apparent, such as Jesus' admonition
against hypocrisy (Matt 23:27–28), in which he distinguishes between the
outer self (appearing as "whitewashed tombs") and the inner self ("full of
dead men's bones and all uncleanness"). It is as if through the scrutiny of
Christ's preaching, the brokenness of the human condition becomes clear.
These inner distinctions, which show forth an ontological frailty, are made
apparent in the parables (for example, Matt 6:2–4: "But when you give alms,
do not let your left hand know what your right hand is doing that your alms
may be in secret . . ."). Welton notes the predominance of the Greek term
"soma" [σῶμα] for the body in the Synoptic Gospels, while the term *"sarx"*
[σάρξ] for flesh predominates in John's gospel.[37] Crucially however, human
bodies may find new theological impetus in the resurrected order instigated
in the risen Christ.[38] Janet Martin Soskice has argued for the inseparability

34. Welton, *The Body*, 247.

35. Even Ezekiel, anguished in the valley of the dry bones, highlights the flesh by
its absence. The bones signify death and the decay of the body, which remind us of the
essential goodness of the living body, which is a union of flesh and spirit. Its loss is the
cause of agony and disarray.

36. See, for example, the heart in Matt 5:8; 6:20–22; 12:34; the eye in Mark 12:11;
Luke 19:42; 24:31; the ear in Matt 30:16; Mark 4:9; Luke 22:51; and the hand in Matt
8:15; Mark 5:41; and Luke 5:13.

37. Welton, *The Body*.

38. New vistas of theological thinking have been opened up by the renewal of

of the call to holiness from the resurrected body as the new temple in which Christians dwell. She writes: "The body of the Christian individual, as well as the 'body' of Christians together, is the Temple—the pre-eminent dwelling-place of God with men and women—and this dwelling-place is the body of Christ."[39]

The call to holiness and its relationship to embodied life is a vocational concern. To what extent is the body integral to a divine call to live a holy life? And in what way does the body speak the language of discipleship, of redemption, of love? It is impossible to ask these questions without some reference to further questions of sexuality and gender. For example, Sarah Coakley laments the hesitation in recent thought about the resurrection to probe beneath the normative "generic male" vision of selfhood she identifies on the surface of that thinking.[40] Coakley is seeking out a fuller account of the transformation that occurs interiorly in the human recognition of the risen Christ; that the "spiritual senses" may play a fuller part in the perception of Christ's resurrected body than what is normally accounted for.[41] As Coakley puts it:

> What levels of the self—what affective or intuitive depths, what interpersonal mysteries of human response, what dimensions of bodily existence (themes normally downplayed in "masculinist" philosophical discussion)—are unavoidable in their epistemic implications if the true *richesse* of encounter with the risen Christ chartered in the New Testament is to be grasped?[42]

Such a *richesse* located in the encounter with Christ denotes a role for sexual difference and gender. This is a search for an account of Christ and the human person that accentuates the fullness of embodied life. Another example is that of John Caputo, who believes that the body of philosophical description, even in phenomenology, all too often remains an athletic,

---

vigorous thought concerning the resurrection. Consequences for ethics, inter-religious dialogue, ecumenism, and many others are now being considered and developed. See for example, O'Donovan, *Resurrection and Moral Order*; D'Costa, *Resurrection Reconsidered*; O'Collins, *Easter Faith*; Moltmann, "The Resurrection of Nature: An Aspect of Cosmic Christology"; Schärtl, "Metaphysical Aspects of the Concept of Resurrection"; Scola and McCarthy, "Jesus Christ, Our Resurrection and Life: On the Question of Eschatology."

39. Soskice, "Resurrection and the New Jerusalem," in Davis et al. (eds.), *The Resurrection*.

40. Coakley, "Response" to William P. Alston, "Biblical Criticism and the Resurrection," in Davis et al. (eds.), *The Resurrection*.

41. Ibid.

42. Ibid.

upright, healthy, whole body, one that expresses its agency in the world freely and without reduction to itself.[43] This is problematic, for in the world bodies remain experiences of personal flesh, of suffering in the substance of embodiment. Scholars of the body ought to beware the temptation to bracket out bodies as they are lived, what Caputo calls the "Jewgreek" body who experiences in his flesh disease, blindness, and all the sensuous frailties of incarnate existence.[44] For Caputo, the suffering body is the location of the weakness of flesh. The flesh is "the body's palpable, living, sensuous, feeling stuff, the site of a purely immanent, nonintentional feeling. The suffering is situated in the reduction to flesh."[45] In the body, flesh is the experienced *locus* of intentionality, while maintaining the means by which the body directs itself to others. Yet, the scriptural witness to the body and to Christ's resurrection is already an account of a full-bodied, incarnate anthropology. The sensory anticipation of future glory glimpsed in the present is very much one in which flesh and bodies play a formative role. The vision of the Son of Man in the book of Revelation signifies a certain *gravitas* upon the resurrected body in its commanding glory:

> The hairs of his head were white, like white wool, like snow. His eyes were like a flame of fire, his feet were like burnished bronze, refined in a furnace, and his voice was like the roar of many waters. In his right hand he held seven stars, from his mouth came a sharp two-edged sword, and his face was like the sun shining in full strength. (Rev 1:14–16)

Now, this vision is one in which all the senses are ultimately touched; they each share in a bodily experience of the eschaton. Nevertheless, theological anthropology cannot dwell completely on eschatological visions of the body, for in the current moment bodies are present in their suffering and their torment.

Levinas notes this truth of existence and out of that suffering alterity he develops a philosophy of responsibility that precedes every conscious thought, act, or commitment.[46] The self's binding to others is made manifest in bodily suffering. This manifestation of the other's suffering has been linked by some thinkers to the manifestation of God. For example, Max Scheler, a major influence on Wojtyla, believed that the binding of the self with others is made possible by the prior act of God, rather than upon one's

---

43. Caputo, *Against Ethics*.

44. Ibid., 206–8.

45. Ibid., 206.

46. See for example: Levinas, *Otherwise Than Being*, 138.

own initiative.[47] For him, the fragile responsibility held for others finds its first orientation in God who acts as the primary giver of all embodied experience. In this way, phenomenological accounts of embodied responsibility find some scriptural correlates for the emphasis upon responsible action for the embodied other. The description of a theological basis for an approach to the body finds warrant in Scripture as well as in the phenomenological language taken up by Levinas and Wojtyla.

The excesses of the body

A theology of the body, scripturally informed, would hold in tension an eschatological hope for a full share in the resurrected life as well as an acute sensitivity to contemporary privations in the bodies of others. Because of this incarnate dimension, it is important to consider the body as a *desiring* as well as a *given* enterprise, an erotic and receptive experience received within a logic of the gift. This requires attentiveness to the body in its alterity, both theologically and ethically. In other words, an embodied alterity is required. And rather than looking beyond the body for its deferred meaning, or only within the body for an interior presence, it must be the human person in its somatic whole which is considered. As Levinas puts it, the body "does not express an event; it is itself this event."[48] As an integrated whole, the embodied person is eventful to excess, revealing a givenness of meaning that exceeds the embellishments and descriptive language it is clothed with. This echoes the New Testament text in Matt 6:25, Christ's rhetorical question in the midst of preaching: "is not the body more than clothes?" The suffering body receives and gives, desires and speaks. Wojtyla and Levinas identify this excess and describe a phenomenality of the body open to phenomenology and theology.

---

47. Scheler, *On the Eternal in Man*, 375.

48. Levinas, *Existence and Existents*, 72.

1

John Paul II and Emmanuel Levinas
An Overlooked Dialogue of the Other

Introduction

JOHN PAUL II HAS been declared a saint. With this declaration of extraordinary holiness, the Catholic Church calls for reflection upon the many contributions that John Paul II (Karol Wojtyla) made to various problems of the age in which he lived, which in the case of the twentieth century is a time of much war, blood, and conflict. Of the examples of friendship and dialogue in which Wojtyla engaged, an overlooked discourse is that which he held with Emmanuel Levinas, a Lithuanian-born French-Jewish intellectual. This particular dialogue cannot be understood without reference to religion, phenomenology, and postmodernity. Moreover, key publications reveal the extent of their interest in the mystery of the human person, and their appeal to the philosophy of phenomenology to describe it. This builds an interpretative framework in which their shared concerns relating to the status and significance of the body can be explored. Such a framework opens up to a theological and philosophical discourse concerning fundamental questions about the other and the complex event of facing the other.

Wojtyla and Levinas: The intellectual and historical shape of a dialogue

Religion

Levinas and Christianity

In a 1987 interview, published as "Judaism and Christianity after Franz Rosenzweig," Levinas comments on the relationship between the two faith traditions and upon the trace of the ethical he identifies in the latter.[1] He acknowledges his reservations about the embodied forms of Christianity he discerns in history, from the Crusades to the Holocaust, moments of horror invested all too often with the symbols and language of Christian faith: "The message of the Gospels has been forever compromised for us by history."[2] Despite this, he speaks positively of moments of authentic Christian self-sacrifice. He notes the contradiction between the sins of the baptized at Auschwitz, and the sacrificial service of refuge offered to Jews by clergy during World War II.[3] Levinas' own wife and daughter were spared death (despite later deportation) by the protection of a Christian cloister, for which Levinas expresses gratitude and a painful joy.[4] He comments upon his development of a view, largely taken from Franz Rosenzweig, that in Christianity and Judaism can be found a common measure of the (ethical) *kenosis* of God, as well as the necessity that God demands of his adherents an incarnate servanthood to the weak, hungry, and the oppressed.[5] For Levinas it is a sad reality that political and social structures assumed by Christian Europe lack evidence that the Christ of Christianity has been heard. This remains a point of departure for the Levinasian notion of Christian-Jewish dialogue. It is from history that the great deviances of Christian praxis seem to speak against their own heritage; and yet it is from history that particular persons appear to speak against the universality of this negation. On the one hand, in regards to the patently execrable actions of some Christians: that the inquisition and the Crusades were "bound to the sign of Christ and the Cross . . ."; and yet on the other, in which Christian persons have acted in sacrificial folly and utter self-deprecation and danger, "Secondly, though,

---

1. Levinas, *Is It Righteous to Be?*, 255–67.

2. Ibid., 256.

3. It must be remembered that Levinas deplored being labeled a "Jewish" or "religious" philosopher. He wished, like Paul Ricœur, to simply be a "philosopher." See Malka, *Emmanuel Levinas*, 197.

4. Levinas, *Is It Righteous to Be?*, 257.

5. Ibid., 256.

and this is important—very important—something you call caritas, charité, misericordia appeared to me. If one saw a black cassock, then there was sanctuary."[6] Levinas' complicated relationship with Christianity is made a positive possibility because of this shared charity.

Levinas owes to Rosenzweig the insight that truth might be received in more than one form.[7] This is crucial to the notion that faith and trust might be shared across certain theological distinctions, without abandoning those distinctions.[8] It is in kenosis for the other that Levinas identifies the shared tradition and therefore is able to locate within Christianity an ongoing development of its own practices.[9] In other words, there remains in Christianity something that is peculiarly Jewish. Kenosis refers not only to Christian belief in its objective and abstract forms, but also and especially in the act of "doing."[10] The ritual of religious practice is bound to the *ethos* which is enacted because of what is believed, what Psalm 35 refers to as the rejoicing of the soul followed by the bones crying out to God (9–10).[11] Because of this, for Levinas, to believe is to act "with your whole body!"[12] Yet in the act of doing, he still perceives the requirement of a messianic figure. That is, some form of messianic hope stands over the self as a summons to act. The human person is called outside of itself to act for others. This necessity to act binds Christians and Jews together.[13] Nevertheless, there remains

6. Levinas appears to misidentify the religious habit of religious sisters with the black cassock of the priest, but if anything, his misuse of the exact attire serves the point more profoundly: religious symbology is complex and nonstatic. See Levinas, *Is It Righteous to Be?*, 257.

7. Ibid., 257. In this case, an equivalence is drawn between Christianity and Judaism. Elsewhere, Levinas expresses his debt to Rosenzweig's influence on his thinking concerning positive possibilities in Christianity. See Levinas, "Judaism and Christianity," in *In the Time of the Nations*, 161–66.

8. A major component of this dialogue is the trend to consider the Jewish claim to be the "people of God" as founded on an enduring covenant, rather than having been succeeded by Christianity ("supersessionism"). For a summary of this theological development, see Braybrooke and Bayfield, *Christian-Jewish Dialogue*, 96–112.

9. Levinas highlights the Second Vatican Council's declaration, *Nostra Aetate*, as positive evidence of the attempt to overcome historical errors in *Is It Righteous to Be?*, 257.

10. Levinas, *Is It Righteous to Be?*, 258.

11. Ps 35 (9–10), referenced indirectly in Levinas, *Is It Righteous to Be?*, 258. The idea that theory is opened up by ritual/practice is also present in the Talmudic commentaries. See Levinas, "From Ethics to Exegesis," in *In the Time of the Nations*, 109–13; also Levinas, "On the Jewish Reading of Scriptures," in *Beyond the Verse*, 101–15.

12. Levinas, *Is It Righteous to Be?*, 258.

13. Once again, this carries the influence of Rosenzweig's mystical and anti-Hegelian work of 1921, *Stern der Erlösung* (English: *The Star of Redemption*).

a crucial distinction in this point of departure. Levinas wishes to emphasize the Jewish trace of the messianic without the Christian insistence on Christ. He says:

> I mean a Jesus without Incarnation, without the drama of the cross. Yet, there is still a moment in which what we share is still quite different. I mean that you begin with "God is love." The Jew begins with obligation. And the *happy end* is uncertain.[14]

This hesitation before incarnate presence is a constant theme in Levinas, which is considered in further detail in chapter 3. Levinas' consideration of the difficulties associated with the Jewish-Christian relationship is essentially historical, although made complex by his rejection of the incarnation. To this end, Levinas says that it is the possibility of "speaking together" that must be maintained as the "most important thing."[15] It is dialogue that becomes crucial to the continuance of a possible relationship, but it remains a dialogue in dynamic relationship with the real events of history.[16] That is to say, the relationship already appears as a concrete historical reality, but its continuance relies on the absolute commitment to dialogical words and actions. It is more than intellectual debate and conversation, but an enactment of social interactions with awareness of one's own tradition in relation to that of the other. As a dialogue informed, but not restricted by history, it feels the need to confront the experiences of violence and suffering in the past. Such a consideration requires a deeper reflection upon the nature of suffering *as it has occurred*, rather than as a transcendent category upon which an abstract language is determined. Suffering is a historical and personal occurrence that demands reflection. Suffering is not considered without its moral problematic; this is not only a question of suffering as it is experienced in the domestic existentiality of human life, or according to the Christian notion of natural evil. Rather, Levinas places an accent on suffering as it expresses the experience of evil acts. Levinas speaks elsewhere of the "excess" of evil, of its intentionality that surpasses expectations, and of the possibility that the soul is awakened to the good because of its awareness of evil.[17]

Evil must also be considered in relation to this dialogue; otherwise it would limit the scope for the dialogue to take its own history seriously. Only in this way, and in dialogue with real moments of redemptive self-offering,

---

14. Levinas, *Is It Righteous to Be?*, 267.

15. Ibid., 257.

16. Most notably, the Holocaust. Levinas, *Is It Righteous to Be?*, 256.

17. Levinas, "Transcendence and Evil," in *Collected Philosophical Papers*, 183–84.

can Levinas observe, "[t]his is how I understand Christianity: to live and die for everyone . . . ," a reverberation, in his view, of what is genuinely human, which is "being-a-Jew, an echoing in the particular."[18] For Levinas, dialogue is not simply the basis of the Jewish-Christian relationship, it is the *enacting* of that relationship. Furthermore, he identifies a shared *ethos* for the other, which is always maintained as an embodied ethics of alterity. Equally, ritual and theological commitment are ethical practices.

Wojtyla and Judaism

As pope, John Paul II directly intervened in Christian-Jewish relations; on one occasion in Germany proclaiming that no one could approach Christ without encountering Judaism.[19] His positive appraisal of Judaism both doctrinally and in personal relations was a matter of principle.[20] In contrast with the controversy which attends the memory of Pope Pius XII, Wojtyla/John Paul II has been called "righteous among the Gentiles" for his commitment to Jewish-Christian relations.[21] The following may be especially noted.

First, Wojtyla's record attests to intimate friendships and collegial relationships with Jewish countrymen; including the loss of Jewish friends throughout the war to anti-Semitism.[22]

Second, as pope, he altered the public theological language concerning the Jews: they were "elder brothers" for the Christian *ecclesia* and the latter was sorrowful and repentant for all acts of violence against what, in effect, was a fraternal relationship.[23] This reconfiguration of language, and

18. Levinas, *Is It Righteous to Be?*, 257.

19. Weigel, *Witness to Hope*, 364.

20. Shepherd, "John Paul II and Catholic-Jewish Dialogue," in Hayes and O'Collins (eds.), *The Legacy of John Paul II*, 229.

21. Wojtyla was given this title by the Israel Arbeiter Gallery of Understanding in Boston, 1999. For the debate about Pope Pius XII's actions during World War II, see for example Cornwell, *Hitler's Pope*; Dalin, *The Myth of Hitler's Pope*. A comprehensive collection of news articles, book titles, opinion pieces, and historical resources is available at "Essential Articles and Resources," in *Pope Pius XII and the Jews*.

22. For example, long-term friendships with Jewish men and women from Wadowice can be seen on the public record. Shepherd provides a reflective commentary on these relationships in "John Paul II and Catholic-Jewish Dialogue," in *The Legacy of John Paul II*, 230.

23. The reference to the Jewish people as Christianity's "elder brother" can be traced to an occasion in 1935 during a rise in anti-Semitism in Poland. Following an evening of public vandalism of Jewish businesses in support of an anti-Semitic economic boycott, Wojtyla's history teacher solemnly rebuked any students who might have joined in. The teacher exclaimed that what happened "has nothing to do with the tradition of our

of the Jewish religion as "intrinsic" to Christian faith, marks a significant development, one that was made during the first papal visit to the Jewish Synagogue of Rome.[24] Consequently, the Jewish-Christian relationship was to be interpreted as intrinsically familial, not simply historical.

Third, John Paul II's "iconic" visit to Israel and the Palestinian Territories in 2000 marked a symbolic moment of repentance and dialogue, during which time he prayed at the Western Wall for forgiveness for sins committed against the Jewish people throughout history.[25]

Fourth, the formalization of diplomatic relations with the State of Israel in 1994 established an open channel for social and political dialogue and negotiation between the Vatican State and Israel.[26]

John Paul II's record is of historical interest, but a further theological point can be made. That is, the opening up of philosophical vistas from thinkers formed within Jewish contexts was now to be a gift to Christian reflection.[27] This could be achieved because of the new *rapprochement* between the two peoples, who had been severed from one another in the breakdown of dialogue in the first century.[28] The dialogue between Levinas and Wojtyla is given some impetus by this context, in which a shared approach to the body and wisdom might begin.

Phenomenology

Phenomenology is the philosophical method largely shared by Wojtyla and Levinas. Edmund Husserl elaborated phenomenology as a method of scientific discovery, claiming a return "to the things themselves."[29] Central

Fatherland." He proceeded to read Adam Mickiewicz's 1848 manifesto which pledges high esteem to the "Jewish elder brother in the faith of Abraham" and a future Poland with equal rights for all. See Weigel, *Witness to Hope*, 39.

24. John Paul II, "Speech to the Jewish Community of Rome," 4.

25. Shepherd, "John Paul II and Catholic-Jewish Dialogue," in *The Legacy of John Paul II*, 241–43.

26. The agreement was signed in 1993 and diplomatic offices and representatives were established the following year. See Holy See, "Fundamental Agreement between the Holy See and the State of Israel."

27. Fifty years after the violence and bloodshed of the Warsaw Ghetto Uprising, Wojtyla continued to connect the memory of the Holocaust with a renewed mutuality of dialogue and friendship between Christians and Jews. Famously, he said: "It is therefore necessary for us, Christians and Jews, to be first a blessing to one another." See John Paul II, "Message of His Holiness John Paul II on the 50th Anniversary of the Warsaw Ghetto Uprising."

28. Weigel, *Witness to Hope*, 516.

29. In the German: "Zu den Sachen selbst." See Husserl, "Introduction," *Logical*

to Husserlian phenomenology is the "*epoché*," the "bracketing out" of the world.[30] In order to describe the data of an object in reality, one must bracket out the world in an act of reduction, which begins with one's own natural attitude. Levinas drew on Husserl's phenomenology whose student Heidegger also had an influence on Levinas. For the summer of 1928 and the winter of 1928–29, Levinas departed his formal studies in Strasbourg to attend Husserl's lectures in Freiburg im Breisgau, Germany. By this stage, Husserl was in his declining years and the young Heidegger was filling lecture theatres with his turn to facticity. Levinas is quoted as saying, "I came to see Husserl, and what I saw was Heidegger."[31] At twenty-three years of age, Levinas became a guest in Husserl's house, where philosophy and other topics would be discussed. Contact with Husserl and Heidegger places Levinas within the first stages of phenomenology's rapid growth from Germany to France. Later events in Heidegger's work and life would deter Levinas and others from aspects of his thinking, but the initial influence remained. Wojtyla, on the other hand, stayed in Poland throughout the war and for much of its aftermath. His contact with phenomenology was partially through a meeting with Husserl's texts, but was, in the mainstay, via the works of Max Scheler. Wojtyla lacked the direct personal association with the movement that Levinas had from an early age, yet the two of them found in phenomenology a methodology and language that could bring philosophy in an ethical direction, one that could take seriously themes such as alterity, subjectivity, and what it means to be human.

Wojtyla and the influence of Max Scheler's phenomenology

For both Wojtyla and Levinas, phenomenology provides a methodology that opens up new discoveries in existence, "almost an attitude of intellectual charity toward man and the world and, for the believer, toward God, the principle and the end of all things."[32] In 2003, John Paul II received a delegation from the World Phenomenology Institute, confirming his lifelong intellectual commitment to phenomenology, which he describes as "first of all a style of thought, an intellectual relation with reality, whose essential and constitutive traits one hopes to gather, avoiding prejudices

Investigations, vol. 2, 252.

30. Smith, *Routledge Philosophy Guidebook to Husserl and the Cartesian Meditations*, 21–22.

31. Malka, *Emmanuel Levinas*, 35.

32. John Paul II, "Phenomenology Represents an 'Intellectual Charity.'"

and schematisms."[33] Wojtyla's *habilitation* thesis was on the thought of Max Scheler, disciple of Husserl, whose ethics fostered a decisive "turn" in Wojtyla's own interest in seeing "things as they are."[34] His thesis, *An Evaluation of the Possibility of Constructing a Christian Ethics on the Basis of the System of Max Scheler*, concluded negatively, but not without developing a permanent interest in phenomenological investigation.[35] This interest, opened up in Scheler's concern for human experience, was integrated with the metaphysical realism Wojtyla had learnt from Aristotle and Thomas Aquinas.[36] In Scheler's attention to "pathos," "ecstasy," and the "*ethos*" of human life, Wojtyla found a philosophical approach that was attentive to understudied aspects of human experience. This was a significant distance from the thought of Wojtyla's doctoral supervisor, the "sacred monster" of Thomism, Reginald Garrigou-Lagrange.[37] The influential Garrigou-Lagrange had encouraged Wojtyla to explore St. John of the Cross for his doctoral research, in which a kind of "phenomenology of mystical experience" is evident, despite the former's reputation for a kind of strictly observed Thomism.[38] In Scheler's account of "value," Wojtyla rejects the description of what is given in experience, not of command or agency in itself but of "feeling."[39] Yet, in excluding Scheler's phenomenology as a basis for Christian ethics, Wojtyla does not reject the discovery of "value" in embodied human experience, or Scheler's affirmation that "values" were "objective."[40] According to Scheler, phenomenology allows for recognition of the transcendent dimension of the human person, a unique trait distinguishing humanity from all other

33. Ibid.

34. Weigel, *Witness to Hope*, 126–27.

35. Wojtyla's Habilitationsschrift, *Ocena mozliwosci zbudowania etyki chrzescijanskiej przy zalozeniach systemu Maksa Schelera*, has been translated from the Polish into German, Spanish, and Italian.

36. Weigel, *Witness to Hope*, 128.

37. The term is taken from an insightful account of the Dominican scholar's involvement in some of the tense moments between the Vatican and Catholic scholars of the twentieth century. See Peddicord, *The Sacred Monster of Thomism*.

38. Buttiglione, *Karol Wojtyla*, 45. The doctoral thesis, *The Doctrine of Faith according to St. John of the Cross* [*Doctrina de fide apud S. Joannem a Cruce*], is discussed later in this book. It was written in Rome, but Wojtyla's Polish homeland was still heavy with the memory of hardship and death and despite a new-found peace, the anxiety of the presence of Soviet intrusion in Polish life was a constant factor. Faith as a conscious act was found by Wojtyla to premise a mystical identity that had the capacity to overcome historical obstacles, redeeming them by a free act of discipleship. See John Paul II, *Faith According to St. John of the Cross*.

39. Simpson, *On Karol Wojtyla*, 20.

40. Modras, "The Moral Philosophy of Pope John Paul II," 683–84.

creatures. By "transcendence," Scheler describes a tendency which moves beyond "vital values" and which is directed towards the "divine" (as a philosophical category and not specifically theological).[41]

Max Scheler himself was born to a Lutheran father and Orthodox Jewish mother, but converted to Roman Catholicism, only to publicly distance himself from the latter. As such, his published work reflects a developing and unstable referent in its descriptions of God or the divine. He complicates the question of transcendence by asserting an inherent instability within the human subject to such a degree that the person becomes an entity without a discernible essence.[42] Such a creature, while open to a heroic directionality towards the "divine," cannot identify an essential description of itself except by reference to its transcendent movement. Yet by this, Scheler does not mean the divinity of revelation. He refuses "the idea of God in the sense of an extant and positively determined reality that is presupposed"; rather, Scheler can only see in his philosophy, "the *quality* of the divine, or the *quality* of the holy, that is given in an infinite fullness of being."[43] The problem arises as to the objective directionality of such transcendence—where does it lead to—or more specifically, alongside who or what does it allow a relationship? This was Hans Urs von Balthasar's problem with the ultimate logic of Scheler's system, that in the matter of self-transcendence, an "ideal" form is present against a nihilistic horizon.[44] That is, the form itself is a positive heroism that appears removed from human experience, while the horizon against which it stands triumphant is an oblivion of signification and meaning. This is not simply the absence of God, but the absence of anything to which a name can be given or with which a relationship might be formed. Scheler's system reaches a juncture where phenomenology opens up to discovery of the transcendent, but disallows the naming of that transcendence in terms to which theology is accustomed. In Aidan Nichols' words, "Scheler's man is utterly alone."[45] Scheler's system remains important for the development of intersubjectivity and of the role of values, but in this respect it is closed to theology. Furthermore, the phenomenological recognition of inherent values within human experience lacks the capacity to recognize good and evil as anything other than values with an emotional content.[46] That is, good and evil may be intentionally perceived in phenomenological analysis, but

41. Scheler, *Formalism in Ethics and Non-Formal Ethics of Values*, 291.

42. Ibid., 292.

43. Ibid.

44. Balthasar, *Love Alone*, 151.

45. Nichols, *Scattering the Seed*, 147.

46. Modras, "The Moral Philosophy of Pope John Paul II," 684.

they only appear in Scheler as objective values in and of themselves; they have no content that is fundamentally and universally applicable. Description may follow, but not ethics.

This observation relates profoundly to the possibility of moral theology. In his thesis on the topic, Wojtyla concludes that phenomenology requires the metaphysical tradition in order to ascertain the ethical applicability of "value" as it is identified in human experience: what he calls "meta-phenomenological or, frankly, meta-physical."[47] In other words, phenomenology, to be authentically open as a science of experience, must have a capacity for metaphysics. Scheler could recognize in religious experience a historical reference to metaphysics, but distinguished between what he called the "metaphysical urge" and the "motivation of religion."[48] He calls the first an emotion that arises from astonishment that anything at all should "*exist*."[49] For Scheler, the latter is a "*way of salvation*," founded in two prior events, the love of God and the longing for a final salvation of "man and all things."[50] On the other hand, the "motivation of religion" is the movement of lived practices as they unfold. It is a way or a concrete actuality, but its motivation is altogether different from that of metaphysics. Scheler acknowledges that there will be shared intentional objects in both metaphysics and religion, and even that reality, as discovered by either, remains "identical" to both.[51] Wojtyla was not displeased with the notion of a shared reality, but found the ethical applicability of this highly subjective distinction difficult to maintain. The real problem for Wojtyla's reading of Scheler was the question of ethics.

Despite the shared basis for metaphysics and religion, there remains in Scheler an objective distance to such a marked degree that philosophy, if it adheres to a phenomenological structure, cannot find in metaphysics anything like an objective criterion for ethics. On one level, Scheler seems to protect religious acts from metaphysical infringement—"These are things which only the religious act grasps and can grasp . . ."—and yet in marking his terms, he closes off religion from an ethical content verifiable by metaphysical enquiry.[52] To be sure, metaphysics and religion share an indivisible foundation. Just as Scheler refuses metaphysics as more than an

---

47. John Paul II, *Ocena Mozliwosci Zbudowania Etyki Chrzescijanskiej Przy Zaozeniach Systemu Maksa Schelera*, 60.

48. Scheler, *On the Eternal in Man*, 138.

49. Ibid., 138.

50. Ibid.

51. Ibid., 139.

52. Ibid., 142.

emotional value (albeit a complex value embedded in human behavior), he also collapses religion and metaphysics in a way that renders impossible the task of describing ethics in terms of reality as it is experienced:

> Only one thing stands firm: that metaphysics and religion—should they ever achieve their goals—must needs lead to one *identical* reality, a reality which lends real and ultimate meaning to the two essentially different intentional objects.[53]

So, the "real and ultimate" meaning of the two different intentional objects share in a final *telos*.[54] Wojtyla's response to Scheler negates this as a basis for Christian ethics, because it relies on an emotional evaluation of ethical acts.[55] That is not to say that the objective nature of ethics itself was not, in Scheler's work, attractive to Wojtyla. For Wojtyla, Thomistic metaphysics provides the basis for a description of ethics that avoids Scheler's emotive-value problem. In Scheler, there is a description of emotion and of value that remains an important insight, but it lacks the objective content Wojtyla had sought. Moreover, Scheler's notion of religion is bound to historical practices that are closed to theology and revelation. Wojtyla took from Scheler a positive appreciation of phenomenology, but combined it with the Thomist tradition in order to find an applicable ethics informed by theology.

Wojtyla: Intellectual influences and the meeting of phenomenology and Thomism

As well as the phenomenology of Edmund Husserl and Max Scheler and the thought of Thomas Aquinas, Wojtyla was influenced by others, including medieval mysticism (especially John of the Cross). Historically, he was associated with the *Nouvelle théologie* school through personal contact and mutual appreciation, but his own project was developed in the Soviet-Polish context, which faced different challenges than those faced by contemporaries like Henri de Lubac, Hans Urs von Balthasar, Karl Rahner, Yves Congar, and others.[56] Indeed, while these thinkers in Western Europe struggled

53. Ibid., 139.

54. Ibid.

55. Modras identifies a difficulty for Anglo-American readers of Wojtyla: because Scheler never achieved a great influence amongst English speaking readers, it is difficult for them to recognize so much of Wojtyla's implicit response to him. See "The Moral Philosophy of Pope John Paul II," 694.

56. See for example the account of intraecclesiastical conflicts and suppression experienced by these theologians in Mettepenningen, *Nouvelle Théologie, New Theology*.

with ecclesiastical censorship, Wojtyla, in Eastern Europe, was faced with the censorship and explicit violence of the state. The kinds of problems Wojtyla faced were experienced in a context of state-based violence against the human person and against the church. The intellectual labors that Wojtyla undertook were in constant dialogue with a rich prayer life that was explicitly mystical and self-consciously Catholic. Michael Waldstein describes the confluence of an austere mysticism with contemporary philosophical thought in Wojtyla as his "Carmelite personalism."[57]

In his spirituality, Wojtyla embraced John of the Cross for his commitment to the total self-giving of one for the other in the life of prayer. The devotional practices of the Carmelites as a radical displacement of worldly experience in favor of complete attention towards the divine (as an objective) were attractive to Wojtyla. This interiorized monastic ideal found a philosophical counterpart in the "personalistic norm," which finds in the irreducibility of the human person a natural command not to use the person as merely a means to an end.[58] Waldstein argues that in both his mystical interests and his personalist convictions, Wojtyla was interpreting the spousal dimension of love revealed in the Trinity; that God's love is a mutually offered self-donation of persons.[59] Emphasis on the Trinity in this personalist interpretation can be seen in John of the Cross (both poetically and theologically), and there remains a strong link between the language of bride and bridegroom in both the mystical doctor and Wojtyla. In this understanding of the Trinity, self-gift is a primary feature. Wojtyla draws from the spousal analogy a concept that has merit for the human relationship to God more generally. The link between the two relationships is the analogous power of the nuptial mystery as it is experienced (even fractured and imperfect) by human persons. For Wojtyla, this theological analogy is strengthened by an appeal to personalism as espoused by figures like Emmanuel Mounier and the journal *Esprit*, as well as an awareness of the role of Immanuel Kant in defining the subjectivity of the human person after René Descartes.[60] Wojtyla saw Kant as a decisive figure in shaping modern approaches to the human person and morality, but departs from him because of the latter's emphasis on the dignity of the autonomous human being.

For Wojtyla, human communion (*communio* between persons) is constituted fundamentally in the relationship of self-giving, which is most

---

57. Waldstein, "Introduction," in John Paul II, *Man and Woman He Created Them*, 23.

58. John Paul II, *Love and Responsibility*, 40–44.

59. John Paul II, *Man and Woman He Created Them*, 22.

60. Waldstein, "Introduction," in John Paul II *Man and Woman He Created Them*, 34–63.

perfectly expressed in the absolute commitment of one person to another in the nuptial mystery. While Wojtyla appreciates the consistent anti-utilitarian argument of Kant, the body's capability of a fundamental relationship with another person is a point of departure between them. Indeed, it is shaped by the nature of the human relationship with God as understood by John of the Cross. Wojtyla learned in the latter that human beings cannot know God as object, but learn him as a person.[61] The nonobjectivizability of God, in the light of faith, is given as a personal encounter (or, an encounter between persons), therefore protecting the person from thinking that a complete intellectual grasp of God is possible. Because it is a relationship and not an attainment of objective properties or knowledge, it remains always in a certain obscurity that can be called the night of faith. These influences on Wojtyla are not the overturning of reason in favor of mysticism, but a relationship of faith and reason founded in a relationship of *communio* of persons.

In *Fides et Ratio*, John Paul II confirms the centrality of Thomistic thought in the Catholic tradition, but lists phenomenology among "those recent philosophies which had the capacity to keep alive the great tradition of Christian thought which unites faith and reason."[62] In that document, he avoids committing the church to a particular school of metaphysics. Nevertheless, he refers to Thomas Aquinas seventeen times, confirming Thomistic realism as an appeal to the objectivity of truth in its capacity to discover not only what "seems to be" but a philosophy of "what is."[63] The more concrete possibilities of an ethics which is both universal and identifiable relies on this because it confirms the possibility of objective truths known in the "experience of the whole"; a creative development of Thomism without simply returning to Thomas as one might return to archaeology or history.[64] The Thomistic approach to the mystery of the person was itself a development, one that has been called an "ecstatic Thomism" for it calls the person out of itself on the basis of God's prior act of love.[65]

Having said this, Wojtyla identifies two specific areas in which Thomas' thought is open to "enrichment" by contemporary philosophy.[66] Wojtyla's treatment of these two underdeveloped areas of Thomistic thought are given in the 1967 essay, *Etyka a teologia moralna*, which was first presented

61. Buttiglione, *Karol Wojtyla*, 51.

62. John Paul II, *Fides et Ratio*, 59.

63. Ibid., 44.

64. Buttiglione, *Karol Wojtyla*, 81.

65. McAleer, *Ecstatic Morality and Sexual Politics*, 138.

66. Modras, "The Moral Philosophy of Pope John Paul II," 685.

on February 17th that year, during the tenth annual Philosophy Week at the Catholic University of Lublin.[67] They were therefore presented in a highly concentrated Thomistic setting and forced to be creative in their work in a pervasive censorial scholarly context because of the Soviet presence in Poland. The first concerns the grounds of moral action.[68] Thomas' metaphysics is teleological, concerned with the ultimate direction and end of persons and their actions. For Wojtyla, "[w]e are concerned today not so much with determining the ultimate end of moral conduct as with giving an ultimate justification of the norms of morality."[69] He takes as axiomatic that Kant's move towards explaining and justifying moral action on the basis of values and norms has become a decisive and irreversible achievement. As moral theology is informed chiefly by revelation, it therefore must recognize a departure from the classical consideration of its moral content in terms of eschatology and teleology, and be more concerned with investigating the meaning of the "Incarnate Word."[70] This christological direction in moral theology views the "God-human" as normative in ethics, for he is the "living model for living people, a model for the here and now . . . ."[71]

The second area is that of anthropology.[72] Wojtyla takes phenomenology seriously as a development which enables a new means of enriching the concept of what it is to be human, doing so in terms of the "whole subjective, 'conscious' aspect," which for him had been "levelled" in the tradition of metaphysical "naturalism."[73]

By no means does Wojtyla reject Thomas or the Aristotelian-Thomistic tradition that developed after him, but rather highlights its inadequacies which contemporary phenomenology offers some hope for repair.[74] The reduction of the human person to a "nature" or a "substance" without regard for the "normative" and "personalistic" dimensions is viewed by Wojtyla as problematic. For him, phenomenology opens reality up to description, which develops the Thomistic tradition rather than usurping it. In fact, Wojtyla's approach is to find in phenomenology a means also to interpret

---

67. John Paul II, "Ethics and Moral Theology," in *Person and Community*, 101–6.

68. Ibid., 103–4.

69. Ibid., 103.

70. Ibid., 103–4.

71. Ibid., 104.

72. Ibid.

73. Ibid.

74. For a helpful account of the centrality of Thomas in Wojtyla's thought from early on, see chapter 3, "A Philosopher from Kraków," in Gregg, *Challenging the Modern World*, 47–75.

reality theologically.[75] The intrinsically theological character of Wojtyla's philosophical openness to revelation unites what he calls dogmatic theology with moral theology within a christological dimension. The more unified relationship of a theology of earthly realities with a normative treatment of moral theology is, to his mind, "basically one: the demand for a more integral 'theologization' of moral theology."[76] This integral theological openness to the avenues of experiential knowledge in phenomenology is fundamentally interested in embodied human experience. Wojtyla is concerned to avoid the flattening out of the human person in its unique subjectivity that he occasionally detects in the Thomist tradition. This is a concern for the person—the other—in its irreducibility and what John McNerney classifies as the common question for both Wojtyla and Levinas.[77] They both develop their projects on the embodied other within the context of phenomenology.

In *Crossing the Threshold of Hope*, Wojtyla reflects upon the entrance of Marxist power in the realm of the university after World War II, in which polemical disputes with Marxist theory centered on the human person.[78] In Poland, the program of dialectical materialism was expressed through an appeal to natural philosophy.[79] Against this move, Wojtyla recalls the work of Kazimierz Klosak, who challenged Marxist theory with the philosophical discovery of the *Logos*, in which "creative thought and order" could be recognized in the world.[80] Such creativity destabilizes the atheistic self-assurance of dialectical materialism, which cordons off the possibility of arriving at any knowledge of a divine Creator. Having said that, the real confrontation was not between atheism and theistic belief, but over the question of the human person. In this context where natural philosophy was "put aside," eth-

---

75. Wojtyla's account of a noncombative relationship between phenomenology and theology foreshadows a later controversy as to the limits of phenomenology. Dominique Janicaud argues that phenomenologists such as Marion, Levinas, Henry, et al. have moved beyond the Husserlian limits of phenomenology by taking a "theological turn." In considering theological themes such as God, prayer, or the transcendence of the Other (*l'Autre*), Janicaud detects a nonsystematic move outside the clear boundaries set by Husserl. For example, Levinas' work is described as a "strategic blurring of the boundaries of the phenomenological and the theological." See Janicaud, *Phenomenology and The "Theological Turn"*, 50. Much earlier, Wojtyla foreshadows a position contra Janicaud, insisting that phenomenology cannot be a science of experience if it refuses any particular aspect of human experience, including religion and religious experience. See the debate in Benson and Wirzba, *Words of Life*.

76. John Paul II, *Person and Community*, 106.

77. McNerney, *John Paul II*, 75.

78. John Paul II, *Crossing the Threshold of Hope*, 198.

79. Ibid.

80. Ibid.

ics became significant for natural philosophers and in this context, Wojtyla developed themes that eventuated in his work *The Acting Person*.[81] Wojtyla admits not having a predilection for the natural sciences, but was primarily interested in the problem and experience of the human person. As he says:

> I was always more fascinated by man. While studying in the Faculty of Literature, man interested me inasmuch as he was a creator of language and a subject of literature; then, when I discovered my priestly vocation, man became the *central theme of my pastoral work*.[82]

Of this "fascination" was born the pastoral dimension of Wojtyla's overall work and ministry. Wojtyla saw in the human condition the marks of creativity, of language, of communal interests and indeed, the power of narrative. Yet, despite Wojtyla's early work as an actor and writer, it was primarily to the realm of ethics that his attention was drawn. This comes directly from his contact with young people after the war. Their questions were "not so much about the existence of God, but rather *about how to live* . . . ."[83] From this came Wojtyla's first book-length study, *Love and Responsibility*, although he acknowledges that the later work, *The Acting Person* "was also born of the same source."[84] In *Love and Responsibility*, he formulates the concept he calls the "personalistic principle," which attempts to "translate the commandment of love into the language of philosophical ethics."[85] As such, the personalistic principle confirms human persons as concrete subjects through which the world may be interpreted. From within the ethical questions and challenges of concrete persons, largely involved in making early-adult decisions concerning vocation, love, marriage, and living towards the good, Wojtyla turns his interest in ethics *against* any philosophical arrangement of persons by which any one might become an "object of pleasure."[86] Love is not an idealistic *telos* for human living; instead it is the normative basis for any genuine ethic of lived experience. In this sense, love as experience rests under the higher signification of love as virtue, by which the former is made a concrete possibility.[87] As a normative basis, the human instinctual sense is that this is impossible, but the command to love, issued

81. Ibid., 199.

82. Ibid.

83. Ibid., 200.

84. Ibid.

85. Ibid., 200–201.

86. Ibid., 201.

87. John Paul II, *Love and Responsibility*, 120 (Polish title: *Miłość i odpowiedzialność*).

directly towards the creation, signifies its very *possibility* in the first place. As a command and as a practical possibility, it is therefore more than an available option; it is constitutive of the order of creation. That is to say, the possibility of love is not an addendum to what is given in the created order. Rather, creation already offers the availability of pursuing love as an integral aspect of its own order. As persons perceive in others their human counterparts, so human experience is already faced with the possibility of love, if not its perfection. Reflected in the human person is the image of God, whose originary power issues love first, such that the command to love is possible. In this way, the command to love as God first loves is the suitable form of witnessing to another person. Wojtyla writes, "[t]he person is a being for whom the only suitable dimension is love."[88] Suitability implies a normative dimension. He insists that justice itself cannot be given by one to another unless love is offered first.[89] It must be remembered that human experience is an experience of the world, of concrete events and of other persons. As such, it is an embodied experience saturated with ethical possibility.

Levinas and the meeting of phenomenology and alterity

For Levinas, "Husserlian phenomenology intervenes at the level of the human," seeking out the meaning of what appears before the self. It is the philosophical movement into an awareness: "where reason signifies the manifestation of beings to a true knowledge, careful of their presence in the original, their presence in their identity as beings, or their presence qua being."[90]

In phenomenology, Levinas is impressed by the appearance of objects without their "remaining in their being."[91] He sees in the occurrence of signs, words, or images the coming forth into consciousness of a resemblance and not of an identity of things in themselves. This resemblance allures and frustrates human reflection. Reason ought to be a self-conscious endeavor, "distrustful of certain games that enchant it," for that which is other appears according to a logic of alterity and not of sameness and not to an immediately assumed lucidity about the other.[92] The phenomenological approach to that which is other to oneself is, for Levinas, not simply an ab-

88. John Paul II, *Crossing the Threshold of Hope*, 201.

89. Ibid., 201.

90. Levinas, *Discovering Existence with Husserl*, 153.

91. Ibid.

92. Ibid.

stract philosophical maneuver in aid of scientific knowledge, but carries an ethical appeal. In daring to approach the meaning of one's intentional gaze towards the other, one is captivated by what the other captures in the gaze back to the self. The other makes an ethical appeal of responsibility, which causes a restless wakefulness in the self. Levinas expresses a moral excitement about this process, in which he exclaims, "[o]ne must not sleep, one must philosophize."[93] For Levinas, phenomenology renders the act of philosophizing an ethics of intersubjectivity. Phenomenology cannot be seen to simply open up objects to the act of knowledge, but reveals the ethical nature of intersubjectivity. One does not evade sleep to think and to write, but to act responsibly for the other.

Levinas' work has been described as the "phenomenology of alterity" and this is in evidence from his earliest works.[94] In the early 1930s, Levinas became the French translator of Husserl's *Cartesian Meditations*, thus forging an important bridge between German phenomenology and its French descendants that blossomed in Paris throughout the latter part of the twentieth century.[95] This translation was followed by *The Theory of Intuition in Husserl*.[96] Nevertheless, it was not until *Totality and Infinity* was published in 1961 that Levinas' original contribution to phenomenology was made manifest.[97] In that book he introduces a radicalized appreciation of alterity in terms of ethics, contra Heidegger, for whom ethics was not a branch of fundamental ontology.[98] This was developed further with *Otherwise Than Being or Beyond Essence*, in the declaration that Western philosophy has, at heart, treated difference and the other with disdain by passing all significance to being as the primary category.[99] This is not the rejection of being per se, but rather understanding it "on the basis of *being's other.*"[100] Unlike Wojtyla, for whom metaphysics in the tradition of Aristotle and Thomas

93. Ibid.

94. Moran, *Introduction to Phenomenology*, 320.

95. Ibid.

96. Levinas, *La théorie de l'intuition dans la phénoménologie de Husserl* (English edition: *The Theory of Intuition in Husserl's Phenomenology*).

97. Levinas, *Totality and Infinity*.

98. Throughout *Sein und Zeit* (1927), Heidegger is concerned with the nature of authenticity in being, in which a defined ethics plays no part. See Heidegger, *Being and Time*. The Levinasian critique has been contested by Heidegger interpreters such as Laurence Paul Hemming, who rejects Levinas' argument that *Being and Time* instrumentalizes the other for the sake of the self. See Hemming, "A Transcendental Hangover."

99. Levinas, *Autrement qu'être ou au-delà de l'essence* (English translation: *Otherwise Than Being, Or, Beyond Essence*).

100. Levinas, *Otherwise Than Being*, 16.

provides a necessary corrective to the limitations of phenomenology, Levinas draws on a reading of Plato as a self-inversion of the Western philosophical tradition.[101] For Levinas, Plato's prioritization of the good beyond being challenges the prioritization of ontology, and reinterprets the philosophical tradition from Plato onwards. Levinas insists that the going out of the self for the sake of the other—absolute responsibility—places the self in the role of "hostage," restless and "gnawing away at oneself," both "inspired" and drawn completely up in one's own psyche for the sake of the good of the other.[102] The body of the other is taken up into the self's own ethical practice, just as it is infinitely distant: "The psyche can signify this alterity in the same without alienation in the form of incarnation, as being-in-one's-skin, having-the-other-in-one's-skin."[103] One is drawn out of oneself, and the other is drawn into the self's ethical practice.

The significance of incarnate presence is chiefly one of ethics, yet the limits of the other's body could be seen here to dissolve in relation to one's own ethical responsibility. Is this truly the other, or is this such a dehumanizing alterity that it avoids the very others for whom Levinas crafts his phenomenological description? This is considered in some detail in chapter 3, but the crucial factor at this point is that Levinas' ethics is not a program, a system, or a cause. It evades these social and political expressions because in the end it remains an attempt, via phenomenology, to authentically describe the appearance of the other. This is despite the problem that Levinas' literary flourishes appear to move fluidly into "mystical" prose and poetic metaphor, rather than philosophy as it is normally conceived.[104]

So, Levinas' phenomenology is not to be conceived in terms of an objective criterion for action. Rather, it is description. And as description, it falls back into an argument that metaphysics is preceded by ethics. Ethics is the *prote philosophia*.

Postmodernity

The postmodern condition provides a contemporary space in which no settlement has been reached as to its meaning or its outcomes. In this context, the body has become an important and contested site of meaning, one that

---

101. See, for example, Allen, *The Philosophical Sense of Transcendence*; Staehler, *Plato and Levinas*; Webb, "Eros and Ethics: Levinas's Reading of Plato's 'Good Beyond Being.'"

102. Levinas, *Otherwise Than Being*, 114.

103. Ibid., 114–15.

104. Moran, *Introduction to Phenomenology*, 321.

Levinas and Wojtyla challenge with distinct approaches towards a possible solution.

Postmodernity and Levinas' turn to the person

Within postmodern thought, the appeal to neutrality has been rejected.[105] In rejecting neutrality, it has been observed that a definition of postmodernity is as likely to "say more about the person offering the definition than it is of 'the postmodern.'"[106] Instead, the category of "condition" describes "modes of thought" as well as "modes of embodiment."[107] In this way, thought and worldly experience are affected by the postmodern condition.

In such a state of flux, Christian thought has reason to be "cautious."[108] As will be seen further in chapter 4, the postmodern body experiences itself as an unstable site of meaning, one whose signification appears to be endlessly deferred. Within this experience of the body, Levinas offers a philosophical language that does not simply reject the language of being as it has been inherited in the broader Western tradition, but reinterprets it as ethics. As an "ethics," Levinas' thought cannot be spoken of in terms of formal or traditional ethical categories, but rather as a descriptive language of that which is ethical, what Edith Wyschogrod calls the epiphany of an appeal, a "direct but nonparticipatory" relationship with other persons.[109] This is a personal appeal from the other person before any constructions, laws, expectations, rituals, or theologies. But it is also "beyond" ontology, not disputing the possibility of describing "being" as such, but radically repositioning it in relation to all other thought. Being must be rethought on the basis of the other, or *"being's other."*[110] The Levinasian turn to the other is not the usurpation of Western philosophy, a conclusion one could reach when reading *Totality and Infinity*, but the reimagination of being in terms of the personal *other*, who appears to the self before all other thought begins. This becomes clearer in *Otherwise Than Being*, where Levinas states, "The way of thinking proposed here does not fail to recognize being or treat it, ridiculously and pretentiously, with disdain, as the fall from a higher or-

---

105. Vanhoozer, "Theology and the Condition of Postmodernity," in Vanhoozer (ed.), *The Cambridge Companion to Postmodern Theology*, 3.

106. Ibid.

107. Ibid., 4.

108. Rosemann, "Postmodern Philosophy and Jean-Luc Marion," in Candler and Cunningham (eds.), *Transcendence and Phenomenology*, 91.

109. Wyschogrod, *Emmanuel Levinas*, 105.

110. Levinas, *Otherwise Than Being*, 16.

der or disorder. On the contrary, it is on the basis of proximity that being takes on its just meaning."[111] In other words, Levinas does not reject being as a philosophical category, but argues that its importance has been misconstrued to the detriment of the other. In proximity to the other person, an appeal for the other's wellbeing is discovered which is not to be described and formulated in the first instance; it is rather to be acted upon. This is not a form of nihilism, but a descriptive ethics of embodiment. In his turn to the other, Levinas' work offers a "striking originality," as Jean-Luc Marion puts it.[112] Yet, could it not be argued that Levinas' conception here of being in a skeptical mode, of a hesitation before philosophy's traditional metaphysics, is directly at odds with Wojtyla, especially with the assertion made in his papal capacity in *Fides et Ratio* of reason's capacity to seek out truth, providing a "solid foundation" for the perception of being?[113] Caution is advisable here, for to place Wojtyla's appeal within the Western Catholic tradition for the truth of being as a philosophical category in direct opposition to Levinas' phenomenology of the other would be a premature judgment. It is worth avoiding the tempting fallacy that Levinas' approach simply belongs to the postmodern mode of suspicion, in which all positive truths and narratives are without foundation. Rather, Levinas can be described as a "minimalist" thinker, one whose suspicion is not of being as such, but of the substitution of being for the ethical difference which arrives in that of the other person.[114] Being is not to be put aside, but rethought and reimagined.

Indeed, one approach would be to accept the difficulties established by the postmodern condition and to read Levinas and Wojtyla sympathetically in such a conflicting context. This is addressed by Roger Duncan, who argues that the traditional notion of the *analogia entis* provides a perspective in which Levinas has much to say in light of *Fides et Ratio*.[115] In the tradition of analogical thinking, being is an inclusive notion that unfolds the unity-in-difference of the world of phenomena; just as it reveals this world as derivative of a divine origin in invisible being. The "ever-greater" difference between God and creation offsets the relation of similarity with God.[116] The analogy of being has its dangers, and this is no place to account for its many derivations within Christian theology. Duncan proposes that Levinas'

111. Ibid.

112. Marion, "The Care of the Other and Substitution," in Hart and Singer (*eds.*), *The Exorbitant*, 201–10.

113. John Paul II, *Fides et Ratio*, 41.

114. Duncan, "Emmanuel Levinas in the Light of Fides et Ratio," 107.

115. Ibid.

116. Ibid., 108.

grounding in the experience of difference uniquely places the latter to be of service in a comprehensive approach to the relationship of difference and sameness within being. Levinas' insight into the preconscious, nonintentional content of being—which is *ethical*—provides philosophers of the *analogia entis* with the challenge to discern in the margins of experience an essentially moral character in being. Duncan acknowledges that at times, the language used for such a description will appear more like poetry than philosophy, but such a Levinasian reading of being confronts postmodernity with the embodied beauty of responsible action; it goes both beyond being just as it describes being at its phenomenally most fundamental.[117] Equally, the theological description of divine being as a triunity of love confronts postmodernity with a wider application of Levinas' notion of being held hostage to the other, of an abandonment to alterity which precedes its own acting-out. That is to say, the self gives itself to the Triune God because the Triune God is the originary event of self-giving love. In both Levinas and the analogous conception of divine being, asymmetry is held in tension with mutuality, necessity, and freedom. Duncan acknowledges rightly that Levinas himself does not defend the *analogia entis*. Yet, if Wojtyla's call for a renewal of the thought of being is to be successful in the postmodern context, Levinas provides a unique apparatus in thinking through and beyond being with regards to otherness.

Levinas beyond postmodernity

The influence of continental philosophers such as Emmanuel Levinas on postmodern thought cannot be underestimated.[118] For example, he is listed among a total of fifty-three individuals and groups in *Postmodernism: The Key Figures*, and his attention to alterity is critically endorsed by Jacques Derrida, whose deconstructionist approach has been taken up by many postmodern thinkers.[119] Yet, a description of Levinas as a postmodernist would be simplistic. For Michael Morgan, it is Levinas' reshaping of philosophy in orientation toward the ordinary and concrete ethics of responsibility that situates him outside of simple modernist or postmodernist categories.[120]

---

117. Ibid., 113.

118. Examples of a direct influence include, but are not limited to Bernstein, *The New Constellation*; May, *Reconsidering Difference*; Beavers, "Emmanuel Levinas and the Prophetic Voice of Postmodernity," in *"Andiron" Lecture at the University of Evansville*; Bernasconi, "The Truth That Accuses," in *The Ethics of Postmodernity*.

119. Bertens and Natoli, *Postmodernism*; Derrida, *Adieu to Emmanuel Levinas*.

120. Morgan, *Discovering Levinas*, 86.

That is to say, Levinas' attention to what seems mundane in the ordinary events of human sociality distinguishes him from the modernist tendency towards "grand action, creativity, and extraordinary religious experience," yet his appeal to the face also moves beyond what Morgan calls the "idealism" in postmodern thought.[121] This is not so much philosophical idealism, but the tendency to idealize particular subjects within a pluralistic optimism. Levinas is neither overly optimistic nor pessimistic, but wishes to receive in the other an epiphany that the self may only describe from a passive posture. In one of his final lectures at the Sorbonne, Levinas argues that the exposure of the face without shelter or reserve is a passivity "more passive" than any passivity, which seems to indicate an ethical nod to the possibility of violence if received on behalf of the other.[122] While there may be a postmodern infatuation with the body, Levinas says that when the other materializes, "he loses his face."[123] Levinas' descriptions of embodied presence resist an easy incorporation into a contemporary idealism of the other, the body, or the face. Furthermore, a growing accumulation of secondary literature is confirming Levinas' indebtedness to older sources, which places him within a broader and ancient philosophical tradition than contemporary, modern, or postmodern thought (even as he interrupts and reinterprets that tradition).[124] "Difference" is the recurring theme of postmodern thinkers, which in itself cannot be an identity, or a single, "originary" term for which a comprehensive account may be described.[125] According to Derrida, "Tout autre est tout autre" [Every other is totally other].[126] For Derrida, the space between every person is one of profound ethical investment. He makes much of the French term *différer*, which means both to "defer to" another and to "differ from" another, confirming that in both space and temporality, the distance between oneself and the other is not "innocent" of ethics.[127] To defer to the other is to place the other before oneself in time. Nevertheless, appearing before one's own eyes is the other's body, which shares features the self identifies. For Christian theology, a fundamental article of faith is that in the incarnation, it is human nature, as a shared and universal reality, which is assumed in the person of Christ and thus redeemed by his sacrifice

121. Ibid., 86–87.

122. Levinas, "Glory of the Infinite," in *God, Death and Time*, 196–97.

123. Ibid., 196.

124. For example, Schroeder and Benso, *Levinas and the Ancients*; Allen, *The Philosophical Sense of Transcendence*; Ajzenstat, *Driven Back to the Text*.

125. Mansfield, *The God Who Deconstructs Himself*, 61.

126. Derrida, *The Gift of Death*, 82.

127. Derrida, *Writing and Difference*, 206.

and resurrection.[128] Is it the case then that the other is totally other? What does it mean that the other *has* or *is* a body? A postmodern context that emphasizes radical alterity and difference renders problematic any reading of the body, however crucial a thematic the body has become in postmodern discourse. Sarah Coakley observes this when she writes, "[I]ndeed the 'body' comes to bear huge, and paradoxical, philosophical weight in postmodern thought . . . ."[129] Wojtyla views this new situation as problematic.

Wojtyla and postmodernity

In *Fides et Ratio*, John Paul II writes: "Our age has been termed by some thinkers the age of 'postmodernity.'"[130] He is concerned at the lack of universality in such an age and associates it with that of a growing nihilism.[131] The lack of certitude regarding formal categories of moral knowledge fosters a "horizon of total absence of meaning, where everything is provisional and ephemeral."[132] Postmodern advocates recognized this early. In *The Postmodern Condition: A Report on Knowledge* (1979), the widespread methodological reduction of meaning was termed the "little narrative"; the legitimization of knowledge in a reduced capacity of competence.[133] In this reduced horizon, Wojtyla, writing as John Paul II, is concerned that the ultimate threat to humanity is one of "despair."[134] The problematic relationship of postmodernity to its antecedents tells strongly in the acknowledgement that there remain enclaves of enlightenment-inspired thinking which maintain a resistance to this despair, but not with a transcendent horizon towards which that hope might direct: "Even so, it remains true that a certain positivist cast of mind continues to nurture the illusion that, thanks to scientific and technical progress, man and woman may live as a demiurge, single-handedly and completely taking charge of their destiny."[135]

The attempts either to live as a demiurge, sealed off within a modernist self-confirming logic, or as an equally self-directing figure against the void

128. See St. Gregory of Nazianzus: "That which was not assumed is not healed; but that which is united to God is saved" [*to gar aproslepton, atherapeuton ho de henotai to theu, touto kai sozetai*], in *Epistle 51*, to Cledonius, in Gregory, *On God and Christ*.

129. Coakley, "Religion and the Body," in *Religion and the Body*, 3.

130. John Paul II, *Fides et Ratio*, 91.

131. Ibid.

132. Ibid.

133. Lyotard, *The Postmodern Condition*, 60.

134. John Paul II, *Fides et Ratio*, 91.

135. Ibid.

of nihilism, confront humanity with the conflict of meaning in a state of historical flux. A lack of consensus on the demarcation of historical periods is identified, so there is no agreement on when, where, or how postmodernity came into being.[136] There remains no consensus on the progression of modernity to postmodernity; is the latter a "severance," a "mutation," a "heretical reconstruction" of the former, or is the relationship itself in such a state of fluidity that categorical description evades possibility?[137] Even the term "postmodern" remains subject to conflicting debate.[138] John Paul II has been identified as having adopted "postmodernist rhetoric and argumentation," and yet the appeal to a postmodern "condition" lacks both consensus and formal description.[139] His concern is to acknowledge that postmodern thinking "merits attention," but also to foster a renewed theological concern for understanding "[r]evelation" and the "content of the faith."[140] Much of Wojtyla's concern for this new context rests upon his commitment to Thomism.

In fact, Thomism is undergoing its own reevaluation on this question from a number of sources. For example, Jean-Luc Marion has altered his views on whether Thomistic metaphysics ultimately collapsed the distinction between Being and beings, or whether Thomism is exempt from the charge of reducing divine being to a truncated metaphysics.[141] Also, John Caputo, in an early work on Heidegger and Aquinas, defends Thomas' distinction between Being and beings as exempt from the postmodern charge of "forgetfulness."[142] Within Thomistic metaphysics, "participation" provides the means by which individuation is included within a divine community,

136. Ibid.

137. See a clear treatment of these categories in Rowland, *Culture and the Thomist Tradition*, 132–33.

138. Even movements that seek to positively appraise the possibilities of postmodernity find that it remains a project in need of completion. E.g., Radical Orthodoxy, which Long describes as turning "the philosophical advantages toward which postmodernity points" and completing them theologically. See "Radical Orthodoxy," in Critchley and Bernasconi (eds.), *The Cambridge Companion to Postmodern Theology*.

139. Harvey, *The Condition of Postmodernity*, 41.

140. John Paul II, *Fides et Ratio*, 91 & 93.

141. See the debate concerning the English and French editions of Jean-Luc Marion, *God without Being: Hors-Texte*. In the preface to the English edition, Marion distinguishes between "esse" according to Thomas and "being" according to contemporary nihilist thought. According to Marion, God does not give himself according to the horizon of being, but of "the gift," and it is in this that the question remains whether Marion is consistent with Thomas or whether this is a radical departure, other later clarifications from Marion notwithstanding.

142. Caputo, *Heidegger and Aquinas*.

but Levinas rebukes precisely the notion of "participation" for what he sees as its enfolding of difference within the same.[143] He wishes to avoid the idea that the other is captive to the divine Other. For Levinas, a social relation with the "transcendent" is possible only on condition that "captivation by the Transcendent" is unavailable.[144] While it could be contested whether the Christian notion of participation is really the total objectification of the subject as Levinas understands it, or something more akin to a *metanexus* in which a transcendent prior cause transforms the freely offered self, the question posed by the postmodern condition centers especially on the human person. Unexpectedly perhaps, it is this postmodern debate about being which returns to the body, for it is through embodiment that the human person arrives at the question of being in the world. In discussing the body, it should also be kept in mind that Christianity shares a complex relationship with postmodernity.

Christianity and postmodernity

It could be argued that the postmodern fascination with the body is motivated by "otherness of faith and the idea of divinity."[145] This fascination recalls a lost past in which a "seamlessness" existed between the body and the idea, as opposed to the modern compartmentalization of these and other categories from communion with each other.[146] This fascination is not an honoring of the giftedness of the body, but a fetishizing of the body. The flesh of the body is idolized in a state of self-serving manipulation. On this account, theology and postmodernity approach the body with different agendas. As Françoise Meltzer argues, there exists a demarcation between Christian theology and the postmodern project: postmodern texts are committed to the "problem of being" and theology, on the other hand, is concerned with "revelation."[147] Theology has a long history of gaining insight from being as a philosophical category, yet shies from mutual self-identification in its name or usage. Indeed, the body itself can be imagined as the originating disclosure of the

143. Levinas, *Totality and Infinity*, 77.

144. Ibid., 78.

145. Meltzer, "Re-embodying: Virginity Secularized," in Caputo and Scanlon (eds.), *God, the Gift, and Postmodernism*, 268.

146. Ibid.

147. This picks up on themes from the early Heidegger: Meltzer, "Re-embodying: Virginity Secularized," in Caputo and Scanlon (eds.), *God, the Gift, and Postmodernism*, 268.

world folding back upon itself.[148] That is, the world is received in the body's senses and rational awareness, and reappropriated, used, experienced, and altered by the body. One witnesses this in the infant who embraces every item with hands and gums, literally seeking to chow down on a world it cannot contain or describe. Despite the postmodern obsession with difference, it remains closed to the overcoming of difference within the embodied redemption which theology alone recognizes, what Meltzer (following Spinoza) names the "*don gratuit* of the body, in the service of faith . . . ."[149] That is, without reference to mind as such, the very possibility of the giving of the body in sheer gratuity echoes a notion of self-donation that is articulated most clearly in Christianity. In martyrdom and in any example of *caritas*, the saints witness to the unity of the idea of self-gift in Christ with the act of self-givenness in the body. Individuation is overcome in the gratuity of self-donation for the other, even while natural distinctions between persons remain. The thought of self-sacrifice or of self-donation becomes not so much the object of thinking, but the embodied *act*. In the martyr, *numena* is indistinguishable from *phenomena*.[150] In this, theology recognizes the redemptive opportunity every singular body affords, but must view within the postmodern condition both a fascination with the body as well as a certain discordance as to its meaning. Kevin Vanhoozer states unequivocally:

> We have learned from the postmoderns that knowledge is not disembodied. On this point, postmodernity and incarnational Christian faith are agreed. What is needed, therefore, is a translation of the Gospel that goes beyond conveying propositions— a translation that would *concretize* the Gospel in individual and communal shapes of living.[151]

In other words, an imperfect Christian echo can be heard in the postmodern concern for the embodied other. However, Christianity names the other as "neighbor."[152] For the postmodern mind, this is an immediate and illegitimate dislocation of power from the process of self-determination rightly ascribed to the self of the other. It is a categorization, a labeling, a positioning of the other outside the realm of true difference and involving

148. Steeves, *Imagining Bodies*, 152.

149. Meltzer, "Re-embodying: Virginity Secularized," in Caputo and Scanlon (eds.), *God, the Gift, and Postmodernism*, 269.

150. Ibid., 270.

151. Vanhoozer, "Theology and the condition of postmodernity: a report on knowledge (of God)," in Vanhoozer (ed.), *The Cambridge Companion to Postmodern Theology*, 24.

152. Ibid.

a complicity in the assertion of political power. This postmodern reading of the other reduces the other; it pervades the space with the relationship of intersubjective naming and the characterization of the other based on *one's own* conditions, shaped by *one's own* agenda; what Levinas wishes to reject by insisting on the self's relationship with a neighbor as an "extreme passivity."[153] Yet, there is a paradox here, because the Christian claim of ethical responsibility for the other is based on the Nicean claim that the naming of the other as neighbor flows from the lips of an incarnate God, the Lord of time and history, whose speech is the linguistic formation of the desires of the union of humanity and divinity. Jesus Christ, proclaiming this ethical vision from a particular cultural context, does so not simply as *a* God, but as *God*. In this sense, divine being is the calling forth of the self exterior to oneself and in service to the other. It cannot do so without an embodied immersion in the world, and in locating the neighbor, both persons are freed to embody the divine command. Through this embodied *ethos*, the world itself is known and interpreted.

This embodied *ethos* presents the human person with a way of being in the world. Its calling is that of service in the form of love, which could be described as praxis.[154] Much recent theological reflection on praxis has been in the context of liberation theology, where a general understanding of Christian discipleship as a practical outworking of authentic community can be seen.[155] Love does not provide a capitulation outside the world, but places persons in service within the world. A number of theorists have contended various complex uses of the term, but an essential characteristic is the manner in which praxis operates as a redemptive work practiced by disciples in the face of systemic and institutional evil. Levinas' approach to the body offers something more fundamental and less politically implicated. The body is that concretization of being in the world and the opportunity for service within it, before human awareness of it. So how might the body be described at this fundamental level in a postmodern context? One example is Maurice Merleau-Ponty, who describes the body-world relationship in these terms: "Our own body is in the world as the heart is in the organism; it keeps the visible spectacle constantly alive, it breathes life into it and sustains it inwardly, and with it forms a system."[156]

153. Levinas, *Otherwise Than Being*, 47.

154. An example of this turn towards concrete practice is the work of Werner Jeanrond, who argues that a theology of love would be interpreted in terms of a transformative "praxis." See Jeanrond, *A Theology of Love*.

155. See for example Gutiérrez, *A Theology of Liberation*; Sobrino, *The True Church and the Poor*; Azevedo, *Basic Ecclesial Communities in Brazil*.

156. Merleau-Ponty, *Phenomenology of Perception*, 235.

Merleau-Ponty's description of embodied life stems from the perspective of the person. He sees the world as sustained and nourished by bodily nature, viewing the world as a spectacle and receiving breath by the inner dynamism of the human body. In this way, Merleau-Ponty emphasizes the abiding connection between body and the exterior world by using the category of system. A systematic relationship between the body and the world reveals a depth of inner commitment between our bodily experience and perception of the world; in other words, a relationship between the self and that which is other. Perception alters the actions of the body. What is perceived in the body of the other will not always be clear or immediate, but is to be interpreted in a greater logic. For both Wojtyla and Levinas, there remains an ethical excess in the presence of the body, one that exceeds the postmodern infatuation with the body and which determines the morality of human actions for the body of an other. Wojtyla and Levinas provide a constructive critique of this postmodern condition in which the body has become a key site of debate. In reapproaching the body in terms of gift (as will be seen in chapter 5), an ethics of responsibility is enacted that falls most appropriately within theological anthropology. Yet, prior to theology, phenomenology provides a method that both unites and distinguishes Wojtyla and Levinas.

Wojtyla and Levinas: The dialogue

In this section, the historical and intellectual dialogue that has already taken place between Wojtyla and Levinas is outlined, including their first encounter, their descriptions of each other's approaches in a number of texts, and meetings and interviews.

Wojtyla and Levinas' first encounter: The problem of I and the other

Of his Lublin essays, one of Wojtyla's most important contributions is his 1975 essay, "Participation or Alienation?"[157] This paper, sent in French translation to the conference on "I and the Other" (sometimes translated as "The Self and the Other"), was ultimately read by Emmanuel Levinas

157. Original title: *Uczestnictwo czy alienacja*, according to the collection, *Person and Community*, which was sent to the Fourth International Phenomenology Conference in Fribourg, Switzerland (24–28 January 1975), later published in *Summarium* 7.27 (1978) 7–16. However, according to Malka, Levinas' biographer, the conference was in fact the second international conference for the World Institute for Advanced Phenomenological Research and Learning. See Malka, *Emmanuel Levinas*, 223–24.

(who was presiding over the session) in Wojtyla's absence.[158] Levinas had been encouraged to attend these international conferences of the World Institute for Advanced Phenomenological Research and Learning by Anna-Teresa Tyminiecka, who was a Polish colleague of Wojtyla and translator of the English edition of *The Acting Person*.[159] Wojtyla had been scheduled to present the opening address but was denied permission to travel outside Poland (a not infrequent occurrence, depending on Soviet politics). Hence, Levinas, one of the copresenters, read the pre-sent paper, which he recalled in the following years with a mixture of "pride and mischievousness."[160] As the first encounter between Wojtyla and Levinas, this event is something of a nonmeeting, in the sense that the two did not meet face-to-face. Such opportunities would present themselves in later years, but the essay read by Levinas in the presence of various scholars has some historical significance. Some years later, Levinas responded to aspects of the paper in the journal *Communio*. Wojtyla prefaces the essay by connecting it with his general concern with philosophical anthropology and particularly *The Acting Person* (which at that time had not been translated from Polish).[161] What follows is really a consideration of the I-other problematic beginning explicitly with the New Testament commandment to love one's neighbor.[162] The primacy of the evangelical commandment is obvious to Wojtyla, but its ethical description is not, for he employs personalistic language in the service of explaining human action that emphasizes a dynamic role for the human subject. For Wojtyla, the commandment to love the neighbor requires some ethical description if it is to be actualized in practice, and remains difficult for many to understand. Beyond intellectual banalization, or saccharine emotional experiences, Christ shows his disciples how to act, and raises a high bar indeed. In Wojtyla's terms, the human person is primarily a subject revealed in the performance of action, which carries within itself an irreducible moral content.

158. John Paul II, *Person and Community*, 198.

159. There is some controversy over Tyminiecka's translation of this text. Upon Wojtyla's papal election, the Vatican withdrew endorsement of the English version based on what they perceived to be inadequacies in her translation from the original Polish. She has been accused of misrepresenting Wojtyla's reliance on Thomistic metaphysical language and reinterpreting his work to fall more closely into line with her own phenomenological conclusions. See Buttiglione, *Karol Wojtyla*, 42. The controversial account is related also in Weigel, *Witness to Hope*, 174–75. For these reasons, the French edition, considered a more faithful translation, has been consulted for comparison and accuracy. See the imprint: John Paul II, *Personne Et Acte*.

160. Malka, *Emmanuel Levinas*, 224.

161. John Paul II, *Person and Community*, 197.

162. Ibid., *The Acting Person*, 197.

Wojtyla highlights two "cognitive situations" in extending his commentary on *The Acting Person*.[163] The first is in the concrete "existence and activity" of a human being—an *I*—who is situated in an existence and activity "in common with other human beings."[164] In relation to this is that of the *other*, who also experiences himself or herself as a human being immersed in a shared sociality. The other is always *an* other, one of many, but the many in this case are viewed by Wojtyla collectively as the "sum of human beings in general."[165] This I-other dynamic encapsulates the personalistic fullness of each individual, who is an other (*autrui*) before and beyond the self is its own "I."[166]

The second cognitive situation is that of self-consciousness, which according to Wojtyla, conditions "the whole structure of the lived experience of the self, the concrete I."[167] From its own perspective, self-consciousness constitutes the "entire world that is simultaneously given to us as a fact."[168] Wojtyla displays here his indebtedness to the basic Husserlian phenomenological structure, in which the self-conscious I receives the data of the world as that which is given and not attained. It is worth noticing that Wojtyla sees this givenness of the world in terms of "fact," a concrete realism that, although open to misinterpretation or confusion, remains nevertheless the world in which one must live. No other world is given to the observing I. This is what Wojtyla means by lived experience.[169] In self-consciousness, the living I discerns its own identity as different from that of the various others who also appear in the world at hand. Wojtyla takes these two cognitive situations as the point of departure for his reflection upon the "I-other problematic," which is not bound to categories of being or existence, but in

---

163. John Paul II, *Person and Community*, 198.

164. Ibid.

165. Ibid.

166. Ibid., 200.

167. Ibid., 198.

168. Ibid.

169. It may be noted that the term "lived experience" is contested. For Levinas, phenomenology reveals that "lived experience" is the encounter of consciousness with objects outside of itself, and of an intentionality that remains in contact with those objects. The person is always intending something towards objects that precede its own existence, which must be interpreted and described. See Cohen, *Face to Face with Levinas*, 14. This resonates but is not identical to Wojtyla's account, in which "lived experience" is the encounter of a responsible self amongst others who remain different. This difference opens itself to the event of *communio*, for the self must act on behalf of others and beside them in a shared intersubjectivity.

the "lived experience . . . of two really existing and acting subjects."[170] From here, Wojtyla moves readily into the importance of action:

> Action is what most fully and profoundly reveals the human be-
> ing as an *I*—and, indeed, as a person, for that which we express
> in categories of being by the concept "person" is given in experi-
> ence precisely as a self (*soi*), as an I.[171]

By this, Wojtyla is not indicating that action is the only determinative aspect of the personhood of a person, or an *other*. Rather, he views action in a revelatory sense; it is the action of a person that reveals to others the way of being. The reality of the I in the mind of oneself is made clear and is only made manifest in the action of the other. The role of self-fulfillment is only reached as an action entirely dependent on the nature of an individual action, which must accord with the inner element of personal conscience.[172] Actions are rarely done in isolation, so that Wojtyla is content to view the series of moral actions (activity) as both "rooted and ingrained" in the human subject as well as the proficiency of "virtues and vices," what the Aristotelian-Thomistic tradition refers to as *de habitibus*.[173] Opposed to actions that pertain to the good is a kind of "antivalue" in terms of morality, which pertains to evil rather than good.[174] Either way, self-fulfillment is another structure within the human person that speaks of its own subjectivity, both its metaphysical reality (actions fulfill us in terms of the good or negate us in terms of evil) as well as its experiential aspect (the existential subject might distinguish its action/s from others, but always within the larger continuity of personhood).

This is an important counterintuitive contribution within contemporary thought because it relies on action and responsibility rather than a directory of rights. Carson Holloway's study of the relationship between Wojtyla and liberal modernity contrasts their difficult relationship as one of correction rather than antipathy.[175] That is to say, Wojtyla's positive appreciation of the achievements of post-Enlightenment philosophy corrects rather than rejects liberal modernity, particularly in terms of this question of the self and personal fulfillment. Self-fulfillment is a moral condition,

170. John Paul II, *Person and Community*, 198.

171. Ibid.

172. Ibid., 234–35.

173. Ibid., 235. The word *"hexis"* [ἕξις] is first used by Aristotle especially in relation to ethics, translated as *habitus*, but also used in terms such as "state" or "condition." See Aristotle, *The Nicomachean Ethics*, 1105b25–26.

174. John Paul II, *Person and Community*, 235.

175. See Holloway, *The Way of Life*.

informed by the good as it contradicts the evil intent within the inner self. As will be seen, the I-other problematic is also important to Levinas.

John Paul II's references to Levinas in *Crossing the Threshold of Hope*

In *Crossing the Threshold of Hope*, John Paul II refers to Levinas three times with a certain gravitas, reflecting the role of the latter in the former's intellectual development.[176]

First reference in Crossing the Threshold of Hope: Levinas and the way to being

John Paul II's first reference to Levinas occurs early, in the fifth chapter under the title, "'Proof': Is It Still Valid?" Until this reference to Levinas, John Paul II had referred to Scripture and some of the early church fathers, as well as to the Second Vatican Council and other thinkers. John Paul II finds in the Bible and St. Thomas the recognition that the interior life of human experience is not itself completely subject to, or explained by, what he calls positivistic thinking.[177] That is to say, both these sources indicate that human experience exceeds the categories found by sensory and scientific knowledge. Further to this, the inner recognition of the human person that good and evil provide the criteria by which an action may be understood reveals that the human self is an "ethical being" who may act with intentions other than simply "profit or pleasure."[178] Prayer verifies this awareness.[179]

In rejoicing in a contemporary advance towards "the ever more complete discovery of man," John Paul II is desiring a more developed intertextual "value of metaphorical and symbolic language" in human self-understanding.[180] Immersed within a symbolic intertextuality, the human person is not bound to objective descriptive criteria, but is rather an excess of meaning beyond those categories. John Paul II cites trends amongst hermeneutical

---

176. Brief reference to Levinas is made in some of Wojtyla's speeches, such as that given to the representatives of Jewish organizations in the USA and Canada. See John Paul II, "Address of John Paul II to the Representatives of Jewish Organizations."

177. John Paul II, *Crossing the Threshold of Hope*, 33–34.

178. Ibid., 34.

179. Ibid.

180. Ibid., 35.

theorists in which God seems to become, once more, a "knowable object."[181] He writes, "[c]ontemporary hermeneutics—examples of which are found in the work of Paul Ricœur or, from a different perspective, in the work of Emmanuel Levinas—presents the truth about man and the world from new angles."[182] This citation of Ricœur and Levinas is based upon their approach to anthropological questions with an appreciation for the symbolic world in which the acting human agent participates, one that remains metaphysical: "We are witnesses of a symptomatic return to metaphysics."[183] By "integral," John Paul II is claiming a knowable wholeness to the human subject that involves the constitutive factor of God.[184] Implied here is the subjective turn in anthropological reflection, defended by Wojtyla in essays such as "The Person: Subject and Community" and "Participation or Alienation?" This turn, as enacted by Wojtyla, is not the revolution envisaged by figures such as Ludwig Feuerbach, who predicted a new philosophy, "the complete and absolute dissolution, without any contradiction, of theology into anthropology."[185] Rather, this is an expression of Yves Congar's prediction which, almost whimsically, foresaw the "union" of theology and anthropology via a "method of immanence."[186] In Wojtyla, alterity is marked by a social immanence, and not by an infinite distance. Levinas' contribution is profoundly affected by his understanding of alterity, which will be explored in more detail in chapter three of this book. Here, Wojtyla, as Bishop of Rome, is drawing Levinas into a personalist approach to the question of being. John Paul II holds to the full validity of Thomas' contribution, but wants to find his way to existence via the mediation of persons in their experiential contexts, rather than abstract categories.

The dialogical I-THOU relationship in Levinas

The second reference to Levinas follows quickly from the first, in which John Paul II refers to Martin Buber and Levinas as the "philosophers of

---

181. Ibid., 34.

182. Ibid., 35.

183. Ibid.

184. Ibid., 35–36. For Thomas Aquinas, the philosophical basis for existence is drawn under the category of *actus essendi*. Thomas' full account of the "act of being" lies outside the scope of this book, but his account can be seen in Thomas Aquinas, *Quaestiones Disputatae De Potentia*, Quest. 7, Article 2, ad 9.

185. Feuerbach, *Principles of the Philosophy of the Future*, 68.

186. This "sense" of theology's future is developed in Congar, *A History of Theology*. The theme is interpreted and developed further in Nichols, *Yves Congar*, 199.

dialogue."[187] In considering Buber and Levinas, two significant Jewish philosophers in the post-World War II era, John Paul II claims:

> [W]e find ourselves now very close to Saint Thomas, but the path passes not so much through being and existence as through people and their meeting each other, through the "I" and the "Thou." *This is a fundamental dimension of man's existence, which is always a coexistence.*[188]

John Paul II calls attention to the origin of Buberian and Levinasian thinking as it coincides with Thomas. He focuses on the nature of ethics as it is presented in their work and asks, "[w]here did the philosophers of dialogue learn this?" answering with reference to "their experience of the Bible."[189] For John Paul II, Buber, Levinas, and Ricœur are not inspired by the text in and of itself, but their experiential relationship with what is discovered in that text. It is profoundly the "experience . . ." of the ". . . Bible" which, imbued with a wealth of symbolic and metaphorical texture, is able to offer a coexistential vision of the human person to these philosophers. John Paul II is wishing to hold together the universal and the particular in an existential-anthropological description. He writes:

> In the *sphere of the everyday* man's entire life is one of "coexistence"—"thou" and "I"—and also in the *sphere of the absolute and definitive*: "I" and "THOU." In Biblical terms, the tradition oriented all human experience towards this "THOU," who is the same God of Abraham, Isaac and Jacob, then of the Fathers, of Jesus the Christ and of those who inherited their faith.[190]

The transcendent dimension cannot be separated from the personalist experience of the God who reveals himself. He is the primary Thou to one's I. This allows John Paul II to claim that to speak of Christian faith is also to consider its sense of the anthropological, in which being and ethics are not understood apart from each other. He goes on:

> Our faith is profoundly anthropological, rooted constitutively in coexistence, in the community of God's people, and *in communion with this eternal* "THOU." Such coexistence is essential to our Judeo-Christian tradition and comes from God's initiative.[191]

187. John Paul II, *Crossing the Threshold of Hope*, 36.

188. Ibid.

189. Ibid.

190. Ibid.

191. Ibid.

It is significant that the orientation towards the divine "Thou" is one that makes of the "Thou" the origins of relationship, including that which occurs between people. The divine initiative is what makes one's "I" an "I" in the first place, because it is designated by the "Thou" who alone has the power to name a particular "I" as a "thee." Communion is thus formed in the power of naming and of divine initiation. For John Paul II, such an initiative is connected with creation and leads to creation. This relates to the Pauline teaching in Eph 1:4, "the eternal election of man in the Word who is the Son."[192] Divine initiative is also one of election, but is extended to the human community most concretely (most obviously en-fleshed) in the Incarnate Word. The Word is not an abstracted *Logos*, but the Christ, who is recognized as a divine person by the signification of the familial term: he is the *Son* of God.

The face in defense of every human life

Further to these first two major points of entry for John Paul II in Levinas' thought, he considers also the latter's philosophy of the face as a defense of the dignity of every human life. In the penultimate chapter of *Crossing the Threshold of Hope*, "The Defence of Every Life," Levinas is appealed to for his defense of human dignity. To understand it, it is important to contextualize the lines of thought present in the preceding interview questions. In the intermediary chapters between the first reference to Levinas and this third reference, John Paul II gives his personal response to questions such as Christian belief in the modern era,[193] religious pluralism,[194] and the pope's implementation of Vatican II.[195] A theme that arises throughout the interview is that of human dignity, referred to often in subtle ways and not always directly. However, John Paul II is asked what he understands to be "authentic human rights" and what he means by "human dignity."[196] His answer helps to explain his interest in figures such as Levinas. He describes human rights as having been inscribed by the Creator in the order of creation, such that human institutions such as the state or international organizations merely express what is written into the created order from the beginning. Human rights, as fundamental to the relationship of human communities to the world around them, do not derive from the Christian witness, but are

192. Ibid.
193. Ibid., 27–59.
194. Ibid., 84–100.
195. Ibid., 170.
196. Ibid.

rather clarified and confirmed by it. As John Paul II writes, "*[t]he Gospel is the fullest confirmation of all of human rights.* Without it we can easily find ourselves far from the truth about man."[197] The reason for this is that at the heart of the gospel is the incarnate Son of God, whose redemptive work restores the fullness of human dignity. It is the liturgy that reminds people of this throughout the yearly cycle, especially during Christmas and the Easter Vigil.[198] John Paul II goes on to describe the historical dimension of his early interest in the dignity of the human person and the gospel demand that human rights are integral to the human condition.[199] Earlier, in *Evangelium Vitae*, objection is made to the liberal statist model of human rights as a minimalist social obligation, one that diminishes the role of love in social ethics.[200] That is to say, human rights are not decided by any human institution, and for this reason they are not limited to the horizontal dimension of human knowing and acting, offered as no more than a limitation of the worst of human tendencies to exploit or hurt one another. Human rights are derived from the divinity that precedes and stands over human institutions, such that they have a vertical dimension, calling human beings out of themselves towards a higher, virtuous sociality.

John Paul II concludes with two mutual confirmations: first that the person must be affirmed *as* a person in his or her fullness, and second that the biblical command to love may be translated into philosophical terms as the self-gift of the person: one *for* others.[201] He establishes these two confirmations as part of his defense of the church's role in protecting human dignity and in the defense of universal human rights.

John Paul II develops further the theme of human dignity with regards to the notion of life itself as a right that is intrinsic to the Christian notion of human dignity. It is in this context that John Paul II once again refers to Levinas. First, he makes his oft-repeated claim that the "right to life" is the "fundamental right," for it provides the foundation for all other human rights, both chronologically and philosophically.[202] It should be noted that the right to life applies to the whole person, from conception until natural death.[203] The protection of this right is connected with the formation

197. Ibid., 197.

198. Ibid.

199. Ibid., 196–203.

200. John Paul II locates in human rights a minimal standard for the beginning of freedom, rather than its fullness or perfection. See *Evangelium Vitae: The Gospel of Life*, 75.

201. John Paul II, *Crossing the Threshold of Hope*, 202.

202. Ibid., 204.

203. Ibid., 205.

of a culture of life, in which responsible parenthood is not overlooked (he encourages it, in conjunction with the freedom that comes from acting responsibly and not to the detriment of any single human individual).[204] Mothers receive special attention in this context. A "radical solidarity" is called for with each woman, such that the choice for life becomes part of a cultural whole, one that honors the role of all persons, including parents.[205] Indeed, the criterion for authentic responsibility amongst every family, human community, and ecclesiastical agency is the intentional witness of an ethic of love. John Paul II views many persons as already fulfilling these criteria. Of them he says, "[i]n their lives we find confirmation of the Christian and of the personalistic truth about man, who becomes fully himself to the extent that he gives himself as a free gift to others."[206] In addition, John Paul II calls for greater collaboration between pastors, biologists, and physicians.[207] By reference to so many stakeholders, this is a universal vision. The pope concludes these thoughts in "The Defence of Every Life" with the following reference to Levinas. It is helpful to quote it in full:

> I cannot dwell here on *contemporary thinkers*, but I must mention at least one name—*Emmanuel Levinas*, who represents a particular school of contemporary *personalism* and of the *philosophy of dialogue*. Like Martin Buber and Franz Rosenzweig, he takes up the personalistic tradition of the Old Testament, where the relationship between the human "I" and the divine, absolutely sovereign "THOU" is so heavily emphasized.
>
> God, who is the supreme legislator, forcefully enjoins on Sinai the commandment "Thou shalt not kill," as an absolute moral imperative. Levinas, who, like his co-religionists, deeply experienced the tragedy of the Holocaust, offers a remarkable formulation of this fundamental commandment of the Decalogue—for him, the face reveals the person. This *philosophy of the face* is also found in the *Old Testament*: in the Psalms, and in the writings of the Prophets, there are frequent references to "seeking God's face" (cf. Ps 26[27]:8). It is through his face that

---

204. This follows the language pattern laid out by Paul VI, who is often quoted as encouraging "responsible parenthood" in *Humanae Vitae*. However, the original Latin of the encyclical uses the term *"paternitatem consciam attingens,"* which, in context, would be better rendered as "conscious parenthood." In this light, English language allusions to the encyclical as having some kind of parallel Catholic approach to what various contemporary institutions understand as "responsible parenthood" lack justification. See Paul VI, *Humanae Vitae*, 10.

205. John Paul II, *Crossing the Threshold of Hope*, 206–7.

206. Ibid., 209.

207. Ibid., 210.

man speaks, and in particular, every man who has suffered a wrong speaks and says the words "Do not kill me!" *The human face and the commandment "Do not kill" are ingeniously joined in Levinas, and thus become a testimony for our age,* in which governments, even democratically elected governments, sanction executions with such ease.

Perhaps it is better to say no more than this about such a painful subject.[208]

This reference to Levinas highlights John Paul II's ongoing interest in the notion of the face as an epiphany of the other. For him, this is intrinsically incarnate, whereas for Levinas—as shall be seen—the face is a nonincarnate epiphany of the other.

Reflections on the John Paul II–Levinas dialogue in Crossing the Threshold of Hope

It is clear that in 1994, when *Crossing the Threshold of Hope* was published, Levinas had made an impression upon John Paul II. Keeping in mind the initial references to Levinas at the beginning of the book, in which John Paul II favored the hermeneutical understanding of the human person of both Paul Ricœur and Levinas as indebted to the language of symbol and of metaphor, these paragraphs extend the interest in Levinas towards a more robust ethical description of the mystery of personhood. This is discussed in the context about the inherent dignity of human life and of ethical responsibility for its protection as well as that of universal human rights. Following the insights of Buber and Rosenzweig on the "I-Thou" relationship, Levinas develops his own ethical understanding of the role of alterity in the intersubjective experience of human living.

John Paul II felt that in the context of an interview about death and the defense of life, Levinas stood out as the name that "must" be mentioned amidst other contemporary thinkers.[209] John Paul II chooses to recommend Levinas as a personalist voice who speaks in harmony with the witness of the Old Testament. This is in direct conflict with some interpreters of Levinas, who claim to find in him an ethics of alterity that favors the other's right to specific acts such as euthanasia and abortion.[210] There is variation in the practical application of Levinas' ethics.

208. Ibid., 210–11.

209. Ibid., 210.

210. See for example Wolfs, "Levinas, Euthanasia and the Presence of Non-Sense," in Burggraeve (ed.), *The Awakening to the Other*, 303–19; Diprose, *Corporeal Generosity*.

Furthermore, the Holocaust plays an important role in the minds of those who, like Levinas, would speak of ethics at all after experiencing its horror. In mentioning this, John Paul II locates the importance of what may be learned from Levinas within the historical dimension in which it emerges, specifically that of the experience of evil at such a large-scale level of bureaucracy and organization. The utter destruction of so many Jewish persons and their communities, as well as those in other minority groups, is not an event that ought to be forgotten in general terms, let alone when considering voices like Levinas who lost much personally in the events of the Shoah.

The "philosophy of the face" is not, in John Paul II's reading of Levinas, an isolated approach to understanding the human person, but rather to be interpreted in close correlation with the divine law.[211] The commandment of the Decalogue—"Thou shalt not kill" (Exod 20:13)—is intimately related to the epiphany of the face as an extension of the transcendence that is present in each *other* person. This reveals that the divine law is not simply passed on in a propositional manner in the form of the law upon the tablet, but is *given* in each individual person. The cry of anguish that emerges from a human face, the contorted facial expressions of urgent plea, "do not kill me," the tilt of the downtrodden face as it bears upon the body's suffering frame; these are revelatory moments, not simply of the intense desire to be liberated from suffering and the threat of death, but are revelatory of God's own command *not* to kill the other. In this way, the commandments of God are written in both stone and in the human heart. John Paul II describes this linking of the epiphany of the face to the Old Testament witness in terms of a "remarkable formulation of this fundamental commandment of the Decalogue."[212] Of course, the face does not simply reveal the presence of the divine law in the order of creation, but "reveals the person."[213] After the Holocaust, it remains crucial to locate the relationship between the event of Sinai and the contemporary requirement of love in human relationships, which remain always the event of being among faces.

Furthermore, there are political consequences from the enjoinment in Levinas of the human face to the commandment not to kill. The relationship of the face and the divine command are "ingeniously joined in Levinas, and thus become a testimony for our age . . . ."[214] As a testimony, this enjoinment speaks directly to ethical concerns, including the manner in which

211. John Paul II, *Crossing the Threshold of Hope*, 210.

212. Ibid.

213. Ibid.

214. Ibid., 210–11.

ethics is made concrete, such as in politics or friendship. While the face is an epistemological vehicle of ethical knowledge, it is not passive knowledge; it is the knowledge that makes a demand, which is the requirement of action. On its own, the words "do not kill" remains a negative construct, lacking the divine fullness of actually seeking out life and affirming, protecting, or cultivating it. Life itself is the demand of such an ethics. John Paul II comments that in our own age, "governments, even democratically elected governments, sanction executions with such ease."[215]

Finally, the comment that "[p]erhaps it is better to say no more than this about such a painful subject" indicates the role of silence before suffering. More could be said, but the thought of what has transpired causes us to falter.[216] In considering seriously the role a Levinasian ethic might have in the further development of Wojtyla's philosophical anthropology, these indications from John Paul II may be taken as a point of departure.

John Paul II's reference to Levinas in *Memory and Identity*

In *Memory and Identity*, John Paul II's final interview and published testimony, he refers to Levinas.[217] He reflects on the nature of freedom and responsibility after the totalitarianisms of the twentieth century.[218] In their collapse, how is a newfound freedom to be used? John Paul II is concerned that utility and pleasure have been the adopted criterion for regulating this freedom, as distinct from what Aristotle understood to be the "just good" (John Paul II refers to the *bonum honestum*).[219] Certainly, utility and pleasure (John Paul II prefers the terms *bonum utile* and *bonum delectabile*) are, in themselves, also examples of goods that ought to be available to human experience, yet they remain limited in their scope for enabling an authentic human freedom when pitted in competition against the just good. In hu-

---

215. Ibid., 211.

216. Ibid.

217. John Paul II, *Memory and Identity*, 42.

218. Totalitarianism in its most explicit varieties cannot be thought of merely as constructs of the past, and too often enjoy contemporary expression. Wojtyla alludes to Soviet Communism and German National Socialism, but others reach into the present moment, including aspects of Chinese Communism, North Korea, Cuba, Zimbabwe, Sudan, Iraq, etc. Some of these are expressed in the state and others in illegitimate and self-proclaimed regimes and movements. See John Paul II, *Memory and Identity*, 37.

219. For Aristotle, the just good (and the good in general) cannot be defined with absolute precision, but remains a true aspect of nature and not of convention. See Aristotle, *The Nicomachean Ethics*, 1094b14.

man action, these goods share a synthetic relationship in which the will plays a lead role.[220] Human action then is the manner in which the human subject is imprinting his or her own rationality upon an experience; desire and freely exercised choice provide the content for the form of an act as it is performed. When a human act is given this form and content, the human person is making a moral decision. That is to say, a "certain good" is chosen that becomes the "goal" of the said action.[221]

The Thomistic appropriation of the Aristotelian schema is dismantled with modern utilitarianism. In divorcing utility from any form of a common good to which the human person might aspire, freedom becomes the availability and pursuit of an individuated pleasure, which is not equivalent to the *bonum delectabile* of Thomistic thought.[222] As one response to this utilitarian vision, John Paul II describes Immanuel Kant's philosophy as providing a foundation for modern personalist ethics.[223] Kant's categorical imperative at least maintains an obligatory character in human moral choices, yet he attempted to do so without an intrinsic reference to the *bonum honestum*.[224] John Paul II summarizes his approach to this fundamental problem of the authentic criterion for human freedom in the three works, *Love and Responsibility*, *The Acting Person*, and in his catechesis *Original Unity of Man and Woman* (his theology of the body).[225] The problems dealt with in these texts are, in John Paul II's reading, the same problems identified in the work of Levinas, alongside figures such as Max Scheler, Jean-Paul Sartre, Paul Ricœur, Vladimir Soloviev, and Fyodor Dostoyevsky.[226] In the "anthropological reality" that is analyzed in their work, John Paul II identifies the emergence of a variety of manifestations of what he names "man's desire for Redemption, and confirmation is given of the need for a Redeemer if man is to attain salvation."[227] This theological conclusion is orientated by John Paul II's reading of significant philosophers from the twentieth century who, in their turn, have engaged with fundamental challenges in human existentiality and in the prospects of thinking and acting after the Holocaust. Levinas' inclusion in the list confirms that to the end, John Paul II viewed him as

220. John Paul II, *Memory and Identity*, 38.

221. Ibid., 39.

222. Ibid.

223. Ibid., 41.

224. See especially Kant's introduction of the "categorical imperative" in *Groundwork for the Metaphysics of Morals*.

225. John Paul II, *Memory and Identity*, 42.

226. Ibid.

227. Ibid.

an influential voice in the philosophical background of his own theological anthropology. John McNerney has described the generous scope for further comparison of Wojtyla and Levinas in this context, the former's philosophy of which he calls the "footbridge toward the other."[228] With this footbridge in mind, Levinas' own references to Wojtyla may now be considered.

Levinas' direct references to Wojtyla

Levinas references Wojtyla in interviews, but his article published in 1980 is a crucial insight into his interpretation of the latter.

Communio article: "To the letter and to his hermeneutic"

Levinas published an article about Wojtyla in the July-August (1980) issue of the French language edition of *Communio: International Catholic Review*.[229] It is an edited version of a presentation Levinas gave to a Parisian conference on the theme "The Philosophical Thought of John Paul II" in 1980.[230] The article is largely overlooked in secondary literature. Strangely, despite the ambition for comprehensiveness in the otherwise excellent resource the *Levinas Concordance*, this article is not listed in that text, nor does Wojtyla appear in the index under any name or title.[231] Nevertheless, the article is a rare insight into Levinas' philosophical appreciation of Wojtyla's work and contextualizes their relationship. Levinas comments on what he appreciates most in his interlocutor's work:

> Within this thought, what is no doubt the most appealing is above all the utter fidelity to the norm of philosophical discourse: the persistence of analysis in a language that is rigorous in the light of day and which is suspicious, if one can say, of theological inspiration. I have to admit, although observing the same norm, I have always allowed myself in my modest writings, to return

228. In fact, the book is referred to in the preface by that title and listed by some retailers as *Footbridge Toward the Other*, which is taken from Wojtyla's poem, *Thoughts about a footbridge*. The final published title is: McNerney, *John Paul II*, xiii, 161.

229. All quotations of this article are the author's own translation of the original article: Emmanuel Levinas, "Notes Sur La Pensée Philosophique Du Cardinal Wojtyla," *Communio* 4, no. juillet-aout (1980).

230. McNerney, *John Paul II*, 84.

231. See Ciocan and Hansel, *Levinas Concordance*.

more often than not to what the Cardinal does, to the letter and to his hermeneutic.[232]

Levinas notes Wojtyla's methodology, which he first encountered in "Participation or Alienation?"[233] Levinas' admiration for the suspicion of "theological inspiration" does not carry the sarcastic edge it seems to betray, but rather the comment of one phenomenologist about another. Phenomenology seeks to rigorously describe objective realities by virtue of their appearance, "describing, not of explaining or analysing," in the words of Merleau-Ponty.[234] While there is now a complex array of different phenomenologists and versions of phenomenological method[235] the roots of phenomenology remain organically fixed to Husserl's vision of a scientific method that is an authentic "aperspectival, theoretical, 'objective' understanding of things."[236] Elsewhere, in an essay titled "Reflections on Phenomenological 'Technique,'" Levinas affirms that Husserlian phenomenology is a method and not an exegesis or history of Husserl's writings.[237] As such, he identifies the success of phenomenological description by virtue of its fidelity to the Husserlian mode of intentionality; beginning with the object and departing upstream in the current that constitutes its presence.[238] As he argues, "[t]o do phenomenology is to denounce the direct vision of the object as naïve."[239] Indeed, this is what enables Levinas to recognize a new philosophical appreciation of the body, in which sensibility is conjoined with the experience of subjectivity instead of simply acting as some kind of object-subject reflection.[240] A certain ambiguity arises in the fact of subjectivity and in its sensory activity in the world; these are not exacting borders but the meeting of observable dimensions of embodied life. Within this complexity, the person can be identified as transcendent to the world and its history, in which the "*now* is prior to the historical manifold that it will constitute, that phenomenology preserves the person."[241] As such, Levinas' identification of

232. Levinas, "Notes Sur La Pensée Philosophique Du Cardinal Wojtyla," 87.

233. "Participation or Alienation?" in John Paul II, *Person and Community*, 197–207.

234. Merleau-Ponty, *Phenomenology of Perception*, ix.

235. Moran, *Introduction to Phenomenology*, 14.

236. Ibid., 12.

237. Levinas, *Discovering Existence with Husserl*, 91.

238. Ibid., 94.

239. Ibid.

240. Ibid., 99.

241. Ibid., 100.

Wojtyla's "strict" methodology is an appeal to phenomenological enquiry as the common landscape in which they both think and write.[242]

In the second part of his article, Levinas compares Wojtyla's phenomenology with Søren Kierkegaard, for whom ethics and religion were separated by a "crack," whose depths divided them in polar opposition.[243] Levinas finds in Wojtyla an overcoming of that separation, but by a phenomenological rather than theological route. Wojtyla's phenomenology of the human person in action is therefore a philosophy of that which appears as ethical. Ethics is not an *addendum* to the embodied person, but an intrinsic aspect of its appearance in the world. Levinas identifies Wojtyla's entry point into ethics as the interior fullness of the action of the human person, of "man as realized in his acts" [personne-accomplissant-les-actions-d'homme].[244] Levinas writes of this ethical-philosophical relationship:

> Also very striking is the particularly sensitive and unfailing solidarity with the entire structure of ethics; which determines a phenomenology of that which is human within that of transcendence.[245]

In other words, transcendence relates to that which is authentically human. It will be seen in chapter 3 how transcendence is one of a number of categories that are problematic in Levinas' approach to the body. Yet in this context he is identifying its philosophical use as an experiential trajectory in Wojtyla's thought, one that affirms the wider possibility of communion with others. Indeed, transcendence is a possibility *ad extra* the human person, predicated precisely on a complex interiority. The external dimension of relationship with others depends on the internal direction towards the other. Levinas rightly views Wojtyla's intellectual project as following one aspect of Kant's approach in critiquing any form of naturalism.[246] Wojtyla learnt from Max Scheler that the embodied human person is the possibility of the presence of values; values and judgments cannot occur without concrete persons.[247] By the same token, human persons relate those values and judgments in a concrete intersubjectivity, which negates modern conceptualizations of the self as autonomous.[248] In the consciousness of the

242. Levinas, "Notes Sur La Pensée Philosophique Du Cardinal Wojtyla," 87.

243. Ibid.

244. Ibid.

245. Ibid.

246. Ibid., 87–88.

247. See especially the final chapters in section 6.B. of Scheler, *Formalism in Ethics and Non-Formal Ethics of Values.*

248. See the graphic example of Friedrich Nietzsche in the second essay in "The

social human subject, Levinas locates the "voice of God" [*voix de Dieu*]. Even at this point, Levinas is hesitant to objectify this voice, but turns to the language of "resonance" [*résonance*] to describe its presence.[249] That is to say, Levinas is not wishing to theologize in terms of any formal religious tradition, but appeals to the common Judaic-Christian inheritance of an association of divine voice with the inner voice of "moral conscience."[250] It is a philosophical observation appealing to a theological sensibility.

In section three of Levinas' article, he comments on *The Acting Person* and its central concern; that of the human subject constituted in action. He comments that Wojtyla's account of participation is uniquely positioned between individualism and totalitarianism.[251] For Levinas, the privileging of the role of the individual in the communitarian context of an ethical sociality bears the marks of a thinker affected by the actions of Hitler and Stalin.[252] Yet this is not simply a mean between two extremes, but a phenomenological description of the human person as *the* subject who acts. Indeed, at no point in Levinas' reading of Wojtyla does he find the latter move the center of gravity in human affairs to the strictly social or even to the sociological.[253] Wojtyla seeks out the "possible agreement between a common goal and the subjective purpose of each member."[254] In other words, no natural antipathy is assumed between the community in which the person participates and any individual within that community. The Wojtylan distrust of the "subordination of the substantial person to the collective soul" locates the vocation of the philosopher within an ethical orbit of others; not bound to one ego and its imposition upon others.[255] It also acts against totalitarianisms of either the Left or the Right, by placing the possibility for community within human subjectivity (which is both individual *and* social) rather than in exterior forms or collectives.

Section four carries two further thoughts on Wojtyla's phenomenology. First, Wojtyla does not claim to have offered a philosophy of consciousness.[256] In this sense, he does not follow Husserl and in fact breaks with the Husserlian turn towards pure consciousness and transcendental idealism.

Genealogy of Morals," reproduced in Atkins, *Self and Subjectivity*, 80.

249. Levinas, "Notes Sur La Pensée Philosophique Du Cardinal Wojtyla," 88.

250. Ibid.

251. Ibid.

252. Ibid.

253. Ibid.

254. Ibid.

255. Ibid.

256. Ibid.

Wojtyla is also far from Heidegger on this point, who Levinas notes is only referenced once in *The Acting Person*.[257] Certainly, the correlation of Wojtyla's approach with the early Husserl (especially of the *Logical Investigations*) places Wojtyla amongst that collection of thinkers who are highly sensitive to the difference between thinking and thought and of the characteristic intentionality of any particular conscience in relation to objects and their value; namely Max Scheler and Roman Ingarden.[258]

Second, Levinas personally attributes to phenomenology a surplus of possibilities, much of which can be found in Wojtyla's written corpus.[259] Levinas seems uncertain as to whether Wojtyla follows the early Husserlian phenomenological method strictly at all other times (despite his earlier comments), but seems to interpret it as a guiding principle in Wojtyla's thought.

Levinas offers two "less academic" observations on the fruitfulness of phenomenology.[260] First, to do phenomenology is to practice intentionality. That is, phenomenology is not an abstracted *theoria* that can bracket the world out with perfection. Knowledge, like the will, is also an intentionality, one that thinks a thought and is able to reflect on the manner of that thinking, itself a new thought present to consciousness.[261] Such knowledge of thought and its thinking carries a directionality within a horizon of knowing. Second, "one can say otherwise" in relation to the above.[262] To do phenomenology is also to request or ask for "everything" that is immediately perceived and understood.[263] It is to accept that which is available before oneself and allow it to narrate its "twists and turns" in a plot performed before an audience.[264] The object's practical meaning can then be perceived in its truest terms. Levinas notes with approval these two aspects of phenomenological enquiry in Wojtyla, but does not elaborate further.

In conclusion, Levinas again notes the integral relationship between acts and embodied personhood in Wojtyla.[265] He asks whether the "phe-

257. Ibid., 88–89.

258. Ibid., 89.

259. It is an interesting side note that Levinas insists in this article on referring to Wojtyla as "Cardinal Wojtyla" or "the Cardinal" [*le Cardinal*] and not by his (by then) papal title. Levinas first met Wojtyla after he had become a cardinal and seems to prefer this title over others.

260. Levinas, "Notes Sur La Pensée Philosophique Du Cardinal Wojtyla," 89.

261. Ibid.

262. Ibid.

263. Ibid.

264. Ibid.

265. Ibid.

nomenological Cardinal" did not begin with these things and find his way towards metaphysical and anthropological concepts and the metaphysical essence of man?[266] In the relationship of person-act-will-choice-decision, the human subject locates both its self-limitations as well as its teleology within free acts. For Levinas, Wojtyla was "perhaps seeking the eidos of man . . . ."[267] The Wojtylan enjoinment of ultimate meaning with personal acts reveals this *eidos*—the form—of what is authentically human, "as if the intrigue of human transcendence unfolded in its own terms the truth of being."[268] These reflections constitute a necessary aspect of the Wojtyla-Levinas dialogue, in which Levinas is concerned to find what is authentically human in the incarnate human subject. The human subject's ethical nature is revealed in action and is fundamentally open to phenomenological enquiry.

In interview and at Castel Gandolfo

Levinas refers to John Paul II as the "phenomenological Cardinal," which links Wojtyla's philosophical interests with his ecclesiastical title and pastorate.[269] In an interview titled *The Vocation of the Other*, Levinas speaks of the "filiality of transcendence," the recognition that the children of Israel are descendants of the patriarchs, that their glory is an elevation, but that further to this recognition is the moment in which the self is recognized as a "son of God."[270] Levinas refers to a "magnificent meditation of John Paul II," teaching that God incarnates himself through Christ in all men. For the Jews this is no surprise, but a confirmation of the literal formulation of divine paternity giving itself to each person as a son of God, such that the words "Our Father" consistently return in the Jewish liturgy.[271] Levinas does not clarify where this meditation originates, but the theme was not uncommon in Wojtyla's teaching that divine sonship is offered to all through the filial obedience of the incarnation. This places the phenomenological interests of Wojtyla in a theological context marked by the sense of the familial; that the people of God have recourse to a divine person known in his fatherhood, which makes him an intimate carer with whom they share a relationship.

266. Ibid.

267. Ibid., 89–90.

268. Ibid., 90.

269. Malka makes reference to this Levinasian term, not said without some humor, in Malka, *Emmanuel Levinas*, 222–25.

270. Levinas, *Is It Righteous to Be?*, 105–14, 109.

271. Ibid., 109.

Many of these themes were explored in other scholarly gatherings. In 1983, Pope John Paul II began inviting scholars and scientists to Castel Gandolfo for annual *colloquia*.[272] According to George Weigel, each participant would present a paper, followed by discussion, concluding with a response from the pope.[273] Levinas was invited more than once and it was an opportunity for the philosopher pope to express his respect for Levinas in an informal scholarly gathering. Unfortunately, there are no minutes or public records of these meetings. Paul Ricœur was another attendee who confirmed not only a personal friendship but a shared intellectual interest between Wojtyla and Levinas.[274]

Conclusion

The dialogue between Wojtyla/John Paul II and Levinas has the potential for a fruitful theological engagement. In their commitment to developing a dialogical relationship between religious traditions, approaches to the body find an interreligious impetus, but without a reduction in either religious tradition. Phenomenology describes a shared philosophical methodology that opens up new possibilities for looking at the person and the body. More generally, the postmodern condition has become a site of increased debate concerning the body and both Wojtyla and Levinas exemplify a desire to overcome deficiencies they see in contemporary debate. In section two, the historical encounters that constitute the Wojtyla-Levinas dialogue were studied. The first encounter, Levinas' reading of Wojtyla's text on the "I-other" problematic, indicates a mutual awareness of human alterity as a crucial factor for contemporary philosophy. This is confirmed in John Paul II's comments in *Crossing the Threshold of Hope*, where he appeals to Levinas' "philosophy of the face" as both a philosophical insight and an ethical obligation. While Wojtyla refers to this philosophy affirmatively, it will be seen that the face is problematic in describing the body. There is a disincarnate logic at work in Levinas' refusal of incarnation in recognizing the human person.

272. Weigel, *Witness to Hope*, 466 and 192, respectively; Malka, *Emmanuel Levinas*, 192–93.

273. Unfortunately, no minutes were taken at these meetings and photos of the occasions (which are said to have taken place of each scholarly gathering) remain in the archives. It is hoped these will be made available to scholars and members of the public in due time.

274. Malka, *Emmanuel Levinas*, 193.

At the same moment in which Levinas appeals to the face most strongly, he denies an incarnational avatar and so disconnects the human body as it is experienced from his account of the other. While most interpreters of Levinas emphasize the descriptions of the other and the face from his major works (*Totality and Infinity* and *Otherwise Than Being*), a more interesting challenge emerges in Levinas' inconsistencies regarding the body. This will be seen in chapter 3 in which it is shown that despite Levinas' argument for an absolute alterity of the other, his own rhetoric remains committed to the sensuous and affective realities which anchor humanity in the embodied experience of the world. Human beings cannot, despite Levinas, escape or deny the body. It is unclear whether Wojtyla recognized this irregularity in Levinas' thought and certainly his appeal to Levinas is inconsistent with his own theological commitments to the language of the body. The dialogue between them is fruitful precisely because of the commanding role the body plays in their accounts of the human person and especially in how this appears in a logic of giftedness. The other person as a gift to be received is for both of them a mystery which remains present in the most mundane and domestic of human encounters; especially the home and in the family. Further comments in *Memory and Identity* and from Levinas in his *Communio* article about Wojtyla indicate that their shared phenomenological interests are immersed in the mystery of the human person as an embodied creature in the domesticity of world. They are both aware of the need to avoid totalitarian tendencies and to describe the person, as it appears to intentional awareness. Indeed, intentionality is on particular display when considering Wojtyla's nuptial mystery in dialogue with Levinas' absolute alterity, for both are intensified in the desiring gaze of one person for the good of the other. A concretized self-gift appears in both their accounts of the body, even though one is theological (Wojtyla) and the other strictly phenomenological (Levinas).

This dialogue deserves reflection and reveals both tensions and opportunities between Wojtyla and Levinas. The inconsistencies of Levinas prove a fruitful philosophical insight into the body because they test his descriptions of the other against the body as it is experienced. That the body cannot be escaped or denied is itself a fundamental challenge and this is made more important when considering Levinas' use of theological language to describe it. Equally, the emphasis on self-donation in the logic of the gift makes Wojtyla's claims about the nuptial mystery relevant to a wider sociality than simply the embodied married relationship. The appearance of the other is an embodied experience that reveals an ethical responsibility, and one that evokes the joy of the good revealed in the other's face. The dialogue between Levinas and Wojtyla is then one that shapes both an ethical description of the encounter with the other as well as one that enables a theologizing of the body with phenomenological attentiveness. With this dialogical foundation, Wojtyla's theology of the body will be explored in the following chapter.

2

John Paul II's Theology of the Body

Introduction

THE PLACE OF THE body in the thought of John Paul II is situated within a prolific literary legacy for philosophy and theology.[1] Here, his original contribution to theological anthropology will be of interest, specifically his development of a theology of the body.[2] This chapter has three sections. The first is on the formative influences upon the younger Karol Wojtyla, the second outlines his theological framework which accentuated his thought as Bishop of Rome, and the third looks closely at *Man and Woman He Created Them*. The latter was written while Wojtyla was Archbishop of Krakow, but presented and published after his election as John Paul II. The place of the body according to John Paul II relates profoundly to his phenomenological interest in the human person. Furthermore, his account of *communio* and the body leads him to take up the nuptial mystery as his principle paradigm of alterity.

---

1. John Paul II's papacy lasted over twenty-six years (October 1978–April 2005) and produced more than 70,000 pages of teaching in encyclicals, apostolic exhortations, apostolic letters, homilies, addresses, letters, and other published texts. See O'Collins, "John Paul II and the Development of Doctrine," in Hayes and O'Collins (eds.), *The Legacy of John Paul II*, 1.

2. As an original contribution, John Paul II's theology is remarkable for reshaping papal teaching by more constant attention to Scripture, both as a point of departure and as an active role in developing his own thought. See Jones, "John Paul II and Moral Theology," in Hayes and O'Collins (eds.), *The Legacy of John Paul II*, 103.

Formative influences and theological departures: the human person in the drama of history

Man and Woman He Created Them has been described as a "theological time bomb," waiting to go off in the life of the church at some point in the twenty-first century.[3] It is true that many, probably most, Catholics have not heard of it, and it is an underutilized lens through which Christian theologians might view the mystery of the human person. Informed readers of *Man and Woman He Created Them* are rare. There tends to be two camps: those who have taken to it with evangelical enthusiasm, and those who have a vague idea that a pope said something about the body.[4] Comprehensive negation of John Paul II's position is uncommon, although argumentation appears in the context of other broader works.[5] It is possible that Wojtyla's election as pope permanently clouds the judgment of those who might engage with his thought on its own terms, stripped of prejudice concerning his official teaching and that of the Catholic Church (whether glowing or condemnatory). As David Albert Jones comments, "[i]n order to appreciate John Paul II as a theologian (without either excessive deference or excessive defensiveness) it seems better to try to forget that he was also pope."[6] Here, Wojtyla will be read as soberly and as fairly as possible, attempting to put aside unhelpful enthusiasm and lazy indifference. In any case, both before and after his papal election, Wojtyla's published works concerned the human person as an embodied creature within a theological framework. The prominence Wojtyla gave to the body in his writing is a response to various anthropological tendencies he encountered. The biographer George Weigel contextualizes it thus:

> By insisting that the human subject is always an embodied subject whose embodiedness is critical to his or her self-understanding and relationship to the world, John Paul took modernity's "anthropological turn" with utmost seriousness.[7]

That is, Wojtyla's *Theology of the Body* was an attempt at answering the turn to the person evident in modernity, with a robustly Christian response.

---

3. Weigel, *Witness to Hope*, 342–43.

4. A well-known popularizer of John Paul II's theology of the body is Christopher West, an evangelist and writer. See his interpretation of John Paul II, *Man and Woman He Created Them*; West, *Theology of the Body Explained*.

5. For example, see Curran, *The Moral Theology of Pope John Paul II*.

6. Jones, "John Paul II and Moral Theology," in Hayes and O'Collins (eds.), *The Legacy of John Paul II*, 103.

7. Weigel, *Witness to Hope*, 343.

The critical relationship between embodiment and the dual comprehensions of one's selfhood and one's relationship to the world is central. Embodiment is a state of being for material creatures that both limits and enables them to act within a wider experience of the world. The body is a particular form of materiality that distinguishes one person from another; limited to what a human person can achieve as a body and enabling it to live and die like others. There is a long-standing tradition in Christian theology of explaining the human person as a unity of the body, soul, and spirit, with particular emphasis on the body-soul relationship. Much debate has ensued on the nature of this relationship, although Wojtyla placed himself in line with a reasonable emphasis on the unity of the body and the soul. For example, the Catechism, authorized by John Paul II, refers to the soul as the "spiritual principle" within the human person that is not only the most authentic inner truth of the person, but also acts as the "form of the body."[8] The soul remains incorporeal and invisible, yet that aspect which, in turn, shapes the body in its spiritual and moral capacities. In turn, the body experiences in itself the imprint of sensory experience and the mental awareness and nonawareness of itself and others. Furthermore, it is organized according to genetic patterns and the opportunities to learn cultural, religious, and social habits by communication with others. The human body also experiences itself in terms of gender—male and female—which is a dimension of human experience Wojtyla attends to with both theological and philosophical interest. As will be looked at in detail, Wojtyla's approach to the body takes gender and sexual differentiation seriously, not as social constructs but as signifiers of the bodily and sexual aspects of being male and female. He does this primarily not to invoke a categorical account of attributes belonging to one sex or the other, but to evoke the analogy of the nuptial mystery as primarily a theological reality concerning Christ and the church that is grounded within the embodiment of relationships between male and female. As such, this evocation is an appeal to an embodied reality in social discourse for reflection on God.

Weigel, along with George Williams, is right to relate this to Wojtyla's more general appreciation of the points of anthropological interest that have arisen in recent philosophy.[9] Weigel refers to an interview with Angelo Scola, who suggests that every thesis in theology could be seen in a new light if theologians were to explore in depth the personalism of Wojtyla's

8. Catholic Church, *Catechism of the Catholic Church*, 363, 65.

9. George H. Williams contrasts Wojtyla's development of Christian anthropology in highlighting the "historical man" against the "abstract" man of Marxism or the abstract "humanity" of the French Revolution and its twentieth-century sequels. See Williams, *The Mind of John Paul II*, 267.

theology of the body, which is presented as a catechesis on human and married love.[10] For Scola, it is the nuptial mystery that unfolds an authentic theological anthropology.[11] He argues that the nuptial mystery acts as a systematic perspective for the *intellectus fidei*. Following Balthasar, both Scola and Wojtyla develop the nuptial mystery with the Trinity as a basis for human relationships. Scola explicitly states that this moves beyond traditional restrictions in prohibiting the Trinity of Father, Son, and Holy Spirit from acting as the iconic model for marital or familial relationships.[12] Those restrictions, in Scola's reading, have now been overcome. A key voice that expresses a more wary, and therefore restrictive perspective on this use of the Trinitarian model is that of St. Augustine. Scola wishes to take Augustine seriously, but move beyond his perspective on the body. Augustine's contribution to the development of Western Trinitarian theology is profound and some comment on how Wojtyla departs from him is important.

For Augustine, the *imago Dei* in man has a Trinitarian structure: either the tripartite structure of the human soul (spirit, self-consciousness, and love) or the threefold aspects of the psyche (memory, intelligence, and will). In the *Confessions*, Augustine says that we are formed for God and that our hearts are restless until they find rest in the Lord, and in *the Trinity*, he states that the divine image orients the human person in invocation, knowledge, and love.[13] That is to say, the human capacity to respond to God's prior act of love is shaped by the Trinity's personal structure of one-in-three and three-in-one. Yet, Augustine warned against overreliance on this mutuality of structures to build a description of human behavior. In *On the Trinity*, he disparages those who "try to transfer what they have observed about bodily things to incorporeal and spiritual things . . . ."[14] Augustine distinguishes God from creation so that the absolute difference of the divine life can be appreciated more perfectly from a human perspective. Again, in Book 8, he speaks against images of the body or interbodily relations as a basis for understanding God: "Indeed any and every bodily conception is to be so rejected."[15] Thus, the Augustinian position is, strictly speaking, one that Wojtyla departs from. It can certainly be seen that Augustine maintains a

10. Weigel, *Witness to Hope*, 343.

11. For Scola, it constitutes one of the "essential aspects of reality, considered both in itself and against the horizon of Christian revelation," yet its depth and multilayered imagery reminds us that it must not be circumvented. It remains a "mystery." See Scola, *The Nuptial Mystery*, 82–83.

12. Scola, "The Nuptial Mystery," 209.

13. Augustine, *The Confessions*, I.1.1; *The Trinity*, IX.3–5.

14. Augustine, *The Trinity*, I.1.1.

15. Ibid., VIII.2.3.

firm difference between God and created things. Nevertheless, despite Augustine's warning about the body as a basis for understanding God, he recognizes that limited human experiences of love are motivated and oriented by God's first act of love. In responding to the higher love of the Triune God, human beings are aware that their first contemplation is upon those acts of love with which the body is accustomed. Augustine states:

> Now love means someone loving and something loved with love. There you are with three, the lover, what is being loved, and love. And what is love but a kind of life coupling or trying to couple together two things, namely lover and what is being loved? This is true even of the most external and fleshly kinds of love. But in order to quaff something purer and more limpid, let us trample on the flesh and rise to the spirit.[16]

Augustine wishes to raise human minds from the lowliness of flesh and bodily love to the heights of the Spirit of God. For him, bodily witnesses to love are merely a lowly step to take on the way to a higher love. Wojtyla does not depart from Augustine in insisting on either the absolute difference between God and creation or the emphasis on God's love as the one perfect love to which all human loves are imperfectly oriented. However, Wojtyla does depart from Augustine by speaking of fleshly love as something to hold in veneration, rather than something to trample upon on the way to God. For Wojtyla, embodied forms of human love—and in particular those relating to sexuality within the nuptial relationship—have the capacity to orient human persons towards God's love without being discarded in the process. This is because embodied forms of love hold no capacity to love without the prior gift of God's Spirit. This is of primary importance, because all experiences of love known by the body find their originary event in the divine Trinity. The directionality of the Spirit is crucial; God reveals himself in Christ and shares the Holy Spirit as a gift to the created order, thus manifesting God's life within the world. The nuptial mystery in this sense is also an affirmation of God's prior self-gift. John Paul II states:

> This gift sustains and develops in the spouses a singular *sensibility for all* that in their vocation and shared life carries *the sign of the mystery of creation and redemption*: for all that is a created reflection of God's wisdom and love.[17]

It is the Spirit of God that offers and maintains the possibility of experiences of the body oriented to love. There is no doubt that Wojtyla defends

16. Ibid., VIII.5.14.

17. John Paul II, *Man and Woman He Created Them*, 131:4.

a strong account of the reflection of the Trinity within some human relationships. Yet it is also true that his innovative work does not fundamentally disregard the tradition before him. Augustine is an important point of clarification in understanding Wojtyla's relation to the tradition, for it can be seen how the absolute difference between God's higher love and imperfect human loves is shared by Wojtyla and Augustine. The innovative work of Wojtyla is a delicate tension between the reflection of God's love within an embodied human love and the prior, perfect, and eternal love that, strictly speaking, belongs to God.

Two innovations in Wojtyla are identified by Scola. The first is the communional quality of our being made in the image of God (humans reflect the Trinity in their relation with others) and the second is his sexually differentiated anthropology of human embodiment (the body is the sacrament of the whole person).[18] Based on these two developments, Scola argues that the nuptial mystery serves as a new opening for systematic theology.[19] As an avenue for understanding *communio* with other persons and with the Triune God, the nuptial mystery casts light on the problem of the other and the dimension of alterity. However, it has its dangers. Two extreme poles come to mind. The first is the maximalist approach, which places an excessive burden of the images of nuptial and sexual relations upon the Trinity itself; in effect to "sex" the Trinity.[20] This is an overextension of the nuptial mystery, misunderstanding its nature as an analogical image within the theological tradition.[21] An opposing pole exists, in which the nuptial mystery is rejected altogether as a perspective for systematic theology.[22] This is often based upon a limited reading of nuptial imagery in the Bible as synonymous in value to the parables, such as the Shepherd and lost sheep.[23] It is viewed as limited in scope, lacking the systematic integration with other areas of thought and doctrine that would give it its inherent theological value.[24] There is no doubt that some danger lurks in the systematic presenta-

18. Scola, "The Nuptial Mystery," 212–14.

19. Ibid., 233.

20. Ibid., 221–22.

21. Examples include D'Costa, *Sexing the Trinity*; Loughlin, *Alien Sex*.

22. For example, Tracey Rowland notes a resistance to nuptial mysticism amongst neo-Thomists in contrast with Balthasarian thinkers, for whom life is theodramatic and therefore ecstatically open to the notions of being as (nuptial or spousal) "gift." See Rowland, "Natural Law."

23. Scola, "The Nuptial Mystery," 222.

24. For example, Fergus Kerr guards against possible excesses of utilizing the nuptial mystery systematically. See Kerr, *Twentieth-Century Catholic Theologians*, especially the chapters: "Hans Urs von Balthasar," "Karol Wojtyla," "Joseph Ratzinger," and "After

tion of the nuptial mystery, but with some care, and with due consideration of Wojtyla's perspective, it will be shown that its use is indeed valuable.

For Wojtyla, the Trinity is the original source for the enactment of *communio* in history. Michael Waldstein has demonstrated how vividly the centrality of triune love appears in the corpus of Wojtyla's writings.[25] In his papal pronouncements, the mystical fruit of the human person "finding himself" in the love of the Trinity is shown forth in the concrete realities of a lived life.[26] Salvation, through the Trinity, centers in each human (bodily) person a redeemed order of love, which in obedience to the source of all good things seeks to offer his or her humanity to Christ in all things (including sexuality). This reordering can only be understood in Trinitarian terms. The kernel of this thinking can be seen in earlier works, such as *Redemptor Hominis*, but the maturity of what could be called a Trinitarian praxis is evident from the earliest years of the John Paul II papacy. The notion of Wojtyla's development of the tradition can be observed in the broader context of moral theology after the Second Vatican Council. David Albert Jones identifies two areas in which Wojtyla makes an original contribution to that development.[27] The first is in his personalist approach to moral questions. That is to say, Wojtyla's phenomenological focus on the content of human experience in explaining the dignity of the person developed moral theology at its experiential and existential foundations. It is because of this contribution that Wojtyla could consider sexuality, not simply in terms of physiology or biology, but in terms of its *meaning* for human persons.

The second area is that of Wojtyla's use of Scripture in moral theology. For Jones, this will be the more enduring legacy, because it takes up the Second Vatican Council's call for a return to Scripture as the "supreme rule of faith."[28] Wojtyla's biblical hermeneutic is to allow the texts to act as a source of argument and disputation in their own right, yet central and primary within Christian moral discourse. Within scriptural texts, Wojtyla in turn views Christ as the hermeneutical key to understanding various threads of differing emphasis, and the Christian *ecclesia* as the proper social context in which those texts are to be manifested in the moral life. The use of Scripture by Wojtyla is an important contribution to developing the tradition. Oliver

---

Vatican II."

25. Waldstein, "John Paul II and St. Thomas on Love and the Trinity (First Part)," 116–17.

26. Wojtyla speaks of man's "living area" [*spatium hominis vitale*] raised up to the level of supernatural life. John Paul II, *Dominum Et Vivificantem: The Giver of Life*, 58.

27. Jones, "John Paul II and Moral Theology," in Hayes and O'Collins (eds.), *The Legacy of John Paul II*, 86–90.

28. Catholic Church, *Catechism of the Catholic Church*, 21.

O'Donovan has referred to Wojtyla's scriptural methodology not so much as a proof for arguments developed in the latter's encyclicals, but "teased out as a way of framing a question in scriptural terms, in a preacher's way."[29] That is, Scripture acts as a fruitful resource of authoritative guidance in Wojtyla's work. Wojtyla's development of the tradition is defended, as will be seen, very much in line with these two contributions, the first in his phenomenological approach to human experience, and the second in his utilization of Scripture as a primary source for moral theology.

A note on two previously unpublished works

It will be many years (if ever) before the full catalogue of Wojtyla's writings become publicly available. Both papal and prepapal correspondence, his early journalistic efforts, at least one play, and some poetry, not to mention personal journals, will be studied in detail before they are each published and translated. A brief comment on two relevant unpublished works needs to be made:

1. In the final years before his papal election, Wojtyla had worked on a sequel text to *The Acting Person* with his former student Fr. Tadeusz Styczeń. This work, begun in 1972 and uncompleted in 1978 when Wojtyla was elected pope, was a step back from sexual ethics as such to consider the more general content of ethics and its relation to the human subject. It has only recently entered circulation in English as *Man in the Field of Responsibility.*[30]

2. There is some controversy over the possible contents of an unfinished manuscript titled (provisionally), *Catholic Social Ethics* (*Katolicka Etyka Społeczna*), which Wojtyla published in a short print run of only 300 copies in 1953–54. Poland's Catholic University of Lublin, which holds the two-volume work, has committed itself to publishing the contents, but has not provided a timetable. The work is controversial because some readers have indicated that Wojtyla expresses sympathy for Marxist philosophy in an analysis of political ideology.[31] Weigel, in his biography, gives one footnote to this mysterious text and argues that the book is really the compilation of notes gained from other scholars, particularly the lecture notes of his

---

29. O'Donovan, "Pope John-Paul II."

30. Wojtyla's final prepapal book became available in 2011. See John Paul II, *Man in the Field of Responsibility.*

31. Controversy has been promoted by some journalists on this theme. See a public debate in Luxmoore and Ihnatowicz, "How an Unknown Text Could Throw New Light on John Paul II's Views on Economics," in *Houston Catholic Worker.*

colleague Jan Piwowarczyk.[32] Perhaps the real problem for contemporary critics is not that Wojtyla expresses a scholarly appraisal of those currents in Marxist thought with which Christians might sympathize, but his criticism of free market capitalism. Given Wojtyla's integral involvement in the collapse of Communism and in the success of counter-Soviet movements in Poland (specifically that of *Solidarność*), it seems incredible that his philosophical consideration of Marxist thought might be interpreted as Communist sympathy.

Wojtyla's interest in anthropology and its historical context

From his earliest writing, including his theatrical productions, Wojtyla was concerned with the mystery of the human person. As he writes in a 1968 letter to the Jesuit theologian Henri de Lubac:

> I devote my very rare free moments to a work that is close to my heart and devoted to the metaphysical sense and mystery of the PERSON. It seems to me that the debate today is being played out on that level. The evil of our times consists in the first place in a kind of degradation, indeed in a pulverisation, of the fundamental uniqueness of each human person. This evil is even more of the metaphysical order than of the moral order. To this disintegration planned at times by atheistic ideologies we must oppose, rather than sterile polemics, a kind of "recapitulation" of the inviolable mystery of the person.[33]

This commitment to the "metaphysical sense and mystery" of the human person is present in virtually every work produced by Wojtyla. It is clear that he did not understand it as an isolated intellectual problem, but as an ethical context in need of recapitulating the "mystery" of the person.[34] Furthermore, it cannot be understood apart from the formative influences upon the younger Wojtyla's thought and life.

Wojtyla's early experiences of the Second World War had a formative effect upon his thought. When he was later elected pope, he was able to speak as a church leader who had direct experience of war and its travesties.[35] Furthermore, Poland suffered through both the war and the Soviet liberation that followed. Poland's relationship with Russia had rarely been

---

32. Weigel, *Witness to Hope*, 130–31.

33. Lubac, *At the Service of the Church*, 171–72.

34. Ibid., 172.

35. Williams, *The Mind of John Paul II*, 8.

comfortably at peace, with a series of wars and insurrections between 1772 and 1944, so its history is marked by transient freedoms and heroic moments of national significance.[36] Indeed, Poland lost the highest proportion of its citizens (both civilian and military) to the war, in addition to those who were shipped elsewhere, placed in camps, tortured, cremated, or killed by the regime of German National Socialism.[37] Bleakly, Wojtyla's previous archdiocese (Kraków) included a death camp, that of Auschwitz (Oświęcim).[38] Wojtyla's formative adult years covered the duration of time between German occupation, Soviet liberation, and, in turn, Soviet Communist oppression. It was over a decade into his papacy before Soviet Communism collapsed and Poland gained a significant level of independence and autonomy.[39]

Wojtyla's theological framework: christocentric, Trinitarian, eucharistic, and Marian

Because Wojtyla published so widely in philosophy before his papal election, his theological contribution can be interpreted solely in terms of official pronouncements and writings such as encyclicals or apostolic letters. Yet his philosophical enquiries were pursued within a clear theological framework that he developed consistently throughout his life. Surprisingly few theologians have systematically engaged with Wojtyla's theology, but exceptions include John Saward, Aidan Nichols, Gerald O'Collins, Michael Hayes, and Antoine E. Nachef.[40] Wojtyla's personal reflections have highlighted the protection of theology as a scholarly discipline, in close dialogue with other areas of study.[41] To understand his later contribution in the area of the body, his theological framework must first be outlined, which is at once Trinitarian, christocentric, eucharistic, and Marian.

36. Ibid., 9.

37. Ibid.

38. Ibid.

39. For comprehensive accounts of the historical background to Wojtyla's life, see Prażmowska, *Poland*; Kemp-Welch, *Poland under Communism*; Davies, *God's Playground*.

40. See especially Saward, *Christ Is the Answer*; Dulles, *The Splendor of Faith*; Hayes and O'Collins, *The Legacy of John Paul II*; Gillis, *The Political Papacy*.

41. John Paul II, *Rise, Let Us Be on Our Way*, 87–88.

A christocentric theology

For John Saward, Wojtyla's theological framework is shaped by a geometric metaphor: it is thoroughly "christocentric."[42] This is in evidence from the opening words of his first papal encyclical, *Redemptor Hominis*: "The Redeemer of Man, Jesus Christ, is the centre of the universe and of history [*Iesus Christus est centrum universi et historiae*]."[43] These words act as a kind of Christian protest against the false ideologies of the twentieth century, and reject the claims of various other possible centers to the meaning of history, such as the state, the proletariat, the market, or the economy. A great number of themes are treated in *Redemptor Hominis*, but the common thread is the redemptive event of Christ, in whose person and work is revealed the mystery not just of God's love, but the vocation of the human person. As *Redemptor Hominis* states:

> Man cannot live without love. He remains a being that is incomprehensible for himself, his life is senseless, if love is not revealed to him, if he does not encounter love, if he does not experience it and make it his own, if he does not participate intimately in it. This, as has already been said, is why Christ the Redeemer "fully reveals man to himself."[44]

John Paul II expresses here the relationship between an encounter with revealed love and the encounter with the self. It is by virtue of the former that the latter is made possible, thus constituting anthropology on a christological basis. Love arrives in the person of Christ; it is this arrival that makes knowledge of one's own self possible. This was taught by the Second Vatican Council, especially "Gaudium et Spes." In that document, the Council explicitly linked anthropological understanding with the self-giving love of Christ. See especially the first paragraph of section 22:

> The truth is that only in the mystery of the incarnate Word does the mystery of man take on light. For Adam, the first man, was a figure of Him Who was to come, namely Christ the Lord. Christ, the final Adam, by the revelation of the mystery of the Father and His love, fully reveals man to man himself and makes his supreme calling clear.[45]

---

42. See his definition of terms in Saward, *Christ Is the Answer*, 1–14.
43. John Paul II, *Redemptor Hominis: The Redeemer of Man*, 1.
44. Ibid., 10.
45. Catholic Church, "Gaudium Et Spes," 22.

Only by Christ can the mystery of the human person be interpreted. Christ fulfills what was anticipated in the first Adam, and completes in his flesh what is lacking in the common human experience of embodied life. In fact, the anthropological teaching of the Second Vatican Council is a constant reference point for Wojtyla's theology.[46] Of course, he had played an active part in the Council. There are various accounts of the exact number of interventions made by Wojtyla, but of them, six were in connection with "Gaudium et Spes."[47] He intervened in the discussion of method and outline (II/5, 298–300); wrote parts on human nature and culture (III/5, 680–83) and various amendments (III/7, 380–82); gave a speech on creation and redemption as well as the topic of atheism (IV/2, 660–63); and wrote further on marriage and family (IV/3, 242–43) and culture and work (IV/3, 349–50).[48] These contributions highlight Wojtyla's interest in "Gaudium et Spes," but also speak to his interest in what Christ reveals to the whole man; to the human person in its concrete experience of the world. The teaching of *Redemptor Hominis*, that at the center of both the universe and of history is revelation, the God-Man Jesus, provides the constant point around which Wojtyla's theology moves and finds its bearings. In Saward's words, Christ acts as the *"nexus mysteriorum"* in Wojtyla's theological constellation.[49]

Crucially, Christocentrism is not a theology of an isolated Christ alone in a circle. The Incarnate one is never received *alone* in matters of faith, as if the center was all that mattered to the circle; it is not "Christomonism."[50] That is to say, Christocentrism cannot be interpreted as if faith consisted of Christ in a monadic form, severed from the bonds of incarnate relationship with the world he has redeemed, or even with his relationship to the other persons of the Trinity. Rather, Christ is both the second person of the Trinitarian *communio*, as well as a dynamic center who is accompanied by his redeemed creation/s, most especially the saints. The Christ to which Wojtyla refers is not constituted most properly within the terms of ontology,

46. Schmitz, *At the Center of the Human Drama*, 70.

47. Dulles counts twenty-three contributions to the Council, against Scola's twenty-two and Grondelski's eighteen. Dulles includes written works under the title "inscribed to speak," which were never given in actual speech form; from the *Acta Synodalia*. See Dulles, *The Splendor of Faith*; Scola, *"Gli Interventi Di Karol Wojtyła Al Concilio Ecumenico Vaticano II,"* in *Karol Wojtyła*; Grondelski, "Sources for the Study of Karol Wojtyła's Thought, Appendix," in Schmitz, *At the Centre of the Human Drama*.

48. In addition to details taken from the Council's official record, Dulles notes the integral relation they have with his other published works. See Dulles, *The Splendor of Faith*, 1–17.

49. Saward, *Christ Is the Answer*, 1.

50. Ibid., 3.

but the dynamic of relations in which he participates.[51] These relations are Trinitarian and human. Avery Dulles points out that while for Wojtyla theology must be christocentric, Christ himself is not.[52] The orientation of the Second Person of the Trinity was always in humble obedience towards the First, who is God the Father (John 4:34). This substantive work of the Son—to do the will of his Father—bears itself out in the three aspects of his mission: that of prophet, priest, and king. This *tria munera Christi* always, in Wojtyla's reading, presents a revelation also of the human condition itself.

Wojtyla's approach to the *tria munera Christi* is detailed explicitly in the work *Sign of Contradiction*, a text that includes his addresses to the papal household of Paul VI during its Lenten retreat in 1976. This work reflects further editorial changes made after the actual presentation of those addresses, and because of its ecclesial context offers a strictly theological work as opposed to Wojtyla's philosophical publications. As such, it is an important account of John Paul II's understanding of the *tria munera Christi*.

CHRIST THE PROPHET

In his prophetic mission, Christ "proclaims divine truth," both enacting it and preaching it to the world.[53] In so doing, Christ prophetically reveals a *telos*, a calling to mind of human dignity as something both present and called to fulfill in the action of life. Human dignity, according to the prophetic witness of Christ, is bound up with truth, which is our "greatest treasure."[54] It is that gravity of self-worth that finds its origins in the Father's love, but that can only strengthen its own witness by its binding to the truth. And truth, by nature, belongs to God and is one with the divine Word.[55] The culmination of Christ's prophetic witness is revealed for Wojtyla in the dialogue with Pilate, in which Christ gives his reason for coming into the world, "to bear witness to the truth" (John 18:37). In Christ, all human persons can locate the perfect synthesis between bearing witness to, and bearing within themselves, the truth.

Against the backdrop of an unruly world, Christ who is the truth stands out in stark relief, and so his prophetic nature is shown in form and outline, even before his spoken words are granted a hearing.

51. Dulles, *The Splendor of Faith*, 31.

52. Ibid., 33.

53. John Paul II, *Sign of Contradiction*, 120.

54. Ibid.

55. Ibid.

CHRIST THE PRIEST

The priestly ministry of Christ is not only a christological reflection for Wojtyla, but also an opportunity to reflect upon the "mystery of man."[56] In addition to Scripture, he refers to "Gaudium et Spes" (10) and to "Lumen Gentium" (22).[57] Building on the Council's teaching in these two documents, Wojtyla emphasizes that it is Christ's own priestly ministry in which both the laity and the ordained ministers of the church participate. Christ's priesthood is a self-sacrificial offering, one that is offered universally and so can be named the "common" priesthood of all the faithful.[58] Although Wojtyla's methodology here is reflective, calling to mind the various scriptural references to Christ's sacrificial priesthood (for example, Rom 12:1; Heb 10:5–7), he shapes this reflection anthropologically, by linking Jesus' soteriological accomplishment in his sacrifice and in the Eucharist to the "existential interrogative" about the human person.[59] That is to say, the existential question about the meaning and purpose of the embodied human creature, who finds itself caught between conflicting limitations, aspirations, possibilities, and the ever-present demands of a choice to be made.[60] The link is one of call and response. The existential question of human existence is the call that demands a response. Wojtyla concretizes this in terms of the lived experience of priesthood (speaking generally of lay or ordained members of Christ's priesthood). In a sense, the priest is making a subjective response both to a divine mandate as well as to the complex alterity of the self, what James Mensch calls "self-hiddenness."[61] In looking to others, we confirm our self-reliance on them, seeking in them a completion of what is lacking within ourselves. A "trace" is identified by the human subject referring to itself incompletely and to others to confirm this "inadequacy" of self-representation.[62] However, this trace is not the whole truth, nor does it have the capacity to tell the whole truth. Rather, the person locates the truth in an ascetic moment of recognizing its subjective inadequacy, and so becomes a more perfect subject to what lies beyond itself.

56. Ibid., 127.

57. Catholic Church, "Gaudium Et Spes," "Lumen Gentium."

58. John Paul II, *Sign of Contradiction*, 129.

59. Ibid., 127–29.

60. Ibid., 129–30.

61. Mensch, *Hiddenness and Alterity*, 89.

62. Ibid., 28–30.

The priest is one who has embraced the truth, and so has become a free subject to the truth.[63] Priesthood, as a quality of vocation that is embodied in a single human subject, is the sacrificial commitment that reveals truths about God, the world, and the human condition. It is an expression of meaning, showing the thread of continuity between the sacrifice of Calvary and the life of each human person. Priesthood plumbs the depths of human experience, reaching "to the depths of the whole existential truth of the created world, and above all the truth of man."[64] As a category of absolute sacrifice, priesthood is self-giving of a particularly high order, which provides an adequate response to the existential problem. Sacrificial priestly behavior "answers" the existential problem with the form of self-giving.[65] It is at this point that Wojtyla turns explicitly to the ordained sacerdotal ministers within the Roman Catholic tradition to explain transcendence in relation to the human condition. The priest is one whose ordination confers the "turning towards God" as an expression of lived transcendence.[66] This transcendence is a reaching towards that which surpasses the world, yet expresses itself precisely in living for others within the world.[67] It is not an expression of the self, but a participation in the priesthood of Christ.

Wojtyla does not summarize his thoughts on the intimate relationship between the priesthood of all believers, the ordained priesthood, and Christ's priesthood by reference to ethics. Instead, he refers to priesthood as prayer, both of man and the world. In fact, he turns to prayer as the "supreme" pursuit of the human person.[68] Prayer is not only an act of hope, but is revelatory of the human condition. In an allusion to Heidegger, Wojtyla claims that "[h]uman existence is 'being directed towards God.'"[69] Yet it is also contemplative, for "it is 'being within the dimensions of God.'"[70] Christ's sacrifice is therefore a participatory aspect of his ministry; one that invites each human person to enter a redemptive course of life that also reveals truths about human experience. It displays the contemporary existential

63. John Paul II, *Sign of Contradiction*, 130.

64. Ibid., 131.

65. Ibid., 130–32.

66. Ibid., 132.

67. This also has resonances with Martin Buber's "Single One" in the body politic: "Otherness enshrouds him, the otherness to which he is betrothed," in Buber, *Between Man and Man*, 64.

68. John Paul II, *Sign of Contradiction*, 135.

69. Heidegger's *Dasein*, lived authentically, is "being-toward-death." See for example Heidegger, *Being and Time*, 247. Wojtyla's Heideggerian reference is made in *Sign of Contradiction*, 135.

70. John Paul II, *Sign of Contradiction*, 135.

problem of human existence, as well as insisting that "Man exists not merely 'in the world,' not merely 'in himself'; he exists 'in relationship,' 'in self-giving.'"[71] In the contemporary setting, it is confirming the "between" of human existence, and does not look to this present world as the final context in which this "between" can be overcome.[72] Within such a transient moment, the kingship and prophetic witness of Christ are profoundly related to the priestly dimension, by which the kingly character is enjoined to the priestly character within the Christian disciple's act of faith.

CHRIST THE KING

Wojtyla reflects upon the third of the three major aspects of Christ's vocation and ministry, that of his kingship. Once again, he quotes the words of "Gaudium et Spes," "Christ, who is the new Adam, by revealing the mystery of the Father and his love, also reveals man to man himself . . . ."[73] The revelation of man's own mysteries have been understood under the titles of prophet and priest, but it is in Christ's kingship that Wojtyla's interpretation is the most paradoxical. He defines a relationship between *Christus Rex* and the human conscience by which the divine kingship is enthroned in the conscious acts of human personality. This is an argument for an integral relationship between the postresurrection Christ as a living God, and the structure of personal moral conscience within the human person. In the latter, the former is enthroned as king, thus putting aside a complete deferral of kingship until the eschaton in favor of a contemporary morality that owes its form and guidance to a contemporary Christ. The paradox lies in the absolute kingship afforded to Christ, while maintaining its humble reliance on the unique moral choices of each individual believer.

    Lumen Gentium is recalled; especially section 36 on the topic of Christ's kingdom.[74] In these words, Christ's obedience unto death and his entering into glory reveal him to be king, to whom all subsequent obedience is owed.[75] As the document explains:

> Christ, having made himself obedient unto death and exalted by the Father (cf Phil 2,8–9), entered into the glory of his kingdom. To him all things are made subject until he subjects himself and

71. Ibid., 132.

72. See especially William Desmond's treatment of desire in *Ethics and the Between*, 292.

73. Wojtyla quotes from Sect. 22 of GS; John Paul II, *Sign of Contradiction*, 137.

74. Ibid., 138.

75. Catholic Church, "Lumen Gentium," 36.

all created things to the Father in order that God may be all in all (1 Cor 15,27–28).[76]

Wojtyla includes the more extensive quote, in which the power of kingship is communicated to the disciples, established in "royal freedom."[77] The royalty in which Christ's disciples share is not one of dominion over others, but a dominion of "self-abnegation and a holy life," in which the reign of sin is overcome within themselves.[78] This interior kingdom also serves in an exterior, heraldic dimension, leading other brethren towards Christ the King, ushering in a time of humble servanthood under his reign.[79] For Wojtyla, this kingly character does not arrive solely by grace, but is already present or "embedded" within the structure of human personality as a kind of anticipative event.[80] In the various secular labors of the faithful, the kingly aspect of Christ shows itself. By acting faithfully within the world, the inner structure of kingship manifests itself outwardly. As such, theory and praxis are united christologically, confirming the Aristotelian notion that they remain complementary.[81]

Conscience is an important category for Wojtyla. For him, the union of *theoria* and *praxis* exists because of the presence of conscience, which he describes as "the most secret core and sanctuary of man, where he finds himself alone with God . . . ."[82] Conscience acts as the moral law, written within the human heart, to which human dignity is obedient. In subjecting human dignity to the moral conscience, Wojtyla is placing himself close to Thomas Aquinas' account of conscience, for which the good of human nature is protected by obedience to a higher good, which is of moral virtue. For Thomas, conscience is the application of "knowledge to activity."[83] It is the knowledge of good or evil as it is applied in particular circumstances that present themselves. The concrete practice of actions that follow a correctly formed conscience is what Thomas calls prudence, but it must be

76. Ibid.

77. Ibid.

78. John Paul II, *Sign of Contradiction*, 138. According to Aristotle, there are three main forms of *energeíai*. They are *theoría*, *poíesis*, and *praxis*. While the first is the highest, it remains in complementary relationship with the last, neither of which can be understood without reference to the second. See Book VI, Aristotle, *The Nicomachean Ethics*.

79. John Paul II, *Sign of Contradiction*, 138.

80. Ibid.

81. Wojtyla names Marxist philosophy as problematic in placing *praxis* before *theoria*. See John Paul II, *Sign of Contradiction*, 139.

82. Ibid., 140.

83. Thomas Aquinas, *Summa Theologiae*, I–II, I.

remembered that a conscience must be formed well and correctly to serve the person in correct moral guidance.[84] Wojtyla takes up this Thomistic approach and develops it within a stronger christological dimension. The human person must live and act in accordance with a high moral call; one of kingly dominion over the self's temptation towards sin and towards the enacting of Christ's kingly dominion over the whole creation. Conscience therefore must be obedient to the divine law, by which "serving Christ in others" equates to "reigning."[85] Wojtyla writes:

> Man's obedience to his conscience is the key to his moral grandeur and the basis of his "kingliness," his "dominion"; and this—ethically speaking—is also a dominion over himself. Obedience to conscience is a key element in the Christian's share "in munere regali Christi."[86]

In this schema, ethics follows the order of self-abnegation, which is a participation in the kingship of Christ. Obedience to God equals a share in Christ's kingly reign. This requires that the human person be obedient to moral conscience. In line with the tradition preceding him, Wojtyla identifies a powerful relationship between conscience and repentance, through which the individual human subject turns from a course of sin and faces the Redeemer.[87] He even associates Christ's kingship with the sinful man who has accepted the truth of his own sinfulness and thereupon repents.[88] This moment of humility, given form in the concrete experience of going down on one's knees in the Sacrament of Penance has, for Wojtyla, "something of the nature of a meeting 'face to face' (1 Cor 13,12)."[89]

The kingship of Christ therefore holds an anthropological promise. By it, the human person is granted its own moment of "kingliness" within the self, shone forth most clearly in the life of self-abnegation and the act of penance.[90] This is established in royal freedom only in so far as human dignity acts in abeyance to the law of love written in the moral conscience. The kingly person is one who has responded to the primary kingship of Christ, and in so doing, anticipates Christ's kingdom by living for others. It is therefore both a response and a participation in the life of grace.

---

84. Ibid., Ia, q. 79, a. 13.

85. John Paul II, *Sign of Contradiction*, 141.

86. Ibid.

87. Ibid., 141–43.

88. Ibid., 143.

89. Ibid., 142.

90. Ibid., 143.

A Trinitarian theology

For Wojtyla, the form of Christ is always in an integral relationship with the *communio personarum* that is the divine Trinity. John Saward describes the ecstatic experience of Christ in relation to the Trinity: "In the case of the 'Christ-form,' mediated in Scripture and the Sacraments of the Church, the glorious 'heights and depths' to which the Holy Spirit transports us are Trinitarian, 'the love of Him who sent Him.'"[91] In other words, the person of Christ opens up to us the life of the Trinity. In light of this intimate relationship between Christ and the other two persons of the Triune communion, Wojtyla's theology is consistently Trinitarian. His Christology is always a Trinitarian-shaped Christology and his Trinitarianism is informed by the concrete presence of Christ. Furthermore, he develops a theology of the Trinity that is fundamentally *experienced* and enacted in the life of the church. The personal cooperation of all three divine persons in the concrete moments of ecclesial life is an unfolding of divine love in history.[92] History then finds its meaning in the life of the church, which does not exist for itself but for the sake of that which breathes life into its body to begin with, the Trinity. The clearest example of John Paul II's Trinitarian theology is summarized in his weekly catechesis on Salvation History, named *The Trinity's Embrace: God's Saving Plan* (contained in volume 6 of a translated series based on his Wednesday catechesis in St. Peter's Square and the papal summer residence).[93] Here Trinitarian theology, perhaps unexpectedly, is concerned with history. As an embodied extension of the public acts and person of Christ, this dramatic enactment in history takes place most precisely in the life of the church:

> In truth, the Church, a "people made one by the unity of the Father, the Son and the Holy Spirit," (98) carries within her the mystery of the Father, who, being neither called nor sent by anyone (cf. Rom. 11:33–35), calls all to hallow his name and do his will; she guards within herself the mystery of the Son, who is called by the Father and sent to proclaim the kingdom of God to all and who calls all to follow him; and she is the trustee of the mystery of the Holy Spirit, who consecrates for mission those whom the Father calls through his Son Jesus Christ.[94]

91. Saward, *Christ Is the Answer*, 12.

92. The tripersonal God has an asymmetrical relationship with the world, which is shaped and determined by God and for God's purposes. O'Collins, *The Tripersonal God*, 182.

93. John Paul II, *The Trinity's Embrace, God's Saving Plan*.

94. John Paul II, *Pastores Dabo Vobis: Post-Synodal Apostolic Exhortation*, 35.

This "carrying," "guarding" and holding in "trust" of the threefold mystery of divine personal being is a deeply ecclesial event. The interior life of the body of Christ is a gift that is carried, and one that gives itself over in proclamation. The interrelation of Father, Son, and Holy Spirit is revealed in history such that it involves each of the three persons. Wojtyla avoids a false magnification of one or two over the other members of the divine life.[95] In holding an intimate relationship between the ecclesial safe-guarding of the Triune self-gift and the inner life of God, he is also providing his response to questions about the relationship between the immanent and the economic Trinity. Antoine E. Nachef highlights Wojtyla's approach to this problem.[96] Nachef notes the fundamental relation between each of three stages in Wojtyla's account of the economy of salvation: creation, incarnation, and sanctification. In each stage, all three members of the Trinity are in operation, but always in sight of the other two. For God, there is no experience of chronology here. In speaking forth creation, God also conceives of his own self-donation in the incarnation. Furthermore, in his self-offering upon the cross and in his resurrection, God conceives and enacts a self-communication in the Holy Spirit at Pentecost. As consubstantially related, each Person acts in a perfect communion of activity with the others without detriment to the unique personal quality of the Father, Son, or Holy Spirit. As Father, the First Person of the Trinity acts as the beginning and the end in terms of salvation history; yet the Son and Holy Spirit complete their work in symmetry to one another.[97]

In *Redemptor Hominis*, this theme is reflected in John Paul II's intensely christological vision of history and anthropology. Here his vision rejects popular visions of the human person or society considered fundamentally secular, including Communism. For example, the opening line of the encyclical frustrates and reconstructs the opening line of the *Communist Manifesto*. Karl Marx's ideology interpreted history in terms of the alienation of the worker against the hegemonic control of a property-owning elite, of class struggle. His opening words interpret history in this way: "The history of all hitherto existing society is the history of class struggles."[98] For Marx, alien-

---

95. This relies on Thomas' unity of distinction in the Trinity, which rests on the notion of "relation." Giles Emery notes that this relies on a "weak" notion of "relation," following Aristotle and Averroes. See Emery, *The Trinitarian Theology of Saint Thomas Aquinas*, 356.

96. Nachef, *The Mystery of the Trinity in the Theological Thought of Pope John Paul II*, 187–98.

97. Ibid., 198.

98. See chapter I. "Bourgeois and Proletarians," Marx and Engels, *The Communist Manifesto*.

ation of one class through a manipulative arrangement of technology and labor can be overcome by revolution. Wojtyla had lived through a practical application of Marxist ideology in Poland and its restrictions of academic and ecclesiastical affairs. In his first encyclical, he offers an alternate vision of history, also summed up in its opening words: "The Redeemer of man, Jesus Christ, is the centre of the universe and of history."[99] By centering Christ in history, Wojtyla offers a reinterpretation of social, economic, and political histories on offer by alternate ideologies, especially Communism. For Marx, history is the narrative of class struggle. For Wojtyla, history finds its logic in the person of Christ. The sensitivity of Wojtyla to broader cultural conflicts and trends reflects his interest in developing a theological anthropology with Christ at the center and with an informed understanding of contemporary intellectual and political arguments.[100]

By centering Christ as the giver of meaning in both space and time, the entirety of cosmic experience finds its origin and *telos* within the Second Person of the Trinity. Wojtyla situates his thought in continuity with his immediate successors and with the Second Vatican Council.[101] The theological anthropology of this encyclical is based upon the person of Christ as both "the eternal Son and the true man."[102] As the eternal Son, Christ is the entrance point for relationship and awareness of the fullness of life that is bestowed in knowledge of the Trinity. As the true man, Christ is not simply a humanitarian guide or the teacher of precepts, but recapitulates all of humanity within the redemptive work of his own personhood. He is the one "who penetrated in a unique unrepeatable way into the mystery of man and entered his 'heart.'"[103] The christological basis for Wojtyla's anthropology is attested to once again in this document, but it remains situated in relation to the Triune community, opening up the vision of the Father by way of the Son and intrinsically within the power of the Holy Spirit, the "Counsellor," who is the Spirit of truth.[104]

The relationship of Christ to the Father is crucial in *Redemptor Hominis*, but in a stylistically understated manner. In Wojtyla's second papal encyclical, *Dives in Misericordia* (1980), the Trinitarian picture becomes even clearer, one that takes its orientation from *Redemptor Hominis*. In this

99. John Paul II, *Redemptor Hominis: The Redeemer of Man*, 1.

100. Kupczak, "The Meaning of Theological Anthropology in the Teaching of John Paul II," 4.

101. He references the Second Vatican Council twenty-seven times in this, his first encyclical, John Paul II, *Redemptor Hominis: The Redeemer of Man*.

102. Ibid., 20.

103. Ibid., 8.

104. Ibid., 7.

work, the divine Father—the First Person of the Trinity—is described in a twofold manner: first, the Father is "rich in mercy," quoting Eph 2:4; and second, to see the Son is to see the Father, in reference to John 1:18 (Cf. Heb 1:1–4).[105] As the origin of abundant mercy, the Father is the point of reference through which an encounter with the Son is made present. Indeed, in the second paragraph, John Paul II makes reference to his oft-quoted line from "Gaudium et Spes," that Christ "reveals man to himself."[106] The revelation of human meaning in the flesh and body of Christ is a double reflection, both of our true selves in him, but also of the Father through him. The anthropological significance of the Father's revelation in the Son is therefore one of both description and eschatological directionality.

That is to say, the human person, in the Son, finds reflected an icon of the merciful Father, in whom a descriptive form of *who* the human person is called to be is shown forth. In other words, that of a personal subject created and loved by a gratuitously merciful divine Father. In an eschatological dimension, the Father also signals through the Son a hoped-for omega within his own presence, one in which all of human longing and desire is met and perfected. Wojtyla cannot describe the possibility of intimacy between human persons and the Father without constant reference to the Son, with the reminder of scriptural accounts of his own teaching, his witness, and the paschal mystery. The account of mercy developed in this encyclical is one given voice and flesh in the life of the church and in concrete acts of charity for those in need.

In the third of his Trinitarian encyclicals, *Dominum et vivificantem* (1986), which is the fifth of his total encyclicals, John Paul II invokes the Holy Spirit in the life of the church and the world with constant reference to the Trinity (a total of twelve times).[107] It is the Holy Spirit, the Paraclete, who makes Christ present in historical experience, by virtue of an intimate bond between them both.[108] The presence of the self-communicative Holy Spirit is for John Paul II the expression of divine self-donation at its most constant. He comments: "It can be said that in the Holy Spirit the intimate life of the Triune God becomes totally gift, an exchange of mutual love between the divine Persons and that through the Holy Spirit God exists in the mode of gift."[109]

---

105. John Paul II, *Dives in Misericordia: Rich in Mercy*, 1.

106. Ibid.

107. John Paul II, *Dominum Et Vivificantem: The Giver of Life*.

108. Ibid., 7.

109. Ibid., 10.

It is because of the redemptive acts of Christ in his crucifixion and resurrection that the Holy Spirit enters the apostolic community in a profoundly new way.[110] By basing the Spirit's presence in the nascent church upon the actions of Christ, John Paul II is concerned to hold to the scriptural witness of marked and definitive vocational attributes to each of the Triune persons, without reducing them one to another. Once again John Paul II links the revelation that God is both one and three with the mystery of the human condition.[111] For him, the Holy Spirit not only empowers the church to recognize and love the person of Christ, but it convicts each individual human being in its sin and calls each person to be mindful of the need for constant repentance. The interior life of the human person is the place of encounter between the Holy Spirit and that same human self: "The way of the Church passes through the heart of man, because here is the hidden place of the salvific encounter with the Holy Spirit, with the hidden God, and precisely here the Holy Spirit becomes 'a spring of water welling up to eternal life.'"[112]

It can be seen how the Trinitarian dimension of John Paul II's thought is inseverable from his Christology. Nachef comments that the late pope answers the possible dichotomy between the economic and immanent Trinity without explicit involvement in contemporary theological debates.[113] John Paul's reflections take place within a long-standing Augustinian-Thomist tradition. For him, the economic Trinity is a true reflection of the immanent Trinity, solely on the foundation of Scripture's witness to the triunity of God. He avoids the problem of knowledge of the immanent Trinity, treating the inner life of God as a mystery, yet, as Nachef argues, maintains an understanding that the divine persons' relationship of love is based on the "unity of the divinity," that is to say, a shared nature.[114] This holds to the traditional distinction between person and nature such that the Trinity encapsulates the only known example of a perfectly shared unity of will and nature within a community of persons. As Gerald O'Collins put it:

> One consciousness subsists in a threefold way and is shared by all three persons, albeit by each of them distinctively. It is as if

110. Ibid., 25.

111. Waldstein argues that Wojtyla's interpretation of the *imago Dei*—that human beings reflect God's image relationally as well as individually and rationally—can be reconciled with St. Thomas. See Waldstein, "John Paul II and St. Thomas on Love and the Trinity (Second Part)," 269.

112. John Paul II, *Dominum Et Vivificantem: The Giver of Life*, 67.

113. Nachef, *The Mystery of the Trinity in the Theological Thought of Pope John Paul II*, 188.

114. Ibid., 193.

God realizes the dream expressed by the saying about persons very much in love with each other: "They are of one mind and heart."[115]

This mystery can be described analogously, but never understood in completeness. It is a shared *personal* nature present in the triune life that constitutes possibly the deepest "mystery" of the faith.[116]

In basing his study of John Paul II's account of the Trinity and history on the triptych of Trinitarian encyclicals, Nachef offers a helpful analysis of the former's Trinitarian theology. However, it is surprising not to find reference here to the 118 Wednesday audiences presented by John Paul II, which carry a more reflective, meditative, and pastoral immediacy in both style and application. This catechesis, collected as *The Trinity's Embrace*, offers a fundamental and engaged approach to the Trinity.[117] For John Paul II, the doctrine of the Trinity affirms that God is *for* the human person in the realm of history. A picture of Wojtyla's long-standing Trinitarian theology is incomplete without reference to his papal catechesis on the subject, so some comment on that is necessary.

The 118 presentations are divided into five sections, in order: "Salvation History," "The Holy Spirit," "God the Father," "The Trinity," and "The Eucharist and the Kingdom." This structure alone tells much about the contextualization that occurs in John Paul II's methodology. The first section begins with the address, "God Is the Lord of Creation and History," situating historical experience under the dominion of God, within an eschatological horizon. John Paul II recalls his plans for celebration of the new millennium, beginning with the Trinitarian preparation of a focus in 1997 upon Jesus Christ, the Holy Spirit in 1998, and the Father in 1999.[118] He sees in the event of the Jubilee a spontaneous calling to mind of the previous 2,000 years, which, despite "difficulties and sufferings," have been a period of "grace."[119] And in looking back on history, John Paul II recalls the *creatio ex nihilo*, by which the triune God reveals himself as "transcendent," "omnipotent," not constrained by "necessity," "absolutely free" and crucially, "dictated only by love."[120] Time unfolds from its divine origins as a continuously dependent agent, yet one given as a gift ("of love").[121]

---

115. O'Collins, *The Tripersonal God*, 178.

116. Dulles, *The Splendor of Faith*, 26.

117. See John Paul II, *The Trinity's Embrace*, *God's Saving Plan*.

118. Ibid., 4.

119. Ibid., 5.

120. Ibid., 4.

121. Ibid., 4–5.

The future horizon, before which time enacts its divine purpose, is a moment known and acted within God's sovereignty. Nevertheless, underneath this transcendence is the invitation to each human person to cooperate in the future, which must be attempted in light of a future-promised grace and the fulfillment of a divine plan of "love for all humanity and for each one of us."[122] This synthesis of creation, time, giftedness, and eschatological hope shapes the rest of this first section, moving through other familiar themes such as the entering of Christ into time, and the historical fulfillment of God's fidelity to his people and all of creation. In fact, despite its title, this first section is really a series of reflections on the way the incarnation redeems history from within, reshaping it, renaming it "Salvation History," and ultimately opening the way for the fullness of life that arrives in the Holy Spirit (see the second section on "The Holy Spirit") and the Father (see the third section on "God the Father").[123]

It is important to note the nuanced relationship between history and divine action in this Trinitarian catechesis. The glories of immanent divine life, which are reflected in the economic activity of the Lord, for all their splendor, do not shirk the basic structures of human experience in creation. In fact, their splendor arrives in the imperfect forms encountered. For example, across the three opening sections of the catechesis, there is reference to the "gradual" nature of Trinitarian revelation within history and especially in Scripture: see the addresses "The True Face of the Messiah Was Gradually Revealed" (in "Salvation History"), "The Holy Spirit Is Gradually Revealed in Scripture" (in "The Holy Spirit"), and "God Gradually Reveals His Fatherhood" (in "God the Father").[124] The gradual revelation in Scripture of each of these three persons, together with the development in time of the church's perception of each, is also the gradual progression of grace acting in history. Moreover, the gradual nature of this revelation and experience of grace is intimately coupled with the transcendence of history.[125]

This becomes clear in John Paul II's reflection on the role of Christ's ascension. In his public ascension, the Son of God enters into glory, returning to that realm which lies above the earthly horizon and stands transcendent to the space in which human existence "unfolds."[126] John Paul II finds in the Lucan account of the ascension a Trinitarian event (see Luke 24:45–47 and

---

122. Ibid., 5.
123. This theme is constant throughout section one. See Ibid., 3–52.
124. Ibid., 9–12, 53–56, 171–74.
125. Ibid., 338.
126. Ibid., 339.

Luke 24:50–52).[127] In the farewell discourse to his disciples, Jesus confirms the saving plan of his Father, who had foretold the death and resurrection of the Son. Yet the Holy Spirit is also glimpsed, who is promised as the source of power.[128] So, recollection of the Old Testament promises of the Father is enjoined through the saving acts of Christ (especially in this context, by way of the ascension) with the promised work of the Holy Spirit. John Paul II finds in this Trinitarian moment also the confirmation of the Trinity's redemptive relationship with history. He quotes Luke's gospel: "And behold, I am sending the promise of my Father upon you. But stay in the city until you are clothed with power from on high" (Luke 24:49).

The promise of Pentecost follows a Trinitarian moment in Christ's ascension. Consistently, John Paul II's accent is upon the action of the Triune God in relation to history, which is centered on the embodied experience of the human person. The human person is thus able to both interpret and act within history. The Trinitarian theology of John Paul II does not depart from Roman Catholic tradition, but enriches it with an anthropological sense of the uniqueness of human experience within history. The sharing of the inner divine life with the human person is indubitably Trinitarian, calling to mind its many uses and descriptions in the New Testament.[129] It is a *communio personarum* that, through Christ, invites participation.

Furthermore, its glory is to be contrasted with the opposing experience of noncommunion, or separation. In his preaching to the papal household, (then Cardinal) Wojtyla had pictured the contrast in stark terms: "This mystery can be explained only on the basis of the truth that man is called to communion, to a share in the fullness of the Trinitarian life of God, the communio personarum. Separation is the opposite of communion."[130]

In fact, Wojtyla had titled this homily with the words of St. Irenaeus, "[t]he glory of God is man alive."[131] Wojtyla rejects the notion that human desires and aspirations are enough to begin a kind of eschatological understanding. Rather, he locates in salvation history's horizon the "last things"; the christological consummation of time and history, by which the Trinity can be correctly interpreted.[132] From the Trinitarian mystery flows the final consummation, which is enlarged by the presence in history of Christ's

---

127. Ibid., 339–40.

128. Ibid., 340.

129. Ibid., 347.

130. John Paul II, *Sign of Contradiction*, 178.

131. Ibid., 173. See the original quotation, "*Gloria Dei vivens homo*" in Irenaeus' *Adversus Haereses*: Irenaeus, *Against the Heresies*, Book IV, 20, 5–7.

132. John Paul II, *Sign of Contradiction*, 174–75.

cross. It is the cross that enlarges the Trinitarian mystery to include the "additional dimensions of man and the world" and initiate the "*missio Spiritus Sancti.*"[133] Anthropology, in this methodology, is now an essential aspect in any consideration of the economic Trinity. And because the anthropological condition is one wrought by the dual experiences of good and evil, hell must play its part in the explanatory foil to the Trinity's open embrace of humanity. Human conscience demands it, pressing the requirement of justice and a final judgment. According to Wojtyla, conscience is responsible for the whole structure of the human person directed towards an "eschatological dimension."[134]

In John Paul II, the Trinity is presented in a dynamic relationship to both history and to the human condition. The embrace of the human condition is the out-working Trinitarian consequence of the work of the Son, whose love for humanity and creation is an invitation to divine participation. Final consummation depends chiefly upon Christ's redemptive work, yet is gradually unfolding in the internal structures of history. The final section of John Paul II's catechesis on the Trinity is titled "The Eucharist and the Kingdom."[135] The eucharistic shape of Christian liturgy and its orientation towards sacramental presence is a further important theme in Wojtyla's theology, along with a Marian arc.

A eucharistic and Marian theology

It has been shown how John Paul II's theological framework is christocentric and bound together within a Trinitarian interpretation of history. It will be further argued that the concrete forms in which this theology is enacted are at once both eucharistic and Marian. They are expressed within the eucharistic practices of the church, which in turn finds impetus and animation within the place of Mary in the life of faith.[136] In a message to the 1996 International Marian Congress in Poland, John Paul II explicitly enjoined the Eucharist and Mary by way of Christ's passion. The Congress' theme was "Mary and the Eucharist," and John Paul II prayed that Mary would lead disciples to the Eucharist:

133. Ibid., 175.

134. Ibid., 178.

135. John Paul II, *The Trinity's Embrace, God's Saving Plan*, 385–453.

136. The theological significance of Mary has a long history. Viewed in light of the Incarnation, the role of the mother of Christ is one of intercessor and first participant in the order of salvation. Her entire orientation is to the glory of her son, as is shown in the helpful historical survey: Graef, *Mary*. The opening quote in this text is from Pope John XXIII: "The Madonna is not pleased when she is put above her Son."

> Every Holy Mass makes present in an unbloody manner that unique and perfect sacrifice, offered by Christ on the Cross, in which Mary participated, joined in spirit with her suffering Son, lovingly consenting to his sacrifice and offering her own sorrow to the Father (cf. *Lumen gentium*, n. 58).[137]

This reflection, given on the Feast of the Assumption, highlights the christological centrality in his thought that makes possible the continual thematic connection between Mary and the Eucharist. Mary is spoken of devotionally and personally in such works as *Crossing the Threshold of Hope*, but his chief Marian documents are his Wednesday catechesis on the Virgin Mary (1995–97), *Redemptoris Mater* (1987), and *Rosarium Virginis Mariae*.[138] In the first, he produced a sustained meditative study of the role of Mary in the life of faith, placing it foundationally within the saving work of Christ in history.[139] In the last, he added specific scriptural narratives to the prayers of the Rosary, named the "luminous mysteries," and explained the focus of its prayers as the contemplation of the face of Jesus, via the "School of Mary."[140] Similarly, the Eucharist is a continual theme in his work, but the only two full-length documents devoted entirely to its meaning are his early letter, *Dominicae Cenae* (1980) and his final encyclical, *Ecclesia de Eucharistia* (2003).[141] Other texts make reference to the Eucharist with similar accents on the role of Mary.[142] In his Lenten sermons in the presence of Pope Paul VI (1976), Wojtyla makes reference to the "fundamental subject" of priestly prayer (liturgical prayer) as well as nonliturgical prayer.[143] In liturgical prayer, it is primarily the Eucharist he refers to. The Eucharist is such a constant presence in the life and ministry of Wojtyla, it might be difficult to

137. John Paul II, "Mary Leads Us to Eucharist: Message to 19th International Marian Congress Czestochowa, Poland."

138. John Paul II, *Crossing the Threshold of Hope*; John Paul II, *Redemptoris Mater: On the Blessed Virgin Mary in the Life of the Pilgrim Church*; John Paul II, *Rosarium Virginis Mariae: Apostolic Letter on the Most Holy Rosary*.

139. John Paul II, *Redemptoris Mater*, 1.

140. John Paul II, *Rosarium Virginis Mariae*, 1, 3, 9, 10, 15, 18, 21, 23, 25, 40, 43.

141. John Paul II, *Ecclesia De Eucharistia: Encyclical Letter on the Eucharist in Its Relationship to the Church*.

142. Other writings from John Paul II with significant Eucharistic themes include the following, the last of which was produced as an apostolic letter in the year of the Eucharist (2004–5): *Dies Domine: Apostolic Letter on Keeping the Lord's Day Holy*; *The Trinity's Embrace, God's Saving Plan: A Catechesis on Salvation History*; *Mane Nobiscum Domine: Apostolic Letter for the Year of the Eucharist October 2004–October 2005*. See also *Sign of Contradiction*, 134.

143. John Paul II, *Sign of Contradiction*, 134.

ɔle in his theology, but along with the Marian arc, it performs a
ration.

‾‾ucharist is the key liturgical rite within Roman Catholic worship,
called by the Catechism the "source and summit" of the Christian life.[144] Liturgy is both the thanksgiving offered by the ecclesial community as well as
participation in that thanksgiving offered by Christ to the Father. It should
be noted that in terms of the church as the receptive body of Christ's own
presence, John Paul II draws on Scripture to paint an ecumenical picture.
It is to all of God's people that this Marian arc directs its eucharistic meaning.[145] John Paul remarks: "It is the divine presence, then, which 'sanctifies'
the community of believers 'in the truth' (John 17:17, 19). The loftiest sign
of this presence is constituted by the liturgy, which is the epiphany of the
consecration of God's people."[146]

By "consecration," John Paul II refers to the sustained (re)commitment
of the people of God to the path of holiness. The process of sanctification requires a free agency in each human subject, by which the subjugation of the
self's desires to God's will is made possible in a free response to God's initiative. The centrality of the Eucharist contains many facets and the Trinitarian
catechesis concludes with a section titled "The Eucharist and the Kingdom."
Those facets include the Eucharist as "celebration," "memorial," "sacrifice
of praise," "banquet of communion," "taste of eternity in time," and "sacrament of the Church's unity."[147] The baptized human person finds in the
Eucharist a uniquely repeatable participation in the one historical event of
Christ's passion and a share in his resurrected life. This is possible in spite of
the historical trajectories of "war, violence, oppression, injustice and moral
decay," which call to mind the apocalyptic visions of the book of Revelation
(cf. 6:1–8).[148] On John Paul II's account, eucharistic worship gives way to an
anthropological route, a hopeful embodiment of the future life pledged in
the eucharistic feast. In other words, the Eucharist is a central point of convergence for the life of persons in *communio*: "For Christians in general, the
concept of *communio* itself has a primarily *religious and sacral meaning, one*

---

144. Catholic Church, *Compendium of the Catechism of the Catholic Church*, 1324.

145. In this sense, Mary's motherhood for the church links itself to her word in the
Magnificat, already in itself an ecumenical text because it is scriptural and liturgical. See
Yeago, "The Presence of Mary in the Mystery of the Church," 165.

146. John Paul II, *The Trinity's Embrace, God's Saving Plan: A Catechesis on Salvation History*, 350.

147. Ibid., 387–90, 391–94, 395–98, 399–402, 403–6, 407–10.

148. Ibid., 435.

connected with the Eucharist, which is a sacramentum communionis between Christ and his disciples—between God and human beings."[149]

The sacral meaning of communio—especially as expressed in the Marian typology of the church—cannot be separated from the eucharistic encounter with the risen Christ. The "sacramentum communionis" is a cosmic social moment, nourishing the human person with the redemptive person of Christ. There is a sense in which John Paul II's explanation of the church's doctrine concerning Christ and his work is, at times, more catechetical than dogmatic. That is to say, he is offering the content of dogma in a pastoral and teaching mode of delivery. Avery Dulles calls this Wojtyla's "method of correlation," by emphasizing the correspondence between the questions of human existence and the divine answers that arrive in the person of Christ.[150] In fact, both the eucharistic and the Marian aspects of Wojtyla's general thought are in constant relation to an appreciation of the existential anxiety wrought in the human condition. The human person exists between multiple plains of meaning, desire, temptation, and only finds the fullness of life in the paradoxical relinquishment of the self in God; this is made concrete in the Eucharist.

The eucharistic encounter with Christ is also the affirmation of the Marian arc, in which the Lord's mother acts as the type par excellence of the church. The typology of Mary also speaks of her as a living disciple in the life of the church, one who is an object of devotion for John Paul II. His Episcopal Coat of Arms carried the Latin words "Totus tuus" [Totally yours], which comes from the mystical Marian writings of St. Louis-Marie Grignion de Montfort in his treatise on Marian devotion: "Totus tuus ego sum, et omnia mea tua sunt."[151] It is to be given totally for the sake of the other and specifically the community of Trinity-Christ-Mary. For John Paul II, to think of one is to act in concert with the others.

In the Apostolic Letter Redemptoris Mater, Mary is presented as central to the gospel mission in the church's life.[152] From the beginning, it is John Paul II's Christocentrism that defines the terms in which Mary is treated. She is the human factor in the Holy Spirit's cooperative work of the incarnation, by which the Word takes flesh.[153] She is the human person whose faithful obedience in the "fullness of time" precedes the conception, birth, and

149. John Paul II, Person and Community, 320.

150. Dulles, The Splendor of Faith, 33.

151. "I am all yours, and all that I have is yours." See Louis Marie Grignon de Montfort's prayers in: A Treatise on the True Devotion to the Blessed Virgin.

152. John Paul II, Redemptoris Mater: On the Blessed Virgin Mary in the Life of the Pilgrim Church.

153. Ibid., 1.

work of Christ, whose gift of her own flesh made possible the incarnation.[154] In the discipleship of Mary's embodied interiority, the church's own pilgrim journey locates its beginning, for she is both *Theotókos* and Mother of the Church.[155] As the Mother, Mary plays a continually active role in the life of the church, so she cannot be relegated simply to historical, typological, or theological significance. In fact, in each of these three categories, her significance continues in the life of the church, for she intercedes as an active agent of grace fully obedient to the Son. The contemporaneous confrontation with sin and evil—the ancient "enmity"—is given impetus and encouragement by the prayerful involvement of Mary.[156] Her involvement is maternal, but always directed towards the same end: Jesus Christ.[157] John Paul II develops the teaching of Vatican II and Paul VI on Mary, with a lively emphasis on the presence of Mary as a kind of arc to the entire Christian life, one that is holy, spotless, maternal, and faithful, for "Mary guides the faithful to the Eucharist."[158] It is clear that for Wojtyla, the possibility for each of these roles in Mary is her concrete vocation as a person in history who was chiefly characterized as the particular mother of a particular person; this is an incarnate and human framework in which the divine enters and works within the world. Without the peculiarly local aspect of Mary's vocation at a fixed point in history (the "fullness of time"), Mary's overarching vocation for the *ecclesia* and to every individual believer would be impossible. A mother is a mother of *someone*. A person is a person *somewhere* and at *some time*. In fact, the Marian arc only makes sense in John Paul II's theological structure because of its shared vocational context in the mysteries of history. "She [the church] sees Mary deeply rooted in humanity's history, in man's eternal vocation according to the providential plan which God has made for him from eternity."[159] The maternal vocation is central in Wojtyla's theology, but only because of the historical particularities of the person of Mary.

The concluding encyclical of the John Paul II papacy, *Ecclesia de Eucharistia*, is a sustained reflection on the relationship between the liturgical rite

154. The term "fullness of time" [*pleroma tou chronou*] is crucial to Mary's role in history. Wojtyla includes in footnote two an explanation of its use in Scripture, especially Gen 29:21; 1 Sam 7:12; Tob 14:5; Mark 1:15; Luke 21:24; John 7:8; Eph 1:10; and Gal 4:4, in *Redemptoris Mater: On the Blessed Virgin Mary in the Life of the Pilgrim Church*, 49.

155. Ibid., 1–2.

156. Ibid., 11.

157. Ibid., 21–22.

158. Ibid., 42–47.

159. Ibid., 52.

of the Mass and the lived practices of the church.[160] The supernatural change of the Eucharistic elements constitutes for John Paul II both the constant presence of Christ in his earthly body and the sacred marking of time in history.[161] In both, the Eucharist acts as the intersection between the Trinity and creation that is manifest most clearly amongst Christian disciples. The emphases in the Trinitarian encyclicals upon the dramatic relationship between the human person and the Triune God are made concretely in the Eucharist. As Tracey Rowland describes, "the most dramatic intersection of all three relationships is to be found in the Eucharistic Mystery."[162] While John Paul II has said the church's beginnings are found in the grace-filled life of Mary in *Redemptoris Mater*, in *Ecclesia de Eucharistia* he says the church is "born" of the Paschal mystery.[163] In the Paschal Triduum, the foundation and wellspring of the church is "gathered up, foreshadowed and 'concentrated' forever in the gift of the Eucharist."[164] The presence that is revealed in this liturgical and communal offering is that of the *person* of Christ. John Paul II describes the showing forth of the "Eucharistic face of Christ," made tangible by an education in the "school of Mary."[165] Furthermore, the eucharistic contemplation of Christ's face within the context of the school of Mary is laid before the church as John Paul's program for the third millennium.[166]

In *Dominicae Cenae*, John Paul II marks the mutually-constituting relationship of Eucharist and the church. He states that the "Church 'makes the Eucharist'" and so "'the Eucharist builds up' the Church" (quoting section eleven of "Lumen Gentium").[167] The Marian arc, of obedience to the Lord and the gradual contemplation of his face, acts as the constant reference point to which eucharistic devotion finds its orientation.

Mary is considered in close approximation to the Eucharist. Indeed, John Paul II concludes his final section (on the Eucharist) in his Trinitarian catechesis with a reflection titled "Mary, Eschatological Icon of the Church."[168] In it, he brings to a close a four-year catechetical program by emphasizing the typological interpretation of Our Lady as the people of God. He takes his point of departure as the account in the book of Revelation of the woman

160. John Paul II, *Ecclesia De Eucharistia*.

161. Ibid., 1.

162. Rowland, "In Search of Real Freedom."

163. John Paul II, *Ecclesia De Eucharistia*, 3.

164. Ibid., 5.

165. Ibid., 7.

166. Ibid., 6.

167. John Paul II, *Dominicae Cenae*, 5; Catholic Church, "Lumen Gentium."

168. John Paul II, *The Trinity's Embrace, God's Saving Plan*, 450–53.

with child, giving birth while the dragon rages against her[169] (Rev 12:1–6). The interpretation of this woman as both the mother of Christ and as a type of the church is not unusual within the patristic traditions of the church.[170]

In John Paul II's thought, the human person is a participant in the same historical drama of good versus evil, acting in a free agency which is fundamentally open to the divine Other. This same divine Other—the blessed Trinity—bestows upon the lowly, poor, refugee, prayerful virgin a powerful intercessory role. In her vocation as the teacher and orientation of eucharistic understanding, Mary, for John Paul II, is "woman of the Eucharist."[171] That role is always orientated in one direction: towards the risen Christ, who, in sight of the eschatological horizon, is present in the Eucharist.

Wojtyla's philosophical theology

John Paul II's theological framework builds on many of the philosophical themes that the younger Wojtyla had explored as an ethicist, philosopher, seminarian, and priest. Because of diverse interests, his personal philosophy cannot be easily categorized in either Thomistic metaphysics or Husserlian phenomenology on their own. Rather, his approach is to construct a positive alternative apart from the excesses in either. As John McNerney describes:

> Wojtyla sets out in *The Acting Person* to navigate the seas of philosophical enquiry and to steer a course between the Scylla of a metaphysical tradition of the person that has left the relational dimension undeveloped, and the Charybdis of a phenomenological tradition that has highly developed the relational aspect but lost its metaphysical grounding.[172]

In steering between the two, Wojtyla allows for both phenomenology and Thomism to find their orientation in the full datum of the human person. In *The Acting Person* (*Osoba I Czyn*, better translated as "Person and Act"), Wojtyla constructs his philosophy in close dialogue with both traditions. John McNerney views these two traditions as complementary and attributes this insight about their relationship to Wojtyla.[173] Yet revela-

169. Ibid., 450.

170. See for example, St. Ambrose, *Exposition of the Holy Gospel according to Saint Luke; with, Fragments on the Prophecy of Isaias*, II.7.

171. John Paul II, *Ecclesia De Eucharistia*, 53–58.

172. McNerney, *John Paul II*, 18.

173. Ibid., 149.

tion itself can be located in these earlier works. George Williams identifies the restorative work of Christ (or the "Second Adam") as an "unstated presupposition" in *The Acting Person*.[174] There, the close correlation between action and the inner dimension of the human person is described as an integral relation in the human subject. In considering persons acting besides or with others, Wojtyla refers to the evangelical commandment of love as a constituting factor in the creation of authentic human communities.[175]

In addition, in *Love and Responsibility*, Wojtyla views sexual ethics in terms of both metaphysics and phenomenology. He takes seriously the concrete experience of men and women in defining the terms in which their embodied relationship can be described. But he also speaks of the commandment to love as a form of the "personalistic norm," thus bridging Scripture and contemporary philosophy.[176] The personalistic norm is the normative principle by which the act of love is made possible in human relationships. It has a positive and a negative aspect. Positively, it contends that the person is a good towards which "the only proper and adequate attitude is love."[177] Negatively, it states that a person is the kind of good that "does not admit of use" and cannot be treated as an object of use or the means to an end.[178]

The human subject must be recognized first as a person and only afterwards as carrying a sexual value.[179] Love, for him, is a virtue and not simply an excitement of the senses or an emotional rapture. Sexual attraction is orientated towards a person and should not be construed as an isolated desire for the body. Wojtyla avoids a glib description of sexuality as essentially a conceptual problem. He acknowledges that "[s]exual sentiment is a continually shifting response to many experiences, to impressions obtained from many persons."[180] In the giving over of one's body to an other in an exclusive arrangement, marriage confirms that the expression of love is not simply a *gift* of self to another, but the *surrender* of that self to the other. Surrender is a crucial feature of the relationship, for it implies a comprehensive relinquishing of rights and privileges over an extended period of time. For Wojtyla, the personalistic norm is the ethical standard by which a person is called to act in relation to other persons. It requires that the other be

174. Williams, *The Mind of John Paul II*, 189.

175. John Paul II, *The Acting Person*, 296.

176. See for example John Paul II, *Love and Responsibility*, 121.

177. Ibid., 41.

178. Ibid.

179. Ibid., 123.

180. Ibid., 124.

affirmed in the value that is present by virtue of personhood. This is a negation of any form of sociality in which a human person is "used" by another
for some other end. Indeed, *Love and Responsibility* begins by analyzing the
verb "to use."[181] The personalistic norm clashes with the utilitarian principle
because of this affirmation of the person *as* a person. The Old Testament
command to love God and one another is, in Wojtyla's reading, presupposed
by the personalistic norm. The irreducible nature of the human person
makes possible the way of love, even before the divine command is given.
Wojtyla argues, a "person is an entity of a sort to which the only proper and
adequate way to relate is love."[182] In this way, the divine command affirms
the natural and rationally identifiable personalistic norm, but follows it with
a particular way of relating to God and human persons, not in justice, but
in the order of love.

Developing the tradition: A catechesis on the body

In chapter 1, it was argued that the body has become a significant topic in
contemporary and postmodern thought, just as it did for Wojtyla in both
prepapal writings and in texts produced as pope. He develops a Christian
approach to the body within a Catholic context, as have other recent theorists. For example, Regina Ammicht-Quinn has called for a contemporary
theological engagement with the body. Along with Elsa Tamez, she argues
that it is "urgently necessary for theology critically and in full self-awareness
to become involved in current discussions about the body . . . ."[183] She is especially concerned at destructive approaches to the body, such as a Western
cultural preoccupation with perfected images of the body that regards the
body acceptable only if it meets certain norms.[184] Popular conceptions of
the body exalt impossible levels of youth, health, and beauty. On the other
hand, Ammicht-Quinn identifies the broken body associated with impoverished parts of the world, where evidence of injury, torture, and brokenness
mark the body in juxtaposition to Western perceptions of normative ideals.[185]
In both extremes, the body is unhealthily thin and sanitized images of either
the perfected or the broken body isolate the form of flesh from events of
authentically social behavior: the model of the television advertisement is
posed in manufactured light and airbrushed tones, never seen in mundane

181. Ibid., 21–100.
182. Ibid., 41.
183. "Introduction," in Ammicht-Quinn and Tamez, *The Body and Religion*, 8.
184. Ibid., 7.
185. Ibid.

conversation, bodily suffering, or the awkwardness of walking through a crowded street in a hurry; the broken body of impoverishment too is isolated from these kinds of social behavior, except that instead of suffering having been bracketed out, it remains the only mark of the body's humanity. Yet, as Ammicht-Quinn argues, suffering is a revelation of vulnerability, which in turn is both the point at which human dignity can be seen as a necessity and a possibility.[186] In other words, the vulnerability of the human person highlights the body's dependence on the care of others, and makes it possible for others to achieve something positive for the suffering person. Even in an age in which the body is increasingly dependent on technological advances or in which technology appears to be moving towards artificial intelligence, the body remains a revelation of human vulnerability.[187]

Popular representations of the body reveal a social imaginary in which the body is fluid; offering a wealth of social possibility and signification, yet also unstable and more like a project to complete than a gift to be received.[188] Testaments to this problem are examples such as cosmetic surgery, juvenile eating disorders, pornography, or iniquitous disparities of access to medical attention in a globalized context. The body is a discordant experience of shifting values and desires for which material attention is not constant or even reflective of what is necessary in any given situation. Indeed, there seems to be a cultural desire for the "perfect body" and a dual repression of the suffering body, as Werner Jeanrond elsewhere describes.[189] This fluidity of the body occurs as an important feature of postmodern culture. The body's vulnerability can be viewed as a revelatory aspect of the human body in such a context, but it is often the occasion of a suffering that awakens the question of evil, for which theology is equipped to answer. Ammicht-Quinn argues that there is no prospect of answering or resolving the problem of evil as such, but rather it must be responded to by solidarity and a Christian praxis.[190] Her theological approach is the emphasis upon a self-reflective Christian activity of care and attention. In this case, the human person is at the center, with a prioritization of consideration for the body of the person

186. Ammicht-Quinn, "Whose Dignity is Inviolable?," 44.

187. Ammicht-Quinn writes that the categorical imperative of popular culture is now "never get a person when you can get a machine." See ibid., 35–36.

188. See for example: Ammicht-Quinn, "Cult, Culture and Ambivalence," in *Fluid Flesh*, 67–81; and Ammicht-Quinn, "Introduction," in Ammicht-Quinn and Tamez, *The Body and Religion*, 8.

189. Jeanrond, *A Theology of Love*, 12, 75.

190. See: Ammicht-Quinn, *Evil Today and Struggles to Be Human* and her work on theodicy and the need to confront evil with a solidarity-praxis as justification of the content of faith: *Von Lissabon Bis Auschwitz*.

in its vulnerability and suffering. The person is an embodied other who reveals its reliance on the charity of others.

For Wojtyla, the body's significance is related profoundly to the mystery of the human person. It has been argued that Wojtyla's theological and philosophical foundations are guided by his interest in the mystery of the human person. This ought to be kept in mind in turning towards his explicit reflections on embodiment: his *Theology of the Body*.[191] The following will argue that the nuptial mystery, which for Wojtyla unveils the meaning of gendered and sexual creatureliness in relation to others, serves as his principle account or paradigm of alterity. The *communio* of the Trinity is reflected in the *communio* of human persons, primarily the church, but especially in the complementary community of bodies that constitute the married relationship.[192] This teaching is perhaps one of the most controversial of Wojtyla's developed understandings of human love, which is described by Charles Curran as neither systematic nor complete, and even "sketchy."[193] Criticism of *Man and Woman He Created Them* will be considered later in this chapter, but in what follows it will be argued that Wojtyla's approach is systematic, but by his own admission, incomplete. As discussed earlier, Wojtyla's work develops the tradition by holding a delicate balance between embodied forms of love (the nuptial mystery in particular) and the higher love of God. Whereas Augustine rejected embodied forms of love as a basis for understanding God, Wojtyla argues that God's Trinitarian self-gift is to be reflected in the self-gift of human spouses.

In Wojtyla's approach to the body, difference becomes the opportunity for alterity to mark out the self's ethical vocation for the other. Unlike Levinas, Wojtyla's account is explicitly theological as well as phenomenological. Wojtyla develops his account of difference between persons in light of the framework above (christocentric, Trinitarian, eucharistic, and Marian), relying on these as fixed terms within his philosophical analysis of the person and of action. Between September 1979 and November 1984, Wojtyla, as John Paul II, presented his weekly catechesis on the subject "Human Love in the Divine Plan."[194] Over the course of 129 Wednesday addresses, he de-

191. This is the term used within his catechesis on the subject and has become the popular title of this series of teaching within Wojtyla's many publications, though it was not the title that he gave the work himself.

192. For Waldstein, Wojtyla sees in the heart of the Second Vatican Council's teaching the "call to deeper personal awareness of love as self-gift rooted in the Trinity." The theology of the body carries the same theological understanding. See John Paul II, *Man and Woman He Created Them*, 89.

193. Curran, *The Moral Theology of Pope John Paul II*, 170.

194. This is Waldstein's translation of the original title, whereas "theology of the

velops a nuanced theological approach to the embodied human person in two parts, "The Words of Christ" and "The Sacrament."[195] In his concluding address, John Paul II reasserts the title "Human Love in the Divine Plan," but acknowledges the more precise title would be "The Redemption of the Body and the Sacramentality of Marriage."[196] In his retranslation of the totality of these texts, Michael Waldstein identifies four prepared addresses that were never given, and so includes them in his published version for the purposes of completeness. This collection adheres to the same theological and philosophical priorities evident in John Paul II's earlier work (described above), but remains the most systematic approach of a Roman Pontiff to the mystery of the human body, emphasizing the original experiences of human embodiment and disclosing the human *telos* within present existence.[197]

Within days of Wojtyla/John Paul II's Beatification in 2011, Pope Benedict XVI promoted *Man and Woman He Created Them*, emphasizing that bodies offer the place where the Spirit may dwell and that because of this, "if we know how to listen, they speak the language of true love."[198] In contrast, the body also carries a negative language. "When separated from its filial meaning, from its connection with the Creator, the body rebels against humans, and loses its capacity to show communion, becoming a place where the other is appropriated."[199] For Benedict, as for his predecessor, the concrete settings of marriage and family are the contexts in which embodied human lives must act ethically for the sake of the other. Human alterity is an embodied encounter.

Part One of Man and Woman He Created Them

In Part One, John Paul II focuses on the words of Christ, with especial significance granted to three textual sources.[200] First, Matt 19:8 and Mark 10:6–9, in which Christ appeals "to the beginning" in his dialogue with the Pharisees concerning the unity and indissolubility of marriage. Second, Christ's Sermon on the Mount in Matt 5:28, where he confirms concupiscence as

body" was a subtitle or alternative title used by Wojtyla. See John Paul II, *Man and Woman He Created Them*.

195. Ibid., 131–462, 63–663.

196. Ibid., 133:1.

197. Anderson and Granados, *Called to Love*, 199.

198. *Vatican Information Service*, "Uniting Theology of the Body with Theology of Love."

199. Ibid.

200. John Paul II, *Man and Woman He Created Them*, 1:1–5.

"adultery committed in the heart." Third, Christ's appeal to the resurrection of the body in the "outer world," common to the Synoptics in Matt 22:30, Mark 12:25, and Luke 20:35–36.

Common to each of these is the authority of Christ to interpret the tradition and correct his disciples. In the first, marriage is held before the Pharisees as the continual service of fidelity, and he bases this upon the return to "the beginning," specifically the book of Genesis. In the second, concupiscence is presented not only as a bodily activity or tendency, but one that is committed within the human heart as "adultery," thus including an interior dimension. Following these two first texts is the final Synoptic narrative, in which Christ says that in the resurrection, marriage will not be enacted, for men and women will be "like angels in heaven" (Matt 22:30). This last perspective is eschatological and confirms the unique place of marital love within this present world, one that anticipates a final resurrection but, in its present institutional and sacramental form, will cease to exist in the final resurrection of the body.

In the first text, the unity and indissolubility of marriage is John Paul II's point of departure in considering his theology of the body. He takes as axiomatic the authority of Christ in interpreting morality in both Old and New Testaments, which forms the christological basis for further reflection on these themes. In fact, this provides the stylistic pattern for the addresses contained in the rest of Part One, in highlighting Christ's recorded teaching and its basis in "the beginning."[201] The response of Jesus to the Pharisees' question concerning Moses' allowance of divorce is crucial, in that he avoids both "juridical" and "casuistic" controversies, turning instead to "the beginning."[202] Explicitly, Jesus makes reference in this dialogue to Gen 1:27: "So God created man in his own image, in the image of God he created him; male and female he created them"; and then to Gen 2:24: "Therefore a man shall leave his father and his mother and hold fast to his wife, and they shall become one flesh." Christ inscribes a relationship of difference in the prelapsarian order of creation. God commands in this same text the phrase, "let man not separate," providing an indissoluble relationship in the ancient order of marriage. But the Pharisees, even in the way their questions are crafted casuistically, are for John Paul II fulfilling a vocation all persons are called to fulfill: that of "interlocutors" with Christ and his words.[203] The same pattern follows in the secondt text, Matt 5:28, and the third group of texts, Matt 22:30, Mark 12:25, and Luke 20:35–36.

201. Ibid.
202. Ibid., 1:2.
203. Ibid., 1:4–5.

In this dramatic involvement of his audience in the scriptural narrative, John Paul II takes his listeners (and readers) through an argument that is understood within a logic of the gift.[204] This is especially important in relation to Levinas' understanding of the other as an embodied gift, one whose body reveals the ethical form of the self's relation to the other. For this reason, the giftedness of the body is the main focus in the following analysis of the first part of John Paul II's theology of the body.

Part One, "The Words of Christ," could be considered John Paul II's existential treatment of the body, while Part Two, "The Sacrament," could be viewed as his theological treatment. Of course, this would be a simplified thematic divide, but it helps give the contextual sense of how John Paul II is thinking through the problem of the body. Having established his methodological approach in looking first at "the beginning" in the Genesis creation accounts through a christological lens, John Paul II turns to three original experiences, which he identifies as constitutive of the prefallen state. These are "original solitude," "original unity," and "original nakedness."[205]

Original solitude

John Paul II refers to the second creation account in Genesis (2:18), in which God—*Yahweh*—says that it is not good for the man to be alone. In contrast to the account in Genesis 1, the creation of man stands in a separate passage, before the creation of the first woman. The language of sexual differentiation is important, highlighting the definition of "male" (אדם) after the arrival of "woman" (אישה). The text speaks of the solitude of man, and in this context the term is not gender specific. John Paul II draws two conclusions: first, that solitude has a meaning derived from man's nature (his humanity) and second, a meaning which comes from the relationship between male and female.[206] The first meaning is prior to the second and describes a "fundamental anthropological issue" concerning human existentiality.[207] Solitary existence is not simply a matter of the first man's numerical value, but of the mood of his being; one that is searching itself out before God's presence. Adam is placed above the animals and grants them their names, and so cannot equate himself existentially on their level. Yet he is granted this authority from God himself, so he has no basis for understanding himself at

204. This is most acute in section 5 of chapter 1, "Man in the Dimension of Gift," but permeates *Man and Woman He Created Them*. See ibid., 178–203.

205. Ibid., 146–55, 156–68, 169–77.

206. Ibid., 5:2.

207. Ibid., 5:3.

the level of the Creator.[208] Man's authority is a delegated power. He is aware of his existence between the higher and lower planes of God and other animals. Nevertheless, Adam specifically identifies himself as different in creation through his self-knowledge, which points towards his rationality. In revealing "himself to himself," he discovers himself to be a human person precisely on the basis of his rational subjectivity.[209]

Yet, the Genesis account does not simply furnish man with self-consciousness, but also self-determination. This occurs in the free will afforded to Adam before the temptations of the tree of the knowledge of good and evil. These basic characteristics of the first man constitute him in his solitude and mark him as a human person. In doing so, the status of being "alone" in the world also makes possible the covenantal nature of a relationship with God.[210] Such a relationship is to be "unique, exclusive, and unrepeatable."[211] The awareness of these relational possibilities are based upon the unique significance of Adam amongst other creatures, but John Paul II reads in the text a crucial role for Adam's body in the knowledge of these things. It is through his body that Adam is aware of his likeness to the animals, and in his own self-awareness, he is able to identify himself as set apart from them. It is the man's body that makes him self-aware. The entire "sketch" of man's original solitude is therefore intrinsic to understanding the human condition in "the beginning" and by which the human person is "a body among bodies and discovers the meaning of his own bodiliness."[212] This is achieved before God and in the visible creatureliness of the world. John Paul II is looking for both the natural role of the body and its intrinsically anthropological significance. Man is a subject, but not simply by the self-consciousness and self-determination that are constituent features of his existentiality; at a fundamental level, it is his body that makes his self-awareness possible. As John Paul II describes it, *"The structure of this body is such that it permits him to be the author of genuinely human activity. In this activity, the body expresses the person."*[213]

---

208. Wojtyla does not wish to depart from Aristotle's anthropological categories, but he recognizes their limitations in explaining the human condition in the contemporary setting and therefore both accepts and expounds those categories. Wojtyla comments that if we are to accept the Aristotelian tradition in logic and anthropology, this element of Adam's existentiality would be named his "proximate genus." Man's uniqueness as a rational animal sets him apart from both nature and God. See ibid., 5:5 and footnote 10.

209. Ibid., 5:6, 6:1.

210. Ibid., 6:2.

211. Ibid.

212. Ibid., 6:4.

213. Ibid., 7:2.

Moreover, the body becomes the site of man's mortality. In the command not to eat of the tree, God confronts Adam with a sense-less word: "die." For the first man, who has not experienced the death of others, this word is meaningless. As he listens to the divine voice, he hears a term that ought to have no meaning, because until now, the narrative has only spoken of the creation of living things. That is to say, death had not yet been experienced. In John Paul II's words, the arrival of such a word appears as a *"radical antithesis of all that man had been endowed with."*[214] In this moment, the body is faced with a limit upon its possibilities. The breath that had been breathed into its nostrils, so to speak, has now been endowed with the possibility of expiration, which John Paul II connects with the determination of man's path in the invisible and not the visible. Life, and in particular, the life breathed into the human body, is a fragile materiality contingent upon the will of God. Such contingency highlights the solitudenal experience of the human person, and such a solitude is intrinsic to his being as a rational embodied creature.

Original unity

In the notion of "original unity," John Paul II outlines the theological significance of the arrival of "woman."[215] While the original solitude of man is crucial to the Yahwist text of Genesis 2, it is not present in Genesis 1. In the latter, the duality of sex and male-female unity is paramount. The creations of man and woman are described separately, but without the disharmony with the *imago Dei* as it is presented in Genesis 2. John Paul II does not wish to do violence to the theological unity between the two accounts, but draws out differing emphases. He identifies a correlation in this mythic narrative between the creative action of Yahweh and human consciousness.[216] The two inform one another as a dialogue of creativity between God's first causality and human self-awareness. In the creative act of God, the world comes into being. In the appearance of self-consciousness, the human person becomes aware of God as his first cause and is able to reflect upon this relationship between creation and Creator. In the creation of the first human being/s, the male-female differentiation also makes its appearance.[217] The original unity

214. Ibid., 7:3.

215. Ibid., 8–10.

216. Ibid., 8:2.

217. This theme is taken up in numerous contemporary theologies of the body. For example, Eugene Rogers, from a different perspective, takes up Rowan Williams' notion that sexual love causes persons to reperceive themselves as loved by an other. Sexual

to which John Paul II refers is that of the *communio* of persons between the two sexes, male and female.

During his sleep—his *torpor*—man becomes the material origin of his helpmate, "woman," who is formed from the man's rib (Gen 2:21–22). John Paul II highlights that in Genesis 2, original solitude is substantially prior to the meaning of original unity, which is constituted in the union of masculinity and femininity. Man is alone in his original solitude, but existentially, he also experiences the "unity of the two" in the male-female relationship.[218] The process of moving from the "one" to the "two" occurs during Adam's unconscious state, which is significant for John Paul II. He sees in the passage from consciousness to subconsciousness a return to "non-being," or the "moment before creation."[219] The body returns to this state by way of sleep, and rises from its slumber in the double unity of male and female. The original solitude (see above) is then broken in the act of sleeping by God's gracious initiative. Because this action occurs with reference to Adam's body, John Paul II insists that a certain homogeneity of male and female is protected by Genesis 2.[220] This is confirmed in the words, "[t]his time she is flesh from my flesh and bone from my bones" (Gen 2:23).

In fact, the acknowledgement by the first man of this somatic homogeneity in his embodied nature is immediate upon waking up. He rises, he sees and identifies, and he exclaims an essential unity.[221] Joy erupts in this moment of the first "face to face." Indeed, in the sensory experience of woman, the impression of the other forges the beginning of both sexual desire and the act of love in its ethical dimensions *for* the other. As Ghislain de Barmon describes it: "Le point de départ est l'impression. Celle-ci est fondée sur la perception. Au contact du monde qui l'entoure, chaque personne perçoit des images."[222] Such impressions of the other upon the self remain both instinctive and ethically saturated phenomena.

---

expression alters self-perception and opens its gaze to multiple perceptions of other persons. See Rogers, *Sexuality and the Christian Body*, 237.

218. John Paul II, *Man and Woman He Created Them*, 8.

219. Ibid., 8:3.

220. Ibid., 8:4.

221. A certain allusion to the future resurrection is given here, whereby the body, by the will of God, falls into a deep slumber ("non-being") and rises to find a perfect unity with the other. In death, Christ's body lay dormant, but in rising, his perfect obedience to the Father is given new impetus by way of new life. In his passion, death, and resurrection, the beginning of the church is made possible, through which we may live in communion through grace. More could be said on this, but it is enough here to acknowledge the textual parallels.

222. [The point of departure is an imprint. It is based on what is perceived. By way of contact with the world that surrounds them, each person perceives these images.] de

In other words, the sensory data of the face-to-face encounter impresses itself upon each of the two persons. In a way, this first reception of sensory data as sensual longing is the foundation of all normative experience in human life. But if this is so, it must be acknowledged that the "original unity" differs from what might be experienced in a postlapsarian world, because it is not sullied with imperfect desire. It remains unique and unrepeatable.[223] Original unity both overcomes the lonely existentiality evident in man's original solitude, but also affirms the human subjectivity established by it. The unity that follows the initial recognition of woman by man as his complementary other is the first "*communio personarum.*" And this *communio* is crucial to John Paul II's reflections on the body.[224] He acknowledges that the term "community" could have been used, but that it is fraught with multiple meanings. *Communio* is more precise, because it conveys the immediacy of being *beside* another person as a help, and also more biblically, it indicates that human existence is authentic when lived *for* the other person.[225] For *communio* to operate effectively, it requires the prior foundation of an existentiality in original solitude (which gives rise to self-consciousness) and the self-determination (subjectivity) that takes place through the awareness of one's own body.[226]

For John Paul II, the emphasis upon the *communio personarum* also indicates something about the creation of man in the image of God. Genesis 1 teaches the *imago Dei* explicitly. Genesis 2 confirms it indirectly by picturing the *imago* as issuing forth not only in the creation of humanity, but in its structure as a communion of persons, differentiated by sex.[227] Man, in John Paul II's reading, is not made in the image of God at the moment of his solitude, but in the moment of communion. In this logic, the human person is not truly human until it is differentiated sexually as male and female. Only in this way are they rendered in the vocation of *communio* towards and with one another. This is a fundamental point in John Paul II's account of the body, and it provides a clearer picture of his theological understanding of its significance. Indeed he acknowledges: "This is obviously not without significance for the theology of the body, but constitutes perhaps the deepest theological aspect of everything one can say about man."[228]

Barmon Ghislain, *Jean-Paul II Professeur D'amour*, 30.

223. John Paul II, *Man and Woman He Created Them*, 9:1.

224. Ibid., 9:2; Catholic Church, "Gaudium Et Spes".

225. John Paul II, *Man and Woman He Created Them*, 9:2.

226. Ibid.

227. Ibid., 9:3.

228. Ibid.

The male-female relationship is an essential dimension then for John Paul II's development of theological anthropology. For him, the human body is constituted formally in its masculinity or femininity, but not limited to mere biological description. Instead, the body is a dynamic image of God's Trinitarian nature, in terms of the *communio* between male and female. In considering the body in these terms, we are at a juncture here between systematic and moral theology. This is a reminder of John Paul II's use of Scripture as a basis for moral theology, because for him the former is not simply the primary witness to the doctrinal content of Christian belief, but the primary guide to Christian living. The images of embodied love that John Paul II finds in Scripture show that Christian truth is both about God's self-revelation as well as the manner in which Christians ought to respond to that revelation. In the context of the married community, the unity between the two has both a sacramental and an ethical dimension, confirmed by the words of St. Paul in speaking of the mystery of Christ and his church and their social counterparts the bridegroom and the bride (Eph 5:29–32). Between the first human parents in the theology of both Genesis accounts, a "reciprocal enrichment" presents itself in the concrete union of the two sexes.[229] The theological meaning goes deeper than the somatic structure of male and female, for it unites the interiority of the *communio* of persons in their embodied states with the interiority of the tripersonal divine community, Father, Son, and Holy Spirit. In this way, the exterior bodily dimension and the interior subjective dimension intersect at the Trinitarian *imago*. Reciprocity in *communio* then is theological and socially implicated.

In this schema, sexual union plays its part in two fundamental ways. First, the conjugal act unites the woman with the man in the "very mystery" of creation.[230] That is to say, the ongoing generative power of creation is experienced in the embodied act of two persons in the conjugative embrace. Secondly, the sexual act is the means of return for both female and male in terms of the original unity of the two. As they unite, they become what biblical language names "one flesh" and reorient themselves towards the good, as it is first envisaged in the book of Genesis. The couple return to that stage of union which is given witness in Gen 2:23 ("bone of my bones and flesh of my flesh"), in which a *communio* is present, not simply of bodies but of persons. By way of this return, original solitude is once again overcome in the mundane and ordinary act of sexual union between married persons. Indeed, a radical ethical move takes place, as one adopts the "solitude of the

229. Ibid., 9:5.
230. Ibid., 10:2.

body of the second 'I'" in one's own self-giving.[231] This is achieved through the free agency of the human person, who exercises the choice of reciprocal giving in relation to the other. If this embodied self-sacrifice and mutual joy is bereft of free choice, it is a meaningless reduction of the body. Openness to the other must be conducted interiorly and personally; it is, as it were, a "door" that may only be opened freely.[232]

So, the two ways of being an embodied human person—masculinity and femininity—appear as two "incarnations" of the "same metaphysical solitude before God."[233] As such, their mutual reciprocity overcomes the original solitude that constitutes the human person. In overcoming it, this *communio* also reveals the *imago Dei*, not as a static inscription upon the human person in the singular, but as an embodied social event of divine witness. God witnesses to himself through the human body in relation to others profoundly in the complementary and radically reciprocal nature of "the two": male and female.

Original nakedness

John Paul II views these reflections as "foundational" to human experience.[234] That is, they do not belong to prehistory, but are the theological account of man's foundational existentiality in history and therefore common to each human person. Because of this, John Paul II's account of the body is also a theology of the mundane and ordinary, of the seemingly banal experiences of man and woman in their waking and in their sleeping. The foundational experiences of original solitude and original unity are present to each person. John Paul II is arguing for a horizon of meaning to which the human body is called, which may be named *communio* or communion, with each other and with God. The third foundational experience, "original nakedness," builds on this perspective. It also is based on a developed reading of Genesis.

According to Genesis, the original unity of man and woman was ruptured by the fall (see especially Genesis 3). In eating of the tree of the knowledge of good and evil, the first parents crossed a boundary in terms of their basic innocence. The two do not simply act contrarily to God, but have their eyes opened to their standing before the divine: "Then the eyes of both were

---

231. Ibid.

232. Séguin, "The Biblical Foundations of the Thought of John Paul II on Human Sexuality," 276.

233. John Paul II, *Man and Woman He Created Them*, 10:1.

234. Ibid., 11:1.

opened, and they realized that they were naked . . ." (Gen 3:7). In response
to this new awareness, clothes are woven together to hide their bodies from
the divine gaze and a new situation arises. This situation is that of "shame,"
which John Paul II views as a new "experience of the body."[235] Shame arises
through the act of disobedience and the imparting of knowledge. Between
Gen 2:25 and 3:7 is a great gulf in the content of the human existential relation to the body. In the former, there is no shame but only innocence; in
the latter, shame provokes a desire to veil the body before the divine other.
Shame, for John Paul II, is therefore a "boundary" or a "threshold" experience, marking the biblical point at which the male-female relationship enters a new self-awareness of the body.[236] Shame also serves as a "foundation"
that watches over the body's involvement in the social and public spheres.[237]

In experiences of original solitude and unity, John Paul II locates the
primordial and foundational events of human experience. In such events,
shame is a nonpresence, notable in its absence from the narrative. According
to Gen 2:25, "the man and his wife were both naked and were not ashamed."
This indicates a fullness of bodily presence, both inwardly and outwardly
for both man and woman, uninterrupted by the feeling of shame. In his or
her nakedness, the body's physicality also indicates its more private, spiritual dimension, and bears itself before its sexual counterpart with ease and
comfort. When shame does arrive, John Paul II notes that the face-to-face
relationship of male to female experiences "fear" of the "second I." The self
experiences the gaze of the other's face and is fearful of its judgment. Furthermore, fear of the "second I" is substantially a fear for "one's own 'I.'"[238]
That is to say, in the face of the other, the self is aware of one's own nakedness and becomes fearful of its effect upon the communion between the two.
The human self desires affirmation and acceptance from the other, but fears
the rejection of the self in its nakedness. This experience is concerned with
the embodied person in its totality, including the interior dimension that is
invisible and complex. In this way, shame links itself to the experience of the
human body in relation both to the exterior "visibility of the world" as well
as the "inner dimension of vision."[239] In fact, the perception of the exterior
and sensory dimension of the world is constituted precisely upon the inner

235. Ibid., 11:4.

236. Ibid., 11:3–6.

237. Mensch, *Hiddenness and Alterity*, 114–17.

238. John Paul II, *Man and Woman He Created Them*, 12:1.

239. Ibid., 12:3–4.

dimension of the embodied human person. Shame introduces a fear about the self's relationship in both directions.[240]

In the Genesis narratives, man and woman experience nakedness before becoming aware of it. In John Paul II's reading, this is bound to the statement in Gen 1:31 that "God saw everything that he had made, and indeed, it was very good." The divine vision of the human person, constituted in a complementary alterity of male and female, encompasses a naked goodness in creation. It entails a level of personal intimacy and acceptance which lacks nothing and which shows itself as representative of the interior communion with both the self and with the other. In Genesis, male and female communicate themselves in the nature of gift; conscious of an embodied meaning in this logic of the gift, the first parents provide the foundation of every other act of *communio*. Masculinity and femininity, in this reading, are integral to the nature of the gift, because they are essentially related to the givenness of the body in the created order. In this way, the human community cannot disregard the body, and is called to maintain a crucial witness to the fruitfulness of an encounter with the other.

Now, a problem must be addressed here: does this mean that for John Paul II, the original experiences of solitude, unity, and nakedness require marriage as the sole means of enacting these foundational experiences? If this is so, it requires a violent reduction of every nonmarried experience of alterity and, practically speaking, foists an impossible benchmark for holiness and ethics. It is important to understand that John Paul II does not describe his anthropology in this way. While it is true that in the married communion of two, the paradigm of man and woman is given as the foundational experience of alterity, it must be understood as intrinsically linked to the first experience of alterity in the God-man relationship. That is, the nature of the divine-human relationship is foundationally a nuptial relationship, which casts light on how to interpret embodied acts of human sexuality. Human marriage is nuptial because God's desire for the human other is a nuptial love, and not the other way around. This is why the church can legitimately identify aspects of sexuality that may inhibit their capacity to analogously reveal divine-human love, as well as describing what acts have the capacity to reveal that love more adequately. John Paul holds the conviction that the combined procreative and unitive dimensions of marriage mark it as the only legitimate expression of human sexuality.[241] Be-

240. According to Radner in "The Nuptial Mystery: The Historical Flesh of Procreation," the fallen state opens sexuality up to an embodied enactment of "vast . . . ignorance." See Jeal, *Human Sexuality and the Nuptial Mystery*, 110–11.

241. Wojtyla's most extensive treatment of the relationship between sexuality and marriage is given in chapter IV of *Love and Responsibility*, 211–44.

cause of the normative function of marriage as a natural institution that crosses cultural boundaries (inclusive of various cultural differences), and as the appropriate paradigm for the begetting and raising of children, marriage also serves a related function in John Paul II's thought: *marriage is the principle paradigm of alterity*. Of course, not every encounter with the other is either sexual or constitutive of sexual difference. Encounters with other persons occur in every variation of human experience, from the violent and tragic, to the wondrous and liberating. The very exclusivity of the married relationship seems to mark it as a particular form of love, rather than love's paradigm in the world. Indeed, the other is encountered in both social intimacy and in the alienation of modern bureaucracy, on-line avatars or the banal commercialism of the suburban shopping center. The vision of marriage, as John Paul II understands it, is not limited to the couple themselves, but opens their relationship up to the opportunity of reflecting in each encounter with any other person the general significance of the nuptial mystery.[242] For John Paul, the foundational experience of two bodies, male and female, who experience an original solitude, a unity and a nakedness, is intrinsically nuptial or "spousal," and relates to that which is "essentially human."[243] Marriage is a paradigmatic way of being in the world that teaches the embodied and sustained nature of love for the other. In other words, Genesis cannot be read as an anthropology in which marriage is an accidental aspect, but one in which foundational human experience is itself nuptial; the mutual givenness of the male-female relationship is an integral aspect of what it is to be human.

The operation of the nuptial mystery in Wojtyla/John Paul II

The original experiences of the human person, foundational to John Paul II's theology of the body, therefore relate profoundly to a further operation of the nuptial mystery. The nuptial mystery refers to marriage as a central theological category, relating first to the wedding feast of the Lamb and his bride the church, and analogously to that of the sacramental marriage between the groom and the bride (See Rev 19:7; cf. Eph 5:32). In both, the body (whether church or an individual human person) remains the form of the self that makes a commitment to the health and wellbeing of a counterpart

242. It could also be understood within its wider "cosmic drama," as one piece of the drama of salvation and "one perspective" on it, albeit a dominant scriptural paradigm, see Jeal, "Visions of Marriage in Ephesians 5," in *Human Sexuality and the Nuptial Mystery*, 126.

243. John Paul II, *Man and Woman He Created Them*, 13:2.

in a communion of persons. Ideally, openness to the further regeneration of life as a divine gift contextualizes each intimate act between the two. The relationship is sustained by the grace of God and not by the frail strength of its human participants. Indeed, in the earthly marriage of a man and a woman, the relationship is marked by constant failures and inadequacies, always in need of further aid from outside the married relationship itself. By offering the nuptial mystery as his primary experience of alterity, John Paul II relates every encounter with the other to the foundational encounter between God and creation. Or, to place this in John Paul II's christological perspective, every experience of alterity is saturated with the meaning of God's first initiative in the incarnation; Christ the heavenly bridegroom, who seeks out, redeems, and binds himself to his bride, in the nuptial language of the New Testament.[244]

The use of the nuptial mystery as John Paul II's principle paradigm of alterity is built on previous intellectual foundations. In *The Acting Person*, Wojtyla describes a phenomenology of the relationship between person and action. He treats the human person as an embodied, integrated whole, a personal subject whose self-manifestation is completed in the drama of the body. Wojtyla is at pains to avoid a reduction of the embodied human person either to its constitutive physical features, or in the opposite direction, to its soul. Indeed, in his view, the person is not constituted holistically in terms of its body, but in the integration of its body and its actions. As he puts it, the "integration of the person in their action, taking place in the body and expressed by it, reveals simultaneously the deepest sense of the integrity of man as a person."[245] For this integration to be achieved, the human person must relate objectively to his or her own actions (and it is the body that makes this possible). Human actions are based on a foundation of personal freedom. The human person is free to act and to forge a personal path. Such a degree of freedom places human possibilities in the category of the transcendent. Phenomenologically speaking, the activity in which intentionality moves beyond the limits of subjectivity is named transcendence. With his account of freedom, Wojtyla is arguing that the directionality of human intentionality is interior rather than exterior, because it corresponds to the truth of the person. According to Rocco Buttiglione, "[t]he relationship of freedom to truth is finally the decisive element of the transcendence of the person in his action."[246] With this freedom to act, the transcendence of the

---

244. See for example, "And I saw the holy city, new Jerusalem, coming down out of heaven from God, prepared as a bride adorned for her husband" (Rev 21:2).

245. John Paul II, *The Acting Person*, 205.

246. Buttiglione, *Karol Wojtyla*, 154.

human person is revealed. By means of the body, the person externalizes the self and makes the body the object of free action.[247] In this way, the person transcends particular circumstances. An act does not ultimately have itself or its consequences as its true object, but rather that of the person who is realized in that act. The somatic whole of the human person is apparent as an integrated structure, for the inner subjective self takes hold of its own body by determining itself in action. This requires both self-possession and self-determination.[248] Wojtyla holds to an Aristotelian-Thomistic requirement that the human subject comes to possess itself as a whole, and to determine itself vocationally in the world.

Yet, Wojtyla highlights features of the human subject that might be surprising. Following Max Scheler, he refers to the emotive dimension of the human being: "All that determines and constitutes the spiritual transcendence of the person—his attitude toward truth, good, and beauty with the accompanying faculty of self-determination—stimulates a very deep emotive resonance in the human being."[249]

It is this inner self to which the externalities of acting point. We must, in Wojtyla's words, "feel its own inwardness."[250] The complex interiority of the human condition is, for him, as psychical and spiritual as it is emotive. In taking seriously the inner dimension, a phenomenological account of human experience takes shape that includes the entire human person and its affectivity. The full integration of the person and action requires consideration of the two as poles, strictly corresponding to one another.[251] Each explains the other without an undue anthropological imbalance. But Wojtyla understood that this account would be redundant if considered separately from the need for human persons to live beside and with others, what would otherwise be called intersubjectivity.[252]

In relation to intersubjectivity (which, as will be seen, relates to the intersubjectivity of the nuptial mystery as his principle paradigm of alterity), Wojtyla highlights the following:

First, the performance of action is itself a value.[253] This value is personalistic, because the action conditions and brings about man's self-determination. In so doing, the action confirms the essential worth of the

247. John Paul II, *The Acting Person*, 206.

248. Ibid., 220.

249. Ibid., 227.

250. Ibid., 206.

251. Ibid., 261.

252. Ibid., 261–99.

253. Ibid., 264.

human person. Wojtyla confirms that being precedes action, but identifies in action the manifestation of the value of the person's own self-determined constitution.

Second, the "personalistic" value conditions the ethical value of the individual action.[254] Notwithstanding the traditionally Thomist conviction that certain actions in and of themselves carry a moral weight, the personalistic value of the action is prior to the ethical content of any action. As a kind of precondition, the personalistic value must bear "efficacy, self-determination, and responsibility."[255]

Third, the personalistic value of action is in relation to "communal action."[256] Wojtyla is concerned to prevent this consideration of the personalistic value of action being reduced to mere volition; the power of the will as the motivation behind action. Communal action, or indeed the entire realm of intersubjectivity, relies on actions that are personalistic. The personalistic value is a revelation and confirmation of ethical values specifically in terms of personal human subjectivity.

In his approach to participation in this treatment of intersubjectivity, Wojtyla is working out his approach to a Husserlian problem, that of how to conceive of the other person. For most interpreters of Husserl, the other is constituted for the self on the basis of one's own consciousness.[257] The real nature of the other eluded Husserl, who could only conceive of the other, or the person, in terms of consciousness. Instead, Wojtyla sees consciousness as an aspect of the human person. Participation with others is therefore a foundational aspect of human personhood. As John McNerney argues: "For Wojtyla the encounter with the other is not just a question for consciousness but it in fact 'discloses a new dimension [of man as a] person.'"[258]

In participation with others, this new dimension reveals itself. The personalistic value is made concrete in the context of intersubjectivity. Wojtyla does not shirk from the complexities of this. For example, he acknowledges that in intersubjectivity, others can limit one's actions to various degrees, by which the term "acting" may simply mean that something "happens" to a particular person.[259] Nevertheless, it is in this acting together with others that the transcendent nature of the personalistic value is revealed and confirmed.

---

254. Ibid., 265.

255. Ibid.

256. Ibid., 266.

257. Moran, *Introduction to Phenomenology*, 178.

258. McNerney, *John Paul II*, 30.

259. John Paul II, *The Acting Person*, 270.

Against this basic insight, Wojtyla contrasts "individualism" and "totalism."[260] In individualism, anthropology is limited to an isolation of the human person. The individual is conceived apart from a common category of the good, which narrows the possibilities for human flourishing. In turn, the "other" or "others," for such an individual, become a source of disturbance and a "source of limitation."[261] On the other hand, totalism is a reversal of individualism but equally rejects the category of participation. In totalism, the community must barricade itself against the individual as its negative other. For the totalist mentality, the individual is a threat to the achievement of the good, which justifies the use of coercion. For Wojtyla, both systems flow from the same error: conceiving of the human being in an "impersonalistic" or "antipersonalistic" definition.[262] It is only in the denial of the personalistic value of human action that either of these two ideological extremes can be embraced and given political and social form. Participation is a means of imagining the personalistic value in intersubjectivity in such a way that the human person—the incarnate human subject—is not reduced to an antipersonalistic definition and therefore not abused and impoverished by the logic of violence which follows.

For the sake of the intersubjective community, a notion of the common good must be achieved which is an authentic reflection of the key attributes outlined above. For this reason, Wojtyla takes up the biblical category of "neighbor."[263] To be a neighbor carries connotations that are more intimate than that of merely being a member of a community. The latter is not necessarily deficient, but lacks the precision of the term neighbor. By this, an ethical proximity to the other person is revealed. In receiving the neighbor, Wojtyla highlights what he names the "humanness of every man," in which participation is manifest.[264] The fullness of participation can only be reached with the universality in the particular of the commandment to love the neighbor, who is revealed in each other's face. Love involves a level of self-sacrifice that reaches paradoxical meaning, in that the self gives itself freely for the sake of others.[265] As Buttiglione describes:

260. Ibid., 273–74.

261. Ibid., 274.

262. Ibid., 275.

263. Ibid., 292.

264. Ibid., 294.

265. There is much in *The Acting Person* that Wojtyla extrapolates in relation to the nature of community, particularly in terms of alienation and various "nonauthentic attitudes" to true community, such as conformism and noninvolvement, but we have restricted ourselves here to what is most relevant to the theology of the body.

> In an authentic human community, according to Wojtyla, the one who participates is open to sacrificing his own particular good to the common good, not because he considers the common good superior to the particular one but because the self-realization of the value of one's own person, which is achieved through sacrifice, is greater and more worthy than what would be gained by achieving one's own particular interest against the common good.[266]

Or, in Wojtyla's own words: "The commandment, 'Thou shalt love,' has itself a thoroughly communal character; it tells what is necessary for a community to be formed, but more than anything else it brings into prominence what is necessary for *a community to be truly human*."[267]

In participation, the personalistic value confirms and makes possible the humanism of encounter with the other, who is one's neighbor. The naming of the other as neighbor constitutes a concrete focus for the commandment to love. Communities come into being because of an intricate relationship of persons, actions, value, and command. Yet, the nuptial mystery is a central theme in Wojtyla's thought that follows the same instinctive desire to uphold community as a participative and personalistic context for human flourishing. The nuptial mystery is a community defined by love and an embodied self-giving open to new life. It is also a participative and personalistic context, but as a theological motif, it achieves something further in Wojtyla's intellectual project; it appears as his principle paradigm of alterity and his clearest iconic presentation of the significance of the body. This is also apparent in Part Two of *Man and Woman He Created Them*.

Part Two of *Man and Woman He Created Them*

Part Two of *Man and Woman He Created Them* begins with the words of Eph 5:21–33, in which St. Paul teaches on the relationship between human marriage and the mystery of Christ and the church. It is a key text in considering a scriptural account of marriage, because it is objectively directed towards both wives and husbands in their practice of the married relationship. Furthermore, it situates that practice in a christological framework, describing the married relationship as analogous to the relationship between Christ and the church. In Paul's words, "[w]ives, be subject to your husbands as you are to the Lord" and "husbands, love your wives, as Christ loved the church and gave himself for her" (Eph 5:21, 25). It is in Eph 5:32 that Paul

266. Buttiglione, *Karol Wojtyla*, 172.
267. John Paul II, *The Acting Person*, 296.

refers to the nuptial relationship as a "mystery" (μυστήριον). The passage is dense with meaning and fraught with a long history of misinterpretation and abuse.[268] Paul thinks of the male as analogous to the role of Christ as head of the ecclesial body and the female as analogous to the ecclesial body in its call to holiness. In fact, the presentation of the bride to the husband is the moment of divine-human encounter, in which the bride (the church) is called to a "holy and immaculate" life (Eph 5:27). In the call to holiness, the male shares an equal part, but is commanded to afford a love for the bride who is both other to his own flesh, and called to be loved "as their own body" (Eph 5:28). With this point of departure, the second part of John Paul II's catechesis on the body is structured.

In Ephesians 5 (especially 21–33), John Paul II identifies two meanings of the term "body."[269] The first is metaphorical, regarding the church as the body of Christ. The second is in its "concrete meaning," by which he refers to the human body in its masculinity and femininity and the "perennial destiny" for marriage.[270] The convergence of these two meanings of the body relate to the spousal analogy of marriage in its concrete form. The sacramentality of the bodily spousal union is a means of grace, but it also speaks of a profoundly other event, that of the spousal event between God and creation, or between Christ and the church. The earthly spousal union is at once a visible sign of God's love, but speaking sacramentally, it also produces grace. In both its visibility and its invisible gracefulness, the spousal union is orientated towards the origin of its own efficaciousness: Christ the Redeemer. Christ is the mystery who manifests his presence in the life of the church and who models forth the life his disciples are called to follow. The spousal union, in its sacramentality, is both a model and an expression of that divine plan revealed in the mystery of Christ.[271] Following this logic, John Paul II reads in Ephesians the basis for the various moral obligations of both society and the family.[272] Once again, John Paul II utilizes the nuptial mystery as his principle paradigm of alterity and its consequent role in determining all experiences of otherness (not simply the concrete married relationship).

Within the nuptial mystery is a strong account of embodied difference. In the differences between masculinity and femininity, John Paul II

---

268. See Jeal, "Visions of Marriage in Ephesians 5," in *Human Sexuality and the Nuptial Mystery*, 116–30.

269. John Paul II, *Man and Woman He Created Them*, 87:3.

270. Ibid.

271. Ibid., 88:3.

272. Wojtyla refers to these as the "Haustafeln"—Martin Luther's term—or "domestic codes." See Ibid., 88:5.

locates the foundational elements of *communio*. Referring to Eph 5:21–33, "be subject to one another in the fear of Christ," he sees an experience of alterity which plays out on two levels. The first is "reciprocal" and the other is "communitarian."[273] Both are possible because of the common fear of Christ (as Ephesians has it), which situates the married couple on the foundation of a shared *pietas* in relation to Christ; of a deep consciousness for the holy—the *sacrum*—referred to by the Old Testament as the "fear of God."[274] The paradox of orientation towards Christ is that through a constant habit of *pietas* towards him, Christ in turn creates the possibility and the means for a shared reciprocity, such that they may become "subject to one another" (Eph 5:21). In this, the "communion" of persons is realized through the community of the married spouses.[275] This is the concrete form of love in its domesticity. The correspondence between the spousal love of Christ and the church with that of the human husband and wife is authentic only in its realization of a self-subjecting of each self to the other. The analogous relationship between both examples of spousal love is only logical when related to the mutuality of the "fear of Christ" and only possible in the event that such fear becomes the habit of *pietas*.[276]

These reflections develop in close correlation to the text of Ephesians, but always in relation to the foundational (or original) experiences of the human condition in solitariness, unity, and nakedness in Genesis. Importantly, John Paul II places marriage at the sacramental service of the church, referring to its lineage long before the coming of Christ. He writes: "One must say, finally, that the sacramentality of the Church remains in a particular relationship with marriage, the most ancient sacrament."[277] This is a fundamental statement of John Paul II's view that the nuptial mystery, precisely in relation to its concrete experience in human history, also serves as a paradigm that saturates all of ecclesial life. It is, at heart, christological, but also serves as a means of participation in the divine life. Its very possibility is based on the prior act of Christ in extending his self-sacrifice for his bride the church. John Paul II sees in the analogous relationship between Christ-church and bridegroom-bride the means of understanding an ethics of the gift. It is that "*aspect of* God's gift of himself to man

273. Ibid., 89:1.

274. Ibid.

275. Ibid., 89:6.

276. Wojtyla refers to this double analogy as a "bi-subjectivity": Christ-church; bridegroom-bride. In the human experience, each partner desires the other in beauty but also desires the good of the partner. This is a "restless" desire, for it has no singular moment of adequate fulfilment or completion. See ibid., 92:4.

277. Ibid., 93:7.

who is chosen 'from ages' in Christ . . . ."[278] Moreover, marriage is situated as the primordial sacrament, of that experience of grace that precedes and therefore provides a foundational experience for all other avenues of grace. We can see here even more clearly how John Paul II utilizes the *communio* of persons in the married relationship (and by extension the family) as his principle paradigm of alterity. According to Gen 2:24, marriage is the social and institutional beginning of the human community, granted a procreative power (Gen 1:28) and the means of expressing that first initiative of the Creator's salvific plan.

In regards to the nuptial mystery, what has been broken in the fall (by original sin) has not been robbed of its efficacy as a sign or a figure of God's gracious first initiative.[279] Because of the fall, historical man is also the "man of concupiscence," whose heart desires the flesh of another solely for self-gratification.[280] John Paul II identifies this as chiefly an interior experience that detaches the human person from the language of the body. The original reciprocal attraction of masculinity and femininity is reduced in its relational horizon, resulting in an opaque vision of what the body might hope for in relation to the other. Its *ethos* is not so much altered but impoverished. This is particularly acute when John Paul II considers the biblical notions of sexual difference and desire in contrast with what he calls (following Paul Ricœur) the "masters of suspicion" [*maîtres du soupçon*].[281] Both Ricœur and John Paul II see a convergence of the thought of Marx, Nietzsche, and Freud, in which the human heart is judged and accused.[282] John Paul II summarizes their positions as follows: Nietzschean hermeneutics understands the nature of the human heart to be enmeshed in a "pride of life"; Marxist hermeneutics sees in the heart the "concupiscence of the eyes"; and Freudian hermeneutics identifies the heart with the "concupiscence of the flesh."[283] While John Paul II acknowledges some level of biblical agreement in these anthropological observations, he insists that the Bible does not stop at these negative appraisals of the human heart. Rather, the biblical witness is to redemption beyond mere concupiscence. In the words of 1 John 2:16–17:

---

278. Ibid., 95b:4.

279. Ibid., 97:1.

280. See especially ibid., 26–33.

281. Ibid., 46.

282. Ricœur identifies a deep relationship between these three and their followers, in which they not only offer three types of suspicion but also deception. See especially Ricœur, *Le Conflit Des Interprétations*.

283. John Paul II, *Man and Woman He Created Them*, 46:2.

> For all that is in the world—the desires of the flesh and the de-
> sires of the eyes and pride in possessions—is not from the Fa-
> ther but is from the world. And the world is passing away along
> with its desires, but whoever does the will of God abides forever.

Biblically speaking, there is little justification for arguing in favor
of a nihilistic pessimism or a fundamental suspicion of the heart or the
world. The latter is, in one sense, passing away, but human beings are not
encouraged to cease hopefulness for a glorious future tense. Instead, the
Bible reshapes an anthropological vision by not restricting it to the state of
concupiscence, and instead moving consideration to that of the redemptive
call issued by Christ. What Paul calls the "redemption of the body" (Rom
8:23) begins with the language of the body itself, which not only speaks
of concupiscence, but also holds an interior call to communion with others. While John Paul II acknowledges that the Word originates outside the
human person, his radical move here is to insist on the interior embodied
call towards grace. With the aid of self-reflection, the human subject finds
within its own anthropological structure the call to *communio* and an appeal through Christ's power to confer love upon the body in its unity and its
difference.[284] In this way, the human heart is not fundamentally condemned
but *called*. It is not the object of restraint so much as it is the subject of
love's redeeming work. John Paul describes this as a calling deeper than
that of concupiscence: "Called as a person in the truth of his humanity, and
thus also in the truth of his masculinity and femininity, in the truth of his
body."[285] The result of being called is to orient the human person and its
body within a directionality of communion with God as the basis for all
other relationships.

John Paul II is not alone in understanding sexual difference as an integral feature of theological anthropology. He was influenced by Hans Urs
von Balthasar, although the latter's name is a rare direct reference in John
Paul's published works.[286] Both thinkers argue that Trinitarian relations are
an appropriate theological basis for reflecting on the male-female relationship. In Balthasar's work, this relationship is not limited to ethical reflection about procreation, but acts as a positive complementary experience
of difference in which persons fulfill the other, which is not limited to the
body.[287] For Balthasar, the Christ-church relationship is "supra-sexual," for
it is a companionship of the former for the latter which is fruitful in terms

---

284. Ibid., 46:5.

285. Ibid., 46:6.

286. Leahy, "John Paul II and Hans Urs von Balthasar," in *The Legacy of John Paul II.*

287. Balthasar, *Theo-Drama,* II:365–66.

of its communion and fellowship.[288] In this way, the nuptial relationship of man and woman is a fundamental good in the creation narratives of both Genesis 1 and 2, but its full significance is revealed in Christ and his love for the church. By "supra-sexual," Balthasar indicates a spiritual relationship that, while not exactly sexed, is not unsexed either. Sexual difference is taken up and restored in the christocentric vision of the human person, and continues to be of great significance. For him, the nuptial mystery of Christ and the church is itself one of agapeic love, yet its spiritual fruitfulness (*of* the Spirit) relies on an analogy to sexual fruitfulness experienced in the world. While Balthasar finds normative consequences of the nuptial mystery by which certain masculine and feminine characteristics formally belong each to the male and the female, John Paul II does not pursue this line of thinking to the same extent.[289] In this sense, Balthasar's account is more prescriptive of male-female relations generally, whereas John Paul II remains circumspect in assigning particular character traits to male and female persons in overly fixed terms.

Another significant defender of a strong account of sexual difference is Karl Barth. There is little evidence for a direct influence of Barth on John Paul II, but it is recognized that Barth influenced Balthasar, who in turn was an important influence on John Paul II.[290] For Barth, the human person is never asexual and the complementary relationship of male to female acts at the heart of Christian anthropology because being truly human means for the man to live alongside woman and for the woman to live alongside man.[291] Barth (like John Paul II and unlike Balthasar) is reticent about describing a normative set of characteristics that belong to either male or female because of his insistence on their "equal dignity and right" before God.[292] He nevertheless comes to the conclusion (based largely on his reading of Ephesians 5) that while a mutual submission of the two is primary, the woman remains the model of Christian discipleship. For Barth, the receptivity of woman is of an active kind, and it therefore serves better as a model for what it means to follow Christ. As Agneta Sutton has observed, while Balthasar turns to Mary as the primary model for the discipleship of the church (and by consequence the feminine), Barth comes to the same conclusion about the

---

288. Ibid., 13.

289. For example, Balthasar views the male as fundamentally active and the female as fundamentally receptive, resulting in the latter as a more perfect image of the Christian life more generally. See Balthasar, *Love Alone*, 77.

290. Mannion, *The Vision of John Paul II*, 162.

291. Barth, *Church Dogmatics. Vol. 3, the Doctrine of Creation*, 166.

292. Ibid., 169.

feminine, but without Mary as his model.[293] In both Balthasar and Barth, a strident attempt is made to base sexual relations on the Trinity, resulting in a theology of sexual difference. John Paul II's approach is, like Barth, to remain close to the scriptural texts in teasing out the possibilities for such a use of the nuptial mystery. And like Balthasar, John Paul II views the nuptial mystery as a biblical theme that may shed light on both male-female relations and the communion of Christ and the church. Unlike both Barth and Balthasar, John Paul II actively paints a picture of the nuptial relationship that views the use of power of one over the other as a distortion of the biblical image. Furthermore, a greater accent on the equal dignity between the two sexes can be found in John Paul II than with Barth or Balthasar, although it must be said that this is not necessarily absent from their works. For all three, both Genesis creation accounts provide the basis for centering the nuptial mystery in theological anthropology. Janet Martin Soskice has commented on the usefulness of discussing sexual difference in a contemporary setting: "The Genesis text also speaks about sexual difference. It is constitutive of human beings, and it is good. It is not good for *H'adam* to be alone."[294] Soskice sees in sexual difference the opportunity for the learning of love. In the reciprocity of the human condition, it is being in relation to the concrete difference of others that makes love possible. Because of this, sexual difference is a "primordial difference."[295] Yet John Paul II's conception of sexual difference as a primordial difference integral to anthropology is not widely accepted, even if it falls within a pattern developed by figures such as Barth and Balthasar. John Paul II's understanding of the human *telos* in becoming a gift for others and witnessing to the nuptial mystery is not without criticism.

The problem of the language of the body: critical responses

The theology of the body is a developing feature of contemporary Catholic thought and has attracted critical attention. For example, Tina Beattie has critiqued the theology of the body as problematic from a feminist perspective, while acknowledging its "promise" in relation to the notion of the body as "self-gift."[296] Her criticism chiefly relates to interpretations of Balthasar, including Wojtyla's. Beattie does not dismiss the theology of the body out of

293. Sutton, "The Complementarity and Symbolism of the Two Sexes," 425.

294 Soskice, "Imago Dei and Sexual Difference," in Jeeves (ed.), *Rethinking Human Nature*, 299.

295. Ibid., 306.

296. Beattie, *New Catholic Feminism*, 46.

hand, but seeks an adequate anthropology from within the Roman Catholic tradition that builds the connections between the human body and experiences of God and the church. Moreover, her work recognizes the crucial role the body plays in the church's worship, liturgy, and hope, even if her conclusions are far from those of Wojtyla.

In the postmodern context, Beattie wishes to bring back the notion that the body (the sign) and its meaning (what it signifies) are intimately related. She disenfranchises the postmodern insistence that signification violates and transgresses the thing it signifies.[297] For her, the Christian narrative refutes this claim.[298] The body and its language is of concern to this debate because Wojtyla's claims depend on the body successfully signifying its own meaning. For Wojtyla, the body, as a text, speaks both towards and beyond itself.[299] Derrida had insisted that there is "nothing outside the text" [Il n'y a pas de hors-texte].[300] He was arguing that a demarcation occurs between a text and any thing it may seem to be signifying. For example, a written report on a person's bodily health remains only a text; it has no immediate significance for the person himself or herself. Furthermore, it could be argued that the text transgresses the person concerned by making claims only the person may signify. Instead, Beattie sees a need for the body to find its appropriate signifier, for life and not death is conceived in the encounter between language and matter. In fact, authentic language is only possible via a creation that has experienced grace; the Word speaks and so words are possible thereafter. This is most acute in the liturgy, which, following the Second Vatican Council and patristic tradition, is described as a foretaste of the heavenly liturgy. In other words, it is a material participation in the timeless liturgy of heaven (for example, Rev 21:1–4).[301] In the Eucharistic rite, a rich multitextured narrative takes place, taking in major themes from across the Bible and early Christian practice, all calling for a full involvement of the body. The body is an active participant in the liturgy, bringing with it a personal narrative to involve itself in the broader, more

297. Ibid., 293.

298. Kevin Hart describes deconstruction (crafted and described chiefly by Derrida) as a criticism of totalizing claims in which a sign is trespassed in its attempt to impose itself on others, however a strict definition is hard to reach. Hart, *The Trespass of the Sign*.

299. In this sense, experience of the body can be likened to mystical experience. Hart comments that language is the medium that reveals mystical experience, "while simultaneously hiding it . . ." Hart, *The Trespass of the Sign*, 180.

300. Derrida, *La Voix Et Le Phénomène*, 136.

301. See also *Sacrosanctum Concilium*; Ferrone, *Liturgy: Sacrosanctum Concilium*.

public narrative of sacramental grace. Bodies are brought to the liturgy. As Beattie describes:

> Sometimes we come as those crucified by suffering or by shame, sometimes we come pregnant with vision and promise, sometimes we come yearning for nourishment, sometimes we come as mystical lovers, filled with erotic desire for the nameless, boundless Other, sometimes we come in nuptial celebration, sometimes we come in funereal mourning, and every time we incarnate him and he divinizes us.[302]

This affirms the traditional notion that through worship, God divinizes persons in both their divine image and likeness. While this affirmation of the role of the embodied person is to be appreciated, it misses a salient point. Beattie's positive reading of the erotic sensibilities of the liturgy overlooks the mundane experience of those whose attendance is marked by boredom and fatigue, weighed down with the habit of Mass attendance as a burden in which there is no recognizable presence of grace, let alone "divinization."[303] Beattie's emphasis upon the extremes of tragedy and glory overlook the graced life of the mundane experiences of liturgy evident for many, if not most Christians, much of the time. It is true that Beattie can see that the fullness of life promised in the text of the liturgy often crumples in its actual performance. The body is promised a foretaste of heaven, but instead is engrafted into a modernist labor of limited participation. Part of the reason might be the limitations of a rite that was reformed in an era of increasing modernist rationality and a diminished sense of the powerful relational symbolics of sex and the sacred. This argument is made by David Torevell who is quoted by Beattie: "We 'learn' to share in the divine life of Christ primarily by the engagement of our bodily senses, not by increasing attention being given to the stimulation of our minds. The power of ritual is achieved through the symbolic use of the body."[304]

Torevell argues that there is a sound basis for a point both conservatives and postmoderns make, that the liturgy has lost its mystical sense, its spiritual awareness, and in turn offers a disembodied, overly rationalistic mode of worship, which is not necessarily in union with Christian mission. Beattie advocates for a new reform of Christian worship on postmodern

---

302. Beattie, *New Catholic Feminism*, 301.

303. Purcell describes the context in which such persons live, of the "terribly ordinary, average, and everyday" which causes falter and hesitation in our steps. Grace operates here, perhaps in its primary expression: the mundane and the ordinary. See Purcell, "Glimpsing Grace Phenomenologically," 79.

304. Torevell, *Losing the Sacred*, 194–95.

terms. Unfortunately, it is not clear in Beattie's work how a richly symbolic liturgical life that values difference is to be enhanced by a reduction in the presentation of sexual difference outside of a contemporary liberal notion of social justice. And unlike other theologians who have written on these themes (for example, Catherine Pickstock), Beattie offers no assessment of the liturgy prior to the Second Vatican Council, of either its virtues or its limitations.[305] These deficiencies do not rob Beattie of her fundamental insight, that the body's role in the liturgy is generally undervalued and bereft of its profound theological language. In this, Wojtyla and Beattie are in agreement. However, Beattie's argument does not account for mundane experiences of the body, of the ordinary interactions of "everyday alterity," and the way the liturgy might have the capacity to incorporate these in stories of grace.

Where Beattie and Wojtyla differ profoundly is in their conceptualization of the relationship between the text of the body and its signification. The body's textual meaning—its language—is never wrought independently of other persons, but rather in that space or gap that exists *between* bodies. It has been seen how Wojtyla's notion of the nuptial mystery operates as his principle mode of alterity between human persons. In this model, the physicality of differentiated sexuality affirms difference at a fundamentally embodied level. Furthermore, it confirms the sense in which the human person discovers and receives its own self by giving himself or herself disinterestedly for the other in the form of "gift of self."[306] Beattie finds positive possibilities in the "relational performances" in the "gap" between male and female bodies, but refuses a theological commitment to its structure of *communio*.[307] By anchoring the difference between persons (especially sexually differentiated persons) within the space that is marked by both difference and distance, human dignity can be valued without recourse to the autonomous subject of modernity.[308] No longer can a theology (or the text) of the body be treated in the singular, but always in the plural. Instead, in intersubjectivity, the form of love makes its appearance, marked by the presence of two for each other, and by a profound attendance to alterity as an embodied event. The convalescence of presence and attendance in the experience of alterity (which is always fractured and imperfect) is evidence of the praxis of love.[309]

305. See Pickstock, *After Writing*.

306. John Paul II, *Man and Woman He Created Them*, 16.B:4.

307. Beattie, *New Catholic Feminism*, 46–47.

308. Ibid., 47.

309. See Elshtain's reflections on the incarnate examples of committed, rigorous

Beattie concedes that those who have taken up John Paul II's call for what he calls a "new feminism," while bound to stereotypes and essentialisms that Beattie rejects, are correct to follow his logic in terms of the body's participation in this logic of the gift.[310] As such, the body is a gift of the self, to the self, towards the other, and stands as a nexus point between God's self-giving and human giving. The marriage of language and the body carries a mystery, one that is "inseparable" from the original mystery of God.[311] Beattie acknowledges that the relationship has a sacramental dimension. In language and the body, the textual meanings of the embodied human person become themselves a testimony to the signifying capacity of the body. Indeed, the rich abundance of nuptial and sexual imagery and meaning in the theology of Balthasar, so influential on Wojtyla and profoundly contradicted by Beattie, owes everything to the communicative power of the body.[312] Beattie is right to identify the central motif of the nuptial mystery in Balthasar's theology: that the primary kenotic initiative is a masculine self-emptying in conjunction with the returned self-gift of the feminine in the consummative act of fruitfulness. The other is always desired within a divine fecundity, by which regeneration in both nature and by grace may also be given as gift.

John Paul II's appropriation of this language in his theology of the body owes much to the nuptial mystery as originating all experiences of alterity. While his account of the body does not fall prey to the self-defeating sexual difference that Beattie identifies, it is certainly an averment of the mutually reciprocal moment of gender and sexual exchange that is occasioned between the first parents. Moreover, it does not reduce the other's body to a biological determinism, but restores difference in bodily terms that allow that same difference to speak as a living text. That text is *gift*. In Balthasar's terms:

> If Eve was taken out of Adam, then Adam had Eve within him without knowing it. Of course, God created her and breathed his breath into her; but God took the material for her out of Adam's living flesh infused with the Spirit. There was something feminine in him, which he recognises when God brings him the woman. And the Creator gives the man the power to be creative in this creaturely womb. But the woman is taken from the man; the substance from which she is made is masculine. She knows

and meticulous love in *Who Are We?*, 67.

310. Beattie, *New Catholic Feminism*, 47–48.

311. Ibid., 48.

312. Ibid., 159–60.

the man from the beginning. She is, together with him, feminine in relation to God, but she also has the actively responding
power with him.[313]

In other words, the embodiment of alterity maintains an integrity of
sexual difference. Hans Urs von Balthasar's account of sexual difference is
fundamentally open to a theological horizon of self-giving. Beattie's concern is to bring a postmodern "carnival" character to sexuality and male
and female embodiment, bringing into stark relief the female body against
its historical silencing in the abyss of the "unsaid" (see Heidegger) or deeper
still, the "unthought."[314] She wishes to move beyond a description of alterity in nuptial terms. Sacramentality, after all the ruptures and inadequacies of modernity and of the postmodern assent, remains dependent upon
materiality and the "presence of bodies."[315] The "unsaid" may, according to
Wojtyla, become a "said" as it becomes an *ethos* of self-gift. It may be that,
following Emmanuel Levinas, the "unsaid" must be given form in the act
of responsibility for the disincarnate other. In both, the gleam of the divine
shows itself in the stirrings of *communio*, which must maintain its embodied experience of the sexual person without reduction. Problematically, the
carnivalesque forms of sexual alterity that Beattie proposes do not free the
embodied person, male or female, to any transcendent experience that is
more human, but rather enfold anthropology within the self-interest of
postmodern theater and poetry.

Beattie is right to look towards a more embodied liturgical performance, but misses the fundamental point: that the body's textual language
speaks in the communion of others, each of whom carries an incarnate
language which is both broken and redeemed, signifying and mysteriously
fecund. In the gift of the other, especially in the arrival of the third (for
Wojtyla, the child; for Levinas, the stranger who is absolutely other; a theme
developed in the final chapters of this book), alterity itself is interrupted
with its truer self; the embodied self who calls out for responsibility.[316] The
significance of this, for John Paul II, is comprehended through the nuptial
mystery, allowing an activity of attentiveness for and towards Christ in the
other's subjective constitution, rooted in the relationship between bride and

---

313. Balthasar, *A Theological Anthropology*, 312–13.

314. Beattie, *New Catholic Feminism*, 298.

315. Ibid., 297.

316. Wojtyla argues consistently that transmission of life is a key aspect of the nuptial relationship in its earthly dimension (the "procreative" end), but says relatively little
about children as active subjects in *Man and Woman He Created Them*.

bridegroom. The spousal meaning carries over into each and every other intersubjective moment.

John Paul situates sexual difference within the logic of the gift. Such a communion of difference is both ethical and sacramental. He argues:

> This unity through the body ("and the two will be one flesh") possesses a multiform dimension: an ethical dimension, as is confirmed by Christ's response to the Pharisees in Matthew 19 (see also Mark 10) and also a sacramental dimension, strictly theological, as confirmed by the words of Paul to the Ephesians, that likewise refer to the tradition of the prophets (Hosea, Isaiah, Ezekiel). And this is so, because the unity that is realised through the body indicates from the beginning not only the "body," but also the "incarnate" communion of persons— "*communio personarum*"—and has from the beginning required this communion.[317]

In other words, Wojtyla's approach to the body holds together the ethical command of Christ to uphold the commitment of marriage together with the sacramental nature of that relationship, which is a graced communion of persons. The dual identity of this *communio personarum* situates it both in the temporal order (in which relationships must be experienced in their local human complexities) as well as in the order of grace, which denotes God's universal self-gratuity. In both its ethical and its sacramental dimensions, the nuptial mystery is relational in that it relies on the self-giving of more than one embodied person. In turn, sexuality is interpreted within a relational context. If it is true—as John Paul argues—that the relational dimension of the original unity of man and woman in God's plan is an integral aspect of man's own personal structures and his very self, then it follows that in the incarnation, such an inseparable part of human identity, was also assumed into the Godhead. In the words of Michele Schumacher, Christ has assumed into himself Adam's natural nature, including the "original" or "natural" sacramental meaning.[318] In Christ, original unity has been raised to perfection in Christ's redemptive work. Sexual identity, male and female, has been perfected within the incarnate activity of Christ, and without any dislocation of Christ's own masculine form. The relationship of these two genders within the resurrected body of Christ constitutes a new heavenly unity. Just as the divine gift of Christ's self-offering is given in complete self-awareness of his own sacrifice, so he orders within his body the constitu-

---

317. John Paul II, *Man and Woman He Created Them*, 9:5.

318. Schumacher, "The Unity of the Two: Toward a New Feminist Sacramentality of the Body," 212.

tive genders of male and female and their self-offering on a conscious level. Wojtyla/John Paul II argues:

> When both unite so intimately with each other that they become "one flesh," their conjugal union presupposes a mature consciousness of the body. Better yet, this union *carries within itself a particular awareness of the meaning of that body in the reciprocal self-gift of the persons.*[319]

In this way, the human body is not a slave to itself. The body is not a mechanistic structure fated by a prewritten program, nor is the human person bound to the trajectory of every natural appetite. Rather, human persons are intimately manifest in the experience of the body and the body cannot be transcended absolutely. That is not to say that much cannot be learned from the critical work of thinkers such as Beattie. From her consideration of Balthasar, the dangers of an oversimplification of human sexual differentiation can be seen more adequately, and this is an important consideration.

As was seen in the consideration of postmodernity in chapter 1, the human person experiences itself in a kind of rupture that includes sexuality. John Paul II's description of a theology of the body takes this into account and situates it in relation to the human existentiality evident in both Genesis creation narratives. While a cursory reading might suggest that "[t]he impression given by the *Theology of the Body* is that passion and sexual pleasure are totally suspect and in need of control," it has been shown how they belong to a wider theological project that is reliant not on the domination or control of sexuality, but in the self-donation of the nuptial mystery between Christ and the ecclesial bride.[320] The achievements of holding a strong account of sexual difference in human experience in creative tension with the theological analogy of the nuptial mystery grounds the scriptural image in the embodied experience of human relationships. In this way, the analogy is not divorced from reality but acts as an interpretive lens through which to understand it, revealing the body as a member of a constellation of human components that speaks a language of its own, not determinative nor prescriptive, but morally and naturally prompting the human person towards the "good."[321] In this way, the good is to be enjoyed profoundly in *communio*, a redeemed sociality.

---

319. John Paul II, *Man and Woman He Created Them*, 9:4.

320. Curran, *The Moral Theology of Pope John Paul II*, 170.

321. For Wojtyla, the "good" is christocentric. "The good has its source in Wisdom and Love. In Jesus Christ the visible world which God created for man—the world that, when sin entered, 'was subjected to futility'—recovers again its original link with the divine source of Wisdom and Love." See: John Paul II, *Redemptor Hominis: The*

Conclusion

Alterity, in this perspective, is an experience that must be reorientated to *communio*. We are saved, John Paul II insists, not *from* the body but *through* it, and in its own unique manner of participation in the principle paradigm of the nuptial mystery. The body, according to John Paul, may be described phenomenologically and bears its own theology. In his theology of the body, the personalistic norm confirms the irreducible dignity of the human person, which acts as a defense of an inherent and universal freedom towards the good. It is through the mediation of the body that the heart is able to speak and commune with others, and this is shown most naturally and most profoundly in the nuptial mystery of male-female intimacy. That intimacy is forged in the difference between the two. The "mystery" of Christ and the church clarifies the distinctions between male and female, at least in the married relationship, constituting a theological correlation for a common anthropological and social experience (Eph 5:32). This is contextualized by Christ's teaching on the theology of the body, which follows the dual sources of the "historical" human person and the Genesis accounts of the "beginning"; the "historical man" is always contemporary and present as the "man of concupiscence."[322] While concupiscence rises within the human condition through the fall as an interruption and ontological disturbance, it does not rob human persons of the possibility of living according to an ethic of *communio*.

Furthermore, it has been shown that in John Paul II's use of such language, the nuptial mystery operates as his principle paradigm of alterity. Faced with the alterity of the other, the human person is placed within an embodied opportunity for either affirming or negating that which is dignified and true in the other. Yet, because the nuptial mystery is first a theological perspective concerning God and creation/Christ and the church, it speaks not only to the concrete forms of human marriage encountered in history but to the general experience of otherness. For John Paul, human persons remain mutually responsible to one another in the direction of *communio*. The body, in its vulnerability and in its sufferings, remains the vexing incarnation of the other. This is as true of the self's own body, which at times seems alien and distant, as it is of the bodies of others. For John Paul, the person who perfectly locates the dignity and freedom of all other bodies is that of the incarnate *Logos*. His body was also vulnerable and suffered exploitation, condemnation, and injury. His crucified body speaks to

---

Redeemer of Man, II, 8.

322. John Paul II, *Man and Woman He Created Them*, 87:2.

each other body in the language of suffering, but in its resurrected state also reminds each wounded body of its intimate, spousal, nuptial concern for the other's healing and personal resurrection. Ultimately, it is through Christ's body that the nuptial mystery is able to operate as a theological principle in the human experience of alterity. While John Paul II is concerned with the same problem of alterity that Levinas addresses, different conclusions result in their accounts of the body.

3

Levinas, Alterity, and the Problem of the Body

Introduction

THE PLACE OF THE body is a problematic feature in the thought of Emmanuel Levinas. Here, it will be considered in light of his Jewish tradition and the ambiguity of the term "God" in his writings, as well as some theological responses. In both his major works, *Totality and Infinity* and *Otherwise Than Being*, Levinas refers often to the body. In the former, he offers a concise description of its dual nature: *"To be a body* is on the one hand *to stand* [*se tenir*], to be master of oneself, and, on the other hand, to stand on the earth, to be in the *other*, and thus to be encumbered by one's body."[1]

That is, the body allows a certain self-mastery, situating the self in the physical world, but it is a limitation as well as an opportunity to serve the other. The significance of the body in relation to the self and to the other here cannot be understated. The body is the mediation which makes responsibility for the absolute other possible. Levinas argues that alterity is itself absolute, and he denies that any other absolute categories may be placed upon the other. This paradox provides the foundation to much of Levinas' thought: that no absolutes may be imposed except the responsibility which makes its appearance in the face of the other, who in turn remains always absolute. Crucially, the body of the other is the beginning of meaning and

1. Levinas, *Totality and Infinity*, 164.

remains the possibility for the soul's presence in the world. Later, in *Otherwise Than Being*, he reflects:

> The body is neither an obstacle opposed to the soul, nor a tomb that imprisons it, but that by which the self is susceptibility itself. Incarnation is an extreme passivity; to be exposed to sickness, suffering, death, is to be exposed to compassion, and, as a self, to the gift that costs. The oneself is on this side of the zero of inertia and nothingness, in deficit of being, in itself and not in being, without a place to lay its head, in the no-grounds, and thus without conditions. As such it will be shown to be bearer of the world, bearing it, suffering it, blocking rest and lacking a fatherland. It is the correlate of a persecution, a substitution for the other.[2]

In other words, the body is an intimate dwelling place for the human person, for whom there is no dire opposition between the soul and either flesh or the body. Levinas makes it clear that the body makes possible an exposure to the world and its violence; sickness, suffering, and death are experienced because of the body. Levinas refuses the excesses of those who would pit the soul against the body. The soulful body turns out to be an extreme passivity, and paradoxically, one revealed in responsible action. This paradox is present in Levinas' earlier consideration of the body's capacity to enact experience in the world, while also encumbering it as it encounters the other.

Levinas, the body, and God

In understanding the place of the body in Emmanuel Levinas, one must engage with the problem of God in relation to the embodiment of the other.[3] Levinas' philosophy is built around the theme of alterity as it appears in the face of the other person, an otherness he understands to be absolute. Alterity offers the possibility of thinking of God within the same event of

---

2. Footnote 12, chapter IV, in Levinas, *Otherwise Than Being*, 195.

3. In the original French, Levinas distinguishes between capitalizing the Other–"*Autre*"–and keeping it lower case, "*autre*," with no formal or consistent methodology for doing so. It appears to act as a rhetorical device, in which the capitalization of *l'Autre* conveys the primary nomination of this *particular* other as *the* Other. As this book refers to the other as treated by a number of writers (including Wojtyla, Derrida, and Marion), who do not follow the same schema, I will only capitalize "the Other" if it appears to be used as such in a particular textual context. For a useful account of Levinas' rendering of these and other terms, see Calin and Sebbah, *Le Vocabulaire De Lévinas*, Vocabulaire De; and also Ciocan and Hansel, *Levinas Concordance*.

receiving responsibility for the other, an event that carries both ethical and social significance.[4] For Levinas, the other is irreducibly other, to the extent that the incarnate appearing of the other is a kind of impossibility; the other may not be described, categorized, or even truly observed. The body of the other is, therefore, disincarnated by alterity and refused description. Despite this, Levinas utilizes language that, despite his own logic, returns time and again to descriptions of the flesh and to incarnation, even as he deploys theological language to describe the experience of otherness. This is problematic. Jacques Derrida noted forcefully that the structure of Levinas' work is not "a theology," and nor is it strictly "Jewish mysticism (it can even be understood as the trial of theology and mysticism); neither as a dogmatics, or as a religion, nor as a morality."[5] Yet in Levinas' writings, the category of "God" appears repeatedly. A strong theological connection between this category and the rest of his work is all too easily observed. At times, Levinas dismisses such a connection, although it has been argued that a subconscious theological openness can be observed in his work.[6] The relationship between Levinas' own religious position and philosophical and biblical notions of God has also been described as one of "equidistance."[7] In this context, it is helpful to consider the other in Levinas as one who remains embodied, despite Levinas' philosophy; in other words, the embodied other. The embodied other will therefore be used as a term which takes up Levinas' reliance on the theme of the body, while acknowledging that his own reference is dominantly to otherness and the other with an indirect reference to the body or embodiment more generally. Levinas made a distinction between his formal philosophical enquiry and his commentaries on the Talmud, which is helpful to consider before turning to the relationship between God, theology, and *l'Autrement* in his work.[8]

4. Michael Purcell notes the parallel between Levinas and Rahner in which supernature and nature are "entwined"; both are experienced existentially and so a linear move from one directly to the other is, phenomenologically, impossible. See Purcell, "'Levinas and Theology'?," 476. See also Purcell's works on similar themes: *Mystery and Method* and *Levinas and Theology*.

5. Derrida, "Violence and Metaphysics," in *Writing and Difference*, 103.

6. Jeffrey L. Kosky has argued for a reading of *Totality and Infinity* as a "disguised or displaced theology." See Kosky, *Levinas and the Philosophy of Religion*, 25.

7. Hutchens, *Levinas*, 116.

8. In an interview Levinas states, "I always make a clear distinction, in what I write, between philosophical and confessional texts. I do not deny that they may ultimately have a common source of inspiration." See Cohen, *Face to Face with Levinas*, 18.

Levinas and the Jewish tradition

The relationship between Levinas and his own Jewish tradition is complex. There is growing secondary literature on the importance of the Jewish tradition to Levinas' philosophy and his unique theological insights as a Talmudic commentator.[9] For all the array of issues that arise in analyzing his relationship to Judaism, the following significant features are highlighted as they pertain to the role of the body and of the face in the context of ethical demand and responsibility. They also situate Levinas' thought on the body in its Jewish context.

A range of specifically Jewish voices are highly influential in Levinas' thought, in addition to his philosophical methodology. For example, Kevin Hart notes the abiding influences of Franz Rosenzweig and phenomenological method upon Levinas' mature thought.[10] Levinas acknowledges his debt to Rosenzweig in his preface to *Totality and Infinity*, especially to *The Star of Redemption* [*Stern der Erlösung*].[11] Levinas is impressed by Rosenzweig's "opposition to the idea of totality" and views it as "too often present" in *Totality and Infinity* to be cited.[12] There is a common and abiding interest between them, as Michael Morgan notes: "For Rosenzweig, revelation is the divine command to redeem the world through love; for Levinas, a similar sense of obligation to accept and help others and to alleviate their suffering is the content of the face-to-face."[13]

The point of difference concerns the nature of revelation. For Rosenzweig, mystical awareness occurs through the event of divine grace.[14] Grace is given in the act of command, or the "summons," as Morgan describes it.[15] For Levinas, the divine summons to love others occurs in the face of the other. The suffering of another person is revealed, and in so doing, it enacts a command of unlimited responsibility for that person. The complication for Levinas is that responsibility precedes concrete experiences of actual suffer-

---

9. See, for example, Wright, *The Twilight of Jewish Philosophy*; Meir, *Levinas's Jewish Thought*; Putnam, *Jewish Philosophy as a Guide to Life*.

10. Hart and Signer (eds.), *The Exorbitant*, 3.

11. Kevin Hart makes reference to this, but also contrasts the "new" philosophy of phenomenology with Levinas' critical reception of Rosenzweig in his own work, in *The Exorbitant* (with Signer, eds.), 3.

12. Levinas, *Totality and Infinity*, 28.

13. Morgan, *Discovering Levinas*, 214.

14. Rosenzweig outlines a philosophy that opens up to a social theology. See Rosenzweig, *The Star of Redemption*.

15. See also Morgan's more concise work in which he treats Levinas' term "summons." Morgan, *The Cambridge Introduction to Emmanuel Levinas*, 99.

ing. Furthermore, his concept of the face relies on an analogous reference to human faces, but it serves as the principle of the other's concrete appearing—an epiphany—and so could be referring to the signification of the other, a trace, a presence, intersubjectivity as a "fundamental event."[16] Despite Rosenzweig's influence, there is much that separates him from Levinas, especially in the latter's conception of the ethical relationship being fundamentally asymmetrical. The intellectual basis of their differences originates in late idealism (Rosenzweig) and Husserlian phenomenology (Levinas).[17] That difference is important, and is also manifest when considering Martin Buber's relationship to Levinas' thought, especially the former's substantial text, *I and Thou* [Ich und Du].[18] The exchange between Levinas and Buber often flounders in the area of alterity, despite their many shared concerns, and has been described as a failure to appreciate the need to "listen" to the presence of the "wholly other."[19] This breakdown in dialogue can be interpreted positively. In a way, it highlights the logic of understanding alterity according to an asymmetry (Levinas) or a radical symmetry (Buber).[20] Each understood alterity differently. The major point of difference between Buber and Levinas turns on the question of the relationship between the "I" and the "thou," the "in-between" or what is named *zwischen*.[21] Is the "between" to be interpreted positively in itself, before all talk of morality or ethics, or is there a particularity to each experience of the I-thou dynamic which shapes its possibilities? In either case, there appears to be a surplus or overabundance of alterity in the presence of another person, such that social possibilities carry an infinity of meaning.[22] Indeed, Buber explicitly connects the I-thou "between" with the experience of divine alterity, who is also a "person," which does not appear to limit otherness but in fact confirms it.[23] His philosophy is notoriously unsystematic, yet his contribution here to interpreting his Jewishness theologically, in dialogue with Christianity

16. Bernasconi and Wood, *The Provocation of Levinas*.

17. Gibbs, *Correlations in Rosenzweig and Levinas*, 7.

18. Buber, *I and Thou*.

19. The primary text collecting Levinas and Buber's dialogue can be found in *Noms Propres*. See Levinas, *Proper Names*, 36–39: To "listen" is not only passive, but requires an active renunciation of one's mastery over the other; also Lipari, "Listening for the Other," 138.

20. See for example Bernasconi's essay "'Failure of Communication' as a Surplus: Dialogue and Lack of Dialogue between Buber and Levinas," in Bernasconi and Wood, *The Provocation of Levinas*.

21. Nikulin, *On Dialogue*, 102.

22. Ibid., 117.

23. Buber, *I and Thou*, 100.

and the I-thou "between," is a helpful contrast to Levinas. In Hans Urs von Balthasar's words:

> Although Buber never falls into over-simplification and does not erect the "I-Thou" relationship into a general, univocal principle which embraces the relation of man to man as well as of man to God, it is nevertheless a principle which Buber regards as decisively indicative of the relation of the creature to God.[24]

So, Buber's understanding of the I-thou relationship is not a general principle as such, but an indicative principle to develop and open new thought. In the I-thou relationship, Buber contests the primacy of the separated Cartesian ego and posits a philosophy of dialogue and communication.[25] His point of departure is the "I"—the self—who experiences its subjective state of being as fragmentation and incompleteness.

In answer to this problem, the "I" must overcome its dichotomy with the objective nature of the world around it and cease its self-isolation. It must become an "I" in relationship, the I-and-thou (or I-and-you). In the presence of an other, the "I" experiences a symmetry of personhood, which is a relationship marked by Buber's idealistic attitude to human sociality.[26] As such, it is the "between," the fragmentary space between the "I" and the "thou" in which a social redemption occurs, which is only ever present *in* the present. Time unfolds with a fixed focus upon the present redemptive moment "lit" by an "eternity" that can only be "glimpsed."[27] This contrasts with Levinas, for whom the other calls the self from *beyond* time, from eternity and from an infinity which appears to the self as timeless; a notion which is common to both his philosophical and his Talmudic works.[28] This is what Levinas calls a signification "beyond" being, by which the trace of the past and the future appear in the face, never allowing the present moment its own temporal "appearance."[29] As Ephraim Meir puts it, "[i]t metamorphoses the I, prior to choice, projecting it into an unseen future."[30] Buber's relational metaphysics is thus shaped by his conception of Jewishness as a

---

24. Balthasar, *Martin Buber and Christianity*, 113.

25. Chiefly, see Buber, *I and Thou*.

26. Meir, *Levinas's Jewish Thought*, 95.

27. Buber, *I and Thou*, 82, 31.

28. For example, see the essay, "Beyond Memory," in which Levinas interprets the Judaic concept of God's proximity in terms of a present consciousness of the narration of past events, the ordering of the "now" by the liturgical memory which is both historical and from "beyond" time. Levinas, *In the Time of the Nations*, 76–91.

29. Levinas *Otherwise Than Being*, 90.

30. Meir, *Levinas's Jewish Thought*, 96.

messianic and ethical call. While his religious origins are similar to Levinas, their positions end in opposition. In Buber, the accent is on relationship and community; in Levinas, on distance, separation, and responsibility. In a sense, mutuality is a nonconcept in Levinas. Nevertheless, it is important to note that both Buber and Levinas begin with a shared Jewish starting point to contest Descartes' emphasis on the thinking self. Meir views their similar projects as constituting the replacement of Descartes "*cogito ergo sum*" with "*respondeo ergo sum*."[31] In replying or responding to the other, one gives oneself to them in some way, thus constituting selfhood through relationship. The self, in other words, is always a self or an other in relation to other selves.

The influence of Buber and Rosenzweig on Levinas is important to understand the theoretical and religious framework developed by the latter, yet it is not one of collaboration. As Robert Gibbs has argued, the more one focuses on these three figures, the wider the "gulf" appears between them.[32] For example, one does not find a direct reference to ethics in *The Star of Redemption*, except as historical description. Its logic is instead both mystical and aesthetic, thereby refusing the denial of time as it enacts its awareness of God's sovereignty within its movements.[33] The Judaic tradition in which Rosenzweig, Buber, and Levinas write is not to be overlooked. Nor can the phenomenological context be overlooked, as Kevin Hart notes. Levinas explicates that his works "owe everything" to phenomenology and furthermore, "[i]ntentional analysis is the search for the concrete."[34] In his reception of various Jewish thinkers, chiefly among them Rosenzweig and Buber, and in the method of phenomenology he received from Husserl, Levinas maintains a critical utilization of various intellectual sources. In this way, his work is oriented towards a philosophy of the particular and the concrete, of the mundane and the ordinary.

As a phenomenologist, Levinas occupies both an indebted and critical relationship with Martin Heidegger and Edmund Husserl. Along with Gabrielle Peiffer, Levinas translated the *Cartesian Meditations* into French, thus introducing Husserl to the French academy.[35] The work is all the more remarkable for being published six years after Levinas' relocation to Strasbourg (he was eighteen when he first arrived).[36] His doctoral thesis

31. Ibid., 98.

32. Gibbs, *Correlations in Rosenzweig and Levinas*, 176.

33. Rosenzweig, *The Star of Redemption*, 357.

34. Levinas, *Totality and Infinity*, 28.

35. Malka, *Emmanuel Levinas*, 38.

36. The German version was never published during Husserl's lifetime. See the

(published a year after its completion), *The Theory of Intuition in Husserl's Phenomenology*, helped to establish Levinas as the original French interpreter of Husserlian phenomenology.[37] Levinas had travelled to Strasbourg in 1923 from his home in Lithuania, a family life in which he had grown up speaking Hebrew, Russian, German, and Yiddish.[38] During 1928–29, he took the opportunity to travel to the University of Freiburg for two semesters. It is an oft-quoted admission by Levinas that he "came to see Husserl, and what I saw was Heidegger."[39] This early involvement with Husserl (who was then in his latter years), had a profound influence on the young Levinas. The influence of Husserl became intertwined with a new appreciation for Heidegger and ultimately moved Levinas to embrace the developing phenomenological method.

In the *epoché*, or the "phenomenological reduction," Husserl's system calls for the "bracketing out" of the world; of all presuppositions and bias.[40] By this, a "pure" science might be developed, one that is philosophically equipped to interpret objective experience. In Levinas' first major post-doctoral work, *Totality and Infinity*, he takes up the reduction and seeks to understand the alterity that appears in the other. In doing so, he challenges Heidegger, in whose work *Being and Time* there is no ethical dimension in his phenomenological description of *Dasein's* being in the world. Levinas also moves against Husserl, in maintaining the existential interest in the world of being, without losing the dynamic existentiality of the human person. Levinas learnt from Heidegger the role of transcendence even in the immanence of human life. Yet, Levinas' notion of transcendence differs from that of Heidegger. In Levinas, transcendence acts as the trajectory that occurs beyond being, or outside ontology. It is the directionality of all truly human existence, in that it takes human beings towards the human other, who is reached by what Levinas calls "metaphysical desire."[41] Transcendence is not simply directionality beyond the self, but beyond being; it confirms difference rather than sameness. Equally, immanence is rethought in Levinas. For him, immanence is the sensible dwelling of the self in the

---

English version, Husserl, *Cartesian Meditations*.

37. See Levinas, *The Theory of Intuition in Husserl's Phenomenology*.

38. Malka, *Emmanuel Levinas*, 38; See also Malka, "Emmanuel Levinas: A Disparate Inventory," in Critchley and Bernasconi (eds.), *The Cambridge Companion to Levinas*, XV.

39. Malka, *Emmanuel Levinas*, 35.

40. For a full account of Husserl's move into transcendental phenomenology and the discovery of the "reduction," see Moran, *Introduction to Phenomenology*, 124–63.

41. See especially section 1.A.4 & 5, Levinas, *Totality and Infinity*.

world, the embodied "at home" of the "I."[42] Immanence is therefore both
a constriction of embodied existence as well as the context of freedom in
which the embodied self might follow metaphysical desire towards transcendence. Immanence must be transcended, even as it offers the place of
being at "home with myself."[43]

Indeed, it is Levinas' concern with this immanence and transcendence
of human life that he remains, always, a Husserlian:

> Is this complacency in mortality (or in historical consciousness)
> exempt from bitterness? The crisis of the modern world perhaps
> lies herein. Is not belonging to an eternal order that exceeds the
> human (be it matter, even) essential to the human? One of the
> most significant aspects of Husserl's phenomenology has been
> precisely its reuniting these two motifs of contemporary con-
> sciousness, namely its quest for the essential and its certainty of
> the importance of the concrete world in which life unfolds, and
> which cannot be relegated to appearances.[44]

The "excess" of the material world, which Levinas refers to as "eternal," is not of a mystical order, but discovered through phenomenological
method. The crisis he identifies is a loss of understanding the essential characteristics of the world as it appears to consciousness. In the appearing of
the world, human eyes miss what is before them. They require a cognitive
reflection before they are able to identify the ethical nature of what is perceived. The concrete life unfolds, even as human persons are immersed in it,
but as Levinas alludes, there remains an invisible aspect to its concreteness.
From beyond essence and from outside ontology: this is the transcendent
beginning for Levinas' notion of ethical obligation, because it is a demand
that issues from alterity and not from being. In the body's passivity, it experiences alterity as a demand from an other who secures the self's full ethical
attention. That is to say, the other must be faced. Levinas does not place
the ethical demand within the embodied presence of any *particular* other,
even though it is this person's suffering he is concerned with. Rather, alterity
invites responsibility without a clear or unambiguous relationship with the
concrete other. In other words, Levinas does not begin his ethics with this
or that face, but of *the* face, of alterity as a living principle. For Levinas, as
Paul Ricœur puts it, "ethics is its own beginning apart from any ontological

---

42. Ibid., 138.

43. Ibid.

44. Levinas, "The Permanent and the Human in Husserl," in *Discovering Existence
with Husserl*, 131.

preparation."[45] Indeed, the hyperbole of Levinas' prose invites the reader into the difficult process of the turn from ontology towards the other. Perhaps this is the only violence Levinas truly condones, that of the wrenching intellectual move from the same towards the other, precisely in the poetic rendering of philosophy.

What for Rosenzweig was a foundational renarration of Jewish life and philosophy—in its turn *away* from seeking after totality—becomes for Levinas' phenomenological analysis the turn *towards* the other person. It flows primarily from the responsibility that one has for the other, even before the self is cognizant of the fact. Rosenzweig's influence upon Levinas in *Totality and Infinity* is considerable. But how does Levinas' Jewishness shape his interest in the ethical responsibility that one has for the other? Michael Morgan highlights the teaching role of Jewish culture in the wider Western context of Hellenic inheritance.[46] According to Morgan's reading of Levinas, Jewish culture is the historical ground in which Greek culture was able to bury deep and from which it could grow. But Greek culture (or Hellenic culture/Athens) is the mode of universality, of essences and tantalizations. The normative cultural expressions of the Greeks are what gave rise to a philosophical tradition focused on being as such. Greek culture is an only child to the Jewish cultural parent.[47] This analogy becomes more pertinent in considering contemporary Europe's slavish commitment to, as Morgan describes it, "definition, precision, universality, structure, and violence . . . ," and paradoxically, "it resists but still remains open to the ancient biblical spirituality, its sense of kindness and mercy."[48] Early in Levinas' career, he proposed a Jewish antidote to the Greek-European problem, which is primarily one of ethics. He calls for the enactment of the learned Jewish tradition of kindness and generosity, in spite of all historical suffering to the contrary.

Morgan identifies two components of Levinas' conception of Judaism.[49] First, the suffering of the Jews is a definitive request for responsible action and justice. Second, the central teaching of the Torah is the primacy of ethics.[50] These mark a new kind of universality in Levinas' approach to

45. Ricœur, "Emmanuel Levinas: Thinker of Testimony," in *Figuring the Sacred*, 120.

46. See especially Morgan, "Judaism, Ethics, and Religion," in *Discovering Levinas*, 336–414.

47. Morgan's reflections are largely based on Levinas' "The Bible and the Greeks" in *In the Time of the Nations*, 133–34; and also his account in Morgan, *Discovering Levinas*, 340.

48. Ibid.

49. Ibid., 342.

50. Morgan argues that these themes are present in Levinas from as early as 1955,

Jewish culture and wider European culture. While he rejects the universality of ethical norms that do not have as their objective a responsible care for the other, he insists that the plea of the suffering Jew is the plea of all Jews and therefore all people. But more than this, that the biblical and extrabiblical textual traditions of the Jewish Law and its interpretation are a wholly new option in ethics, "an entire world . . . a literature and a civilization."[51] In making ethics primary, the Torah becomes the measure of an ethically ordered Jewish life, one tending to mercy and obedience; in other words, an embodied social ethic. Therefore, the *telos* of the Jewish people is truly rabbinical in a universal sense, for it is to teach others the ways of merciful living, seeking out justice as an irreducible necessity. It does so fully aware of the manifestation of divine hiddenness, of the God who hides his face from the ensuing savagery of the world, and in doing so, opens up the possibility for each person to exact an ethical response to that same savagery.

Indeed, it is in this nonexperience of God that Levinas' notion of Judaism becomes more radical still. In his early essay "A Religion for Adults," Levinas situates the presence of God in the context of intersubjective experience, by which he casts away any importance placed on a singular divine mystical experience. In rethinking his own tradition, Levinas demandingly seeks a "disenchanted" and "demystified" Judaism, one that might become an "austere humanism" enacted from the teaching of Torah, Bible, and Talmud.[52] It is an approach that focuses the texts and interpretations of that tradition through the lens of responsibility. The way in which such responsibility manifests itself in the community is not immediate, but learned through a *habitus* founded on the divine commandments. The nature of this *habitus* unfolds in Levinas' writings, but the problem of divine personality is clearly present from the outset. There is reference to a "God" here, founded upon the Hebrew Scriptures, but to what extent are the divine commandments truly issued by a personal God?

Beyond the category of God and the problem of transcendence

Is this God who is known in the face of the other person the God of Abraham, Isaac, and Jacob? Is this the God revealed by the other, or is this an employment of "God" as a category of alterity to serve out Levinas' ethics?

---

evidenced in "Loving the Torah More Than God" in Levinas, *Difficult Freedom*, 144–45; see Morgan, *Discovering Levinas*, 342.

51. "Judaism," in Levinas, *Difficult Freedom*, 24–26.

52. Ibid., 344.

Levinas' lack of clarity on this point makes a direct answer impossible.[53] Nevertheless, some comments can be made on Levinas and the problem of God, especially in relation to the category of transcendence.

There is a problematic relationship between the categories Levinas employs when discussing the body, God, or the other within his notion of alterity. While these categories tend to fall within the remit of philosophical language per se, in Levinas they also carry a theological investment, even if their theology is not necessarily confessional. For Morgan, Levinas' use of philosophical language with a theological purpose is a methodological maneuver in aid of his philosophy. As Morgan puts it, "Levinas has exploited the tone and texture of religious and theological vocabulary for his own philosophical purposes."[54] Levinas' language remains problematic from a theological perspective. The category of "transcendence" serves as a particular example, which appears often in his early works such as *Time and the Other, Existence and Existents,* and his two major philosophical works, *Totality and Infinity* and *Otherwise Than Being,* as well as essays in *God and Philosophy* and *God, Death and Time.*

Levinas commits the first part of *Totality and Infinity* to "Metaphysics and Transcendence."[55] In it, he speaks of transcendence in terms of a beyond being, that which cannot be understood as an existent or a being as such. In fact, he opens with the troubling words, "[t]he true life is absent." In this absence, a lack, or negative experience of reality, Levinas argues that metaphysics, a "toward yonder," has developed.[56] "But," he says, "we are in the world. Metaphysics arises and is maintained in this alibi."[57] This fact of being in the world is a kind of "dwelling," in which the world is present to the self as a primary event: "Dwelling is the precondition of all representing even though subsequent representation engulfs all dwelling after the fact."[58] Persons remain always within the dwelling place of the world, and it is this binding in which metaphysical thought is possible. The earthly grounding from which metaphysical discovery embarks is always oriented towards what is "other" and which will remain "other."[59] Metaphysical desire

---

53. The theme of "God" is treated in the collected essays, Levinas, *Of God Who Comes to Mind.* However, in these essays it is very much a philosophical approach and a reflection on the question of language possibilities, without recourse to theology in any confessional or traditional sense.

54. Morgan, *Discovering Levinas,* 198.

55. Levinas, *Totality and Infinity,* 33–52.

56. Ibid., 33.

57. Ibid.

58. Wyschogrod, *Emmanuel Levinas,* 73.

59. Levinas, *Totality and Infinity,* 33–35.

opens up into the experience of transcendence, at least in so far as it remains metaphysical. It must remain authentically disinterested and always looking for the other, honoring he or she within a dimension in which the self resists that which is wicked, domineering, and fostering misery.[60] In this sense, the experience of transcendence is not a negativity but a positive pre0onto-logical movement.[61] It precedes ontology because it is the ethical reality that overturns Heidegger's primacy of being over existents.[62] For Levinas, alter-ity is not simply primary, but it actively comes before being and acts as the freeing up of the self in active responsibility. Transcendence is not observed; it is experienced. More so, it is experienced as a demand that exceeds the objective datum in which it might be identified. "To think the infinite, the transcendent, the Stranger, is hence not to think an object."[63] Transcendence in this sense is always from a beyond, and cannot be described in a language that unintentionally limits its possibilities. That is not to say that it lacks an absolute character, which for Levinas is a crucial aspect of what is truly transcendent. He holds that in the transcendence that arises in the appear-ing of the other, the person does not so much share in otherness, but is faced with the confronting responsibility which is itself absolute. Transcendence is beyond the self and beyond the world, and it cannot be reached by any means other than the desire that begins in the world.

In *Otherwise Than Being, or, Beyond Essence*, the meaning of transcen-dence is developed further.[64] Its radical difference from being is maintained, but the relationship between the two is described in more detail. While transcendence can never be captured by being and enters into and with-draws from being, it actively invests being with goodness or value.[65] Levi-nas speaks of affectivity "on the way toward transcendence."[66] Affectivity is interpreted broadly, concerning both emotional experience as well as the five senses of the body; all things "touched, marked, moved, or inspired."[67] Philosophy itself begins in love, which is inspired and guided by a sense of transcendence as good and divine.

60. Ibid., 35.

61. Ibid., 40–42.

62. Ibid., 45.

63. Ibid., 49.

64. Sarah Allen has studied this development in detail. See Allen, *The Philosophical Sense of Transcendence*.

65. Ibid., 6.

66. Ibid., 7.

67. Ibid., 8.

This idea of a "philosophical sense" has been questioned.[68] For example, Sarah Allen problematizes Levinas by arguing that the point of departure for philosophy is its enigmatic lack of clarity. It begins in darkness and must therefore invoke in its practitioner a humility, never quite knowing its "origin or limits."[69] Allen identifies a gradual development in Levinas in which transcendence itself undergoes significant change. Levinas approaches interpersonal affectivity as erotic love, but then as a desire that maintains a link with erotic love and finally as a desire or love purified of *eros* in his later works.[70] Allen sees in Levinas' treatment of erotic love a glaring "ambiguity."[71] This ambiguity arises through the mixture of sensibility and the nonsensible, of light and dark and the enticing presence of voluptuousness. It ambiguously mixes the self as the other, even as it is forged in the reality of an absolute distance between the self and the desired, embodied, enjoyed, other.[72] The future which *eros* here opens up is in reference to Levinas' notion of the transcendent, but it appears to push phenomenology beyond that which it has the capacity to intentionally identify. Allen asks whether, in Levinas' later thought (certainly from *Totality and Infinity* onwards), he is still moving within philosophical thinking at all. For Levinas, it is genuinely philosophical because of its consideration of the event of otherness met in the other person. In other words, it is a phenomenological approach of reflection on a prior human event full of ambiguity. Can a theological dimension be viewed within this ambiguity? Two significant responses to this problem point towards an answer.

Two responses to the problem of theology in Levinas

A rejection of Levinas' theological language

Tamra Wright has questioned whether Levinas' ethics is theological.[73] Or, to put it another way, Wright asks whether "Levinas' description of the ethical relation can be understood without reference to 'God.'"[74] For example, it is impossible to ignore "God" in *Totality and Infinity*, which serves as an indispensable category to picture the event of otherness that arises in the

---

68. Ibid., 9.

69. Levinas, *Totality and Infinity*, 24.

70. Allen argues this is present in *Totality and Infinity* and *Otherwise Than Being*.

71. Allen, *The Philosophical Sense of Transcendence*, 227.

72. Ibid., 228.

73. Wright, *The Twilight of Jewish Philosophy*.

74. Ibid., 71.

face. Levinas posits the need for a faith "purged of myths," and the rejection of the religious idea of participation in divine transcendence.[75] He describes the need of a "metaphysical atheism," by which the impossibility of divine participation is negated most fully and in its place is welcomed the event of a veritable relationship.[76] For Levinas, infinity does not begin in a divine transcendence that remains invisible, but in the concrete presence of the face. He cannot see how participation in an invisible God can manifest a true relationship, because it relies on a metaphysical investment in that which is disembodied. This is the rejection of positive religion by way of surpassing the metaphysical tradition. It is not the rejection of "God" per se, but the location of the divine in the intersubjective relationship.

It is through this consideration of religion that Levinas is able to establish the primacy of infinity and its origins in the face. As he puts it, "[t]he dimension of the divine opens forth from the human face."[77] While Levinas uses this language in a strictly philosophical sense (this is not meant to explicitly refer to God as understood by the Scriptures), he uses language that normally belongs to Scripture and theology. The infinity that flows from the face and its designation as *autrui*, typically reserved for other people, takes up theological language divested of its typical meaning.[78]

For Wright, there is a further aspect of the relationship between the human face and God that is important to Levinas. According to Levinas, the relationship with the other is not a means of pleasing or drawing closer to a personal God. Rather, it is the way in which a relationship with God is enacted and sustained.[79] The relationship with the other is not that of a relationship *with* God (as the Judeo-Christian tradition would normally think of it) *as* God, but is the enactment of divine presence in the sociality of the intersubjective. This is linked to the *proviso* that the other is not a divine incarnation. Levinas prefers to think of the transcendence of God as manifested in the social event, rather than as a personal divine presence: "The Other is not the incarnation of God, but precisely by his face, in which he is disincarnate is the manifestation of the height in which God is revealed."[80]

God's height—his transcendence—is known in the encounter with the other. This is not an argument for an essential divine presence, nor is it a

---

75. Levinas, *Totality and Infinity*, 77.

76. Ibid.

77. Ibid., 78.

78. Wright accepts this conclusion with the comment that Levinas is also avoiding a correlation of "the Other" with "God." See Wright, *The Twilight of Jewish Philosophy*, 72.

79. Ibid., 72–73.

80. Levinas, *Totality and Infinity*, 79.

claim of divine self-revelation. Rather, it is a paradoxical argument for the location of divine transcendence in the immanence of the human face. The singularity of the face, known in the experience of "infinity," faces the self as "hostile, friend, my master, my student."[81] The face is a provocation with many titles, and stirs up the self because it is the divine trace that unsettles one's comfort and ease. Its status is the reason Levinas can refer to the face to face in terms of monotheistic religious language, which guarantees an undivided responsibility towards *one* other. The monotheistic discourse to which he appeals is based on a concrete presence of the other, to which the self responds. In recognizing the other, human persons therefore "come to him across the world of possessed things, but at the same time to establish, by gift, community and universality."[82] In the face-to-face experience of this infinity of possibility and meaning, the experience of transcendence emerges, and with it, ethical responsibility. For Levinas, the various uses of terms such as religion, infinity, invisibility, transcendence, and God serve the purpose of explaining the nature of ethical responsibility. Wright recognizes these distinctions, but then argues that for Levinas, they are not unambiguous theological categories. Wright goes further, by viewing in *Totality and Infinity* an assignation of God as a notional subject by which Levinas makes a negative argument concerning the other.[83] In other words, there is a limit to the use of "God." It neither means God's "existence" or contains any "positive meaning."[84] Rather, the category of "God," at least in *Totality and Infinity*, exists as a critique of "positive religion."[85]

In the latter parts of *Totality and Infinity*, Levinas makes more explicit the nature of the ethical demand in the face.[86] In his initial explorations of the face, Levinas refers to transcendence and categories that concern the ungraspable and the distant. He then embraces language that evokes the immanent struggle of intersubjectivity. In the face, a relationship with the other is made possible. It is by this relation alone that the dimension of transcendence is introduced, which is "totally different" from cognitive and sensory awareness that might normally be associated with human "experience."[87] Levinas finds in the sensation of vision an essential openness

---

81. Ibid., 81.

82. Ibid., 76.

83. Wright, *The Twilight of Jewish Philosophy*, 79–80.

84. Ibid., 80.

85. Ibid.

86. See section III, "Exteriority and the Face," in Levinas, *Totality and Infinity*, 185–247.

87. Ibid., 193.

to the transcendence opened up in the face. This is because vision opens up a relation to what is other but, paradoxically, cannot do so in full accord with the otherness of what it envisages.[88] It is like light refracting through the eye and creating a mental impression. It is constituent of the dimension of the transcendent as that which "cuts across sensibility," primordially (and precognitively) bearing itself as a new kind of vision. There is that which is offered to the sensible gaze (the "obverse") and there is that which can be turned over to new discovery (the "reverse").[89] Levinas wishes to hold to the sensible descriptions of both of these kinds of surfaces, but insists on the complex array of meaning possible in that which exists as a *façade*. It both reveals and hides its true essence all the while bearing itself in a relational manner different from how sensory impressions and vision is typically experienced.[90]

For Levinas, the face is both a negation and an affirmation. It is a negation in the sense that it refuses to be imposed upon by the categories of sameness. As he describes, "[t]he face is present in its refusal to be contained."[91] The face marks the moment of absolute difference between the self and the other, for it cannot be described purely in terms of logic. It breaks in relation to the world all that is common to both. It must be remembered that the face is spoken of here as the epiphany or presence of the other, not necessarily bound to the particular features of any given incarnate face. From this context, speech issues forth as language and accomplishes transcendence in relation. Language, as spoken, appears as a rebuttal of the power of the same, in that it both confirms the reality of difference between the self and the other while also acting as the bridge of meaning between them. In a telling phrase Levinas writes: "The formal structure of language thereby announces the ethical inviolability of the Other and, without any odor of the 'numinous,' his 'holiness.'"[92] The trace of divinity in the face of the other is a provocation more than it is a presence.

By the status of speaking, language confirms difference and the face acts as an affirmation. It affirms the divide that exists between the self and the other. There remains a relation between them, but one marked by distance. For Levinas, distance is an infinity that invites an endless capacity for ethical responsibility. It is an active ethical posture by the face of the other,

---

88. Ibid., 191.
89. Ibid., 192.
90. Ibid., 193.
91. Ibid., 194.
92. Ibid., 195.

issued forth as a "moral summons."[93] As an ethical relational structure, this positive demand of the face of the other frees the self to act responsibly. Furthermore, the ethical affirmation of the face assumes the negative aspect of the face into its own moral agenda.[94] That is to say, the infinite negation of the same is taken up into the positive appeal to responsible action.

This betrays Levinas' reliance on an incarnate, embodied reality, despite his insistence otherwise. The negation he describes becomes, paradoxically, an affirmation of the body. Communication relies on particular expressions of universal signs and symbols. The face, the part of the human body that is most regularly exposed to the world, issues a language that is interpreted by Levinas as a totalizing alterity, yet this imposes on the face an agenda it may not embrace. The localized and particular face does not only speak an ethical language, but may enter conversation in a language and in a culture. Concrete words follow the concrete presence of the face. The evil of one face towards another is itself a particular event and words concretize the person in a communicability with others, despite Levinas' negation of the particularity of the face. Furthermore, motivation to pursue the good of the other is limited by an austere alterity without reference to particular faces. In Levinas' turn to language and an allusion to particularities, he reveals the limitations of his notion of otherness as absolute. He all but admits this in various asides, such as his comment that "[v]iolence can only aim at a face."[95] A contradiction can therefore be seen in Levinas on this question.

The inconsistency in Levinas' approach shows us what is most interesting in Levinas' approach to the body: that his attempt to describe a form of ethical absolutism is interrupted in his system by the nature of bodies themselves. The body refuses the absolute otherness assigned by Levinas and issues a presence that, while not avoiding universals, remains particular. Some have interpreted Levinas' excessive claims of absolute alterity as a form of useful hyperbole, designed to shock his readers (particularly Christians) out of thinking of excess as itself useful, when not allowing the excess of the other to be primary.[96] There is truth in describing it as a form of hyperbole, and it remains a constant reference point for Levinas in a philosophy both rich and inconsistent.

When considering the evil of one person towards an other, particular faces come to mind in their suffering and need. This is part of the inner problem in Levinas' approach, although he does not ignore the possibility of

93. Ibid., 196.
94. Ibid., 197.
95. Ibid., 225.
96. Webb, "The Rhetoric of Ethics as Excess," 14.

evil. He considers especially the act of murder, which for him is not an act of "power" per se, but of annihilation.[97] The infinity of the other, the limitless extent of possibilities that appears in the event of the face, is not destroyed by murder, even if blood is spilt and the other's life is lost. It is not for Levinas a real struggle between powers, or a battle of friend and foe, for otherness itself cannot be destroyed. Otherness resists the murderer's violence, even if the murderer has annihilated the living body. The face of the other precedes all thought and learning, and as such, it evades that which the murderer attempts in the annihilation of the embodied other.[98] This is illustrated in the way a victim is remembered by the guilty party, at times seeming to haunt the murderer years after violence was issued. For Levinas, so much of what the face reveals is possible only because of language. Equally, signification is made possible because of the foundation of language.[99] Levinas depends largely on the work of Maurice Merleau-Ponty, whose phenomenology of language insists on the body's immersion in a system of signs and symbols that unite thought and language in an embodied experience of knowledge.[100] The face of the body shows itself as a signification that makes language possible. Yet it is more, for the body appears not only as a means of signification, but of a signifying language in itself. The face *speaks* and the self *responds*. The self's consciousness of the other is the first response to that which preempts thought: the signifying face. On Levinas' reading of the face, language is also a form of reason, for the "first rationality gleams forth in the opposition of the face to face . . . ."[101] Language is not only an embodied tapestry of signs and meaning but a rationalizing tendency towards that which can be perceived and understood. It is because rationality finds its origin in the embodied presence of the other that Levinas' later thought in *Totality and Infinity* denies any equality between the self and the other. In the other's body, the self locates the origin of all that constitutes the self: language, sense, signification, meaning, responsibility, and reason.

Levinas describes the relationship with the other in a kind of antidemocratic turn. He sees the realm of the interpersonal as—*contra* Martin Buber, although he does not name Buber here—"asymmetrical."[102] There is no essential symmetry between oneself and the other. The self does not

---

97. Levinas, *Totality and Infinity*, 198.

98. "The other is not for reason a scandal that puts it in dialectical movement, but the first teaching." Levinas, in ibid., 204.

99. See especially, ibid., 204–9.

100. Merleau-Ponty, *Phenomenology of Perception*, 164.

101. Levinas, *Totality and Infinity*, 208.

102. Ibid., 215–16.

view an equal when looking towards the other, but rather one it is called to serve. The infinity of possibility that appears in the epiphany of the face is grounded in a worldly, suffering body, but speaks with a theological accent. This accent is based on the dimension of transcendence that exists as the dimension of height, or of glory, that exceeds every category the oneself might impose on the other. The excess of categories and of description is a breaking apart, a kind of "disincarnation" of the other; one that makes relationship between different persons possible in the otherness of social drama.[103]

Levinas invokes Old Testament language by referring to the dominion of the other as located precisely in "the stranger, the widow, and the orphan, to whom I am obligated."[104] The insistence on analogous terminology that originates in the face and the body, or of particular bodies, grounds Levinas' theological language in the experiences of human flesh, but in *Totality and Infinity*, he argues that this is not love as such.[105] Love is the ambiguous combination of factors that goes beyond the other in self-sacrifice, but falls short in a self-seeking desire. *Eros* provides Levinas with an example of the complex morality of embodied human desire that secures the turn to alterity rather than the traditional philosophical category of being. More will be said on Levinas' understanding of desire and the body in the following chapter on *eros*.

The latter descriptions of the face in *Totality and Infinity* are ethically robust, but do not refute earlier references in that same text. Wright does not recognize the connecting threads between the early and later parts of *Totality and Infinity*, instead referring her attention to Levinas' later works, such as *Otherwise Than Being*. She highlights his introduction of the term "illeity" in an essay published after *Totality and Infinity*, which becomes important in *Otherwise Than Being*.[106] In the later book, Levinas considers the self and the complex problem of responsibility. Every encounter with the other is predicated on the notion that there are other others to be encountered. Each other person is already an existent in a wider sociality. Outside the singularity of the face-to-face moment is a swathe of other persons, most of whom the self will never meet. This third dimension of responsible relationships constitutes a challenge to the face to face. "The third" also evokes a responsibility in the self. The seeming disembodied

---

103. Gibbs, "The Disincarnation of the Word: The Trace of God in Reading Scripture," in Hart and Singer (eds.), *The Exorbitant*, 38.

104. Levinas, *Totality and Infinity*, 215.

105. Ibid., 254–55.

106. Levinas, "The Trace of the Other," in Taylor (ed.), *Deconstruction in Context*.

status of those who constitute "the third" (one can neither see, nor touch, nor hear them at any one time) guarantees that the self's responsibility for them is not immediately obvious. It is neither chronological nor empirical, but comes from an elsewhere, a trace of which arrives in an "irreversible, immemorial, unrepresentable past."[107]

In *Otherwise Than Being*, Levinas further develops the basic structures of the I-other relationship that he describes in *Totality and Infinity*. It consists of two parts, "The Argument" and "The Exposition." The first part deals with "Essence and Disinterest" and establishes the essence of alterity as received in the acting human subject. It outlines the character of responsibility that the self (the subject) has for the other, arguing for the primacy of responsibility for that which is different to the self. The second part deals with the following topics: "Intentionality and Sensing," "Sensibility and Proximity," "Substitution," and "Subjectivity and Infinity." The sustained theme in this second part is the nature of sensibility as it relates to the experience of alterity in the other. That is to say, the effect of the other upon the self is explored in detail and unpacked, as it were. One of the chief rhetorical devices used here is the exploitation of analogy. Levinas' use of analogy to describe the results of the interruption the face brings to the self is repetitive and constant.

Of these analogies, "proximity" stands out in relation to the face of the other.[108] What was generally referred to as the face in *Totality and Infinity* becomes "proximity" in *Otherwise Than Being*.[109] The emphasis upon distance between the self and the other in *Totality and Infinity* is described as an ethical nearness. Hovering intimately before the face of the self is an other, but one whose embodied presence must appear as *the* other. In the sensory language by which this is identified, "signification is sensibility."[110] Sense becomes a "said," a "something, a thematized," which must appear before philosophy.[111] Levinas considers the nature of the "psyche," which is ambiguously related to the phenomenological theme of "intentionality."[112] The psyche is both complex and confused, only really becoming itself as it acts in an embodied fashion for the other. In relation to the self, the psyche

---

107. Levinas, *Emmanuel Levinas*, 69.

108. Morgan views the shift in Levinas' emphasis as moving from a consideration of the Other to a concentration upon how this effects the subject who faces the Other. The face remains central to the experience. See Morgan, *Discovering Levinas*, 80–84.

109. This becomes explicit in chapter II, "Sensibility and Proximity," in Levinas, *Otherwise Than Being*, 61–97.

110. Ibid., 67.

111. Ibid., 68.

112. Ibid., 68–72.

is "the other in me, a malady of identity," it is both inimical to the self and yet "at odds" with the self.[113] The embodied other stands before the self (this is not literal; the other's proximity is ethical, not chronological) and the psyche is disturbed, called outside of itself by the act of responsible service.

It is here that an example of Levinas' inescapable preoccupation with the body is witnessed. The primary manner of proximity in relation to the self comes via the body. For Levinas, the body, enlivened by the responsible psyche, is a premoral fact, saturated with moral possibility: "Such a signification is only possible as an incarnation. The animation, the very pneuma of the psyche, alterity in identity, is the identity of a body exposed to the other, becoming 'for the other,' the possibility of giving."[114]

The body becomes a moral call issued through the signification of its own presence. Furthermore, there is no room here for a synchronous intelligibility; for a signification of meaning found *before* the other.[115] The other is identified in difference, but not described in any sense of completeness. In fact, the self's attempts to identify another person by the use of categories and formulas of "the same" collapse under the presence of the embodied person. There is a moral "gravity" at work in the other, an ethical dynamism that is experienced as demand and bound to the body.[116] The result of this "gravity" is an absolute "non-indifference," described by Levinas as "an animate body."[117] This could also be described as the animation of care for the other. The body of course can only recognize the otherness of an other because it is able to enjoy what it might sacrifice for the other. What Levinas refers to as "enjoyment" in "sensibility" is really the satisfaction of what is both necessary and desirous.[118] He uses the example of bread for the hungry, which can only be a satisfactory sacrifice for the other when it is torn from one's own mouth; in which one's tongue has tasted and "enjoyed" it.[119] Proximity in this sense does include some shared sensations, which allow for the sensibility of the nearness of the other.

This proximity is shared primarily by ethical creatures. "Only a subject that eats can be for-the-other, or can signify. Signification, the-one-for-the-other, has meaning only among beings of flesh and blood."[120] This embodied

---

113. Ibid., 68–69.
114. Ibid., 69.
115. Ibid., 70.
116. Ibid.
117. Ibid., 70–71.
118. Ibid., 72–74.
119. Ibid., 74.
120. Ibid.

proximity then is predicated on a shared embodied identity. Despite the emphasis in Levinas on alterity, there remains some semblance of what theologians refer to as "*communio*," of a shared relationship of persons.[121] The human person, as a rational creature of flesh and blood, is uniquely capable of answering the ethical call to the embodied other. It is this fact that appears as a contradictory term in Levinas' thought, for despite it, he wishes to avoid its constitution as an absolute philosophical term. The body's incarnate form is a fact he holds to, but not as a means by which any totalizing language might take hold. The body is not to be imposed upon, but received and acted for. Further to this, the body, its flesh and its psyche, form an integrated whole. Levinas avoids the possibility of separating consciousness or the psyche from the body. As he argues: "Incarnation is not a transcendental operation of a subject that is situated in the midst of the world it represents to itself; the sensible experience of the body is already and from the start incarnate."[122]

The modes of sensibility, of "maternity, vulnerability, apprehension," act as a bind between the self and others, even as a precursor to the bind one experiences with one's own body.[123] This is true for Levinas because of his ethical equation that subjectivity equals sensibility. That to be a subject is to appear within the form of flesh and blood, skin and bone, hunger and satisfaction, is to act within a sensible relationship with those who are different to the self.[124] These facts precede language, yet can only be known through language. For Levinas, traditional categories are rendered meaningless, for the embodiment of ethical responsibility is too alive, too sensible, too fleshly, to be circumscribed in categories and formulations. They exceed categorization, and so can only be described. The proximity by which the subject-subject relationship is revealed beats with the pulse of blood through a conscious body. Such proximity is asymmetrical, for one body is ultimately substituted for an other (*the* Other).[125] This approach to the body and to flesh and blood is constituted in terms of a signification of absolutes. That is to say, the otherness of the other bears the demand of responsible action so greatly that it appears as an absolute responsibility; not shared or mediated, but given in completeness and demanding a complete return of ethical responsibility.

121. See for example, Anderson, *Called to Love.*
122. Levinas, *Otherwise Than Being*, 76.
123. Ibid.
124. Ibid., 77.
125. Even against the backdrop of a third party, the "I" remains "hostage" to the Other. See ibid., 158.

For Wright, as with Morgan, Levinas's appeal to the face and to the body are not theological in the traditional sense. While Levinas's use of the category of "God" is both scriptural and appears in the idiom of theological language, it nonetheless cannot be strictly identified with a self-revelatory God. The erstwhile nearness of the divine lingers as a linguistic reminder of the immanent ethical call of the embodied other:

> "Thanks to God" I am another for the others. God is not involved as an alleged interlocutor: the reciprocal relationship binds me to the other man in the trace of transcendence, in illeity. The passing of God, of whom I can speak only by reference to this aid or this grace, is precisely the reverting of the incomparable subject into a member of society.[126]

This "passing" is a movement of perception, in which the language used (theologically) for God reappears as an (ethical) responsibility for another person. But the absolute difference between God and the human person, the divine alterity, is transferred from God to the human other and so theology reappears as ethics. For Wright, this means that texts such as *Otherwise Than Being* may still be read seriously by atheists, because Levinas' references to God are not in the form of a divine command which precede his ethics, but in the form of a latently noticed fact: God's command is noticed *after* one is issued a responsibility for the other.[127] Even the term "God" is radically open to the infinite and in its saying cannot be thematized into the same. Levinas is at pains to argue this:

> It is an extraordinary word, the only one that does not extinguish or absorb its saying, but it cannot remain a simple word. The word God is an overwhelming semantic event that subdues the subversion worked by illeity. The glory of the Infinite shuts itself up in a word and becomes a being. But it already undoes its dwelling and unsays itself without vanishing into nothingness.[128]

The glory of the infinite then is found in this "event" called "God." Levinas, in both *Totality and Infinity* and *Otherwise Than Being*, utilizes theological language in a nontheological manner. The "Infinite," "transcendence," and "God" serve as referential ethical descriptions, bound to the embodied event of the other and serving an ethical end. Nevertheless, as will be seen in the following counter-response to Wright's strict interpretation

126. Ibid.

127. Wright, *The Twilight of Jewish Philosophy*, 91–92.

128. Levinas, *Otherwise Than Being*, 151.

of the theological question in Levinas, the incarnate moment in Levinas' thought remains fraught with theological possibilities.

On doing theology with Levinas

In the response to Levinas from philosophers such as Tamra Wright, described above, it would appear that the "God" of Levinas' writings, especially in his two most influential works, *Totality and Infinity* and *Otherwise Than Being*, is not the God of Abraham, Isaac, and Jacob (Exod 3:16; Deut 6:10; cf. Acts 3:13). His use of the term is philosophical and not bound to a self-revelation as understood in the Judeo-Christian tradition. However, a theological interpretation of Levinas can be described which takes up his references to divinity and to God as holding more reliance on theological usage than Levinas might have insisted. It will be seen that such an interpretation is more generally thematic, drawing on a range of voices, including David Ford, Michael Purcell, and Glenn Morrison. More fundamentally, the following text from the book of Exodus offers a point of convergence between Levinas' thought and a theological interpretation: "And he said, 'I am the God of your father, the God of Abraham, the God of Isaac, and the God of Jacob.' And Moses hid his face, for he was afraid to look at God" (Exod 3:6).

God's self-identification in the burning bush is a major point of revelation in the Old Testament.[129] It is the moment where Moses is given his vocation to lead the people of Israel out of the land of Egypt. Moses witnesses the bush consumed by fire and not destroyed. He protests his lack of eloquence and skill, but his complaints are put aside by the impatient voice of the divine, who promises signs and great power to achieve the tasks he lays before his nervous servant. Forty days and forty nights pass as Moses sits before God who, paradoxically, remains outside the limitations of space and time. God who is the supreme Other, reveals his name. The statement, "I am the God of your father . . . ," is both a personal statement of familial continuity and an assurance of tribal and cosmological continuity, for He is "the God of Abraham, the God of Isaac, and the God of Jacob." This God who can consume his creation without causing it decay, whose face inspires a holy fear and humility, who sees into the hearts of his people, names himself as the same who was worshipped by the patriarchs and prophets of old. In

129. Michael Purcell has described the burning bush as a *"locus classicus"* for understanding the irreducible, nonconsumable dynamic of human sociality in light of Levinas' insistence that the Other decenters and calls us. See Purcell, "Nec Tamen Consumebatur. Exodus 3 and the Non-Consumable Other in the Philosophy of Emmanuel Levinas."

every following scriptural reference to God, this same divine figure is called to mind, whose essential characteristic is not simply power that commands, but mystery that issues a demand. God reveals himself in the same moment in which he is hidden from human perception. As the Russian Orthodox theologian Sergius Bulgakov puts it, "doxophany is not theophany."[130] The Mosaic access to God is cut short, made incomplete in Moses' turning away from the divine face, and in his hiding in the mountainside's cleft as the Lord's power passes by. The point is clearly made: God's mysterious power is complete and fearful, but it is the origin of the Mosaic covenant and the promises of liberation are issued from his face, hidden to human eyes. When reading these texts after Levinas, one recognizes the tropes of the "face," of a "demand," of the "trembling" before the other, all too easily.

The God of "Abraham, Isaac, and Jacob" remains the same God worshiped in the New Testament. In the postresurrection narrative of Acts 3, Peter's sermon upon Solomon's Portico invokes this title. Upon raising the leper to walk, Peter makes christological claim to the "God of Abraham, the God of Isaac, and the God of Jacob," invoking the glory of the Lord of the people of Israel as the same glory which shines in Christ and according to whose will Christ was raised after his crucifixion. The intricate scriptural connection between salvation and ethics is founded upon a radical continuity between the God of Israel and Jesus Christ. Peter's admonishment to his listeners to turn "from your wickedness" flows seamlessly from his reference to the Abrahamic covenant and its promise of great blessing to future generations (Acts 3:25–26). So despite the insistence of scholars such as Tamra Wright that the theological language Levinas employs in his ethics cannot be construed theologically in any classical or traditional sense, there remains a glaring problem. That is, Levinas' references to categories such as "God" are so frequent, and so profoundly drawn from language in the Hebrew Scriptures that it is textually deficient to blithely divorce them from their original contexts. Even if Levinas himself denies a role for positive religion or theology as such, the deep and historical relationship between theology and ethics (salvation and a godly *ethos*) indicate other possibilities. These have a peculiar bearing upon Levinas' understanding of the body.

David Ford has described Levinas as both a "profound critic" and a "copious source" for theological thinking.[131] In Levinas' insistence on ethics as "first philosophy," he provides such a radical new turn in Western philosophical thinking that his relationship to theology could not be anything other than a combination of these two characteristics. As a critic of

130. Bulgakov, *The Burning Bush*, 119.

131. Ford, *Self and Salvation*, 32.

theology, Levinas' Jewishness is important and complex (see above). His recasting of philosophy as a primarily ethical task implicates theology in its thought and practice. It could be argued that Levinas' identification as a source for theology follows directly from his classification as its critic. That is to say, as one who rebukes theology in its enmeshment to positive religion and its avoidance of the ethical content of alterity, his rebuke becomes a source for theology's own renewal and reform. Importantly, it is not Levinas' references to God or religion that Ford finds useful in this renewal and reform of the theological enterprise, but something unexpected: it is the way that Levinas' vocabulary is so closely associated with "ordinary living."[132] He finds in these terms Levinas' insistence that the human self experiences itself fundamentally in terms of "separateness," to which terminology such as "breathlessness," "enjoyment," or even "the face" attest.[133] Even the face, so central to Levinas and as the unique epiphany of the human person in sociality, acts as a divide within the self. It is the point of division between outward expression and inward emotion; between what is seen and what is thought. It is a boundary experience between the self and other persons who each have their own unrepeatable face. One might think of the manner in which people reveal their emotions in the expressions of their faces, but might on other occasions use their faces to conceal their feelings. The meaning of the face is given in language, which is the communication of signification. Sentiment and action are included in this, which require of the face its intimate relationship with a body of flesh. If it does not, the analogy of the face is rendered impotent.

In terms of Levinas' critique of theology, Ford summarizes it as a philosophical negation of idolatry.[134] The language of tantalization, of domineering of the other or of suppressing transcendence, constitute what Levinas names "the Said" [le Dit] and which appear as idolatrous objects.[135] In contrast to "the Said," "saying" [le Dire] renders a relationship with the other that avoids contamination by the imposition of the same (or a tantalization) that is experienced as "synchrony."[136] In this synchronization of otherness and of difference, theology commits itself to an idolatrous reading of every other it encounters, including God. For Levinas, God is known in the gleaming presence of the face and in the call to responsibility it invokes. The kind

---

132. Ford lists a number of terms, including the "face," "enjoyment," "breathlessness," "restlessness," "insomnia," "home" and "hospitality," "the caress," and others. See Ford, *Self and Salvation*, 33.

133. Ibid., 34.

134. Ibid., 49–52.

135. See especially Levinas, *Otherwise Than Being*, 37–38.

136. Ibid., 38.

of "anti-idolatry" that Ford finds in Levinas' poetic and rigorous language is, for him, a resource from which theology may learn and re-orientate itself accordingly.[137] Ford's understanding of theology's own concern with God and the other person is shaped by the theology of Eberhard Jüngel who is brought into dialogue with Levinas. The significant point to be made of Jüngel's contribution is the ethical content of his soteriology. In Ford's reading of Jüngel, the effect of Christ's scandalous particularity for each believing human subject is so absolute that it calls into question the self-substitutionary possibility for any human person besides Christ.[138] Jüngel's insistence on particularity is important to Ford's appropriation of Levinas, yet it differs substantially. For the latter, each individual other remains uniquely other, marked by an absolute alterity which is itself an ethical arrangement of differentiated persons. As Ford summarizes:

> The hungry other; the particular beloved; the particular teacher: to begin to differentiate like this helps in conceiving both how one might be extravagantly grateful before one particular face, as Jüngel is, while yet maintaining the witness to substitutionary responsibility, as Levinas does.[139]

Ford holds in tension the identification of Jesus Christ as an adequate substitutionary self (in life, death, and resurrection) and the substitutionary self in relation to the other by way of Levinas' radical responsibility.[140] The face of Christ is an incarnate epiphany of perfect responsibility, but it is also the infinite possibility of the responsibility of each believing subject.

For Michael Purcell, Levinas' understanding of the holy allows ethics not simply to be construed as "first philosophy," but as "first theology."[141] By this, he indicates that the discipline of theology is itself implicated in Levinas' reinterpretation of Western philosophy. If Levinas' accusation that philosophy has reneged on its responsibility for thinking and acting for the other holds, theology is not excused. Its complex historical relationship with philosophy makes it a crucial thread of argumentation and thought that also allows itself to overlook or undermine difference and the other. Purcell's claim is that this is not to be interpreted negatively, but rather as a positive opportunity for theology to draw deeply from its own wellsprings to

---

137. Ford, *Self and Salvation*, 54.

138. Ibid., 69. Ford compares this with Bonhoeffer's insistence on a substitutionary self as made possible by the substitutionary passion of Christ, in which the freedom to be responsible is made available to each human being.

139. Ibid., 70.

140. Ibid., 72.

141. Purcell, *Levinas and Theology*, 5.

consider the other more clearly and more ethically. Instead of thinking only in categories and sequences of logic, theology might consider the human subject in its alterity, thereby renewing the task of the theologian and the church's practice of theology. Purcell highlights Levinas' comment on the holiness of the other person in a 1992 interview: "Holiness thus shows itself as an irreducible possibility of the human and God: being called by man. An original ethical event which would also be first theology."[142]

Despite Levinas' disparaging critique of theology, he makes here a positive point about its possibilities. As an expression of the fundamental ethical character of authentic thought and action, theology might also be truer to itself, prioritizing an incarnate alterity over the temptation for totalizing the other. Theology, in this sense, is a posture before the holiness of the other. It is less a system, but more an ethical *response* to an embodied alterity. Purcell highlights Levinas' preface to the second edition of *Of God Who Comes to Mind*.[143] Here, Levinas explicates the event of holiness as anterior to theological performance:

> We have been reproached for ignoring theology; and we do not contest the necessity of a recovery, at least, the necessity of choosing an opportunity for a recovery of these themes. We think, however, that theological recuperation comes after the glimpse of holiness, which is primary.[144]

Levinas identifies theology as fundamentally ethically orientated and motivated. Furthermore, he does not see in the discipline of theology the requirement of revolution or razing, but of recovery. The recovery of theology will be an intentional activity, achieved before an incarnate presence. Theology must fundamentally recover its ethical orientation before the holy gleam of the other, or, as Purcell puts it, "[t]he human existential is fundamental to the theological enquiry."[145] Earlier, in 1988, Levinas had spoken of service to the other as a vocation.[146] He finds extraordinary surprise in the vocational act of "being-for-the other," what he names "[o]ntological courtesy," summed up in the sudden ceding of the first place of the self, "[a]près vous, Monsieur!"[147] Levinas reaffirms his insistence that language precedes thought and that he does not wish to pit being against the other in some

---

142. "The Awakening of the I," in Levinas, *Is It Righteous to Be?*, 182.

143. Purcell, "'Levinas and Theology'?," 468.

144. Levinas, *Of God Who Comes to Mind*, ix.

145. Purcell, *Levinas and Theology*, 156.

146. "The Vocation of the Other," in Levinas, *Is It Righteous to Be?*, 105.

147. Ibid., 106.

kind of contest.[148] Rather, he finds the call of responsibility towards and for the other as the primary call for peace and in discovery of what is truly human. Typically, "God" is invoked in close proximity to these thoughts on the provocation of the human being towards the good:

> What would push us? You want humanity to be born from processes that are purely material? Humanity is not some kind of explosion, egoist in the original egoism of being itself. It is the voice of God which reverberates in being. I would maintain the revolutionary character of the apparition of the human.[149]

Such a revolution in the world, of the human who acts humanely, is motivated by a spiritual dimension, what Levinas elsewhere has called the transcendent.[150] The voice of God, called upon to explain this mystery, is a call to pause before the significance of the other. Of this responsibility, Levinas is asked how love might be related. He answers: "responsibility is the love without concupiscence."[151] Love then is disinterested and transcendent, bound at all times to the embodied other. The event of love is an intrinsically personal response of one's own body to the body of an other, but with the advent of a desire that is for the sake of the other, rather than for one's own satiation.

Glenn Morrison has responded to the theological challenge of Levinas with the call for a "Trinitarian praxis" in Levinasian terms.[152] To achieve this, theology must envisage a coinciding of both *theoria* and *praxis* in its pronunciation of God in relation to ethics.[153] Morrison brings Hans Urs von Balthasar into dialogue with Levinas, insisting that the pivot point for his Levinasian consideration of the possibilities for theology's renewal is Jesus Christ.[154] Jesus the Messiah is not a system or a totality, but fundamentally

---

148. Ibid., 107.

149. Ibid.

150. This revolution in worldly terms has been considered as a resource for liberation theology in such works as Mayama, *Emmanuel Levinas' Conceptual Affinities with Liberation Theology*; Alcoff and Mendieta, *Thinking from the Underside of History*; and similar themes in Veling, "In the Name of Who?"

151. "The Vocation of the Other," in Levinas, *Is It Righteous to Be?*, 108.

152. Morrison, "Renewing Christian Theology with Levinas," in Burggraeve (ed.), *The Awakening to the Other*, 137–59.

153. Ibid., 139.

154. See also Morrison, "Levinas, Von Balthasar and Trinitarian Praxis."

and always a *person*.[155] With this in mind, Morrison proposes three factors that must be present for such a Trinitarian *praxis* to operate successfully.[156]

First, ethical transcendence, in which the transcendence of one's own objectifying consciousness makes ethics possible. The ethical transcendence Morrison learns from Levinas is the overcoming of the self's constitutional subjectivity, to the point of being overwhelmed by the presence of the other. This results in terminology such as "fear, fission, trauma, diachrony, anarchy and persecution."[157] Phenomenality is interrupted, to the collapse of time. That is, the call of the other overcomes all phenomenal appearing, and arrives as something from beyond history and memory, an ethical call not bound to the march of time. This trace lingers as an ethical call outside the bounds of temporality, in the sense that the call to responsibility arrives not from the past or the future, but a universal origin beyond being.

Second, there must be eschatology. For Morrison, Balthasar's notion of eschatological experience is enriched by an encounter with Levinas' ethical transcendence. In Balthasar's eschatology, the union of the cross and resurrection so "fills the human vessel" such that Christian experience is one of *knowing* God.[158] In this knowledge, which is always ecclesially grounded, the eschaton is foreshadowed and given foretaste. The objective nature of God's self-revelation is always in relation with the subjective experience of the human self, who savors and sees the glory of the Lord. This is a self-limitation in Balthasar's thought, for it brackets out the ethical from the experience of transcendence. Rather, transcendence ought to be fundamentally open to the ethical obligation to others (and to each *other*), and so fulfill the Pauline injunction that Christ's disciples have nothing, yet possess everything (2 Cor 6:10). The eschatological dimension of this ethics is in the self-awareness of anticipating God's ultimate reconciliation, which is only possible because of the cross and resurrection. In experiencing the other in Christ, the self anticipates the *praxis* of God reconciling all in Christ and in the Spirit.[159] This is in the mode of the passivity before the other of which Levinas speaks.

Third, Morrison claims that the Eucharist provides the concrete context for these first two to be experienced and enacted as a practical

155. Morrison, "Renewing Christian Theology with Levinas," in Burggraeve (ed.), *The Awakening to the Other*, 142.

156. Ibid., 143–56.

157. Ibid., 144.

158. Balthasar, *The Glory of the Lord*, VIII.494.

159. Morrison, "Renewing Christian Theology with Levinas," in Burggraeve (ed.), *The Awakening to the Other*, 150.

Trinitarian ethics.[160] The passivity in which the self begins to anticipate an eschatological horizon of Trinitarian reconciliation is paradoxically one of responsible action that is envisaged eucharistically. Morrison names this "Trinitarian *praxis*."[161] The motivation for this action is precisely in what he understands to be the gifted nature of such praxis, or "gifted passivity."[162] Morrison takes up Balthasar's idea of the passion of Christ initiating an ontological shift *before* any conscious act of faith.[163] In Balthasar, the rite of the Eucharist is an ontological incorporation into the passion that effects the ongoing perfection of the human person. *Praxis* is posterior to the ontological shift wrought in Christ's sacrifice. In this perspective, the Eucharist is an ethical experience, in that the other in Christ is encountered otherwise than being. In the eucharistic species, one's hunger does not end in reception of the body and blood of the risen Christ, but reconfigured as the other's hunger in the self. The self no longer hungers for that which satiates the self, but in the trauma of the encounter with Christ. A fissure opens up which initiates a hunger for "salvation, justice and mercy."[164] In this Eucharistic understanding of the way alterity opens up the self to the practice of Trinitarian reconciliation, Morrison conducts both theology and a Levinasian consideration of the ethical effect of alterity. As he puts it, "[e]xpiation is a difficult condition, but I want to argue that it is a condition *par excellence* that gives rise to theology."[165]

Yet, this isolates singular moments of ethical devotion from the broader narrative of a lived Christian life. As theologically rich as these steps are, they remain reliant on the eucharistic event as carrying an ethical significance that can be recognized and interpreted. For this to be achieved, the Eucharist must be thought beyond its own eventfulness and in the broader context of the narrative of Christian life, the *imitatio Christi*. Even the Eucharist must be contextualized in terms of one's personal experience of the "synthesis of the finite and the infinite, the temporal and the eternal."[166] The Christian life, interpreted through the eucharistic lens, remains the commitment of experience in all these forms, and not the experience of a moment or of a singular event. The body of a human person is given over

---

160. Ibid., 144.

161. Ibid., 140.

162. Ibid., 153.

163. Ibid., 153–54.

164. Ibid., 155.

165. Ibid., 156.

166. Minister, "Works of Justice, Works of Love," in Simmons and Wood (eds.), *Kierkegaard and Levinas*, 240.

in this experience of a life lived for Christ who is other; a life lived in a "linear" movement in orientation to God who is not bound to temporality.[167] Furthermore, the Eucharist is also an event normally experienced collectively, as a people bound in a body.

Indeed, Purcell comments upon the passivity in which the work of the people—*leitourgia*—is given in order to return to God. Especially evident in the Eucharist is "a work that is begun in us by what is other than us and is brought to completion, again by an other than us."[168] Moreover, eucharistic presence is not governed by consciousness, but governs as a provocation: "presence as phenomenal excess provokes attention, and thus is liturgy and life itself a response to a prior initiative, to a gift already given."[169] Purcell explores further the ethical significance of the Eucharist as an activity that intends a world other than what is, and which is structured according to the Levinasian description of responsibility as the "for-the-other."[170] In the ethical transcendence taken up by Morrison, the encounter with what is other can be construed theologically most acutely in relation to the event of Christ and in the eucharistic liturgy.

In the work of David Ford, Michael Purcell, and Glenn Morrison, the contours of a theology after Levinas are anticipated. Other thinkers, such as Eberhard Jüngel, Dietrich Bonhoeffer, Hans Urs von Balthasar, Jean-Luc Marion, and Maurice Blanchot appear as dialogue partners. Despite the perplexing rhetoric and dialogical complexities of the various extremes to which Levinas appeals, and despite his own suspicion of theology, there is growing evidence that a fruitful theological encounter with his thought is making progress. The constant concern amongst Levinas interpreters for the concrete and incarnate experiences of human life highlights the crucial importance of the body to Levinas. The fact that this is arranged with so many tangential theological possibilities proves the point that Levinas himself was less closed to theology than he might have thought.

On hospitality towards the other

What is the practical outworking of a Levinasian ethic of alterity? And with its incarnate sense of the body as the means by which subjectivity equals sensibility, despite his rejections of the body, how would the embodied

167. Izzi, "Proximity in Distance," in Schroeder and Benso (eds.), *Levinas and the Ancients*, 208.

168. Purcell, "Glimpsing Grace Phenomenologically," 85.

169. Ibid.

170. See Purcell, "Eucharistic Responsibility," in *Levinas and Theology*, 155–67.

person enact the radical responsibility Levinas invokes?[171] The problem of Levinas' practical ethics can be highlighted in terms of hospitality, in which his motif of the solitary other is experienced concretely alongside other people.[172] The possibility of hospitality to multiple persons in varying levels of responsibility is challenged by this reality. In any case, hospitality remains central to how Levinas envisages an embodied care for the other. As David Ford articulates, "hospitality" is a crucial means by which the other person is welcomed, cared for, and placed in priority before the self.[173]

Understanding the complete and demanding nature of Levinas' notion of hospitality towards the other requires an awareness of how the body acts as a site of hospitable action; that in the face of the other, the body recognizes an infinite requirement of care, and becomes fundamentally open to the other's well-being and success. The face of the other speaks profoundly against its own murder, but it speaks just as profoundly for a positive activity of responsibility. In connecting the two calls (one of inaction and the other of action) together in the epiphany of the face, Levinas makes a philosophical statement about the incarnate and embodied nature of care, which is not unknown to our historical recollection. That is, history reveals the human capacity to both care for, and to reject the other. Levinas has said that where history manifests a relationship between persons within an impersonal spirit, its integration is "cruelty and injustice."[174] In disallowing the other an absolute alterity (in effect, to be *the* other), the only genuinely possible absolute in history is ignored. Levinas remarks: "History is worked over by the ruptures of history, in which a judgment is borne upon it. When man truly approaches the Other he is uprooted from history."[175]

Embodied gestures, words, postures; these enact human history, but they are also imbued with ethical meaning. Michael Purcell invokes Levinas' insistence on hospitality in an essay on homelessness, in which the homeless other makes the self a hostage to an immediate needfulness.[176] This is problematized in Jacque Derrida's *On Cosmopolitanism*, in which he deals with European examples of local alienation amidst migratory communities

---

171. Kosky has outlined a compelling case for the ethical applicability of Levinas, while also calling for further careful thought and study. See Kosky, *Levinas and the Philosophy of Religion*.

172. See for example Fagan's debate with Loumansky in "The Inseparability of Ethics and Politics"; also Loumanksy, "Reply to Fagan. Hanging God at Auschwitz."

173. Ford, *Self and Salvation*, 30–72.

174. Levinas, *Totality and Infinity*, 52.

175. Ibid., 52.

176. Purcell, "Christ the Stranger."

seeking national and state-sponsored hospitality.[177] In these concrete moments of history, the idea that the latter is a linear movement open to description or comprehension is interrupted. The face of the other is desperate, dwelling within a context of nondwelling, without home or sustenance, and so the self's own body is issued with the need to respond. Homelessness, for Derrida, becomes akin to a fact of being, and not just of history. This is profoundly true not only of citizens without a home, but of those who have fled their place of citizenship due to fear and intimitation, and await bureaucratic processes in a new country regarding their future. They are, by definition, homeless in a troubling and desperate situation. Hospitality is not a figurative ideal that has transient flesh in philosophical debate, but a desperate need for many. In this sense, those who seek asylum across transnational borders experience both a need and a desire for hospitality. For Levinas, hospitality to the other, made possible through the face of the other, also provides a condition of peaceful coexistence for its participants. However, it is not a legal condition but a more fundamental condition that occurs in a precognitive manner. It is for Levinas the practice of "religion," at least insofar as he defines it: "We propose to call 'religion' the bond that is established between the same and the other without constituting a totality."[178] It occurs in the incarnate moment of intersubjectivity and, as has been seen, invokes the language of theology.

Levinas and the body: critiques

A number of critiques have been made of Levinas, casting his approach to the body in a negative light.[179] For example, B. C. Hutchens identifies three

---

177. See especially part one, which deals with the legal and jurisdictional complexities of hospitality, in Derrida, *On Cosmopolitanism and Forgiveness*.

178. Levinas, *Totality and Infinity*, 40.

179. Critiques can be found from a variety of voices, including: Žižek, "Neighbors and Other Monsters," in Žižek, Santner, and Reinhard, *The Neighbor*; Vries, *Minimal Theologies*; Critchley, "Five Problems in Levinas's View of Politics and the Sketch of a Solution to Them"; Derrida, *Writing and Difference*. Some notable feminist critiques can be found in: Katz, *Levinas, Judaism, and the Feminine*; Chanter, *Feminist Interpretations of Emmanuel Levinas*; Bernasconi and Critchley, *Re-Reading Levinas*. In addition to David Bentley Hart, theological critiques can be seen in: Milbank, *The Word Made Strange*; Blond, *Post-Secular Philosophy*. Partially critical, but generally positive accounts of doing theology with Levinas can be found in: Morrison, "Levinas, von Balthasar and Trinitarian Praxis"; Purcell, "'Levinas and Theology'?"; Hutchens, *Levinas*. Alternatively, Janicaud rebukes Levinas for betraying phenomenology by taking a theological turn, see: Janicaud, *Phenomenology and The "Theological Turn."*

major elements of Levinas' approach that are problematic.[180] The first is the problem of scale, in which Levinas' theory applies on too many conceptual levels.[181] The Levinasian insistence on placing alterity at the forefront of all ethical concern is applicable on such a grand scale that there does not appear to be anything in human culture it does not apply to. This means that, as Hutchens argues, if Levinas is mistaken or unclear about the problem he describes, then "nothing else in his thought" can be acceptable with "any great confidence."[182] The scale is at the level of a grand narrative or totalizing approach. The second problematic element is the questionable relevance of Levinas.[183] Because of his shrugging off of normative ethical theory, there is a disjuncture between applicable ethical approaches and his ethics of the other. In what way can Levinas' approach apply in helpful or relevant ways to particular problems? Even if Levinas is correct in his general judgments, there is no guidance on how his descriptions relate to a prescriptive approach to concrete moral problems. The third element is one of detail.[184] Hutchens refers to Levinas' central motifs of the face, illeity, etc, or indeed his understanding of the God who passes by and leaves a trace that "really is not merely a trace of itself" as "nebulous concepts" which are of little use in the technical work of the moral philosopher.[185] This leaves the work of moral philosophy without any guidance as to how Levinasian concepts can be implemented. In effect, these three problematic elements—scale, relevance, and detail—result in a dissonance between Levinasian ethics and the work of ethical theorists (theological or otherwise).

These three elements are genuine difficulties in Levinas' thought. In each of the areas of scale, relevance, and detail, Levinas' approach hinges on the absolute difference between oneself and the other. The pseudotheological language used to describe this difference shows Levinas' commitment to an otherness in which the trace of divinity appears and paradoxically remains invisible. The absolutization of the other denies the constitution of the self because it is overcome and traversed by the impending presence of alterity. In contrast to Levinas, Paul Ricœur has argued that an authentic metaphysics for moral philosophy must account for the way in which each other person is constituted as a self. That is to say, a fully determinate self must already exist before the injunction of responsibility in the other can

---

180. Hutchens, *Levinas*, 155–66.

181. Ibid., 155–56.

182. Ibid.

183. Ibid., 156.

184. Ibid., 157–58.

185. Ibid., 157.

be heard. The asymmetry of the relationship between the other and oneself, which Levinas insists is absolute, implies a capacity in both persons to respond as a *self*, to be able to say "I am."[186] The form of asymmetrical responsibility for the other described by Levinas denies such a constitution of the self. For Ricœur, there remains a dialectically complementary relationship between the self and the other, so that Levinas' asymmetry fails in its application as an absolute principle.[187] Instead, the same and the other remain constituted as authentic selves, neither of whom owe the other an absolute capitulation. This critique is fundamental to both a philosophical and a theological response to the problem of the body in Levinas. In this light, and approaching Levinas with a similar critique, two further negative judgments of Levinas can be considered. The first is that of the secular Marxist theorist, Alain Badiou; the second from the theologian David Bentley Hart. Both indicate what will be called the problem of the disincarnate body in Levinas' account of the other.

Levinas and the body: A secular critique

One of the most energetic critiques of Levinas comes from Alain Badiou. For him, the problem with Levinas' conception of the other (the "Altogether-Other") is its theological annihilation of philosophy.[188] The appropriation of language that is theological (especially references to "God") in Levinas' assertion that ethics is "first philosophy," renders ethics as a "category of pious discourse."[189] This reduction of philosophy to ethics, via theology, is also the reduction of spirituality, because it posits a piety without normativity; theologically bracketed and stripped of dogma. It honors the *ideas* of difference and alterity, but is bound to understanding them within "the same." It would seem that theology and its tradition of maintaining (paradoxically) multiple concurrent differences is also reduced in this reading of Levinas. Badiou's Marxist critique (he was for a while a Maoist) understands the category of "difference" in Levinas as too beholden to contemporary liberalism which only respects the other while the other appears to confirm a dominant Western paradigm: "parliamentary-democratic, pro free-market economics, in favour of freedom of opinion, feminism, the environment," etc.[190] Language

---

186. Ricœur, *Oneself as Another*, 355.
187. Ibid., 393.
188. Badiou, *Ethics*, 23.
189. Ibid.
190. Ibid., 24.

of the other, as it is appropriated from Levinas' thought, remains caught in a *bourgeois* privileging of the self.

According to Badiou, the appeal to alterity cannot really contextualize or "shed light" upon any concrete situation.[191] The experience of otherness cannot define or describe ethics, but is rather the origin of one (and only *one*) approach to the construction of an ethics (and of a Law). There cannot be, in the end, only one ethics (for Badiou), but rather a series of "subjective types," which correlate to different truths: "political, scientific, artistic, and amorous."[192] These truths are not unified, nor are they necessarily complementary. Rather, they coexist, and the task of philosophy is to construct a "space of thought" in which these four types may coexist and be expressed by the singular truths of the time in which such philosophy is set out.[193] Philosophy is therefore always contextual and always dynamic. Badiou's rejection of Levinas is based upon a fundamental misunderstanding of philosophy and a desire for ethics to become a universal category to the upset of both philosophical and theological traditions. The decomposition of religion to ethics is for Badiou a deceit, one that results in *"de la bouillie pour les chats"* (a colloquial English equivalent would be a "dog's breakfast"), a reduction of the other and of all philosophy.[194]

Badiou highlights the problem of describing ethics solely in terms of alterity. The possible confusion in working a way back from otherness to an embodied ethic of care and responsibility may, in the end, turn out to be only one possible route, as Badiou points out. Yet, the Badiouian critique of Levinas assumes too quickly a theological ease in which the latter's work immerses itself. As was argued above, a theological appropriation of Levinas is certainly useful, but it must be aware of the arrangement of terms in Levinas' problematic accounts of alterity and the other.

Levinas and the body: a theological critique

In David Bentley Hart's theological aesthetics, he defends a robustly Christian metaphysics in opposition to postmodern philosophy, and includes a trenchant criticism of Levinas.[195] At times, Hart's critique of Levinas is as acerbic as Badiou's, but his methodology is emphatically theological.[196] For

191. Ibid., 27.
192. Ibid., 28.
193. Ibid.
194. Ibid.
195. Hart, *The Beauty of the Infinite*.
196. ". . . as will presently become clear, I have no sympathy for Levinas's thought

Hart, the Christian understanding of "transcendence," or "the Christian infinite," is first aesthetical and, *contra* Levinas, *then* ethical.[197] This is so because the infinite is not the disinterested ethical openness to an endless obligation (as Levinas puts it) but rather it is marked by a uniquely antidisinterest in the other. Hart argues that for Christian thought, the infinite refers to God, who opens up both being and beings to love, "only within the free orderings of its beauty, inviting a desire that is moral only because it is *not* disinterested."[198] This contrasts with Badiou's investment in a concrete ethical pluralism with no transcendent referent. The God who confirms alterity and particularity is, for Hart, a rebuke to both Levinas and Badiou. Because God reveals his own beauty, the aesthetic nature of theologizing, of reflection upon God and his acts, becomes also an ethical or a moral awareness. In Hart's perspective, the Levinasian darkness of an infinite obligation disregards the radically visual beauty of Christian tradition. He identifies the aesthetic power of the icon, which acts dynamically in the in-between of the divide between idolatry and the ethical abolition of all images.[199] The icon redeems and liberates the visible, and opposes the "contextless, unlocalizable, inescapable face of the other" in Levinas' ethics. The icon, unlike Levinas' appeal to the face, acts as a locater of beauty upon the particular and of course its exemplar is the incarnate Word, whose infinite nature deigns to take finite human flesh in time and space, thus revealing infinity through finitude.[200]

It is in this appeal to the category of the infinite and its relation to the ethical that Hart and Levinas differ essentially.[201] The infinite is, for Hart, opened up by the postmodern appeal to the "sublime," which is a magnified version of Kant's discussion of the third Critique.[202] Hart finds in the postmodern philosophers of the late twentieth century an appeal to the sublime which, while taking Kant as a point of departure, tends to dwell upon sublimity without regard for the integration of other factors noted by Kant, such as the beautiful as envisaged in imagination. In fact, this morose concern for that which the sublime refers to—absence, the indeterminate,

---

. . . ." Ibid., 14.

197. Ibid., 15.

198. Ibid.

199. Ibid.

200. Ibid.

201. They differ in many other ways as well, including their use of language. Hart describes Levinas' writing as a "prodigy of incoherance." See ibid., 75.

202. See Kant, *Critique of the Power of Judgment*.

a concealment of understanding, an "absence" or the "veil"—constitutes for Hart the chief concerns of postmodern philosophers (including Levinas).[203]

Hart outlines four examples of the sublime which mark the nihilistic tendencies of postmodern philosophy: the "differential sublime" (particularly Derrida and the prioritization of difference, change, absence, and exteriority); the "cosmological sublime" (this is philosophy in a "Nietzschean impulse," most especially exemplified by Gilles Deleuze and following him, Michel Foucault, by which power is given as a kind of peace, carrying an anti-Christian prejudice with a high estimation of the will); the "ontological sublime" (the post-Heideggerian thought of Jean-Luc Nancy especially preserves the immutability of the phenomenological collapse of the "it is" into "it appears," rendering the world's passage as, ultimately, a passing away); and finally the "ethical sublime."[204] Most relevant to the current consideration of Levinas is this fourth and final example.

Hart understands Levinas to offer a vision of the "ethical sublime," in which Kant's categorical imperative appears in a mutated form, not governed by an interior moral law or reason.[205] This is, of course, what Levinas understands as the ethical demand that appears in the experience of alterity. In the arrival of the other *qua* Other, the self is confronted with an opposition to the Heideggerian impulse to assimilate the other person into a totality of Being. It is here that Hart asks the most relevant question of Levinas' logic:

> though it ostensibly concerns the Other, such is the severity of its logic that the other—to remain truly other—cannot in any way actually *appear*: neither by way of phenomenology's analogies and reductions, nor by way of any prior understanding of being and beings, nor within the reach of simple recognition (in every case, one remains within the confines of the Same). Rather, alterity is intimated solely in moments of rupture or discontinuity; the otherness that makes demands of us is alien to us, from beyond the totality.[206]

This is profoundly important to the problem of the body in Levinas. Is this other person, who is always *the* Other, a truly embodied presence for Levinas? Is he in fact thinking of a veritable, observably present person, of flesh and bone, whose unique face speaks in the temporal-spatial context of lived materiality? If he is not, there remains a question as to whether

203. Hart, *The Beauty of the Infinite*, 44–45.
204. Ibid., 43–93.
205. Ibid., 75.
206. Ibid., 77.

Levinas' other is not in some way a counterfeit human person, one who, under scrutiny, performs the quality of an ethical structure but who cannot act in the currency of typical human sociality. We have seen above how much Levinas' consideration of the body is propitiously bound to both physicality (flesh, hunger, the face) and to theological categories (infinity, transcendence, God). Are these terms purely analogous, or do they relate to the uniqueness of actual human persons?

The argument Hart unfolds against Levinas is precisely in these terms: that the otherness which Levinas invokes in his appeal for responsibility is the disembodied sublime. He says:

> In this impalpable contact or formless encounter, I am addressed by an injunction issuing from an absolute and immemorial past, never present to me in continuous time; I find that even before I am, I am responsible.[207]

The repetitive language that Hart finds "convulsive and ostentatious" is ultimately not problematic in its seeming magnification of the other's hold upon the self, but rather in its reduction.[208] That is to say, Hart finds worrying the "reduction" of the other to the theme of "persecutor," a "sacrificer of hostages," an "accuser," a "stranger to gratitude."[209] By this *reductio*, it seems that the other, despite Levinas' rhetorical insistence upon alterity, carries no particular features that distinguish it as other at all. In fact, the otherness that invokes one's responsibility serves *one's own* ethical purity, rather than serving the need of the other. Because every other is the Other, the other person no longer remains distinctive and simply acts as an occasion for one's personal ethical perfection.

In fact, something further occurs, because in this decontamination of all that is uniquely distinctive, the other is denied the opportunity to be "distinct, desirable" in any incarnate experience, thus removing also the possibility of "need, dependency, or hope?"[210] There can be no community or authentic sociality in Hart's reading of Levinas; no love, no romance, no friendship. The good is pitted against the ontological (being and anything which speaks of the same) in such fashion as to secure the self's relation with alterity in a war for purity rather than a joyful embrace of difference. The good, in this reading, is really a negation: "For Levinas, the good is so opposed to the ontological that it can have no reality except as a *pri-*

---

207. Ibid., 81.
208. Ibid., 82.
209. Ibid.
210. Ibid.

vatio mali, prompted into paradoxical 'existence' by the aggression of the Other's arrival; the good can only 'be' good as the negative of a *substantial suffering*."[211]

If this is so, then Levinas' ethics is fundamentally at odds with a theological appreciation for the body. Hart notes in passing that Levinas says nothing about the increase in another's joy; only in the cessation of suffering.[212] But it is from the incarnate realities of the body's movement and social discourse that love and ethics are made possible. "Ethics is a social love, born from the preoccupations of the flesh . . . ."[213] So there must be some recognizable counterpart in the other which the self has the capacity to witness, some analogous means by which the glimmer of community springs to mind. Hart calls upon Husserl's *alter ego* (which had been rejected by Levinas) as an experience-based category by which otherness can be the successful point of departure for a true ethics.[214] Here, the recognition of another person by virtue of what one recognizes in oneself is a virtuous and rational activity. Analogy is the means by which the oneself and an other subordinate "the same" into the relationship of difference. The term avoided in much of Levinas' work—community—is for Hart the basis from which the joys of being are manifest (one might think of feasting, conversation, sport, song, laughter, art, debate, let alone the consolations of shared suffering in the face of a common loss).

David Bentley Hart finds no value for theology in Levinas' ethics. He sees in it an approach to the sublime that is disincarnate, not just from the physicality of the embodied human creature, but from the thematizations, cultural traditions, geographical limitations, and even religious commitments that exist in every human interaction. Otherness itself is not problematic, but rather its description as an absolute. At the heart of Hart's critique of Levinas is the problem of ethics and infinity. Hart insists that Levinas' consideration of the infinite as a projection of endless responsibility for the other is in direct opposition to Christian ethics, which must follow the primacy of aesthetics; in other words, the beauty of that which is revealed in revelation. For Hart, ethical action is a response to a beauty that is revealed, a beauty of the particular in the face of Christ. Against the central motif in Levinas' ethics, "the face," Hart insists:

> The face of the other, for Christian eyes, must of necessity be visible *only* in the peculiarities of its features, and only within an

211. Ibid.
212. Ibid., 84.
213. Ibid.
214. Ibid., 85.

unforeclosable sequence of perspectives and supplementations; it is always an aesthetic event. The other is "placed" within being, within the infinite, not as a mere localized essence, but as a unique and so adequate expression of the infinite. The other has a world, and therefore the world has in him or her a face.[215]

So, the face remains central to the body's presence, but the other is reduced in the denial of his or her particularities. In fact, Hart describes the kind of ethics based on an absolute alterity and Levinas' accompanying rhetorical devices (his entire view of the world, in fact) as "a little depraved."[216] Hart's theological rejection of Levinas is based on the idea that being equals goodness. This Christian affirmation has its fundamental origins in Scripture: "And God saw everything that he had made, and behold, it was very good" (Gen 1:31). The good of the creation, affirmed by Scripture and the tradition, is not negated by history's experience of sin and evil, but in fact shows it up as a glaring and contrasting reality. That material reality might itself both be affirmed in its goodness and its difference equally affirms the place of alterity in the created order, not enfolding it diabolically in "the same," but unfolding the same as a servant of the beauty of the other.

Levinas' approach to the body is criticized by David Bentley Hart for its disincarnate tendency, which is unable to recognize the positive nature of what might at times constitute sameness. It is what is shared between the self and the other that makes possible an infinity of possibility, an ethical openness that is affirming and not chiefly negative. In both the face and the voice of the other, Hart follows the thought of Gregory of Nyssa and sees in the category of desire the possibility of correspondence to a "determinate infinity of super-abounding beauty."[217] Rather than Levinas' expiation of desire for the sake of the other, Hart describes the desire that opens up the gaze into an "infinite aesthetic order"; one that invites an obligation and responsibility via beauty, instead of the ethical sublime.[218] Creation is a music to be heard and the other constitutes a world that opens up both the self and others to that music in its glory. It is because the music of creation is a positive infinity that the other is seen in the context of an aesthetic of beauty and not as a servant to one's own pristine ethics.

The infinite responsibility to which Levinas refers is itself not rejected by Hart, but the cause and motivation of its execution differs radically. Hart sees Christian metaphysics as proffering an ethics that begins and is

215. Ibid., 144.
216. Ibid., 75.
217. Ibid., 288.
218. Ibid.

sustained by beauty and not by a negative difference. He views Levinas and the postmodern as an anti-aesthetic, one that effaces the reality of creation as much as it misunderstands human relationships as incarnate and embodied communities. While for Levinas the self is an insomniac in hostage to the demands of the other, for Hart, "when the other is lost, all music is forsaken."[219] Incarnate bodies feast as well as fast, and so Hart's complaint is valid. There are no bearings within Levinas to take seriously the embodied experiences of those whose every love and desire concerns particular objects of affection. Has anyone truly loved an other to the point of sacrifice for the sake of that person's *otherness* alone? Particular faces, names and bodies; each gives itself in signification and meaning by virtue of an incarnate presence in the world.

The problem of the disincarnate body

In the two negative judgments of Levinas above, his approach to the body is shown to be problematic. For Alain Badiou, an ethics based solely on alterity fails to appreciate the complex field of human experience or "shed light" on concrete situations.[220] Badiou also finds the use of religious language in Levinas an obstacle to the work of ethics as a universal endeavor. For him, religion is an absurd complication that denies the local and particular in what it is to be human. For David Bentley Hart, the problem with Levinas is also the absolute otherness that determines the ethical relationship. Hart argues that the appearance of the other is first an aesthetic moment of transcendence, *then* an ethical moment.[221]

For this reason, Hart differs from Badiou in viewing theological language as not only appropriate, but necessary. Hart argues this on the basis that Christian theology has the capacity to recognize in the transcendent moment the opening up of God's own beauty, which promotes a desire for the good of others based on a particular and localized interest.[222] What motivates the oneself to act is not a disinterested response to a demanding alterity, but an otherness that bears a distinctive beauty which attracts. This is similar to Augustine's view of the motivation for desiring the good. In *Spirit and Letter*, he turns to the notion of "delight" as the motivating factor granted by the Holy Spirit to seek the good.[223] Rather than the trauma of

219. Ibid.
220. Badiou, *Ethics*, 27.
221. Hart, *The Beauty of the Infinite*, 15.
222. Ibid.
223. Augustine, *St. Augustine on the Spirit and the Letter*, 2.4.

being drawn into self-substitution for the other, Augustine speaks of the delight in seeking what grants an authentic experience of that which is true and beautiful. Elsewhere he speaks of the Trinitarian persons as the true objects of enjoyment, even as the Trinity is indeed the cause of all objects.[224] For Hart, the infinite itself is an opening up to that which is truly beautiful, and in that experience a delight for pursuing the good is made possible. Hart's appeal to a theological basis for ethics affirms the body because of its intrinsically incarnate openness to the infinite. As he argues, the other is an embodied presence through which the face is not an austere command of otherness, but the "unique and so adequate expression of the infinite."[225] There is no place for such a motivation in Levinas. For him, the other cannot be described in a phenomenality of presence, but as the very "principle of phenomenality."[226] This is pronounced further in Levinas' account of the face, in which the other, who is the destitute one and the stranger, appeals to the oneself as a "Master."[227] The mastery of the other over the oneself derives from the nudity of the face, which appeals as the prophetic evocation of alterity and not as the irreducibly unique embodiment of a particular person. It bears itself over the self in a gravity of ethical authority. Indeed, the face speaks in what Levinas calls the "Unsaid," an ethical language that precedes the spoken word and issues from an infinite glory residing in the face.[228]

This glory is the excess apparent in the experience of alterity, irreducible to disclosure or the narration of "anything that shows itself."[229] Levinas goes further, in that he also denies in this ethical "Saying" (what he paradoxically also calls the "Unsaid") any experience of the person in a tangible or somatic sense: it is "without noematic correlation" in its obedience to such a glory.[230] The body passes on the way to alterity. Ethics is a demanding responsibility and the body is denied, despite Levinas' constant return to it. In fact, the body in Levinas is a disincarnate subject, more the phantom of incarnation than its presence.

As a disincarnate subject, Levinas' body is intrinsically problematic when considering themes of sensory experience and moments of touch. One example is the way in which Levinas refers to the erotic as holding

---

224. Augustine, *On Christian Doctrine*, 5.

225. Hart, *The Beauty of the Infinite*, 144.

226. Levinas, *Totality and Infinity*, 92.

227. Ibid., 213.

228. Levinas, *Otherwise Than Being*, 145.

229. Ibid.

230. Ibid.

no possibility of what he calls "fusion" between two persons.[231] As such, embodied moments of erotic exchange are attempts to overcome the impossible distance between two persons, in which reciprocity cannot be achieved. Passion is not the attraction to a concrete and particular other, but, in the words of one commentator, it is the act of being drawn to an "absolute Other," who remains "inevitably untouchable and out of reach."[232] This is an approach that disincarnates the body from the experience of human bodies in the world. This is an argument developed by Luce Irigaray, who claims that Levinas' accounts of erotic encounters are unhinged from concrete encounters with the body. For example, on the theme of "voluptuousness," she says that Levinas reveals an intuitive lack of imaginative rigor concerning the body.[233] The body becomes an ethereal construct that serves an ethics, rather than a subject for which an ethics must work and respond to. For Levinas, sensory experience is a monumentally solitary encounter, although in the encounter with voluptuousness, in which one "caresses" the other, enjoyment is "shared" to some degree.[234] Levinas says: "A phenomenology of voluptuousness, which I am only going to touch upon here—*voluptuousness is not a pleasure like others, because it is not solitary like eating or drinking*—seems to confirm my views ... on the absence of any fusion in the erotic."[235]

Levinas denies that a fusion exists in the sexual act between two persons, even as he admits that it is unlike other pleasures. Irigaray argues:

> He knows nothing of communion in pleasure. . . . For Levinas, the distance is always maintained with the Other. . . . This autistic, solitary love does not correspond to the shared outpouring, to the loss of boundaries which takes place for both lovers when they cross the boundaries of the skin into the mucous membranes of the body, leaving the circle which encloses my solitude to meet in a shared space, a shared breath, abandoning the relatively dry and precise outlines of each body's solid exterior to enter a fluid universe where the perception of being

231. Levinas, *Time and the Other and Additional Essays*, 89.

232. Moyaert, "The Phenomenology of Eros," in Bloechl (ed.), *The Face of the Other and the Trace of God*, 41.

233. The English term "enjoyment" in translations of Levinas is used in place of the French *jouissance*, the latter of which conveys a heightened, lovely, delightful sensory experience. Levinas often uses *jouissance* when discussing the sensory experience of the erotic, rather than the typical French word for "enjoyment" or "pleasure," *plaisir*.

234. For his discussion on "touching" and especially "caressing" the Other, in which Levinas acknowledges a unique "shared" enjoyment, he insists that it remains paradoxically a "solitary" encounter. See Levinas, *Time and the Other and Additional Essays*.

235. Ibid., 89.

two persons becomes indistinct, and above all, according to another energy, neither that of the one nor that of the other but an energy produced together and as a result of the irreducible difference of sex.[236]

This heightened sensory description is one of experience, rather than a formal consequence for embodied notions of the erotic. Irigaray is seeking an adequate phenomenological description of the embodied experience of sexual pleasure. She uses the term communion and describes the world of shared space that opens up in the erotic intertwining of two bodies of opposite sexes. For her, Levinas' account is wholly inadequate, because it denies the human body the ecstasy of union with the other person. There is a kind of democracy of shared sensory pleasure she insists that is not tarnished by Levinas' concern with absolute otherness or alterity as the defining category for relationships of responsibility.

A defense of Levinas in this regard has been made by Simon Glendinning, who describes Irigaray's criticism as something of a "flight of fantasy."[237] He wants to defend Levinas' idea that the demand the other places upon the self is nonreducible to the self's own pleasure or enjoyment. He refers to the caress of the other, insisting that even in the shared touch, the other and the self remain "totally distinct, absolutely separate."[238] He defends the absolute boundaries between the flesh of the other and the self, arguing for a conception of appearance in the visage of the other that confirms the event of sexual (or any kind of sensory) pleasure but does not reduce it to that which is the same. There is a great limitation placed here on the kind of knowledge the conscious body may discover of another person. Glendinning's defense of Levinas is based on the absolute distinctiveness of each embodied other, such that difference requires a language of the disincarnate to maintain the integrity of the other. Yet this fails to articulate any opportunity for the body of the other to be met in the concrete experiences of caress and embodied enjoyment in a shared social presence. Indeed, Glendinning concedes that the limits of sensory experience outlined by Levinas are problematic, highlighting the strange *impasse* reached in Levinas: "For Levinas, the revelation of the face of the other is a revelation *beyond* sensible experience, beyond anything perceptually available in the world."[239] This places Levinas' approach in the realm of a disincarnate subjectivity.

---

236. Irigaray, "Questions for EL," in Bernasconi and Critchley (eds.), *Re-Reading Levinas*, 111.

237. Glendinning, *In the Name of Phenomenology*, 171.

238. Ibid.

239. Ibid., 174.

For Levinas, the face is beyond sensory, bodily, or incarnate experience. There remains a dissonance between the face located in temporality and the face of Levinasian otherness. Iragaray recognizes clearly the paradox that while the body remains identifiable in its supreme individuality, the erotic embrace is such that the "perception" of a couple between "two persons becomes indistinct."[240] Of the intersubjective relationship, the body is the means by which both alterity and particularity can be maintained in tension.

For theology, a central problem in this disincarnate body of Levinas' thought is that while the other is a revelation "beyond" the sensible, it evades the most basic structures of a material creation honored by its Creator with the term "good."[241] If immersion in the world is marked primarily by a responsibility for the other, there seems little space for sensory enjoyment of any kind (in the pejorative and not the Levinasian sense). The notion of absolute responsibility is of course not foreign to Christian self-understanding; the command to "love one another" carries no scriptural caveats (John 13:34). Yet the new commandment is issued from the Christ, whose incarnate and resurrected body offers the disciple not sleeplessness, death, and entrapment, but rest (Phil 4:7), life (John 10:10), and freedom (Gal 5:1).[242] Union with the divine Other is predicated upon an encounter with Christ, whose human *ousia* is intimately shared with the human subject. In Christ, the same is enfolded in difference, without reduction in each individual person. Because of this, Christ's command is made in conjunction with the offer of communion in which fulfillment of the command is not predicated on the human strength to achieve it. The disciple fulfills the command by obedience and grace which themselves are given as gifts to be received. For Levinas, there is no mediated strength or communion from which to draw the necessary resources to fulfill the absolute command.

If a defense is to be made of Levinas on this point, it could be said that his thought is not pitted against Christian theology as a system, but is written as an ethical appeal. That is to say, his ethics is not intended as an ethical system as such, but an attempt to describe phenomenologically the ethical responsibility that is already present in the face to face. As Derrida puts it, "let us not forget that Levinas does not seek to propose laws or moral rules, does not seek to determine a morality, but rather the essence of the

---

240. Bernasconi and Critchley (eds.), *Re-Reading Levinas*, 111.

241. See the "goodness" of Gen 1:31.

242. Of course, the Christian *evangel* does not promise the absence of suffering, but indicates the union of suffering with that offered upon the cross, and indicates a more fundamental peace that opens up ultimately onto the *eschaton*.

ethical relation in general."[243] Levinas' phenomenological approach is what results in a descriptive ethics, rather than a normative or practical ethics. It has been seen in chapters 1 and 2 how John Paul II uses aspects of Levinas' thinking constructively within a Christian paradigm. Nevertheless, John Paul refers to the face in Levinas as if it is always intended as an incarnate presence, when in fact, as has been shown in this chapter, this is certainly not the case. There is a constant problem in Levinas' approach in that the form and presence of the body is disincarnated from human experience. Erotic sensory experience provides a helpful example of this, because of Levinas' denial of an authentic embodied encounter with the other.

This problem in Levinas requires a corrective. One possibility is found in the work of G. J. McAleer, who proposes a renewal of Thomistic thought as a Christian corrective to Levinas' interpretation of the world as one of inherent violence and misappropriation of others; in which bodies are disincarnated from their concrete human counterparts.[244] He does recognize some common ground between Levinas and Thomas Aquinas, in that for the latter, the natural law precedes any act of personal freedom, which is echoed in Levinas' notion of the ethical call preceding "the said" from time immemorial.[245] McAleer notes Wojtyla's positive appraisal of Levinas and wishes to locate points of continuity in the former's theology of the body and the biblical personalism he reads in Levinas.[246] Essentially, McAleer finds the closest similarity between Thomas and Levinas in the way they seek out a foundational agreement between the revealed law (the Commandments) and the natural, prior to the response of human beings to either. McAleer calls this a synthesis of metaphysics and ethics at the "pre-original" level.[247] In Levinas, the face issues a command to resist murder ("Do not kill"), but for Thomas, it remains a rational norm, one that structures the natural human appetite by virtue of its participation in the eternal rational law.[248]

Moreover, there is an affective side to Thomas that McAleer also highlights. For Thomas, the wound of love is the order of nature; the concrete (embodied) person is ecstatic in its very being and its essence is "abandoned to glory."[249] That is to say, the wounds of the cross open up the order of nature to the infusion of grace, in which the natural law is both rational

---

243. Derrida, *Writing and Difference*, 138.

244. See McAleer, *Ecstatic Morality and Sexual Politics*.

245. Ibid., 70.

246. Ibid., 28.

247. Ibid., 29.

248. McAleer references st. I-II, q. 91, a. 2, in ibid.

249. Ibid., 70–71.

and theologically open. In Thomas' reading of the nature-grace relationship, it is important that Christ's wounds do not heal over but scar "as glory."[250] In other words, Christ's incarnate self-offering signifies the centrality of self-sacrifice in the space of alterity within the world. The order of being is not only the venture of conquest that Levinas reads in Western philosophy's long tradition, but also the experience of vulnerability. McAleer acknowledges this theological difference between Levinas and Thomas, but locates between them, together with John Paul II, an identification of the theological-ethical revelation of woundedness and vulnerability. He argues, "[f]or Thomas, Levinas, and John Paul II then, it is the love that wounds the lover that shows forth 'the glory of God.'"[251] In McAleer's reading of the three, a shared appreciation for the role of vulnerability confirms the body as the site for both revelation and the natural law to complement and fuse together in the moral actions of the incarnate human person.

Now, this is a positive correlation of the body's vulnerability, but it does not solve the problem of the disincarnate body in Levinas. Because his philosophy is completely broad-ranging and offers no particular circumstances in which it may be applied, it has the capacity to either engage the full breadth of human experience or to fail at the first moment of encounter with human experience. Its scale is so far-reaching it makes Levinas' project fragile. Levinas' approach to the body is not delicate and nuanced so much as dizzyingly far-reaching, at least in its rhetorical description. As has been argued in this chapter, it is not the body that Levinas formally refers to, but a disincarnate body that acts as the means by which alterity is appealed to. It is true that he cannot escape the body fully, and so the most fruitful work of interpreting Levinas is in this inner tension between his formal descriptions of the body as separate from incarnate experience and his rhetorical appeals to metaphors of bodily experience. That is to say, the body's inescapability in Levinas' thought itself speaks to the crucial role of bodies in human experience and their role in opening up human life to transcendence and an authentic ethics. It can be said therefore, that McAleer's approach goes part of the way in showing a positive role for Levinas, but only if John Paul II (and the Thomistic tradition to which he remains faithful) is included as a positive corrective.

250. Ibid., 71.
251. Ibid., 72.

Conclusion

Levinas' approach to the body is problematic. He renders the body disincarnate, despite the inescapability of the body in his thought and his rhetoric. As absolutely other as the other may be, Levinas cannot make his argument without constant reference to the enfleshed mode of being in which the other is made known to one's sensory awareness. Following this is the startling way in which Levinas—who finds his thought revolving, as it were, around the human person as an embodied event rather like the moon around the earth—has recourse to theological language concerning the body. Indeed, in furthering the analogy, one could call upon the sun as the theological resource that casts light on the earth-moon relationship. It is a reflected, imperfect light that brackets out the dogmatic content of theological language, but it is substantively theological in its meaning and direction. Levinas' phenomenological reflections about the other cannot escape the embodied nature of the human person, yet in looking for a descriptive language which does justice to the human person as an embodied event, he turns not primarily to ethical or even philosophical language per se, but to *theological* language. It has been illustrated how Levinas uses language drawn from the linguistic and textual traditions pertaining to theology in a Jewish-Christian sense. It would be naïve to put this aside uncritically. Levinas' careful rendering of theological language concerning the human person and human body is significant, for it proves an important point: that in considering the human body in its profoundly phenomenological sense—*as it speaks to us*—theology gifts an appropriate language with which to describe it. To think of the body is to think theologically. This is seen by reflecting on the role of the face. In this way, an ethics of the human body cannot be achieved without an awareness of an integral role for theological language. Having said that, it would be dishonest to impose upon Levinas' thought a Christian interpretation in an explicit sense.

Nevertheless, in subsequent chapters it will be argued that the sense of alterity present in the nuptial relationship between Christ and the church is indicative of a Christian contribution to the problem of the body. *Communio* has become the collective term referring to a retrieval of scriptural and early church emphasis upon the body of Christ as a deeply relational community, defined in part by creeds, councils, and proclamation, but given flesh in its most fundamentally eucharistic threads of giving and receiving, of gifting and of recognition of the gift. At its heart is the experience of a nuptial, asymmetrical alterity. In this light, it can be seen how the place of the body in Levinas' thought is an energetic and ambiguous account of the embodied other that is ultimately inadequate to his own objectives. Levinas' disincarnate body is finally a destabilizing presence within his thought. It is alienated from human experience of the body as well as theological accounts of the body that take the human body seriously. Levinas' recourse to theological language shapes his attempt of an account of the body based on alterity as a theological resource, even if it renders his philosophy problematic. This differs from John Paul II, but is cause now to turn to the problem of *eros* and the body in John Paul and Levinas.

4

Eros and the Desirous Body

Introduction

A PRESSING CONTEMPORARY PROBLEM is that of the relationship between *eros* and desire in the body. How does the dialogue between John Paul II and Levinas shed light on this problem? First, the problems of *eros*, desire, and sexual ethics are described in relation to the place of the body in these two theorists. Next, the sexual person will be studied as a realm of concrete problems for the body; and finally the problem of the body will be explored in light of Jean-Luc Marion's thought, who crosses the boundaries between philosophy and theology. Marion owes a significant debt to Levinas, although the former's work is fundamentally open to theology.[1] This chapter considers what is *desired* in the body and alterity, before proceeding later to the logic of the gift.

The problem of eros

John Paul II and Levinas both envisage the person as an embodied other, albeit with contradictory results. John Paul turns to the nuptial mystery as

1. For example, Jean-Luc Marion offers a phenomenological reading of the story of Emmaus, in which Christ reveals himself eucharistically to two travelling disciples. For Marion, the phenomenon reveals itself in its invisible excess, and is open to theological reflection and phenomenological interrogation. See Marion, "They Recognized Him; and He Became Invisible to Them."

a theological analogy with universal application, which follows from his theology of the body. In Levinas, a dissonance appears between his refusal of the category of incarnation in the other and his commitment to the other in his or her concrete human experience. Indeed, Levinas cannot escape the language of embodiment or theology, which for John Paul remains intimately related. While both consider the body in light of suffering (the body is a suffering body), the body is also a desiring body, and sexuality has become an important theme in contemporary and postmodern reflection. As an erotic body and as an embodied creature informed by *eros*, the human person is embedded in a conflict of various desires and motivations, encumbered by its sinful inheritance and open to new possibilities through grace. Erotic love, when reduced solely to sexuality, can be experienced negatively, for it lacks an integration with the whole body in its relationship to itself and to other persons, much of which is not laden with sexual desire. Indeed, the reduction of *eros* to sexuality results in a clouded judgment upon what is to be defined as the good, because desire is too narrowly focused. Love itself can be experienced as a kind of violence when it upholds the good against the trespass of evil.[2] Jean-Luc Marion draws attention to this problem when he says, "[n]ot lying; the face of the seducer, who does not love but makes himself love, shines indeed with a perfect sincerity: in this way he can calmly betray with a kiss."[3] Marion is commenting on the gleam of perfection that appears in erotic love, masking an involution of hopes and desires which in the end become egotistic and self-serving. There is a tension between what is hoped for and what is received.

The erotic demand is profoundly experienced in bodily terms in sexuality. It seems to "grip" the whole person, revealing an interior infinitude that cannot be mastered by finite means.[4] The desire of the lover is a complication of profound hope, sometimes to the point of obsession for the flesh of another, but never provides the satiation promised in its initial gaze. Indeed, as Marion points out, the sincerity with which the lover presents himself (or herself) can become the opportunity for betrayal, given form and flesh in the kiss. A desire for the supreme Other, the divine communion of love, might be an ultimate experience of *eros*, but it, in turn, is difficult to describe without falling into excessive mystical rhetoric. The body remains within a tension between the worldly experience of desire and a desire beyond the world. This is because the body is not only the locus of subjectivity, but as

---

2. See Gschwandtner, "Love as a Declaration of War?," in Wirzba and Benson (eds.), *Transforming Philosophy and Religion*, 185–98.

3. Marion, *The Erotic Phenomenon*, 168.

4. Desmond, *Desire, Dialectic, and Otherness*, 161.

Michel Foucault notes, the condition that makes convenient its "peculiar and irreducible spatiality" within the world.[5] That is, human subjectivity is conditional upon the experience of the body. The conflict of desires within this experience (both immediate and worldly desires as well as a desire for that which is beyond the world) is made possible by the body in its immersion in a material world. The signification of desires within the body places it in a state of knowing both the world and intuiting something beyond it, which makes social, cultural, and political commitments unstable. Foucault went further, arguing that in contemporary capitalist economies, the body lies beyond signification, existing in a freedom beyond the impositions of culture and history, only acting, rather than bearing a formal sign or signs as a participant in an endless exchange.[6] This is contested by Levinas and Wojtyla. Both of them confirm *eros* as an embodied signification open to theological possibilities. In what follows, this is dealt with as an ongoing problem for the body in relation to *eros*.

While themes relating to erotic love are found in the New Testament, the word *eros* is singularly unused. Its authors never saw it as the appropriate term to use, instead using categories such as *agape* and *philia*. These are stable, less fickle examples of love, making them more appropriate when discussing the reliable character of God's love or the constant love his commands call for in relation to others. In contrast, the ancient Greeks saw the need to discuss and debate *eros* with some vigor. Plato's *Symposium* is a classic example, in which *eros*—sensual and sexual longing—is a good that can be perfected in the person who moves from its concrete enjoyment to the beauty of perfect forms.[7] In this way, the soul is made pure as it reaches towards a transcendental experience of the good, the true and the beautiful. *Eros* originates as the Greek god of love, and continues to carry a wider meaning than simply sexual attraction, although sexual desire has become its chief reference in popular usage.[8] Amongst the postmoderns, *eros* is important once again, and for this reason, a theological approach to the term is relevant and useful. There is need to correct the assumption that a theological account seeks to limit and control passionate love, such as in the complaint of Friedrich Nietzsche:

---

5. Foucault, *The Order of Things*, 342.

6. Ibid., 195.

7. Plato, *Symposium*.

8. For a comprehensive account of the relationship between desire (especially as *eros*) and its wider political consequences in community and in the Greek polis, see: Ludwig, *Eros and Polis*.

doesn't the Church, with all her commandments and prohibitions, turn to bitterness the most precious thing in life? Doesn't she blow the whistle just when the joy which is the Creator's gift offers us a happiness which is itself a certain foretaste of the Divine?[9]

For Nietzsche, *the church poisons eros*. In his first encyclical, Benedict XVI cites Nietzsche's complaint and recognizes the need to respond.[10] Benedict contested Nietzsche by insisting that Christian accounts of *eros* rely on the notion that God gives himself passionately for the other, and that Christ redeems and restores erotic love, rather than destroys it. Before Benedict, John Paul II's study of the multifaceted nature of love in *Human Love in the Divine Plan* considers the themes of embodiment and sexual expression in light of *Humanae Vitae*.[11] Here, an indivisible connection between the procreative and unitive dimensions of sexuality is defended on the basis that there remain limits to the human "power" [*potestati*] over the body.[12] Paul VI had defended the position that sexuality was intrinsically related to procreation within a horizon of sexual limitations concretized in marriage. This complements John Paul's approach, whose argument in texts such as *Love and Responsibility* sought to explain the "no" of *Humanae Vitae*; and in his "theology of the body" articulates the church's "yes" to the body.[13] In the nuptial perspective, *communio* is an expression of human alterity that is theological (*given* by God) and phenomenological (it is *descriptive* of the concrete possibilities of human community). In this context, desire is complicated by concupiscence and requires the work of grace to reach beyond immediate satisfactions and long only for God. For Levinas, desire must be distinguished from need. This makes possible his description of transcendence, which is experienced as an outward directionality originating in the other. Levinas' notion of metaphysical desire is therefore directly relevant.

---

9. Nietzsche, *Beyond Good and Evil*, 168.

10. Benedict XVI, *Deus Caritas Est*, 3.

11. *Humanae Vitae* provides a magisterial teaching context, but John Paul II draws attention to Paul VI's appeal to Christ's "integral vision of man," which can be formed by going back to "the beginning" in the anthropology of Genesis. Again, John Paul II does not depart from the encyclical and chooses to reframe the problem in personalist terms. See John Paul II, *Man and Woman He Created Them*, 23:3.

12. Paul VI, *Humanae Vitae, on the Regulation of Birth*, 17.

13. John Paul II bases his discussion of the dignity of sexuality, marriage, and the family in the words of Christ to the Pharisees, constituting a christological foundation for a theological account of human dignity, against utilitarian temptations. John Paul II, *Man and Woman He Created Them*, 59:5–7.

Levinas, eros, and "metaphysical desire"

As chapter 3 showed, Levinas developed a notion of desire he described as metaphysical. "Metaphysical desire" is a longing for the other that can be described erotically, but is bound to a notion of responsibility in the field of alterity. In fact, Levinas regards metaphysics "as Desire."[14] Metaphysics is a movement outside of the self, recognizing that being produces itself as "goodness and as beyond happiness," and as being for the other.[15] The correspondence of desire with metaphysics implies the need to think outside the body's immediate context. True desire is not directed to that which can be obtained; that which may be grasped in a concrete moment. Rather, its object is the nonobjective presence of the other within the directionality of transcendence. Metaphysical desire is therefore a passage to transcendence. It is the means of remaining connected to that which is otherwise and to the "transcendent proper."[16] This account of metaphysical desire is therefore reliant on there being some kind of transcendence to reach; some object to look towards. Levinas is sensitive to the notion that his conception of desire as metaphysics is too optimistic; too much like a "romantic dream."[17] To this temptation, he insists that desire is a reality that imposes itself upon human beings and in which they may choose to live. To grasp this, it is necessary to recognize that it is in the relationship with the other that desire is awakened. In this sense, desire is nonsatiable and always other-directed. There is no objective moment in which a description of satisfaction can be proffered and no point at which the other is reached. Rather, desire is an activity situated beyond either satisfaction or nonsatisfaction, in which one hungers for the sake of the other, desirous of the other's well-being and contentment.[18] Levinas prefers a descriptive and poetic phraseology, but there are times when the sheer demand of the other alters his writing to a more prescriptive style. On the question of desire, his work is both prescriptive and descriptive for it is based on that desire which is already felt. It is an unmet desire, in which "no voluptuosity comes to fulfill, nor close, nor put to sleep," yet which is accomplished in the act of responding to the other's "absolute" alterity.[19]

This brings discussion to the limits of the body. For Levinas, the body finds its meaning and signification in the other. The body cannot reach

---

14. Levinas, *Totality and Infinity*, 304.
15. Ibid., 304.
16. Dalton, *Longing for the Other*, 137.
17. Levinas, *Totality and Infinity*, 179.
18. Ibid., 179.
19. Ibid., 33.

satiation either in enjoyment of itself or in any other body. Rather, it must desire without satisfaction in the ethical response to otherness. Alterity bequeaths the self to the self. While the body acts as that condition in which the person receives alterity and offers itself in return, it constantly grounds itself by a limitation in what it thinks it desires. At its basest, the body desires the meeting of its hunger and its thirst. Yet for Levinas, it deludes itself in thinking that basic consumption, let alone the higher acts of "caress" and "liturgy" can ever be met in the visible world.[20] Rather, metaphysics is a call to nobility, aware of the immediacy of human misery and therefore acting not out of care for the particularities of the other, but of the embodied presence of the other who must be received in absolute alterity. The body acts as a means by which the metaphysical enterprise can set sail, both reaching positively towards the good of the other as well as resisting stubbornly the descent to what Levinas calls wickedness and animality.[21] So, desire is not only made possible and enacted in the response to the other's absolute alterity, but in turn makes desire itself absolute.[22] In desiring the other in this ethical dimension, metaphysics leads to the transcendence offered in the other. This account of desire marks the limits of the body, which has an absolute vocation and an absolute limit. Its vocation is to and for the other, while its limits are found in the shallow hopes it offers itself. The face to face demands the body to act, even though it will never find satisfaction in the drama of metaphysical desire. No, metaphysical desire "arouses rather than satisfies."[23] This is an ethical arousal for the other, a wakefulness to alterity that brings with it a need.

Of course, the body has its natural appetites, some of which are desires and some of which are needs. Levinas' notion of desire is predicated on a distinction between desire and need. Desire, as can be seen above, is an outward movement to obtain something as an addendum to the self. Levinas understands alterity to interrupt its limited scope and extend it as an ethical desire for the other. However, need is an altogether different category, for it invokes the experience of needfulness within the body; need is an incarnate longing for satisfaction. Whereas desire is in excess of need, need results from the experience of a hollowness to be filled, a *"less"* that requires satisfaction.[24] As will be explored further in the next chapter, need follows desire because time itself is presupposed by need. That is to say, need is given to the

---

20. Ibid., 35.
21. Ibid.
22. Ibid., 34.
23. Ibid., 50.
24. Ibid., 116.

body as an appetite, which can only be met by the body's labor in time.[25] In feeling hungry, one's body tends towards a future tense in which one must labor for the production of food so that a hunger is met. Appetites are never met immediately but require time and labor to find their limited satiation. The bodily experience of "metaphysical desire" is a fundamentally outward movement of the human person that presupposes both time and need. In need and desire, the future is offered: "in need I can sink my teeth into the real and satisfy myself in assimilating the other; in Desire there is no sinking one's teeth into being, no satiety, but an uncharted future before me."[26]

The body is directed towards the future in a dimension of moral height, but the requirement to reflect on need and desire remains. In fact, when desires, loves, and needs seem to provide satisfaction, they are deceptive: this is so because they are not pure and can only "resemble" metaphysical desire.[27] There remains a gulf between need and desire. Parallels can be drawn between metaphysical desire and the theological notion of desiring God, especially in an apophatic sense.[28] This becomes problematic in *eros*.

In erotic desire, Levinas' idea of the limitations of the body is transgressed. The problem of interpreting Levinas' account of *eros* is well documented, and difficulties have been raised by feminist readers in particular.[29] In *Totality and Infinity*, Levinas describes the feminine in terms of a radical alterity, the "Loved" who is the "Beloved."[30] She holds forth a regime of tenderness, manifesting itself as an "extreme fragility, a vulnerability," an "ultramateriality" that is exorbitantly present in its embodied alterity.[31] The relation to this alterity remains embodied, but it seeks after what it cannot locate, an object that remains less than nothing and an excess of presence without signification. Levinas places great emphasis here on the erotic touch—the "caress"—that anticipates that which will not be grasped or seen.[32]

The caress is certainly sensed in the body, but in the act it seems to lose itself, displaced between being and not-yet-being. Levinas writes, "[i]n the

25. Ibid., 117.

26. Ibid.

27. Ibid., 34.

28. This is considered in Kosky, *Levinas and the Philosophy of Religion*, 180–81.

29. See, for example, Chanter, *Feminist Interpretations of Emmanuel Levinas*; Katz, *Levinas, Judaism, and the Feminine*; Bell, "On Ethics and Feminism." Also see an excellent summary in Sandford, "Levinas, Feminism and the Feminine," in Critchley and Bernasconi (eds.), *The Cambridge Companion to Levinas*.

30. Levinas, *Totality and Infinity*, 256.

31. Ibid.

32. Ibid., 258.

carnal given to tenderness, the body quits the status of an existent."[33] The
body is transgressed here in the feminine, through which the other and the
self lose their place in being, and move beyond being. In this "voluptuosity,"
it never obtains what it seeks, but remains constantly in the directionality of
desire.[34] In this sense, the experience of the other's body can become ideal-
ized, evading all description. In the words of one commentator, the "Other"
becomes "almost supernatural, supersensible."[35] This is shown by Paul Moyaert to be an experience in which both mutuality and complementarity are
impossible.[36] The erotic experience of another's body both transcends and
interrupts one's typical intentionality towards him or her, and is insatiable,
even as the caress or the touch occurs. As an experience beyond conceptualization, Levinas is unclear as to whether erotic desire is always metaphysical
desire. To what extent does this experience (which he also describes as "pure
experience") depend on the intentionality of the participants?[37] Furthermore, how is it that he can say of femininity that an alterity from beyond the
face comes into one's presence, when the face itself was the epiphany of the
other? In *eros*, it would seem Levinas is at his most poetic, reveling in the
play on words in which voluptuosity is "not a sentiment to the second power
like a reflection, but direct like a spontaneous consciousness."[38]

The incarnate male-female experience of being a sexed body in relation to another is left within a poetic thrill with little orientation towards its
ethical application. Sexual difference remains an assumed and unresolved
feature of Levinas' thought, which results in a question as to whether the
"I" and the other are to be considered sexed or not.[39] In other words, does it
matter to his project that the self or the other might be a man or a woman
with particular sexual desire? Elsewhere, femininity becomes the means by
which radical alterity is made possible, further complicating the notion of
embodied alterity. What remains is the excess of otherness brought by the
other, in which Levinasian language is indebted to a masculine-feminine
distinction, even while its concrete application remains ambiguous. For example, Levinas refers to the maternal body in metaphorical terms to indicate
that which is most intimate, sensible, and proximate to the self, informing

33. Ibid.

34. Ibid., 259.

35. Moyaert, "The Phenomenology of Eros," in Bloechl (ed.), *The Face of the Other
and the Trace of God*, 32.

36. Ibid., 37.

37. Levinas, *Totality and Infinity*, 260.

38. Ibid., 265.

39. Katz, *Levinas, Judaism, and the Feminine*, 75–76.

the self about the "palpable quiddity of things."[40] Yet the metaphorical appeal to maternity, a feminine characteristic, thematizes the body in a masculine-feminine dialogue of embodied difference. This is an appeal for the feminine in ethics.[41] Despite Levinas' wider project, this approach results in an alterity that is not truly absolute, but particular. It has been described as the "sensible transcendent" in Levinas, problematizing the distinction between metaphor and sense, always seeking to enact the ethics he describes.[42]

Erotic experience is described phenomenologically in Levinas, but leaves itself open to conflicting interpretations. *Eros* and erotic desire are equally central to John Paul II's project, as was seen in chapter 2, most acutely in his use of sexually differentiated language. Also for John Paul, the desiring body is embedded in a conflict of desires, requiring a theological interpretation.

John Paul II, eros, and sexual ethics

Eros, for John Paul II, is a form of love open to redemption. This is a theological commitment, but it deeply influenced his later studies of the human person, of human dignity, and his reflections on sexuality. For the younger Wojtyla, sexual ethics is as much about the morality of acts as it is about the fullness of individuals as persons; in fact, his thought precludes the notion of reducing one to the other, or of too strongly emphasizing one over the other. Furthermore, it concerns the interior dimension of the human person. The interior life is bound up with its embodied experience of the world, but it is a mystery that can only be partially described, because it is also situated within Wojtyla's christological focus. According to John's gospel, Christ held back from entrusting himself to others early in his ministry, "for he himself knew what was in man" (John 2:25). In this sense, only the divine *Logos* knows the full complexity of interior human life and this places Wojtyla's philosophy in a humble position in relation to his theology. The revelation of meaning concerning human interiority (which of course includes the properties of sexuality) is a difficult process to describe, but for Wojtyla it is possible through an activity of reciprocal love with the same *Logos* who "knew what was in man," which has both a mystical and a worldly dimension. Michael Waldstein has highlighted the importance of St. John of

---

40. Levinas, *Otherwise Than Being*, 76.

41. For some time there has been debate between feminist scholars as to whether there is indeed a "feminine" which can be of use to postmodern ethics. See a developed argument in Benhabib, *Situating the Self*, 203–41.

42. Bevis, "'Better Than Metaphors'?," 319.

the Cross for Wojtyla's analysis of the reciprocal relationship. For example, the following words of John's poem *The Living Flame of Love* are indicative of the mystical-wordly relationship:

> O lamps of fire!
> in whose splendors
> the deep caverns of feeling,
> once obscure and blind,
> now give forth, so rarely, so exquisitely,
> both warmth and light to their Beloved.[43]

St. John of the Cross speaks of the warm intimacy of the other, in whom obscurity and blindness is overcome. The interior life, described poetically and interpreted by Wojtyla, is not an isolated phenomenon. It may be experienced in a kind of solitude, but fundamental knowledge of its nature is known in the relational structure of reciprocity with the divine persons, primarily through the figure of Christ. In his doctoral thesis, Wojtyla had concluded that the union of the soul with God was a consummation of the self with the Trinity, one that begins in the first caverns of the "intellect."[44] Indeed, the final consummation between the human person and God results in the soul becoming "God by participation," possessing the divine life itself.[45] The mystic's description of the progression from feeling as "once obscure and blind" gives way to a spousal reciprocity, in which both "warmth and light" are given to "their Beloved."[46] This is the problem of divine *eros* and its mystical application to human *eros*. That is to say, divine *eros* is indeed a spousal experience, but the language is bound to human nuptiality. The experience of human *eros*, of a desirous longing for another *particular* person in the flesh, is the most fruitful point of departure in the search for a language that can describe the experience of divine *eros*, in which a love for the divine other is the focal point of human longing.

The caverns of John of the Cross contrast with the famous allegory of Plato's cave in the progression from darkness to enlightenment. For Plato, the self must exit the darkness of the cave and receive the direct light of knowledge; for John of the Cross and Wojtyla, the self must move deeper into the "deep caverns of feeling" and draw closer to the divine Other, even in darkness.[47] In doing so, the self finds the lamps of fire which are of the most intimate knowledge, for they do not result in a hierarchy of obligation

43. John of the Cross, *John of the Cross: Selected Writings*, 705–6.

44. John Paul II, *Faith according to St. John of the Cross*, 230–33.

45. Ibid., 230.

46. John of the Cross, *John of the Cross: Selected Writings*, 706.

47. See book 7, Plato, *The Republic*.

and order (such as in Plato, for whom the self must return as the philosopher to govern and free the other slaves in the cave), but of perfect humility
in the face-to-face reciprocity of divine bridegroom to faithful bride. Plato's
light remains outside the cave, requiring a distance from the body and its essence for fear of catching alight; the fire is "distant," "behind," and "above."[48]
Even having witnessed the sun, the figure who returns to the cave risks being "swamped" by the darkness.[49] In John of the Cross, the exterior light
becomes an interior illumination, thus lighting up not only the cave but its
"deep caverns," even extending to a knowledge of "feelings."[50] For him, it is
the relationship with the other, known primarily through the act of faith,
in which the light and warmth of personal knowing becomes "exquisite."[51]
The contrast between John of the Cross and Plato helps to clarify Wojtyla's
attempt to include the subjective experiences of affectivity and of reciprocal
attention in his account of erotic love. For him, the mystical and the ethical
are bound to one another in the body.

The mystical ascent to God is also an ethical descent to the realm of the
other. Wojtyla's sexual ethics is informed by a theological meaning behind
all social relationships, by which phenomenology informs the theological
image of *communio*. In this way, John Paul II is the first of the popes to
develop a sexual ethic that is phenomenologically informed, as well as taking seriously the questions of embodied identity in later developments in
modern and postmodern thought.[52] He observes the deep relationship between any discussion of sexuality and the category of nature and the need to
explain both. He describes two subjects present in the problem of Catholic
sexual ethics, "nature" and "person," which "continually intersect, somehow
overlap, and mutually condition one another . . . ."[53] These two subjects present themselves, not as two kinds of stable essences, but as concrete realities
that are open to development. Sexuality is a property of the human person,

48. Ibid., 220.

49. Ibid., 222.

50. John of the Cross, *John of the Cross: Selected Writings*, 705–6.

51. Ibid., 705.

52. Primarily, this is evidenced in *Love and Responsibility*. For example, Wojtyla
explicitly states that the sexual gratification of orgasm is to be reached "harmoniously"
in both married parties and not in the male alone. He does not privilege either the
husband or wife over the other, but acknowledges an entirely different order of sexual
experience in each, which can be overcome by mutual self-giving. Historically, the
realm of female sexual pleasure as a sphere of divinely ordered gifts is not one usually
spoken of publicly by popes or popes-to-be. See John Paul II, *Love and Responsibility*,
272. This book began as a series of lectures given in the University of Lublin in 1958–59,
largely inspired by questions asked in pastoral encounters with students.

53. John Paul II, *Person and Community*, 284.

who at all times remains the *suppositum* of human nature. The reality of human nature here is that it is not simply present *in* an individual human person, but is always present *as* an individual human person. In terms of sexual identity, nature (and specifically human nature) can be understood not as a form or structure that acts of its own accord, but as present in the act of the *suppositum* (the person).[54] In the human person, sexual identity is known primarily through action. Because the human *suppositum* is the bearer of flesh, it implicitly points to a possible *telos* such as that found in the animal world (biological regeneration, for instance), but also towards an ethical *telos*, revelatory of human meaning. In this sense, sexuality is a presence already found within the human structure, but is also present as an opportunity through which human identity may be expressed.

Early on, Wojtyla had posited fundamental questions about the role of "moral theology" in considering sexual ethics.[55] He defines moral theology thus: "Moral theology is a science that, in the light of revelation, makes justified statements concerning the moral value, or goodness and badness, of human actions."[56] This description of moral theology places the emphasis upon actions in the light of revealed religion. It views moral theology as scientific in the sense that it must measure accurately the moral value of specific actions in their performance and meaning.[57] Furthermore, it is related strictly to revelation. Wojtyla is concerned to avoid a nonexperiential approach to morality, while at the same time viewing sexual ethics as a science of justification based upon a universally revealed morality.[58] He holds strongly the notion that moral theologians must creatively explain the church's teaching on sexual (to name but one category among many) matters, but seek to do so with due regard to the actualities of human experience. Human experience, in the case of sexual ethics, consists primarily of matters concerning relations between persons (though he acknowledges the smaller portion that deals with persons as individuals) and, most representative in human communities, of actions "connected with the relation—

54. Ibid., 285.

55. Wojtyla expresses his concern that the branch of science known as "Catholic sexual ethics" appears to transfer the property of the object to the subject. He clarifies that it is not ethics that is necessarily sexual but rather the material object of which this ethical reflection is directed. As such, it would be more accurate to use the term "the ethics of sexual life" or "the ethics of sexual issues." He is happy to tolerate the usage of this term as long as it is understood that the object of our study is sexuality as a problematic in the context of human actions. See John Paul II, *Person and Community*, 282.

56. Ibid., 279.

57. Ibid., 280.

58. Ibid., 281.

mutually oriented—between persons of the opposite sex, between a man and a woman."[59]

In approaching the male-female relationship under the category of sexual ethics, an obvious question arises which Wojtyla acknowledges. That is whether, according to a genuine Christian sexual ethics, only actions explicitly connected with sexual intercourse, including all that leads up to and results from it, fall within the remit, or whether the material object of such a branch of ethics is "simply the relation between persons of the opposite sex, with particular attention to the sexual relation."[60] Wojtyla answers this in favor of the second option, against the general consensus of many of his colleagues in the period immediately prior to the Second Vatican Council. This contextualization of all sexual ethics is crucial to what unfolds in his later work (especially his "theology of the body"), which bears a personalist instinct. His approach privileges the relationship (without diminishing the moral power of the actions in and of themselves), as he says, "according to which we focus primarily on the relation between persons of the opposite sex and view the sexual relation in the context of the former, the interpersonal relation."[61] By focusing his moral gaze upon the relationship itself, Wojtyla shapes his further consideration of specific actions in the context of the *sexual* relationship, foreshadowing his later development of sexual ethics in *Love and Responsibility*. This book first appeared in print as *Milosc I Odpowiedzialnosc* in 1960. In its original form (as university lectures in Lublin), it was written approximately a decade before the publication of *Humanae Vitae* (Paul VI, 25th July 1968).[62] As observed in the 1981 introduction, its date places it well before the highly charged atmosphere of "animosity, of polemic and counter-polemic," which took hold after Paul VI's pronouncement against artificial birth control.[63]

In *Love and Responsibility*, Wojtyla argues for a sexual ethic that derives from a just application of the "personalistic norm."[64] At the heart of this text is a personalistic outline of sexual ethics which Wojtyla deems strong enough to contradict a utilitarian sexual ethic, the model he views as the great cultural challenge in the realm of sexual morality. As chapter 2 argued,

59. Ibid., 282.

60. Ibid.

61. Ibid.

62. Paul VI, *Humanae Vitae, on the Regulation of Birth*.

63. John Paul II, *Love and Responsibility*, 12.

64. What Wojtyla means by the "personalistic norm" is described in chapter 2, but can be summarized as the normative principle that confirms that a person is not an object of utility and is most adequately treated when acknowledged as an object of love. It makes possible the commandment to love.

sexuality in the human person is that aspect of embodiment that reveals the self's dependence on the embodied other, not just as an object of the self's desire, but as the meeting of an authentic communion of two bodies. In Wojtyla, *eros* is an opportunity for *communio*. Debates about sexual ethics are broader than simply a conflict between Wojtyla's application of moral norms and utilitarianism, and an account of the realm of competing sexual ethics requires attention.

The problem of sexuality and the body

Having outlined the two approaches of Levinas and John Paul II to *eros* and themes relating to sexuality, the problem of the body may now be treated in the context of competing sexual ethics. While Levinas is concerned to describe the erotic embrace within a phenomenological framework, along with fecundity and what he calls voluptuosity, John Paul views it within the wider dimension of his theology of the body. Broader debates signify the contested nature of the place of the body in regards to sexual ethics and how these matters remain largely unresolved. It is important to gain some perspective on this broader context to show how the dialogue between Wojtyla and John Paul helps to answer some of these problems.

The body, sexuality, and invisible realities

Sexuality, as a property of human being, may also denote the characteristics of other sexual beings as they are observed; procreation, for example. But for human persons there is a *telos* that exceeds even this natural good. A theological reality can be witnessed in the economics of desire that pervades interbodily relationship/s. There is, in each experience of sexual desire, a *longing* for that which lies outside of the self. To be sure, there is desire that may long for control, for the exercise of power, or for satiation. This is possible in all sexual relationships and acts. However, in terms of an economy of desire that transcends the most immediate and obvious experiences of sexuality, human personhood hides longings that are simply not fulfilled in any kind of entirety, at least not in terms of an enfleshed joy or ecstasy. They are not obvious and can fall within the realm of the theological. For example, Martin Heidegger speaks of those nonappearing truths whose invisibility makes possible knowledge of their existence. In *Being and Time*, he writes: "Appearance, as the appearance of 'something,' thus precisely does not mean that something shows itself; rather, it means that something makes itself known which does not show itself. . . . Appearance is a not showing itself."[65]

For Heidegger, the nonappearance or the "not showing itself" gives itself to consciousness as a reality beyond immediate intentionality. Jean-Luc Marion takes up this theme in the notion of "excess."[66] An example is that of illness, in which there are invisible realities that point to a lack of health and the presence of inhibiting factors to one's well-being. The body experiences pain and the inhibition of its typical ease and movement, thus producing indications of an invisible presence. Without rejecting the idea of essential realities in human persons that remain irreducible (for example, male and female and the need to explicate what this means), there is in the complex economy of desire a series of alterations that the ensouled body experiences, finding itself caught up in a "web" of multiple "dimensions" and "signifiers."[67] These signifiers, when considered in light of desire, are of the moral order and not only of material or biological orders. The body is caught in a dynamic fluidity, fleeting between false idols and icons of true, divinely gifted desire. Indeed, this fluidity between what is expressed in the body and the directionality towards multiple meanings (desire or being desired, various emotions, memories, interplays of power, and so forth) is a major point of departure between Husserl and Derrida.[68] Husserl had identified the difference between expression (*Ausdruck*) and indication (*Anzeichen*).[69] The first concerns the meanings that are attached to any sign that is given in expression; the latter refers to the onward indications that are given in that expression. For example, a smile might express the occasion of a pleasing memory (its *Ausdruck*), but be directed towards a friend with whom that memory is shared (its *Anzeichen*). This indicates a shared hope for similar experiences in the future. Husserl concluded that in phenomenology, indication has no part to play, for it lies outside the field of objective experience, whereas for Derrida, it constitutes a major feature of his deconstructive project.[70] In terms of the body, the concrete presence of the flesh refuses Derrida's refusal: its presence signifies its dependence on the other (see Wojtyla's account of alterity and the nuptial mystery), while its experience—its givenness in expression—does indeed remain subject

65. Heidegger, *Being and Time*, 74.

66. See Marion, *In Excess*.

67. Derrida, *Of Grammatology*, 45.

68. For Derrida's extended treatment of language in Husserl, and Derrida's departure from it, see Derrida, *Speech and Phenomena, and Other Essays on Husserl's Theory of Signs*.

69. See the First and the Fourth Investigations: Husserl, *Logical Investigations*.

70. Mulligan, "How Not to Read," 202.

to conflicting interpretation. In the body, Husserl's disallowance of indication and Derrida's refusal of signification are made problematic. The sexual meaning of the body may be experienced as an unstable reality, but it remains significant for its continued integration within the whole embodied narrative of each human person.

Heidegger is right to emphasize the self-expressive quality of this appearance, but in terms of the ecclesial experience of God's Trinitarian life, there is a momentous and subtle givenness in the economy of desire that calls to be honored with the reflection of God's self-giving of the divine persons. In invoking the triune icon of love, there is the need to both contextualize sexuality and avoid its reduction to an over-emphasized individualization. That is to say, sexuality must not be seen simply as self-expressive or such a powerful property of being that it overshadows other human possibilities. Neither can realities be ignored in which sexuality directs intentionality, even if sexuality does not meet the need or the desire of the body.

Spheres of indwelling: Sexuality and spirituality

Sexual ethics is caught in a web of perspectives, bias, and emphases.[71] This is no less true of theologians than others. That human sexuality is a territory of theological debate ought not be surprising given the wider changes in sexual understanding and knowledge that have taken place over a few generations.[72] Nevertheless, debate and discussion do not lead naturally to clarity of sexuality or of human personhood, let alone of the theological ramifications of these realities.

Sexuality does not constitute the person in its entirety. Nevertheless, it remains a property of personal being whose complexity is open to misunderstanding and intense emotional investment. From a Christian perspective, it can be difficult to mark the line clearly between the sexual descriptions of *eros*, passion, longing, and fulfillment with the same descriptive categories in the spiritual realm. A notable artistic example of this is Gian Bernini's famous statue, *The Ecstasy of St. Teresa* (1652), in the Cornaro Chapel, Santa Maria della Vittoria, in Rome. Teresa's bodily pose, as much as the sheer delight upon her face, are difficult to interpret outside of the language of sexual embrace. In fact, the poetic descriptions of the divine embrace, mystically

---

71. See for example Stuart and Thatcher, *Christian Perspectives on Sexuality and Gender.*

72. For a critical philosophical study of the shifts in Western approaches to sexuality and reason, see West, *Reason and Sexuality in Western Thought.*

experienced by Teresa, do not make the image any less sexualized. In her autobiography, St. Teresa writes:

> I saw in his hand a long spear of gold, and at the iron's point there seemed to be a little fire. He appeared to me to be thrusting it at times into my heart, and to pierce my very entrails; when he drew it out, he seemed to draw them out also, and to leave me all on fire with a great love of God. The pain was so great, that it made me moan; and yet so surpassing was the sweetness of this excessive pain, that I could not wish to be rid of it. The soul is satisfied now with nothing less than God. The pain is not bodily, but spiritual; though the body has its share in it.[73]

This passage is visceral with an interplay of love, sexuality, violence, spirituality, and the body. It is not used to argue that spiritual experience should be construed in obliquely sexual terms (or indeed violent ones). But it does illustrate that in explaining or depicting spiritual experience (in this case mystical ecstasy), the social imagination deploys imagery that can also be construed as sexual. The interpenetration of images both sexual and spiritual is an ongoing problem for the body, which finds itself living a plethora of embodied knowledge.[74] On the one hand, the body experiences something concrete in the dual spiritual-embodied state—intellectual, emotional, perhaps even ritually and in memory—yet paradoxically the embodied person bears no simple answer to the meaning of this experience.[75] The acutely felt sensations of sexual and spiritual experience appear

73. Chapter XXIX, part 13, Lewis, *The Life of S. Teresa of Jesus, of the Order of Our Lady of Carmel.*

74. This approach to the problem of the human person, seemingly existent between multiple spheres, owes much to Graham Ward's concept of theology's relationship with its cultural-historical context/s, although, in what follows, Ward's understanding of the complexity of the space in which theology speaks is pushed further. For him: "Theology has no ability to transcend its historical embeddedness." Theology's means, methods, and materials are composed "from what is available" in its temporal-spatial setting, but finds impetus and vocation in Revelation. Any authoritative form taken by a particular theology is not disembodied but must be "mapped" onto other bodies, whether physical, gendered, social, institutional, sacramental, etc. But as it does so, it finds itself coexistent with other discourses, much of which (but not all) it will offer as a critique from its distinctive relationship to "the cross, the Trinity, the Spirit, incarnation, salvation and the Church." But theology also speaks to experience, which includes the realm of the spiritual, and so the interrelation of various spheres of knowing becomes evident. Theology bears a distinctive identity which cannot be colonized in any entirety, yet is able to identify, critique, and correct the relationship of those spheres, as they each are mapped onto, and experienced, by the embodied human person. See Ward, "Theology in a Culture of Seduction" in Hannaford and Jobling (eds.), *Theology and the Body*, 48.

75. Experiential problems of the body are related to ongoing scholarly debate across

as interpenetrative spheres. Although the human person remains a subject who exists in these spheres (but is not limited to them), it is no simple task to locate the lines of demarcation between them, or provide an account of the theological meaning of the relationship. This chapter treats the body as experiencing a perplexing state of anxiety in the occupation of these multiple spheres of human living, which is the space of embodied existence. So what is the sexual body and how is it experienced?

Jean-Yves Lacoste, in beginning his anthropological study, *Experience and the Absolute*, writes:

> No experience of the self can bracket the body, and thus bracket the relations of proximity to which the body binds us; the experience of the self is the experience of place as much as of time. Interiority can certainly be transformed by an anchoretic desire; it can wish to erase from itself all that is not conscious. But this desire is irrational. My body is thus inescapable for me: both as a condition of consciousness and as perpetually present to consciousness.[76]

Lacoste views the body as the condition for consciousness, both making the self present while being present to consciousness. Sexuality is a characteristic of the body's experience in this consciousness. The human person is a sexual person, whose bodily desires are generally outward, directed towards the embodied event of an other (or others). Wojtyla calls it an "urge" in which a measure of both determinacy and necessity are apparent (the human species embodies the urge to procreate).[77] This outward movement occurs in a broader intersubjective context, one of motivation and exchange. The sexual person experiences its bodily attraction in an economy of desire, participating in a cultural context alongside other sexual persons.[78] Such an economy is complex, but not closed to theological reflection. This is made clear from discussion about sexuality in the public square. For example, Sarah Coakley has observed that sexuality is experienced in the contemporary cultural climate in the form of crisis.[79] While she notes significant mass

---

disciplines about the mind-body-spirit structure. A uniquely christological response, under the influence of Karl Barth, is offered in Cortez, *Embodied Souls, Ensouled Bodies*.

76. Lacoste, *Experience and the Absolute*, 8.

77. John Paul II, *Love and Responsibility*, 51.

78. See the various cultural contexts considered in Salzman and Lawler, *The Sexual Person*.

79. Coakley, "Rethinking the Sex Crises in Catholicism and Anglicanism," *ABC Religion and Ethics* (2010), http://www.abc.net.au/religion/articles/2010/07/14/2953473.htm.

media attention to two sexually related issues, those of sexual abuse in the Roman Catholic Church and homosexuality in the Anglican Communion respectively, Coakley posits that these are aspects of a wider cultural predicament. While this predicament concerns the moral status of particular sexual acts, the fundamental problem is one of "erotic faithfulness."[80]

To explain this, Coakley refers to three cultural contradictions.[81] The first is a deeply held, widely assumed view that a lived life of celibacy is *impossible*.[82] It is derided as churlish to assume it and unrealistic to expect it. Yet the contradiction occurs when some choices *against* sexual activity are made, most notably that of sexual activity between an adult and a minor. If celibacy can be required and expected of this relationship, in which serious differences of maturity, age, legal responsibility, and power are at play, why not of those whose sexual attraction falls within the gambit of mature, informed adults? The second cultural contradiction Coakley describes is the wildly exaggerated differences between heterosexual and homosexual relationships.[83] It is assumed that the traditional form of heterosexual commitment—marriage—is no longer a sustainably permanent option, while homosexual relationship commitments, when condoned, are most positively affirmed when they live up to some standard of permanence. The third cultural contradiction Coakley identifies is the assumption that celibacy and marriage are opposing forms of sexual commitment.[84] There is an ill-defined notion that celibately lived lives are ones of unnecessary, archaic resistance to a natural good and that married lives are awash with as much, or as little, sexual activity as two reasonable adults would like. Coakley makes the point that this does not bear out in concrete experience. It is, as she puts it, "a perplexing cultural fantasy that does not stand up to scrutiny."[85] Relying on the work of Richard Sipe, Coakley further observes that contrary to a widespread cultural contradiction, celibate persons and married persons are acutely aware of their sexual identity and pattern of life in heightened,

---

80. Coakley quotes the public commentator David Brooks who outlines a popularist conservative defence of homosexual marriage to help curtail what he calls a problem of "moral commitment" in any kind of social and sexual fidelity. See ibid.

81. Although she does not here define what (or which) culture she means, Coakley's comments seem to apply chiefly to the Anglo-American cultural *milieu*, in which Anglican/Catholic comparisons are most common and in which her prime examples originate.

82. Coakley, "Rethinking the Sex Crises in Catholicism and Anglicanism."

83. Ibid.

84. Ibid.

85. Ibid.

but different, ways, requiring from observers a more nuanced approach to personal experience in both categories.[86] As Coakley argues:

> Not only does faithful (or what Sipe calls "achieved") celibacy generally involve a greater consciousness of sexual desire and its frustration than a life lived with regular sexual satisfaction. But married sexuality, on the other hand, is rarely as care-free and mutually satisfied as this third "cultural contradiction" might presume. Indeed a realistic reflection on long and faithful marriages (now almost in the minority) will surely reveal periods of enforced "celibacy" even within marriages: during periods of delicate pregnancy, parturition, illness, physical separation, or impotence, which are simply the lot of the marital "long haul."[87]

This understanding of both celibate and married lives shows a greater awareness of the reality that sexual identity and its experience is subject to change and different levels of maturity and reflection. Furthermore, such a disparity between actual human experience in the realm of sexual identity and certain cultural assumptions can be challenged by situating sexuality within a concrete social context, one governed by an economy of desire. This economy of desire, in which sexuality participates but is not driven chiefly by sexual identity, locates sexuality as one property of a wider social exchange of meaning.[88] The concrete experience of persons involved under the various categories of sexual identity is central to understanding this economy, for chiefly it is an exchange of *difference* between persons.

This difference is premised on different degrees of desire. Graham Ward has observed the economic dimension of the operation of desire, especially of *eros*, and situates it theologically.[89] Specifically, Ward calls upon the doctrine of *creator Spiritus* in speaking to the social (re)production, promotion, and consummation of desire in contemporary materialistic cultures, which he deems central to embodied cultural experiences.[90] Ward provocatively describes the material found in those local economies of confected sexual desire, the "Private Shop," which, for all its convoluted promise of immediate, prolonged, or complete satiation, "can neither maintain nor

86. Sipe, *Celibacy in Crisis*.

87. Coakley, "Rethinking the Sex Crises in Catholicism and Anglicanism."

88. Ward refers to this economy chiefly as a "culture of seduction." Ward, "Theology in a Culture of Seduction," in Hannaford and Jobling (eds.), *Theology and the Body*, 49.

89. Ward owes parts of his analysis to the sociologist Zygmunt Bauman. See Ward, ibid.

90. Ibid., 49.

fulfil what it appears to promise."[91] The promise of satisfaction mirrors, if more explicitly, a promise offered in the wider culture of the fulfillment of what is hoped for, even if that which is hoped for is manufactured. Its fulfillment echoes the event of revelation, of an embodied rising, of new life, of ecstatic satiation which overflows into a joy which is beyond words. Ward quotes the French sociologist Jean Baudrillard who says that pornography is "directly descended from a metaphysics that supposes the phantasy of a hidden truth and its revelation."[92] But the promise made in the signs and products of the "Private Shop" betray what they hope to overcome: the absence that lies beneath. There is the chasm of an embodied *lack*, an emptiness to overcome, and it is to this emptiness that the economy of desire (or for Ward, the "culture of seduction") is most profoundly directed. Because the emptiness lies between the person and a hoped-for desire, but emerges as a sexual longing-for in the mediation of contrived economies of desire, it shows itself as the difference between persons. In fact, the distinction between the two dissolves in the act of marking the other person *as* the object of desire. This is the utility of the other person both John Paul II and Levinas reject. It is a banal erotic desire that manifests itself, for it cannot provide what is hoped for, and cultivates the desire nonetheless, almost as a base, suburban mysticism.

Following this process, Ward identifies the "desire-without-consummation" axiomatic for any anthropology in dialogue with the work of a number of critical theorists[93] and observes, "[t]he body (rather than the Enlightenment mind or consciousness) now becomes the principal site for the operation of power in modern society."[94] The body is both the cultivator and the object of erotic desire, in either case remaining the nexus of desire's economy. Michel Foucault understood that in sexuality, economy and expenditure have been recognized features since at least the time of the Greeks, but probably long before.[95] Consummation for the body is a fleeting moment that never reaches totality; there is always "remain."[96] As

91. Ibid., 51.

92. Baudrillard, "Language and Silence," 98, in Ward, "Theology in a Culture of Seduction," in Hannaford and Jobling (eds.), *Theology and the Body*.

93. Here Ward identifies Jacques Lacan, Gilles Deleuze, Jean-Francois Lyotard, Emmanuel Levinas, Luce Irigaray, and Julia Kristeva.

94. Ward, "Theology in a Culture of Seduction," in Hannaford and Jobling (eds.), *Theology and the Body*, 54.

95. See the account of historical economic contexts for sexuality throughout: Foucault, *The History of Sexuality, Vol II*.

96. Ward, "Theology in a Culture of Seduction," in Hannaford and Jobling (eds.), *Theology and the Body*, 54.

such, Ward argues that it is seduction which acts as the ever-present horizon to which sexual desire attends; it is a deferred pleasure, constituted by its absence, experienced as an endless possibility in the "ongoing economy of exchange between self and other."[97] It is a complex web, yet becomes more apparent in its unmasking, for the mode of seduction is heightened in its ecstasy by the veils and appearances which mark its passage. Seduction then is inescapable. Ward views seduction as so pervasive that it is able to slip from the grasp of the symbolic order, which is why so many prohibitions, dangers, and rites of passage have been accumulated into its structures. Of desire at its fundamental, Ward sees "the liturgical pleasure of desire itself."[98] This "liturgical pleasure" is inimical to the created order, for desire—its creation, cultivation, production, and reception—is not simply a cultural construct, but an economy which precedes cultural constructs and proceeds even the choices made for the body.[99] In other words, the body experiences the economics of desire as fundamental to its constitution.

Sexuality, worship, and the sacramentality of the body

John Paul II views sexuality as fundamental, but insists that it remains directed and informed by the framework of subjectivity in which the person experiences itself:

> A man and a woman may be treated primarily as subjects who are (Träger) bearers of a sexual urge, whereas they ought to be treated primarily as conscious and free subjects, endowed with the ability to create genuine spiritual goods, particularly moral goods, in a variety of spheres, including the sexual.[100]

Sexuality is one of a variety of goods in the human condition. It is not primary, but neither can its importance be dismissed or ignored. John Paul has treated sexuality extensively, and as the above words testify, he contextualizes it in relation to human persons as "conscious" and "free."[101] It is an

97. Ibid., 55.

98. Ibid., 56.

99. This is not to say that desire dictates the direction of the body but that it does come before the advent of immediate choices. Desire might be redeemed or redirected, which is where we might speak of grace, but its presence comes before choice/s.

100. John Paul II, *Person and Community*, 285.

101. From Wojtyla in his 1960 introduction to the first edition of this book: "In the commonest view it goes without saying that problems of sex are above all problems of the body. Hence the tendency to allow physiology and medicine an almost exclusive right to speak on these matters—psychology is allotted only a secondary role. The same

important theological category also, for it may be a human property which is urged towards acting for the good of others, as well as revealing something of the nuptiality which describes the relationship between God and the Christian *ecclesia*.[102] The body as sexually described can be understood through a liturgical and theological lens.[103] Its rich intertextual meaning is most profoundly revealed under these two categories when its roots in biblical literature are considered. From a philosophical perspective, Donn Welton has acknowledged the "rich heritage of ethical, social, and political practices" concerning flesh and the body evident in Hebrew and New Testament texts.[104] For all the postmodern attempts to overcome Cartesian dualism, it may be that the scriptural witness to the human body and its ongoing interpretation in the life of actual Christian communities offers a *praxis* of bodily understanding that is already thoroughly integrated. Welton argues against the postmodern assumption (and before that, the Cartesian assumption) that Jewish and Christian philosophical interpreters of their scriptural canons have exhausted the possibilities of these texts. They are disparaged, as if their ongoing study and application, at least insofar as they deal with the body, has found its final stage in the thought of Augustine or Aquinas.[105] It is worth quoting Welton's observation of the biblical picture of the body:

> The very notions that the body is thick with desires and actions, that it is configured not so much by "causes" as by motivational matrices not of its own making, that the organization of its own powers can be returned to it in ways that enslave it, that it is bound up with the trajectory of our ethical and religious life, are all found in these texts.[106]

The experience of the body in biblical texts is the terrain of all human experience. It encompasses freedom and enslavement, liberation and

---

sciences are also supposed to be capable of generating ethical norms unaided. This book puts the problem in a fundamentally different perspective. Sexual morality is in the domain of the person. It is impossible to understand anything about it without understanding what the person is, its mode of existence, its functioning, its powers. The personal order is the only proper plain for all debate on matters of sexual morality." John Paul II, *Love and Responsibility*, 18.

102. Of note is Angelo Scola's study of this theme in "The Insuperable Difference," in *The Nuptial Mystery*.

103. For example, McAleer (especially in "The Wedding Feast of the Lamb") has argued for a profoundly ecclesial dimension to sexual difference, liturgically shown forth eucharistically and ministerially. McAleer, *Ecstatic Morality and Sexual Politics*, 137–55.

104. Welton, *The Body*, 230.

105. Ibid.

106. Ibid.

entrapment. It is important to acknowledge the reality of the biblical witness as together forming a *living* textual canon.[107] Debate concerning the manner in which that canon lives is wide and far-reaching, but suffice it to say that it is dealt with most profoundly in its mediation among the worshipping communities of the church. That is to say, Scripture, as it is repeated in litany, psalm, hymnody, and chant, or as it is read and proclaimed from lectern and pulpit, is chiefly experienced as a text for the worshipping body of the church.[108] This is so in Christian communities across linguistic and cultural divides. Even the small group of disciples gathering in the domestic home for mutual study of Scripture tends to follow a prayerful, theocentric liturgical pattern—they are unlikely to alter their general pattern week by week—and their thought and prayer are disciplined by the *habitus* of a local congregation.[109] Both communal and individual reflection on scriptural texts engage the person not only intellectually, but also in the act of allowing the texts to shed light on current problems and questions in particular contexts. In worship, biblical accounts of the body become profoundly ethical, for worship becomes an intersecting moment of worshipping bodies with the witness of the texts themselves.[110]

As an intersecting moment, the body finds itself experiencing both a text and the performative activity of worship. In this context, Louis-Marie Chauvet's contribution to the development of a postmodern theology of liturgy is helpful. For him, the *exemplar* of Christian liturgy is sacramental worship, although of course not all liturgy is sacramental. Chauvet refers to

107. For example, see "Canonical Theism," a movement described in Abraham, Vickers, and Kirk, *Canonical Theism*.

108. In regards to the Roman Missal both pre- and post-1969 reforms, the Mass is likened to a "cacophony" of words and texts that bear no chronological order or respect for their historical contexts. All liturgical texts are quotations, "citations," from within the tradition that has developed the liturgical rite/s. As Renaud-Chamska puts it, "a phrase addressed by Paul to a first-century community replies to the salutation made by Boaz to his harvesters in Hebrew antiquity. In succession we find an apologia from the high Middle Ages (I confess to God), a biblical cry which runs right through both Old and New Testaments (Lord, have mercy), the early poetic development of the song of the angels reported by Luke . . . ," etc., the believing subject becomes a living participant in the texts and stories in which they worship, enjoining their body with the cited texts and thus actively layering on the embedded meaning/s of the liturgy in relationship to it. See Renaud-Chamska, "The Liturgy as Citation," 79–80.

109. On the notion of *habitus* and the role of habit in human dispositions and relationships, see the influential Ravaisson, *Of Habit*. Cf. Jean-Yves Lacoste, for whom the habitual practice of liturgy denotes the whole *coram Deo* experience: Lacoste, *Experience and the Absolute*.

110. For a study on the relationship between worshipping bodies and the ethical and political consequences thereof, see Tan, "Bodies of Christ in Seas of Change."

liturgy broadly as the worshipping community's acts of praise, but empha-sizes the sacraments as high points of divine disclosure to the human body. For Chauvet, a sacrament is the Word written on the body. The human body itself shaped via a threefold body of history, society, and the world, is a "speaking body" and mediates spirituality in its corporeality.[111] It has done so since its conception. But its speaking is achieved in a common exchange of symbolic *meaning*. The body, in such operations as posture, voice, tone, word, gesture, presence, and absence, *speaks* to others within a symbolic order that precedes it.[112] Of words said and unsaid, the body is the chief point of reception and expression, which is of especial importance in the sacramental economy that is based on particular moments of the "exchange between humanity and God" ("ecclesially mediated").[113] To be sure, the exchange is "extra-linguistic" and flows from the possibility wrought *extra nos*, in the person and work of Christ.[114] By virtue of what is wrought in Christ, the body remains a mode of operation by which it receives (freely) a language or grammar, and does so in the form of a linguistic "binding" to that which precedes and informs it (in this case the divine other).[115] In the sacraments, efficacious of grace, the other traces a mark upon the body in the form of a liturgical sense impression that places the embodied subject in an ethical and symbolic reordering. Chauvet writes, the "body is the bind-ing, the space in the middle where both identity and difference are sym-bolically connected under the authority of the Other."[116] The sacraments of Christian liturgy are the means by which the body is able to receive such communication.

Sacramental worship is a convergence of the body at its most pro-foundly spiritual, paradoxically even at its most corporeal or sensual.[117] In

111. Chauvet, "Editorial: Liturgy and the Body," viii.

112. Chauvet, *The Sacraments*, 2; also at 65, in which Chauvet concludes that the sacraments themselves are "the symbolic expression of the passage . . . from the letter [of God] to the body, that is to say, from the Scriptures to ethics."

113. Ibid., 123.

114. Chauvet, *Symbol and Sacrament*, 140.

115. Chauvet is indebted here to Derrida's *L'écriture et la différence* and *De la grammatologie*, as well as Levinas' *Totalité et infini*. The body allows human beings to overcome otherness in the sense of enjoining the embodied subject to humility before them. Alterity is then not quite the absolute difference that Levinas requires, although it remains central to Chauvet's project. See ibid., 144–47.

116. Ibid., 147.

117. Similarly, in his final encyclical, John Paul II addresses the embodied reception of the eucharistic body of Christ as a pledge of the future resurrection, by which the hu-man body receives the fullness of Christ's resurrected body and writes that same body into the eschatological horizon. The human body must taste, consume, and digest the

other words, the sensual and the spiritual inform and animate one another in the experience of the body at worship. In Chauvet's symbolic exchange, a divine mediation occurs, in which the Word precedes the human subject but mediates himself through word and matter.[118] Language is central to the liturgy and establishes it, but only because God's Word acts as the preemptive sanctuary by which all language has meaning. In this way, liturgy, inasmuch as it is the heavenly sanctuary that precedes the earthly liturgy, also precedes human language. Liturgy is the participation in the active worship of the incarnate Word, whose own body is given as self-donation. The human body finds its divine origins within the discourse of language, and profoundly so in the symbolic exchanges of sacramental grace. The activities of liturgy and sacrament therefore are not passing events or static experiences, but activate a retranslation of erotic desire towards a theocentricity. In the sacraments and in the broader liturgy of Christian worship, bodies have the capacity to reinterpret and orient their natural desires on a theocentric basis. This reorientation means in one sense that bodies are at their most authentic when at worship, but the reorientation is not strictly limited to worship practices. After all, the sacraments are viewed as means of grace-filled encounters with God, and so the grace received in those liturgical moments is to extend within the Christian life at all times and places. The true end of bodily existence is indeed worship, and the *ethos* of a faithful rendering of the body finds its motivation and resources within a life of grace. And as Chauvet shows, the body is already inscribed with liturgical possibilities before it enters the sacramental economy.

More broadly, the human person lives and moves in an economy of desire, what Graham Ward calls a "culture of seduction."[119] Sexuality is central to human experience, especially as it mediates this erotic desire in the flesh, yet is a profound event of the body whose *telos* is liturgically oriented, scripturally described, and bears the possibility of divine participation. Despite this, the person (as a sexual person) experiences itself in postmodernity in profoundly antiliturgical, nonscriptural, and nonparticipatory ways. It is to that experience that attention is now given.

---

nourishment of Christ's postresurrected flesh. See John Paul II, *Ecclesia De Eucharistia: Encyclical Letter on the Eucharist in Its Relationship to the Church*, 18.

118. Willis, "Language as the Sanctuary of Being," 879.

119. Ward, "Theology in a Culture of Seduction," in Hannaford and Jobling (eds.), *Theology and the Body*, 47–61.

Privileging the body: contrasts between the angels and postmodernity

In privileging the body, materiality becomes a locus of attention in contrast to a purely spiritual reality, such as the category of the angelic. Angels are described biblically as those spiritual messengers of God, who are without material form. Unlike the angels, human persons experience the world through their bodies. Yet humans are not mere matter, for the sexual person—body and soul—is an integrated embodied subject.[120] In fact, because human persons are embodied creatures, sexual and spiritual realities operate in the same space. Wojtyla writes:

> The human person is not just a consciousness prolific in experiences of various content, but is basically a highly organized being, an individual of a spiritual nature composed in to a single whole with the body (hence, a suppositum humanum).[121]

An understanding of the body proceeds with the recognition that it remains the site of conditional consciousness and as opportunity for human presence in the world.[122] In the body, the person experiences the passage of time and it is through the body that consciousness is manifest. For any theology of personhood or human community that takes seriously the

---

120. In *Love and Responsibility*, it is not until chapter 2, "The Person and Love," that Wojtyla addresses the wholly integrated nature of the human person. In chapter I, "The Person and the Sexual Urge," he has two sections, "Analysis of the Verb 'to Use'" and "Interpretation of the Sexual Urge," which gives a phenomenological description of the nature of sexual desire and the important distinctions between terms such as subject, object, love, to use, and so on. Having set the context, in chapter 2 he provides three sections, namely "Metaphysical Analysis of Love," "Psychological Analysis of Love," and "The Ethical Analysis of Love." It is in the second part of this chapter in which he deals with the "Affirmation of the Value of the Person," even though it sits in the background of the book's approach and priorities. In this part, he clearly affirms the first value in the human subject as their personhood and which "only secondarily possesses a sexual value" (*Love and Responsibility*, 122). Much of sexual desire is really a response to this secondary value, which is sexuality. Intellectually, or consciously, a person may assign the value of personhood to an other, but their embodied sexuality presents a problem here, for it is experienced as immediate and prior to our conscious assignation of the value of the person to the human subject before us. This is crucial because love is not merely emotive, but is also a virtue and is produced in the will (which is free) of "one person (the subject), resulting from the truth about another person (the object)." See John Paul II, *Love and Responsibility*, 121–25.

121. John Paul II, *Person and Community*, 287.

122. History shows that this opportunity is vulnerable to violent reduction and manipulation through the embodied imposition of others. See, for example, the historical study in Foucault, *Discipline and Punish*, 135–69.

phenomenon of life *as it is experienced*, the body becomes a primary site. There is a danger in theologizing concrete experience, for one might be assuming too much of either experience or theological tradition. For example, Gerard Loughlin views theological analogies of sexual acts as "parodies" of Trinitarian life, thus to be treated with some suspicion.[123] The danger of parody must be recognized so that it might be avoided. Indeed, the tension and distance between human sexuality and Trinitarian life offers the opportunity for closer analysis. It is the bodily nature of the human person that makes possible the desires and temptations of carnality, and the importance of this aspect of being human cannot be overlooked. Or put another way, it must be remembered that human beings are not purely spiritual beings. On this theme, Lacoste states what should be obvious: human beings are not angels. By virtue of their having bodies, humans are "placed" in a way that purely spiritual creatures are not.[124] Blaise Pascal observes that the human person is part beast and part angel, in a rhetorical flourish to sum up the strange duality in which humanity finds itself.[125] This is called humanity's "miniature dignity" by Catherine Pickstock:

> This apparently grotesque hybridity is our miniature dignity. Unlike angels, we combine in our persons every level of the created order from the inorganic, through the organic, through the animally psychic, to the angelically intellectual.[126]

What Pickstock calls human "grotesque hybridity" is not an aesthetic comment, but sums up the strange uniqueness of the embodied human condition. Being neither angels nor beasts, humans are unique and this uniqueness provides access to what is also beautiful in the material creation. The nature of embodied existence, despite its unique hybridity, allows access to the kinds of enfleshed community to which only those with bodies share the key and upon which only those with rationality may reflect. Levinas thinks of this as the opening up of the senses to the "absolute difference" that animates the body, resulting in the "signifyingness" of "non-indifference."[127] Touch, voice, taste; all sensory data are only available to those with a body to experience them. The angels have no pathway to such experiences.[128] There is a christological dimension to this distinction also, in

123. Loughlin, *Alien Sex*, 147.

124. Lacoste, *Experience and the Absolute*, 8.

125. Pascal, *Pensées*, 329.

126. Pickstock, "Liturgy and the Senses," 721.

127. Levinas, *Otherwise Than Being*, 70–71.

128. Even the *Nephilim*, the offspring of the sons of God and daughters of Eve (Gen 6:1–4 and Num 13:33), for all their mythical oddity and dubious heritage, do not alter

that Christ's redemptive work in the incarnation included in its summation the fully experienced *pathos* of human suffering. In his bodily suffering, the divine-human form of Christ assumed the full breadth of human experience (including, of course, death) and thus extended salvation to human beings. Conversely and in the opposite direction, for the disciple to suffer pain and to shed blood or simply to sense the lonely isolation of human experience is to share in the sufferings of Christ. John Paul II takes up this theme of the creative dimension of "redemptive suffering" in *Salvifici Doloris*.[129] He takes his point of departure the text of Col 1:24 in which Paul writes: "Now I rejoice in my sufferings for your sake, and in my flesh I am filling up what is lacking in Christ's afflictions for the sake of his body, that is, the church." There, Paul rejoices in sufferings for the sake of other disciples and makes the bold claim that in his own flesh, he completes some aspect of Christ's own afflictions. Within the flesh of the body, a link is made between the self-offering of the Son of God with the localized and particular sufferings of each other person.

For John Paul II, the "totally voluntary" nature of Christ's movement towards the cross is crucial.[130] By embracing the content of the crucifixion, Christ takes hold of the sufferings of the human person (body and soul) as a perfectly free agent and extends its fruits to humanity. He bridges the divide between his consubstantial Father and the ordinary human person, who whatever his or her lot in life is, remains embodied in a state open to suffering and death. The reach of the suffering body of Christ to each concrete event of suffering is completed by virtue of the grace given to creation in the work of Christ. This is true also of the manner in which personal sufferings may complete Christ's own afflictions. Furthermore, he does not simply offer redemption to each person, but, in John Paul II's words: "Each one is also *called to share in that suffering* through which the Redemption was accomplished."[131] Redemptive suffering is therefore a sharing in the sacrifice of Calvary. It is a conscious activity in that its orientation and basis is the work and sacrifice of Christ and not within one's own personal convictions or desires. Nor is it merely martyrdom for its own sake; the unique privilege

---

this truth, for they themselves are embodied creatures. Their lineage may have been partially angelic, but their embodied existence places them in a similar position to those of normal human beings. What would be more interesting is to consider their parents, those angels who—according to a literal reading of these passages—"knew" human women. It is they who transgress the body/spirit distinction. This, however, would be a purely speculative activity.

129. John Paul II, *Salvifici Doloris*, 24.

130. Ibid., 18.

131. Ibid., 19.

of the human person is to offer the body to share in what it is not worthy to share in. John Paul II describes this activity as "indispensable," occasionally "dramatic," but particularly, "blessed."[132] This is because suffering is not an end in itself, but a humble gesture of self-abnegation offered with a faith in the resurrection of the body: this also is a sharing in what is first achieved by Christ. The suffering of the human person enables the possibility of participating in Christ's own suffering, which can now be interpreted within an eschatological horizon of the redemption of all creation.[133] The angels are barred from this experience, for they lack bodies in which to suffer, let alone in which to rejoice, in the embodied sensations in which the human person is immersed. This privileging of the body is theological, but it takes on a different kind of privileging in the postmodern context, where the body is destabilized. As Sarah Coakley describes:

> Indeed the "body" comes to bear huge, and paradoxical, philo-sophical weight in post-modern thought: just as its Enlighten-ment partner, the "mind/soul" of Cartesianism, is seen off with almost unexamined vehemence, so, simultaneously, what is left (the "body") becomes infinitely problematized and elusive. It is all that we have, but we seemingly cannot grasp it; nor are we sure we can control the political forces that regiment it.[134]

What occurs in nature appears fragmented, unstable, lacking in a clear moral order. There is no common cultural basis for an appeal to the natural law, at least insofar as it was understood in the post-Tridentine era. For this reason, Benedict XVI has referred to natural law as a "blunt instrument" in contemporary discussion.[135] It is not that it has become redundant, but is unpersuasive in dialogue. For a Christian moral witness to be persuasive, it must acknowledge the realities of bodies in such an unstable context. The language used to describe the embodied person is significant because it fol-

---

132. Ibid., 31.

133. See especially the postredemption wounds of Christ, appearing as they do despite the miraculous and now unlimited bounds of his body, which can extend through time and space. The risen Christ is the form of heavenly abiding, which we look to as time's horizon because of that same Christ's redemptive work. The placing of Thomas's fingers in Jesus' wounds represents then a eucharistic moment, for Thomas' flesh touches the blood of heaven and mingles in its flesh, and so in his fragile, doubting, human body, manages to taste the heavenly body of Christ. He tastes and then he sees and then he confesses, and only when these three are achieved is he able to carry the gospel into the world; this follows the pattern of eucharistic worship.

134. Coakley, "Religion and the Body," 3.

135. Benedict XVI, "Dieses Instrument ist leider stumpf geworden," in *Values in a Time of Upheaval*, 38–9.

lows the identification of the context in which the person appears. Privileging the body in terms of its uniqueness in creation is helpful in discussing
sexuality, while the destabilizing context of postmodernity clarifies the extent to which descriptions of sexuality and *eros* are also embedded in a wider
economy of desire. Describing the phenomenality of sexuality in relation to
the body points not only to needfulness but also desire, as Levinas indicates.
Furthermore, the body appears in dramatically different arrays of meaning
and desire. This can also be seen in the work of Jean-Luc Marion, whose
work transgresses traditional boundaries between theology and philosophy.

Idols and icons: The desired and given body

A phenomenological approach to the problem of the body in postmodernity
is a theological resource as much as it is a philosophical one. The thought
of Jean-Luc Marion attests to this, especially his "radical critique" of the
"entire ontotheological project of modernity" to outline how the category of
God has been misused.[136] Marion learns from Levinas the appeal to alterity, but situates it within a broader theological-philosophical horizon. In his
major work on this theme, phenomenology considers the meaning of the
other's directionality towards the self. Marion contrasts the category of the
icon with that of the idol, in which the ethical relation with another can be
articulated.[137] This is presented in the same work in which he suggests that
Nietzsche's proclamation of the death of God is the announcement of the
death of the God of the philosophers, and not of God as Christian revelation
understands him to be.[138] For Marion, the question of the death of God is
the context in which idols and icons may be discerned, for it is a context in
which prior idolatrous notions of God (as a philosophical category rather
than a scriptural object of worship) can be overcome. Following questions
from others (such as Hegel, Hölderlin, Nietzsche, Heidegger, and others),
Marion calls for an admission that if one is to avoid the "concept-object"
understanding of God, in which the category of God is an object according to which one attaches an empirical description, one must view God as
central to a discourse which is ordered by that same God.[139] That is, God is
not one category in a philosophical methodology, but the one who orders
the methodology itself. This relies on an account of the difference between
God and false objects of worship, idols. As Marion notes, there is a finite

136. Lakeland, *Postmodernity*, 94.
137. Marion's central theses on this topic are given in *The Idol and Distance*.
138. Ibid.
139. Ibid., 4.

distance between *Gott* and *Götze*.[140] In what follows, it will be seen how the body may be interpreted within a logic of the idol or the icon; the difference is one of intentionality. In this way, the problem of sexuality and of erotic desire is interpreted within the idol-icon distinction.

The erotic body in phenomenological perspective

Eros, in regards to love and the flesh, is of course a theme in John Paul II and Levinas. In Marion's work, it is given phenomenological attention against the backdrop of philosophy's general silence on the theme of love. In the absence of a contemporary philosophy of love, Marion acknowledges a certain appropriateness in that the silence of the philosophers conveys the truth, "they know, better than anyone, that we no longer have the words to speak of it, nor the concepts to think about it, nor the strength to celebrate it."[141] Into this silence Marion proposes his phenomenology of love,[142] or more specifically, *eros*.[143] He argues that as much as it might be wished that the experience of love might be limited, or described and sealed off, human experience actually attests to love as a widely experienced context, more so than what intellectual argument might achieve. He states:

> we are, insofar as we come to know ourselves, always already caught within the tonality of an erotic disposition—love or hate, unhappiness or happiness, enjoyment or suffering, hope or despair, solitude or communion—and that we can never, without lying to ourselves, claim to arrive at a fundamental erotic neutrality.[144]

That is to say, human persons are always *erotic* creatures. This echoes the arguments of both Levinas and the early Wojtyla. For Marion, the erotic phenomenon is known in the infinite traverse of distance between the lover and the loved. He considers the means by which an erotic reduction is achieved, based not on one's intentional sexual embrace of an other, but

---

140. Ibid., 4.

141. Marion, *The Erotic Phenomenon*, 1.

142. Of love, Marion laments the imposition of "love" and "charity," insisting on an indivisibility in the concept of love, despite the various terms for love which arise from the Greek onwards. Ibid., 5.

143. Rather than simply a philosophy of things erotic, Marion is seeking out the contours of an "erotic rationality," which speaks not to what is, as such, but also to what is not yet, or no longer, or undecided. It is a "love without being." Ibid., 5–6.

144. Ibid., 7.

in the question, "[d]oes anyone out there love me?"[145] This places the self in the context of receptivity, of reducing one's erotic desire phenomeno-logically and thus considering the manner in which *eros* is established and manifested by, through, and because of an other. He writes of the seductive advance of lover to the beloved, which, to be substantial, must start and start again, not departing from the path of erotic desire.[146] To depart from this path is not to desire too much and walk away, but to desire too little and to abrogate erotic responsibility.[147] Upon the fleeting event of satisfaction, there is a mutual reception of flesh that cannot be construed as perfectly re-ciprocal. It is an utter self-giving, in which one's own pleasure and that of the other are mingled without confusion, and in which one does not drown in the immersion of another's body or flesh, but becomes confronted with the spectacle of another who is known in embodied givenness.[148] This differs from Levinas' refusal of a fusion between two bodies. Importantly, Marion notices the manner in which the erotic embrace confronts the person with those themes previously mentioned, especially of the mutual indwelling of the sexual and the spiritual. He says at some length:

> Erotic speech provokes excess and wants only to tell this very excess—to wit, that every accomplishment must become a new beginning. Thus it must inevitably borrow words from mystical theology, which also, and first, tells and provokes excess—the excess of union, and thus of distance. All the same, the process of eroticization only lasts for as long as it says, "Again!" But what does "Again!" mean? I cannot say (and intend), "Here I am!" except by also intending (and saying), "Come!" which is, to the letter, the final word of the Book of Revelation and thus of mystical theology, which is rooted there. We must conclude that erotic speech cannot be performed without the language of spiritual union of man and God, any more than it can avoid the two other lexicons—the obscene and childish.[149]

145. For example, Marion rejects the question of "being" as central to this enquiry, but locates in the question about love the radical engagement with what gives itself to me. See ibid., 40.

146. Ibid., 82–89.

147. More could be said on the rhetorical structure of Marion's thought, which re-flects a certain French flourish in its consideration of the erotic. He writes, "The lover bears everything." Ibid., 85.

148. Such eroticization is occurring for Marion between various lexicons, includ-ing the obscene verbalizations which occur within the sexual embrace and the clumsy fumblings of any sexual act. Ibid., 106–50.

149. Ibid., 149.

In other words, once again, the spiritual and sexual spheres occupy the same space. Marion's observations of the erotic phenomenon center upon the distance between lovers, the lack of real satiation (even as desire is fulfilled it is barren and requires a reseduction at some future juncture), the revelation of another by embodied self-giving and the necessity of theological language in relaying the phenomenological realities of these enfleshed moments of *eros*. For Marion then, the erotic rationality, which pervades human experience, is itself revelatory of the nature of the human person. "Man is revealed to himself by the originary and radical modality of the erotic."[150] With the (possible) exception of the angels, humanity uniquely experiences in each of its subjects the defining excesses of love (and hate), regardless of any reasoned choice before or after the fact.[151] It is in the crossing of difference between lover and beloved that the complex field of human interiority is enjoined with the enfleshed discourse of embodied *eros*.

In response to this reading of Marion, two points can be made. The first is that the human person does not simply have a sexual body; it is an erotic body. The problem of the erotic is inclusive of all human persons, although understanding it reasonably requires maturity and discipline. This includes those in which there is no capacity or maturity for sexual activity, because the problem of sexuality is linked to the broader difficulty of erotic desire, which is not limited to sexuality. The second is that as an *erotic* body, there is no erotic neutrality in the embodied person. Each is subject to the phenomenality of a personal erotic desire for an embodied alterity, despite the lack of complete satiation. There is no bracketing out one's erotic sensibility, although it may be redirected or interpreted within the broader field of human experience.

The idolatrous body

The erotic body experiences itself within the wider intersubjectivity of other bodies. This includes the experience of the iconic and the idolatrous. For Marion, the idol is not the image of a false god in the sense that the latter fosters the cultivation of its own image. The idol is the worshipper's production of an image that flows from subjective experience to which a face is given. Having fashioned an image in metal, wood, or stone, the worshipper seeks from an object an investment of divinity in the form created. The task finds its origins in the experience of the worshipper, who assigns a perceived series of best self-features within a particular physical object. What remains

150. Ibid., 7.
151. Ibid.

is the lingering identification of the divine in the face of the fashioned idol, which flows from an interior experience of the maker. As Marion puts it, "[i]n the idol the human experience of the divine precedes the face that that divinity assumes in it."[152] The best (or at least, what is perceived to be the best) of human experience is located in the idolatrous face. In this crafted body, human hands inscribe an anthropological horizon within a representation of the divine.

In the physicality of the idol, the divine trace is located within a fixed relationship of distance. By crafting and blessing the form as an object of worship, it also fixes the god to whom it relates in a physicality that is concrete and assertive. Its assuring presence shows that its availability is primarily in the gaze upon the world. But as a fixed point of divine presence, the idol does not in fact reflect a divine object from outwith experience back into the gaze. It achieves precisely the opposite. The idol can do no more than reflect back into one's gaze the source of its own origins: human experience.[153] It is significant that the idol does not represent the person who crafts it as such, but rather the subjective experience of the divine by that artist, which in turn has been ordered by the artisan.[154] What is desired in the idol is a personally directed intentionality.

This is similar to John Paul II's description of the results of an objectifying gaze towards the sexual other, instead of a response to its subjective dimension.[155] In terms of the human body, this can be called concupiscence, but here it is the nature of the directionality that allows the idol/icon distinction. The gaze towards the other is the intentionality of meaning. In this gaze, John Paul is concerned that the meaning of the other is reduced to the bodily availability for the self's own bodily desires, the sense of "need" that Levinas refers to.[156] The fashioning of wood and iron into an idol follows the same logic that the sexual objectification of the other follows in its refashioning of the other's body into the meeting of personal appetite. However, the result does not bear a moral equivalence. This is because of the

152. Marion, *The Idol and Distance*, 5.

153. Ibid., 4–7.

154. Marion finds in politics our first and most obvious example of the ongoing need for idols (they are not all fashioned in wood and stone), even in a postpagan era. Examples include "Big Brother," the "Great Helmsman," the "Führer," or the "Man we love best." Even in more recent times, political examples are obvious such as the American presidential candidate offering "change we can believe in." In a sense, personal political commitments are irrelevant. Common to all of these is the projection of personal experiential hopes and desires upon the (political) object of love and devotion. See ibid., 6.

155. John Paul II, *Man and Woman He Created Them*, 40:4.

156. Levinas, *Totality and Infinity*, 116.

irreducible and unrepeatable quality of the human person, as was discussed in chapter 2. It may be recalled that for John Paul II, unlike even the most beautiful of created objects, the only "adequate" response to the embodied human person is "love."[157] The description in Marion of the idol's rendering of the self's own limited horizon of meaning and desire clarifies that the reduction of the other to the body is an idolatrous investment in the corporeality of human alterity.

The iconic body

For Marion, the icon speaks from a different order to the idol.[158] That is to say, the two originate as different kinds of images and with a different moral value. The icon does not reflect back human experience, but is the visible image of the invisible (Col 1:15: "Icon of the Invisible God"). It is the withdrawal of the divine from the absolute and unknowable to the concrete and the intimate. Of course, the icon cannot be a perfect or complete revelation; it continues to paradoxically conceal that which it also reveals. Contained within the icon is an immutable distance between the Father and his creation, which is overcome in the work of the Son. The image Marion uses to convey the difference between the idol and the icon is that of a mirror (the idol) and the typology of the prism (the icon), by "which a multiplicity of colors breaks down, or rather orchestrates, that which a prism multiplies according to our power to see . . . ."[159] To this end, the colors, sensations, concepts, and thoughts which are identifiable in the icon move towards the viewer by entering the viewer's gaze and speaking directly. In Marion's description, the idol may be viewed as the example of embodied mastery or of divinity as enslavement and the absolutization of human experience.

Yet, in the icon, one finds an object that remains embodied. It is situated in the order of a self-donating seduction, of the retention of distance in relating the human to the divine, and therefore the negation of concepts such as the death of God, for the phrase itself becomes meaningless. In the act of givenness, the icon makes itself known to perception, and keeps hidden its own self. It is a revelation that remains concealed. In other words, the "what" and the "how" of love and the knowledge of love are immersed into one logical sequence.[160] Divinity speaks to the one who gazes and not from the gazer's experience. The idol fixes distance as a thing to be sub-

---

157. John Paul II, *Love and Responsibility*, 41.
158. Marion, *The Idol and Distance*, 8.
159. Ibid.
160. Horner, "The Weight of Love," in Hart (ed.), *Counter-Experiences*, 238.

jected within the cosmos, whereas the icon retains its own liberality to be experienced in relationship. The latter rejects the hegemony of control and instead speaks to the gazer in a spirit of common relationship, albeit asymmetrical. Marion refers to the icon's property of manifesting "the nuptial distance that weds, without confusing, the visible and the invisible . . . ."[161] The icon achieves what is impossible, whereas the idol imposes the order of that which has already taken place.[162]

At a fundamental level, the icon-self event is a relational event. Marion identifies relational examples, such as the distance between God and man, in which it is their incommensurability that makes divine-human intimacy possible.[163] In other words, "alterity alone allows communion . . . ."[164] The otherness of the God-human relationship is built into the iconic gaze. Yet, the body may be interpreted by the self in either an iconic or an idolatrous gaze. One might be tempted to idolize one's own body or those of others, or alternatively choose to allow the body to be interpreted in light of its creator, thus mediating the iconic through the body. In any case, it can be seen that the iconic relationship is one which enables the self to experience itself and others in authentic communion, as opposed to the idolatrous relationship, in which one experiences only fantasy and a recreation of one's self-reflection.

With this in mind, John Paul II's argument for an ethical asymmetry between the self and the other within the context of sexuality is poignant. He reinterprets Matt 5:27–28 in terms of personal intentionality within the gaze and calls into question intentionality itself rather than the gaze.[165] For him, Christ's statement that to even look with lustful intent is to have committed adultery confirms the significance of intentionality within the recognition of the person as an irreducible subject of love. Rather than looking away—the traditional moral guidance of generations of confessors—John Paul II advises to look more intensely at the object of desire as a subject of "personal dignity."[166] He places the problem within the intentionality directed towards the other (in this case a woman, but John Paul insists it is the

161. Marion, *The Idol and Distance*, 9.

162. Marion's second interlude, "The Distance of the Requisite and the Discourse of Praise: Denys," draws on Pseudo-Dionysius to discern the role of distance in freeing the impossible. It "gives itself—not to be comprehended but to be received." Ibid., 155.

163. Ibid., 198.

164. Ibid.

165. "You have heard that it was said 'You shall not commit adultery.' But I say to you that everyone who looks at a woman with lustful intent has already committed adultery with her in his heart."

166. John Paul II, *Man and Woman He Created Them*, 42:7.

same for all persons, male or female). Intentionality is directed towards the body of an other and its reduction to one's own carnal needs and desires (for the two become intertwined in the reductive gaze), thus constituting a reductive utilitarianism in the I-other dynamic. In this reading, John Paul II is problematizing the idolatrous approach to the body that hovers unceasingly near to the intentionality towards the other. By interpreting the idolatrous gaze in terms of a reduction to the self, the icon's power in reinterpreting the self becomes all the more apparent. If the other person is received as an icon, one's intentionality becomes the occasion for a profound receptivity towards embodied alterity. In the iconic *exemplar*, Christ, the intentionality apparent in each human perception of the other takes on the possibility of an iconic performance of the self being authenticated by the other. The other, as Levinas would have it, "affects us despite ourselves."[167] In retaining the importance of the category of distance in connection to relational language, Marion opens a way to perceive the redemption of the body.

Distance and the redeemed body

So, the human body may be intentionally objectified such that it becomes idolatrous, or it may be intentionally received such that it speaks as an icon. Distance is the means by which an intentionality brings about the event of the other's appearing in its fullness and it is in the transgression of distance that God takes up human flesh and acts within the human drama. The good to which such action directs itself is one that reveals the redemptive quality of distance, properly understood. For Marion, the "infinite seriousness of the Incarnation" is the risk with which the entire human condition is dealing; it is the divine investment of humanity with an unreserved greatness, "abandoning himself," not to a "particular being," but to the "fundamental constitution of Dasein that he puts on and renews."[168] In Christ, the divine icon restores lesser images and returns the body on a wholly new axiological basis. This "fundamental constitution" is of phenomenological importance, for it views the incarnation as an embrace of human phenomena that has suspended any bias or preferential interest. It would be too much to say that it equates perfectly with the Husserlian reduction, but there is a kind of divine humility occurring here, by which the invisible Father embraces a fullness of human experience, without disdain or circumspection of any kind. It is distance that makes this possible. Despite this, Marion insists upon the separateness of the categories of distance and difference, in which

167. Levinas, *Otherwise Than Being*, 129.
168. Marion, *The Idol and Distance*, 213.

one does not constitute the other. More specifically, distance is not formally predicated upon difference.[169]

The divine distance (from creatures) is taken from the ontological difference between Being and beings. For Marion, there is no abode (divine or otherwise) in Being that can be identified as that belonging to God as such, or to which he belongs. Conversely, the latter is true also of the world and its history, in which no presence, abode, preparation, event, or person acts as a preparatory abode for the divine. Marion takes an apophatic route in arguing that the distance between God and human history acts as a revelatory feature of the truth of a God who is beyond Being. There is no human or creaturely construction or space that is suitable for a God of difference, known in the ontological distance in which he chooses to participate. This is in evidence in a supreme way upon the cross, where no "divine abode" is made and there before human eyes the figure of messianic hope is stripped naked of any visible divine trace.[170] It is "[k]enosis, disdain, and rejection" that mark the divine revelation in history, in which He "withdraws in the distance, unthinkable, unconditioned, and therefore infinitely closer."[171] The kind of relationship this entails is one made possible because of the nature of the divine inner life. It is not simply the nature of the divine-human distance or the divine-Being distance, but of the intra-Trinitarian difference, as revealed by the Second Person of the Trinity. As Marion links these concepts:

> The condition of the revelation of the Father in the figure of the Son, or better, its stakes and its completion consist precisely in the failure and collapse of any "divine abode": in the darkening of the sky, where no azure outlines the glorious figure of any Greek god, the Christ dies and the Trinitarian distance reveals itself forever.[172]

In this way, the iconic form of Christ refuses every imagining of the gods of violence, thunder, and heavenly theater. The gift that is being given is of a perfect kenosis that is not merely given *for* the human person and all of creation, but *beyond* being. Marion does not at this juncture refer to it as such, but this represents a divine eroticism, in the sense that the nuptial state of union being ushered between God and human persons is one of an inverted relationship of alterity. God, as absolute being, is precisely a community of divine persons bound in a state of perpetual kenosis, who arrives over an absolute distance. To return to the character of the icon, is

169. Ibid., 215.
170. Ibid., 214.
171. Ibid., 215.
172. Ibid., 214.

there some form of mediation by which the overcoming of this distance takes place? The icon fulfills such a role in the sense that icons may be formalized in certain ecclesial traditions, yet they are equally present as human persons in particular roles; in communities and in relationships. In this sense, Levinas' statement that the divine shows itself in the human face is both scripturally affirmed and ethically conceived (see the *imago Dei* in Gen 1:27).[173] The erotic divine-human relationship is not yet a face to face, but is most profoundly known in the iconic mediation that interrupts and overturns the self-referential idols of which human persons are no less cluttered. It is through the iconic face of Christ, Marion argues, that the collapse of the idols and a journey through their forms can take place.[174] And this is crucial: the embodied person, to interrupt and overcome the sense of the body (in the self or in the other) in an idolatrous intentionality, cannot avoid the idols, but moves through them in an *ethos* of abandonment to the icon. The body receives its possibility of redemption because the iconic face of Christ gifts itself in a gaze towards that which it loves. It is freely given, and so the possibilities of iconic givenness overcome the intentionality of the idolatrous not by passing over them, but moving freely through them as if they were stripped of their power.

The erotic body in theological perspective

It has been seen that *eros* is a term used for both sexual desire as well as the possibility of a transcendent desire with theological possibilities. For Wojtyla, love for human beings remains a spiritual matter concerning the interiority of each person. Nevertheless, the person remains a *desiring* person in a conflicted context in the postmodern context. Sexuality appears as a characteristic both central to contemporary concern and problematical in its meaning. A lens is required through which the desires of the body transcendent to animal sexuality and attentive to sexuality in its concrete experience can be interpreted.

Eros is experienced within the anxious human subject. For example, Heidegger's *Dasein* is the human person whose "being-towards-death" is written through with anxiety about its spatial temporality.[175] The basic characteristic of human persons is one of existential anxiety, constantly in need of self-analysis.[176] The anxious riddle of the embodied human self is

173. Levinas, *Totality and Infinity*, 76.

174. Marion, *The Idol and Distance*, 25.

175. For example, see Heidegger, *Being and Time*, 232.

176. It has been argued that Heidegger's use of the terms "existentiality," "facticity,"

one in perpetual need of a theological answer, for only in the latter can love become a fixed possibility for human bodies in their lived context. Sexuality here plays a central aspect of human experience as much as it is political, ethical, or theological. In sexuality, it is too simplistic to rely on the outward signs of sexuality to describe a sexual ethic, for it restricts the body to its most primal physical characteristics. John Paul II locates in human interiority the accurate point of departure for such an ethic. Of love and its relationship to the body he observes:

> However powerfully and explicitly it is dependent on the body and the senses it is not the body and not the senses alone that form its peculiar base and its peculiar character. Love is always an interior matter, a matter of the spirit. To the extent to which it ceases to be an interior matter and a matter of the spirit it also ceases to be love.[177]

Love, according to John Paul, is an interior disposition that comes upon the person unexpectedly, but which must be expressed through the body in a rationality. This rationality is ethical in that it calls for an awareness of the full dignity of the person.

The body is better able to be viewed as fundamentally open to the possibility of divine love, which is marked chiefly by self-donation, or self-gift, which of course fundamentally privileges the other person, even to the extent of being "put in question" before the sensuality of the other.[178] More importantly, thinking itself may be better placed before the One who knows the interior human life better than others, including its hopes and desires, its fragilities and temptations; the *Logos*, who shirked those most zealous to prove their loyalty to him, and who alone "knew what was within man." This places the person within a posture of humility before the experience of sexuality and of *eros*.

Much is to be gained by situating these themes christologically. Erotic desire, as understood in purely sexual terms, is inadequate. But an understanding of such desire as belonging to the order of the sensual and the affective delivers a gift-centred, incarnate notion of the complex economies of desire in which the human person acts. The scriptural account of St. John the Baptist, desiring the increase of the divine Other, perhaps provides a clearer theology of *eros* than can be gained by simply grounding a study in

---

and "Being-fallen" originates in his reading of Augustine's *The Confessions*. See Wardley, "'A Desire unto Death'"; Paulo, "The Augustinian Constitution of Heidegger's Being and Time."

177. John Paul II, *Love and Responsibility*, 116–17.

178. Levinas, *Otherwise Than Being*, 75.

sexuality and sexual ethics. "He must increase, but I must decrease" (John 3:30; in reference to the messianic hope of John's christological foreshadowing in Matt 3:11). In the presence of the other, the self may desire with all of one's body for that which is good in and for the other. John Paul's relationship between *eros* and *ethos* achieves a similar trajectory.[179] For him, like Plato, *eros* represents an inner power that draws the human person towards the transcendentals: the good, the true, and, in terms of its intoxicating power, the beautiful.[180] Yet, because of the reality of concupiscence, *eros* manifests itself especially in a "subjective intensity of tending toward the object due to its sexual character (sexual value)" in which the "attraction" that we speak of "extends its mastery over man's emotive sphere . . . ."[181] This is not the only semantic meaning of the term *eros*. It is because of its deeper significance in being the opportunity of a call towards that which is good, true, or beautiful, that within the sphere of the erotic a way opens up which is oriented in line with the *ethos* of redemption.

A coincidence of that which is erotic and that which is ethical takes shape by meeting in the human heart and bearing fruit: "What is worthy of the human 'heart' is that the form of the 'erotic' is at the same time the form of *ethos*, that is, of that which is 'ethical.'"[182] John Paul interprets this relationship between *eros* and *ethos* in the context of the Sermon on the Mount, in which Jesus goes beyond the law against adultery and insists that the interior desire of the heart is the foundational motivation towards what is good (Matt 5:27–28).[183] Moreover, John Paul wants to promote an *ethos* that is fundamental to the Christian life—a habitual framework of action and disposition that acts ethically and is in tune with a healthy desire for the good—and so *ethos* and *eros* coincide. It is cultivated within the embodied self, but given over for the sake of the other.

That human persons are sexual beings is not contested, nor the fact that human awareness of sexuality is distinctive in all of creation. In fact, the dually interpenetrating spheres of sexuality and spirituality provide a means by which the coincidence of *ethos* and *eros* may be observed. The analogy of the two interpenetrating spheres provides an image that situates the human person in a complex economy of desire, but with a fundamental openness to the other. *Eros* and *ethos* already coexist within embodied human

---

179. Especially in "Eros as the Source of the 'Erotic,'" in John Paul II, *Man and Woman He Created Them*, 47.

180. Ibid., 47:2; Plato, *Phaedrus*, 249E.

181. John Paul II, *Man and Woman He Created Them*, 47:3.

182. Ibid., 47:5.

183. Ibid., 47:1–6.

experience. In sexuality, the human person senses both desire and need for the other. The dependence on the body of the other for the fulfillment of one's own need and desire constitutes an opportunity for desire—as understood by Levinas—to open up to a greater desire for the good of the other. *Eros*, the passionate love for another, is both experienced and hoped for.

The human person, precisely in its iconic nature as the other who saturates the intuitive gaze subverts natural erotic desire and opens up further possibilities. Immediate sexual attraction has a power of its own, but it does not, in itself, provide a means of erotic satiation that is permanent or final. Even in the immanent experience of its fulfillment, it quickly passes into other forms of emotive results, which, in a matter of time, develop a further desire for sexual satiation. Situating it in the normative mode of marital fidelity in the Christian tradition, it can be open to the generation of human life, but even that is not a completion of the gift of the other. Rather, human *eros* is contextualized in relation to divine *eros*, by which the nuptiality present in the Trinitarian communion gives itself over to human erotic desire, grounding it in the divine kenosis. That is to say, Christ's self-emptying within the Trinity grants to human experience the power to enact its kenosis for God and others. Self-giving does not replace the desire of another. Instead, by converting human sexual longing into the longing for a divine presence, desiring what is best *for* another can take place. This is not puritanical, for it does not exclude natural sexual longing, but reconfigures it towards the Godhead and so makes it a means by which the good of the other can be hoped for, whose human face speaks erotically, but not necessarily by way of sexual satiation.

Conclusion

Through the ethical demand of the other, *eros* is redeemed. As such, *eros* is seen not to be the highest love, but to serve and complement those forms of love indicated in the New Testament: *agape* and *philia*. In the first, the unconditional love that is deeply invested in the particular and in the selective is manifested. In the second is witnessed the love that forms the bonds of friendship, which remains both dispassionate and interested in common endeavors. *Eros* serves the ends of *agape* and *philia* by forming itself in deference to the greater love, which is for God-who-is-love. This should not be seen as a prosaic process, for it is constituted in the immediate complexities of human sexual personhood. It is the christological redemption of the ancient Platonic notion of *theia mania*, a madness for the flesh of another, and the redemption also of desire at its foundations, in forming the figure of the ethical person by divine self-donation. The erotic madness is not cured or erased; it is redeemed, reordered, redirected towards the divine persons, who are the first to offer the erotic plenitude in Christ's own body.

For Levinas, metaphysical desire has little reference to embodied forms of love, except in the alterity of voluptuosity. Instead, this is the means by which transcendence is reached and the alterity of the other is experienced. For John Paul, *eros* plays a crucial role in his theology of the body, in which an inherent nuptial meaning is inscribed. Yet, what results in the erotic embrace? The role of *eros* is a sustaining theme for the body only if its logic is followed. *Communio* may be thought of as the opening up to the beauty of an embodied alterity in tenderness and passion, but there is something more concrete to consider. In both John Paul II and Levinas, as well as in Marion, the erotic embrace is an openness that might give way to a third, the child, who is understood—to different degrees—in terms of a logic of the gift. This theme is pursued in the following chapter.

5

On What is *Given*
A Gift-Logic of the Body

Introduction

THE PLACE OF THE body in John Paul II and Levinas has been studied
in detail, as well as major themes that emerge from both, especially
eros and sexual desire. It has been seen how the problematic understanding
of the body in postmodern thought might be theologically situated. While
consideration was given to that which is *desired* in the body, this chapter
considers what is *given* in the body. In addition to the dialogue between
John Paul and Levinas, the work of Jean-Luc Marion will be considered
further, whose work explicitly crosses the divide between philosophy and
theology. Marion's "saturated phenomenon" provides a descriptive language
with which to deploy John Paul's theology and Levinas' phenomenology
while maintaining a distance between their positions.

First, a genealogy of the gift will be traced, before outlining the problematic shape of the gift that Jacques Derrida and other postmodern voices
highlight. The bodily gift in Levinas and John Paul will be considered, especially the notion of the third—the child—who both appears as the gift
while giving to others the gift of responsibility. Certain dangers need to be
considered in this approach in relation to a theology of the body.

"The gift" is a volatile site in continental philosophy and theology,
because it touches on pivotal questions about the body, God, the person,

community, and giving.[1] In postmodern theology, its pedigree has become immense, to the degree that Sarah Coakley calls its repetition in the literature a "mantra."[2] Biblically, it is used in a variety of ways, tending to emphasize the self-gratuitousness of divine grace. According to Jas 1:17, "[e]very good gift and every perfect gift is from above, coming down from the Father of lights with whom there is no variation or shadow due to change." In terms of the category of the body and of the embodied person, the New Testament speaks of the gift of grace as having been given to the person for the sake of serving others (1 Pet 4:10), as a sacramental grace for the ordering of the church (1 Tim 4:14), and as the gifting of salvation itself (Eph 2:8). More recently, the gift has become a common theme in theological anthropology. In his social encyclical, Pope Benedict XVI writes, the "human being is made for gift, which expresses and makes present his transcendent dimension."[3] In the same passage, Benedict argues that charity in truth places man before the "astonishing" experience of gift; that gratuitousness [gratuitas] is already present in the natural sphere of life, but clouded from our moral vision by consumerist and utilitarian perspectives.[4] In this context in which the gift has become an important theme, John Paul, Levinas, and Marion mark out a positive contribution to theological anthropology in the notion of the *embodied* gift.

Tracing the gift

A genealogy of the gift is traced by Sarah Coakley, along with a critique of some popular tendencies in postmodern theology. For instance, John Milbank and Kathryn Tanner, while following different methodologies, remain centered upon the category of "gift" in understanding the human person and grace. In her critique of Milbank and Tanner's use of the category of "gift," Coakley describes a genealogy of the term since Marcel Mauss' *The Gift* [Essai sur le don, forme archaïque de l'échange], in 1924.[5] Mauss utilized a broad and unorthodox interpretation of the nature of primitive bartering and economic exchanges in France to find a renewed and fairer basis for economic exchange to take place. In effect, what began as anthro-

1. As a category of debate in the social sciences, it was first popularized by the controversial work of Marcel Mauss. See Mauss, *The Gift*.

2. Coakley, "Why Gift?," 229.

3. Benedict XVI, *Caritas in Veritate: On Integral Human Development in Charity and Truth*, 34.

4. Ibid., 34.

5. Coakley, "Why Gift?."

pological description ended as a social and political agenda. Mauss viewed the pre-modern and precapitalist state of economic exchange as based on a system of codified interactions, which combined to form a cohesive society characterized by the basic offering of the "gift," rather than the seller/purchaser exchange of more contemporary capitalist economics.[6] These codified interactions were the giving of presents embedded in an economy of exchange. Evidence was found for these premodern economies across literature, art, song, painting, custom, and so forth. Depending on the nature of the local logic of the gift, great danger and taboo could bedevil one who shirked the obligations of gift-giving. See, for example, the following verse from a long-standing Scandinavian song, quoted by Mauss:

> It is better not to beg [ask for something]
> Than to sacrifice too much [to the gods]:
> A present given always expects one in return.
> It is better not to bring any offering
> Than to spend too much on it.[7]

Mauss reinterprets these observations into a utopian economic vision, thus transforming a particularized anthropological investigation into a philosophical theory to be applied as a practical program. Coakley views this as stage one of the genealogy behind the modern dialogue concerning gift theory. The trouble with Mauss is that his gift-based system is a repetitive, and therefore unending, process of exchange; there is no horizon to which this process is aimed and no objective to be reached, even tentatively. Positively, he at least recognizes that one needs to look beyond formal pretence and social deception to find a logic of the gift.

The idea of gift as a basis of exchange has been carried over into other disciplines to which Jacques Derrida has issued marked criticism.[8] Derrida argues for the seemingly fantastic concept of the "pure gift," which overcomes the endless repetition of Mauss' gift-exchange; a gift without calculation or any kind of obligated return.[9] As elusive as a "pure gift" might be, it provides an apophatic and endless deferment of meaning, culminating in the finality of the last gift, or the ineffable and unbesmirched gift given in each lived instant: the gift of death.[10] In this way, the pure gift is nullified

6. Mauss, *The Gift.*

7. Unknown author, "Havamal, a Poem of the Scandanavian Edda," stanza 145, translated in *The Theory of Social Economy.*

8. An influential cross-disciplinary collection can be seen in Osteen, *The Question of the Gift.*

9. Derrida, *The Gift of Death,* 112.

10. Ibid., 79.

in its reception, for to receive it is to cancel its operation as unsullied by economy or the chains of exchange. The gift appears in Levinas, rarely without reference to what is given in the other and what, in turn, the self must give by way of response. He writes: "To recognise the Other is therefore to come to him across the world of possessed things, but at the same time to establish, by gift, community and universality."[11]

Through the other, gift, community, and universality come into being. Derrida's work relies significantly on Levinas, who says that "[d]eath opens to the face of an Other [d'Autrui]."[12] As has been seen, the face plays a crucial function in Levinas' thought. It is the epiphany of the other and ultimately serves as the means of recognizing in other persons the confusion of language about death.[13] Human beings encompass death in the language of being, denying its incomprehensibility.[14] Death becomes the only available example of a gift without personal investiture, of a bleak sacrifice beyond the horizon of an economic order that requires a counter-gift. John Milbank argues that this has become a common postmodern trait:

> Recent ethical thinkers have certain characteristic answers to these questions. The only real *gift*, they claim, is one that expects no counter-gift in return. Unless a gift is in this fashion sacrificial—the giving up of something—it is argued, a gift reduces to a hidden contractual agreement, governed by a principle of self-interest; and actions out of self-interest, as Kant pointed out, are not pure gifts.[15]

Milbank views within recent debate an emphasis upon the question of the *pure gift*. His analysis is that the language concerning debates around the gift has been transformed from one in which gift exchange is a recognizable and understood trope transcendent to cultural differences, to one in which the very possibility of the (pure) gift is at stake. He refutes this as a logical consequence of the study of the gift, especially Derrida's claim that all appearances of the gift are entrapped within a measurable exchange of benefits that, after all, is the identical repetition of the same.[16] Milbank in-

---

11. Levinas, *Totality and Infinity*, 76.

12. Levinas, "Thinking About Death on the Basis of Time," in *God, Death and Time*, 106.

13. Levinas, "The Scandal of Death," in *God, Death and Time*, 88.

14. Ibid., 91.

15. Milbank, "The Ethics of Self Sacrifice," 34. Milbank appears to be referring to the argument in the section "Methodology of Pure Practical Reason," in Immanuel Kant, *Critique of Practical Reason*.

16. Milbank, "Can a Gift Be Given?" 152.

stead contrasts what he calls "perpetual Eucharist" against that of "identical repetition," drawing theological language into the defense of a pure gift, even in its incorporation into a form of gift-response, upon the basis of the biblical covenant/s between God and Israel.[17] Within the logic of the Eucharist (perpetually offered in participation with God's first Eucharistic initiative), a self-giving God of flesh initiates a *prior* logic of loving self-donation, one that incorporates lesser logics of the world not into the same, but as a giving for the other. A response-gift is not so much required by a juridical framework, but given freely as the anticipated-yet-spontaneous erotic reply. In Milbank's words, this is true in being and grace because faith offers:

> The trace of a real donation, demanding, not first knowledge as possession, nor yet the suspension which is *ennui* but rather wonder, desire, gratitude, banishment of *angst* and acceptance of continuous passage into death.[18]

As a token of the divine, the enticing gift of grace gives itself as its own consummation, passing through Derrida's gift of grace without the dark abode of fear. This circumvents the contrasting allure of death, which in many ways remains unattainable as an object of ownership or control and therefore out of reach, and in fact redeems the Maussian exhibition of a primitive exchange of gift in both immanent and transcendent terms.

Similarly critical of the latent postmodern approach to the gift, Jean-Luc Marion adjusts Derrida's "gift of death" exchange (at once singular and seemingly eternal) with his idea of the "saturated phenomenon" as an "unconditioned phenomenon."[19] Marion maintains that a phenomenon may both give itself in its appearance, while also exceeding its intuitive capacity.[20] Unlike Milbank, he does not rely on a strictly theological example (the Eucharist) for this phenomenon to operate successfully as an excess of givenness, but turns to the erotic, in which two experiences of embodied flesh rely upon the other for the sake of pleasure.[21] Paradoxically, the flesh experiences the world as a resistance, a gift that forbids and sets limits, while also giving itself in the traverse of the limits of one's own flesh; the flesh of another makes room for the self within its embrace, even as the world refuses such an enfolding of difference within it.[22]

17. Ibid., 150–52.
18. Ibid., 152.
19. Marion, *Being Given*, 212.
20. Ibid., 215.
21. Marion, *The Erotic Phenomenon*, 119.
22. Ibid., 118–19.

Coakley describes how the saturated phenomenon reconceptualizes the presence of divine action as a resummoning of the divine by an intuition that can never be humanly conceptualized.[23] She views in Derrida's critique and Marion's reinterpretation what she names stage two of the gift genealogy:

> So we might say that it is the very category of revelation that is at stake at this stage 2 of the "gift" saga, the possibility that post-modernity—and continental phenomenology—still hides in its pocket the capacity for the recognition of the divine presence whilst avoiding the pitfalls of what Heidegger termed "onto-theology."[24]

In this account, Coakley views Levinas and Derrida, as well as Marion and Milbank, as sharing some common phenomenological concerns. Each wishes to describe the event of the gift in its phenomenality, while remaining intrinsically apprehensive in allowing it an identifiable form.

In a public debate with Derrida, Marion evinces his project as having moved on from the question of gift to the lived phenomenon of givenness.[25] Both Derrida and Marion identify an important aspect of the question of the gift, which is whether a gift, having been given, can be determined in its presence. Derrida wishes to remove the gift from the problematic circle of exchange (following Mauss) and describe a nonidentifiable presence, one that does not "exist" as such.[26] The image of the gift that normally springs to mind has three elements: the giver, the gift, and the receiver. This assumes some objective qualitative content in the gift itself. But in the absence of an objective criteria to describe the gift phenomenologically, against Derrida's definition of pure gift, existence is not a label that can be ascribed to the gift. Rather, the phenomenon of givenness may be better described in terms of excess. Marion correlates it with negative theology, what he prefers to name "mystical theology," in which objective language and forms of signification are overcome by an event that cannot be described phenomenologically.[27]

Stage three of the gift genealogy, Coakley argues, constitutes the framework in which Milbank and Kathryn Tanner are operating as protagonists of a gift-based, theologically-informed, grace-infused Christian economics, what Coakley describes (and Milbank uses the term) a reinvigorated

---

23. Coakley, "Why Gift?," 226–27.

24. Ibid., 227.

25. Caputo and Scanlon (eds.), *God, the Gift, and Postmodernism*, 56.

26. Ibid., 59.

27. Ibid., 69–70.

"Christian socialism."[28] In Milbank and Tanner, the Derridean concept of pure gift has been overturned in favor of a Christianized version of the original enterprise enacted by Mauss. For Milbank, Derrida's overarching transcendent objective of a gift without blemish is really a phantom of modernity. He wishes to purge the language of pure gift by asserting Christian *agape* as a "purified gift exchange," always enfleshed within a real metaphysic of being.[29] As such, the purified logic of gift-giving is an ecstatic moment bound to human experience. It is located in the higher logic of a *Logos* who gives himself freely, repetitively, and nonidentically in the act of giving. Human participation in the gift of divine exchange must by nature be a fragmented and unequal interchange of giving and receiving.

Tanner rejects the Milbankian logic of the gift by asserting that the Christian economy of grace is veraciously noncompetitive.[30] Coakley is also suspicious of Tanner's reading of John Calvin, but it is to the latter that Tanner owes her embrace of divine "unilateralism" undergirding the human-divine exchange, excluding what she sees as the false contractualism inherent in Mauss and Milbank.[31] Coakley describes the Milbankian view of exchange as a "circle" of divine gift and human, participatory response, whereas Tanner rejects utterly the competitivism that derives from capitalist economic systems and replaces it with a horizontal, or unilateral and unconditional gift, flowing from the noncompetitive persons of the Trinity.[32]

This is what brings the present study of the gift to its third stage, at which point the concept is seen as the nexus point of a theological confrontation with dehumanizing economic forms. Coakley argues that competitive capitalism is "the fundamental economic problem to be addressed" and some form of patristic-based Trinitarianism is fundamental to a response.[33] The broadly socialist dynamic in which Tanner and Milbank engage is as a result of their notion that human persons participate in the self-gifting communion of the Trinity, which in turn is a form of socialism. The gift of a noncompetitive exchange is already present; the problem is describing the possibility of a pure gift. While the form of the exchange between human discourse and the persons of the Trinity is very different, the need for this exchange is shared by both Tanner and Milbank.

28. Coakley, "Why Gift?," 227; Milbank, "Socialism of the Gift, Socialism by Grace," 910.

29. Milbank, "Can a Gift Be Given?" 131.

30. Tanner, "Economy of Grace," 181.

31. Coakley, "Why Gift?," 228.

32. Ibid.

33. Ibid.

In chapters 2 and 4 of this book, it was argued that Levinas and John Paul II find the body inescapable, bearing in itself a language of the gift. In the case of the former, it occurs despite Levinas' denial of the body's significance as such. It will be argued that the self-kenosis that Levinas describes in the self's responsibility for the other fleshes out his approach to the gift, which adds to the common interpretation that for him, death stands as the true gift. For John Paul II, a similar denotation is given in the act of responsibility, but it is preceded by a contemplative pause before the irreducible in the person. In his approach to the body and the gift, *ethos* must be purged of its inadequate desires so that it might become the normative form of *eros*. Indeed, in the erotic embrace, sexuality opens up to a broader logic of the gift in which the child—and by consequence each human person—is both the gift and an authentication of disinterested self-donation. What the body fundamentally desires is union with the redemptive gift in the Word (Rom 3:24). Biblical references to the gift are predicated on a prior awareness of gift logic; of a conceptualization of what it is to give and to receive. This is problematized in recent continental philosophy, especially by figures such as Derrida, and complicated further in John Paul and Levinas in relation to the body.

Kenosis for the other: The embodied gift in Levinas

Giving for the body of the other

The following words from *Otherwise Than Being, Or, Beyond Essence*, characterize two important features of Levinas' understanding of the gift:

> Hospitality, the-one-for-the-other in the ego, delivers it more passively than any passivity from links in a causal chain. Being torn from oneself for another in giving to the other the bread from one's mouth is being able to give up one's soul for another. The animation of a body by a soul only articulates the-one-for-the-other in subjectivity.[34]

First, Levinas indicates that the giving of the self for the other is a true sacrifice of one's own good for the life of the other person. Second, Levinas describes the self-gift for the other—pronounced in the tearing of sustenance from one's own lips for the needs of the other—as an embodied self-offering. It relies upon the body and its sensation. It is an offering configured in the substance of flesh, profoundly figured in the movement

---

34. Levinas, *Otherwise Than Being*, 79.

of bread torn from one's teeth for the sustenance of one who is hungry. Its visceral nature is described as an embodied action, rather than acting as a mere allegory of giving for others.

As such, Levinas' giving of bread for the other is both a spiritual and an enfleshed exercise in which the action of giftedness to and for the sake of another grants proper form to a relationship between the two. It is not simply the concrete presence of one's body that gives oneself; it is rather the sacrificing of one's body for the other that gives form to one's true self. Ethical action in Levinas is a revelatory exercise in authenticity. As revelation, it is ethics as excess.[35] Because it is excessive, it opens up the space in which the "conditions" of giving are made possible.[36] By this, it can be seen how the gift of bread to an other (which in every circumstance is *the* other) is more than simply a gift given (or more crudely still, simply a body) but truly a gift received, for it gives form to the nature of the self. At all times it is being called to itself in service to the other, even while it lurks in the mire of unethical inauthenticity. Also the bread, as primordial an image of embodied reliance upon the most basic of life-giving forces, bears a theological significance: it coincides with eucharistic language.[37] The ethical shape of self-offering provides an incarnate extension of the eucharistic symbols; lighting them up as a reality that issues forth from the altar to the domestic and the everyday. Inversely, the ethical shape of self-aggrandizement or violence done to the other (such as the refusal of bread to the hungry) might become a symbol of the withdrawal of God's self-giving nature for those who are hungry. It is helpful to recall Levinas' comment, "after I became acquainted with the concept of the Eucharist, that the authentic Eucharist is actually in the moment when the other comes to face me . . . ,"[38] in which he places an accent on *presence;* of the face to face as precisely a eucharistic mo-

35. Webb, "The Rhetoric of Ethics as Excess." Webb identifies a natural link between the categories of ethics and excess, rooted in the Jewish (and Christian) concern for the widow, the stranger and the poor. He views the Scriptural demandingness of the ethical as a constant "extravagance" over the demands of the everyday and normally expected. To be ethical is not to meet an expectation, but to go beyond it.

36. Mansfield, *The God Who Deconstructs Himself,* 112.

37. Chauvet, *Symbol and Sacrament,* 392. Chauvet speaks of the designation of bread in the biblical witness firstly as the one food substance that is necessary to all, but secondly as a metaphor for all food in general. Bread, for Jesus, would have represented both a metaphorical interpretation of the gift of God as well as the gift of the whole earth and human work. In this way, "cult" and "culture" are joined incidentally with a common etymology of the two terms in Hebrew, Greek, and Latin. Further to this, bread evokes in the religious memory the integral relationship of "bread-manna-word of God-eschatological banquet." Ibid.

38. Levinas, "Judaism and Christianity after Franz Rosenzweig," in *Is It Righteous to Be?,* 256.

ment. Levinas rejects the Christian distinctiveness of the eucharistic liturgy, misunderstanding its fundamental role as an act of worship in obedience to God who gives himself in the act. Levinas also seems to misrepresent the Eucharist by disregarding the Christian claim that God remains absolutely other, and so when, in Christ, he is present in the Eucharist, Christians might relate to this activity as one of humbling responsibility. However, it is true that the eucharistic elements represent something fundamental to the human condition. The bread presents itself as an organic requirement of the hungry stomach, as well as being the sign by which the eucharistic presence of the Christ is received in the entire range of senses that bodies empower human persons with.[39] The breaded sign of eucharistic devotion is a symbol of divine giftedness, carrying within itself the power of its own signing, along with the rich festive qualities symbolized in wine. Such a correlation in Levinas of eucharistic giftedness and ethical self-offering constitutes a concentration on subjective embodiment as an intersubjective experience; an experience which is only made possible because of a language of the body that seeks both nourishment and festivity. Although his interpretation of the Eucharist misconstrues its relevance within Christian worship as an encounter with the person of Christ, it confirms once again his reliance on the body.

Describing the gift

If there is any correlation between Derrida's notion of the gift of death and Levinas' approach to death, it is anchored in the latter's understanding of the former. In his final lectures at the Sorbonne (1975–76), Levinas developed further the themes that had been published in *Otherwise Than Being*.[40] Death is the subject of a number of presentations, and it is clear that in considering the ethical relationship with others, he does not think of death as the pure gift. Levinas follows Ernst Bloch in thinking through the astonishment at existence itself, which follows the provocation of beauty ("a leaf stirred by the wind, in the beauty of a melody, the face of a young girl, a child's smile, a word").[41] The human being who has awoken to the intensity of the other and of the "me" [*moi*] comes to be at home in the world, and death loses its

39. It is no surprise that Levinas, speaking from within the Jewish tradition, would not recognize eucharistic presence in the way recognized by Christians. But it is significant that for him, the eucharistic moment remains one that can point, indirectly perhaps, to a gifted alterity; one that makes a person act humbly and justly for the sake of another.

40. Levinas, *God, Death and Time*.

41. Ibid., 101.

possessive sting.[42] The awakening of the self to the other relates profoundly to the binding of the self to the world in which it inhabits, expressed by Levinas as the *"tua res agitur"* [your interest is at stake].[43] Paradoxically, it is by identifying the interest (the need, the suffering, the desire) of the other that the human person is brought to self-knowledge.

Levinas here inverts the Heideggerian perseverance in Being, in which the self is preoccupied with its own essential mood in the world's objective theatre. Furthermore, he explicitly subordinates being and the world to the ethical order, "to the human order, and to completion (the end of exploitation) . . . ."[44] Further, Levinas views time within this fundamental ethics: time is detached from the idea of nothingness and attached to the utopian completion. That is to say, time becomes the basis upon which death is thought (and not the other way around). It refuses the thought that man lives towards his own death (as either nihilism or gift), and insists rather that death is a kind of nonbeing (which is not the same as nihilism per se) and, in fact, man may find his home in the world on the basis of his ethical responsibility. In fact, via the other, the world becomes the gift of a radical domesticity, a being-at-home for the other. To be sure, death must still be encountered: "We encounter death in the face of the other."[45] Yet in this context Levinas uses the word "love" (as "strong as death" according to Song 8:6), because it sums up the notion that the death of the other affects the self in excess of any emotional realization of one's own death.[46]

For Stephen Webb, Levinas provides a way for the gift to be thought without Derrida's problem of the futility in the process of exchange. In Webb's words, can "giving precede Being?"[47] What appears to be given in Levinas is the self. The other appears before the self but is not given for one's own need or desire; instead the other awakens the gift of responsibility in the self. Responsibility thus moves in two directions: it gives ones own self to the self, and it gives itself in kenosis for the other. This precognitive unfolding of the ethics of alterity has its form before Being can be identified. As Webb argues: "Ethics thus precedes metaphysics just as giving precedes exchange."[48] Levinas is not denying ontology. But in the move-

42. Ibid., 102.

43. Originally, the phrase comes from book I, epistle xviii: *Nam tua res agitur, paries cum proximus ardet,* in Horace, *The Odes.* For Levinas' use of the term see Levinas, *God, Death and Time,* 102.

44. Levinas, *God, Death and Time,* 103.

45. Ibid., 105.

46. Ibid.

47. Webb, *The Gifting God,* 76.

48. Ibid., 77.

ments of givenness he is seeking out an ethics of ethics—more even than a metaethic—because it preordains being and all its objective criteria with the order of a descriptive alterity. It rescues the "Said" from the "tyranny of concepts," allowing the category of Being to be viewed more adequately as being-for (the other).[49]

Need and desire

Need and desire mark out the territory of the gift in Levinas, which relies upon language to carry its meaning. Chapter 4 outlined how the need/desire distinction operates in Levinas' thought. Need is always a return to the self, whereas desire opens itself up as a "goodness" seeking out that which is desirable and consequently nourishes the self with "new hungers."[50] In both need and desire, the self and the other express a language that is not limited to linguistic expression or even the gestures of the body. It is a language of ethical desire; or in other words, a form of speech that indicates the requirement that one acts responsibly for the other. For "language," "speech" may be used as an equivalent term, for this is the term used by Levinas in its broadest meaning, which he explains in terms of its ethical quality.[51] Primarily, his considerations of this theme can be seen in section I of *Totality and Infinity*, "The Same and the Other."[52] By this stage, Levinas has established his definition of metaphysics, by which he proposes an uprooting of man from history in relation to the infinity of the other.[53] Levinas accepts an inherent "metaphysical desire" for otherness coming from an outward movement, but rejects the notion that this movement finds satisfaction in those realities that I can "feed" off "as if I had simply been lacking them."[54] Here the alterity of the bread one eats, or the land of one's dwelling, or the landscape contemplated before one's eyes are simply reabsorbed into one's own identity, as if a person could relate to them as a "possessor."[55] Such

49. Duns, "Being in the Face of Nameless Mystery," 104.

50. Levinas, "Meaning and Sense" (originally *La Signification et le Sens*), in *Collected Philosophical Papers*, 92–94.

51. Levinas, *Otherwise Than Being*, 147. "Speech" here is used in close correlation with Levinas' use of the terms "saying" and "voice," in which he explains the manner through which exteriority to the oneself is known in the dimension of interiority.

52. Levinas, *Totality and Infinity*, 53–81.

53. Section I. The Same and the Other, A. Metaphysics and Transcendence, 1. Desire for the Invisible; Ibid., 33–52.

54. Ibid., 33.

55. Ibid.

a notion of desire relies on the concept of a need or needfulness, such as hunger, sexual appetite, or moral and religious needs.

Yet this needfullness as a basis for desire lacks the result of a pure satisfaction, or equally negatively, it might end in the experience of non-satisfaction.[56] For Levinas, metaphysical desire is not met with material satisfaction, but is identified as a form of generosity that only deepens in its act of desiring, without regard for fulfillment, for it can only be "like goodness."[57] In this Levinasian sense, what one desires is an absolute transcendent in relation to the oneself; one that stands over the self in relation to one's self-knowing, offering no immediate satisfaction or even acknowledgement, and draws the self towards it in a spirit of givenness that offers no alternative. As such, it is described also by Levinas as a form of "death," an "absolute, unanticipatable alterity."[58] The idea of the infinity of the other always relies on an infinite distance between oneself and the other. Even in the act of touch (Levinas uses the term "caress" [*caresse*]) or common understanding, the other is an infinity, exceeding any category or attempt at description.[59] This infinity is experienced as a "height" one could die for, which includes, but is not bound to, individual embodied acts. Levinas describes the "height" as an "invisible" dimension of glory in which the other stands above and beyond one's immediate reach. The "Invisible" is "the very elevation of height and its nobility" [*mais l'Invisible, est l'élévation meme de la hauteur et sa noblesse*].[60] Levinas wants this category to be present in a fundamental and evocative way, and so emphasizes its character by reference to height and nobility. Richard A. Cohen has described this in terms of a nonspatial elevation of moral meaning. By "height" Levinas means the moral urgency encountered in the face of the other.[61]

This is developed by Richard A. Cohen in light of the use of proximity and distance, in which the (infinite) distance between the I and the other speaks to the oneself, calling it "higher than the faculties, capacities, or possibilities whose reflexive structure, whether ideational or existential, define selfhood in its autonomy, its 'as for me.'"[62] In Cohen's reading, this elevation

---

56. It must be remembered that Levinas' early uses of "desire" lacked his later distinction in *Totality and Infinity* between need (*besoin*) and desire (*désir*). As discussed in chapter 5, need is a hole to be filled or a gap to be nourished, whereas desire is the seeking after excess. For an acute definition, see ibid., 117.

57. Ibid., 34.

58. Ibid.

59. Ibid.

60. Ibid., 35.

61. Cohen, *Elevations*, 185.

62. Ibid., 186.

depicts an asymmetrical intersubjective morality. The other draws the self out in a speech that is defined by its lack, precisely by the absence of an audible voice. In so doing, it calls to attention the foci of a metaphysical desire, one that is invisible and yet not insubstantial, that the entire person is desirous of the good of another who is infinite in meaning.

How might metaphysical desire be understood as a kind of giftedness? In answering the question, it is important to hold in mind Levinas' principle of speech; that for him there is a moral language that arises from the infinite meaning of the other in tandem with the distance experienced between the other and the self. It is a speech without quantifiable content, an excess of ethical signification. This speech—a language of the other that is a signification—recalls similar embodied experiences of speechless speech; for example the scream of the frightened, the cry of the tortured, the whimper of the child.[63] Such a speech does not flow primarily from need, as the distinction between need and desire (above) makes clear. Rather, this kind of speech gifts the self to the other in a way desirous of the good of the other.

Levinas' notion of "unsaying" has been described by Jeffrey L. Kosky as problematic in at least two ways: first, it appears to make a "speech without phrase" indistinguishable from the cry of the needy.[64] If Levinas wishes to succeed in describing the distinction between ethics (as responsibility) and need (rather than desire), speechless speech offers no support for such a distinction. Instead, in Kosky's view, such a kind of speech might only invest itself in the closing off of alterity from the other.[65] In other words, otherness is kept at a remote distance, rather than one that exceeds its presence and enters the vicinity of the self. Levinas' notion of otherness is kept at bay instead of being authentically other, and so is an austere presence discontinued from trespassing upon the self's domain. Contrary to Levinas, there remains an eloquent language that appears in the person of genuine and immediate suffering which carries its own embodied requirement of care. The face-to-face moment bears an ethical signification that speaks from one to another. In this way, Levinas' philosophy carries a meaning he only alludes to and not by the purpose of his argument: the *language* of the suffering body, by which the true nature of the transcendent is revealed.[66] In

---

63. Levinas, *Otherwise Than Being*, 79. Levinas describes signifyingness as a *"for-the-other"* that marks an approach in relation to the Other, rather than an inscription in nature or an essence. It is rather a kind of nonthematizable sensibility.

64. Kosky, *Levinas and the Philosophy of Religion*, 42.

65. Ibid.

66. In this way, Levinas points in the direction of closing the gap in Wojtyla's work, what José Granados calls the "missing chapter" of the suffering body. See Granados, "Toward a Theology of the Suffering Body," 556.

this way Levinas' distinction between ethics and need fails a test of human experience.

Second, Jeffrey L. Kosky asks, "if speech offers nothing, can it still be a gift?"[67] Kosky notes that for Levinas speech is ethics[68] insofar as it "offers things which are mine to the Other."[69] Across the spectre of possessed things Levinas' speech without phrase is a passivity disclosing a dynamic ethical content. Levinas holds the paradox of a gifted speech without words, in which a language of the ethical is spoken, or more accurately, *enacted*. Kosky allows for such speech to be a form of pure ethics, but leaves open the question of whether, after all, it remains "language."[70] Nevertheless, Kosky affirms that on this reading of Levinas, "ethics is the gift of the world to the other."[71] In Levinas is a "speech without speech," or alternatively "speech without phrase," by way of Derrida's conviction that there is nonviolence only if the act of keeping silent remains respected, yet concurrently, otherness itself is allowed to speak.[72] This appears axiomatically incoherent and a direct contradiction. Levinas argues that it is an important paradox, on the basis that it allows speech to be recognized as ethics while maintaining the distance crucial to his metaphysical project. It must be argued that contrary to Levinas, the appeal to a silent language of the body that remains ethical may only operate successfully if it is recognized that the spoken word also communicates suffering in a concrete way. Speech and silence together embody a gift that precedes other more recognizable gifts, yet they are embodied all the more fruitfully for the human person when a fuller account of communicability is provided. This can be seen in Louis-Marie Chauvet, who argues that speech and language also constitute a liturgical and sacramental communicability.

The ethical-sacramentality of the body

For Louis-Marie Chauvet, the body is the site of an ethical language without words. That is to say, corporeality—the state of being a body and participating in the world through the body—offers a language that preexists other forms of communication. Furthermore, the body has its own sacramentality; a material openness to the operation of invisible grace, both confirming

67. Kosky, *Levinas and the Philosophy of Religion*, 42.
68. Ibid.
69. Levinas, *Totality and Infinity*, 76.
70. Kosky, *Levinas and the Philosophy of Religion*, 42.
71. Ibid.
72. Derrida, *Writing and Difference*, 116.

and disclosing grace within the world. In its ethical and sacramental dimensions, the fact of corporeality acts as "the body's very speech."[73] The activity of formal communication (words, gestures, habits, etc.) is always a kind of writing that humbly consents to mediation.

The body is the mediator of such writing. Yet this is not a simple or static process. There is conflict between the objective of mediating the body's ethics and sacramentality authentically and the way human beings hinder the "body of the written trace."[74] The demand to communicate well is in constant need of repair and clarification, always tempted to either overplay what it signifies or underplay its possibilities. Within this conflict, Chauvet contends that the body does not so much have a language, but *is* a language, which through its intersubjective relationship with other bodies bears a demand to speak and therefore to communicate. Furthermore, the sacramental economy of grace liberates the body's speech and hinders the limiting temptations of thwarting that speech. The body is also revealed as the receiver of the gift of language in which it participates in a transcendent self-offering of God. The body participates in this movement of grace in the first place by its immersion in the world, and as such, the world is rooted in the dynamic experience of the body (which is never an object, but the presence of a person). Such bodies manifest a claim upon themselves in the act of speaking, which is never limited to verbal exchanges, but reveals the nature of embodiment before acting. Chauvet owes to Maurice Merleau-Ponty the insight that, "like the painting of an artist, 'language is not the illustration of a thought already formed, but the taking possession of this thought itself.'"[75] Yet Chauvet's analysis of the relationship between body and sacrament is also an interpretation of Levinas' notion of the embodied subject's appropriation of the world it inhabits. To quote Chauvet at further length:

> The body is *the primordial place of every symbolic joining of the "inside" and the "outside."* It seems to us this is what E. Levinas means when he envisions the body "as the regime of the separation" that allows us also to "overcome the very otherness of what [we] must live by." Such is the distinctive "economy" of human beings: the body is the human "way" of inhabiting the otherness of the world as a home, a familiar dwelling. The body

73. Chauvet, *Symbol and Sacrament*, 146.

74. Ibid., 145.

75. Ibid., 146. Chauvet quotes from the French edition of Maurice Merleau-Ponty's *Phénoménologie de la perception*, 446. Chauvet also builds his case by reference to Merleau-Ponty's *Le visible et l'invisible: Notes de travail*, especially 302.

is the *binding*, the space in the middle where both identity and difference are symbolically connected under the authority of the Other.[76]

The body is for Chauvet the point of intimate connectedness with the world, in which the oneself is already immersed. It is what Martin Heidegger assigns the "Dasein-with," by which "Dasein understands itself proximally and for the most part in terms of its world; and the Dasein-with of others is often encountered in terms of what is ready-to-hand within-the-world."[77] What for Heidegger is the proximate worldliness of objects and their utility is for Chauvet the openness to ethical life and sacramental grace within the materiality of the world. This describes an image of the body as cooperating with the person rather than operating as a property owned or controlled by the person. Understanding and reflecting on the body would therefore be an appropriate response to one's embodiment as it authenticates both ethics and sacramentality. In this way, the vision is one of an ethical sacramentality of the body.

Now, Chauvet's sacramental economy, in which the other is a saturated appearing, is enlivened by the Levinasian notion of the body also as the point of departure from the world; the separation that Chauvet locates in the phenomena of embodiment in the state of worldliness. This separation appears as a gift, for it designates the manner in which the I is distinguished from that in which it has been immersed. As such, the embodied separation from the world—persons are not merely affected by the cause of the world's current, moving each onwards with no willful interaction—also remains the means of interaction with the world.[78] The body is not so much freedom *from* the world, but the means by which the self is enabled to freely act *within* the world. In other words, the body does not make possible an extension of the self beyond the world, but instead liberates the self to act within the world. Furthermore, this freedom to act makes the world a home in which one acts. As Chauvet argues, the strangeness of the world becomes a domestic abode through the sensations of the body. This experience of liberation remains also a kind of binding, the setting of limits in which the symbolic exchange with the other is made possible. In Chauvet's reading of Levinas, identity and difference are equally caught up in the symbolic exchange of meaning, through which the meaning of the I and the world

---

76. Chauvet, *Symbol and Sacrament*, 147.

77. Heidegger, *Being and Time*, 156.

78. As G. K. Chesterton observes, "A dead thing can go with the stream, but only a living thing can go against it." See part II of *The Everlasting Man*.

are shown to each other in both separation and intimacy. It is to the other that the body is oriented.

So, the world is given to the oneself by way of the body, as the body assumes (in a precognitive act) the structures and being of the world. As the body takes form in the womb, and as it extends its presence in language and culture in its own right, it is always assuming from the world the fleshliness in which it participates. However, the body's form always bears the marks of limitation, such that it can find a separation from the world, but never from worldliness: comportment to the world and others is "saturated."[79] The body can move freely and interact and withdraw from the world as the world presents itself, but it remains always immersed in the pervasive reality of worldliness. The embodied subject, as much as it receives the mundane givenness of matter and form from the world, also makes an undemanded and unsought gift of itself to the world. Within interiority, a language of personhood is carried as well as that of worldliness. As such, the body of writing that is the human person speaks already in a symbolic order that is indelibly cosmological. It points to a higher order to which a theological language is appropriate. The sacramental order, in which corporeal objects are ritually brought into a language play with the corporeal personhood of human beings, is the taking of this symbolic order and gracing it with the movement of divine *ekstasis*. To this end, it can be said with Chauvet that: "The anthropological is the place of every possible theological. And the sacramental—can it be anything else but the arch-symbolic space for this economy?"[80]

Being conscious of the gift

Having considered a way in which Levinas' presentation of the world to the oneself and vice versa can be interpreted, it is now possible to ask whether the self is conscious of the gift of the other. Chauvet establishes the primacy of language in issuing the sacramentality of the place and form of the body. For Levinas, it is in the face that the sensory experience of the self is confronted with the infinity of the other. In section III of *Totality and Infinity*, "Exteriority and the Face," Levinas develops his earlier and substantial idea of the face as an epiphany which ruptures the process of one's intentionality. He begins, "[i]s not the face given to vision?"[81] Levinas first develops his appraisal of the manner in which the objective and the affective find their rela-

79. Steinbock, "Saturated Intentionality," in Welton (ed.), *The Body*, 179.

80. Chauvet, *Symbol and Sacrament*, 152.

81. Levinas, *Totality and Infinity*, 187.

tion in sense awareness, where the psychological intentionality of the self registers the sensed experience of an objective reality. Colors, for instance, do not merely appear in a particular shape and texture upon a canvas. They are experienced in consciousness precisely as a totality of shape and texture in a painting. A sum of parts is experienced more so than a set of categories are listed and ordered.

For Levinas, a phenomenological examination of this process rehabilitates a close intimacy of the colors and shapes of a painting with the viewer. That is to say, the appearance of a painting is interpreted by the viewer according to a totality of features that occurs subjectively and not objectively.[82] Furthermore, a phenomenon never appears as an objective totality in itself, but is experienced in a particular *as such*. The colors on the canvas are experienced by a consciousness as a painting in the terms and categories in which a painting is recognized. Levinas rejects what he calls the Kantian inheritance of "transcendental aesthetics."[83] He locates in Kant the idea that sensory data have a meaning that is predetermined as a form of objectification, which denies for him the kind of subjective experience of a painting (or any object) he emphasizes. Levinas sees a role in the manner of sensory data's presentation to the self, but it bears a "transcendental function," a meaning beyond objectifiable limitation.[84] What Levinas defends is an absolute transcendent character, exemplified in the face, which both discloses and hides it. He connects the transcendental nature of the inter-subjective distance between the self and the other with the face:

> The nakedness of the face is an extirpation from the context of the world, from the world signifying as a context. The face is precisely that through which the exceptional event of the *facing* [*en-face*] is produced, which the façade of the building and of things can only imitate. But this relation of the *coram* is also the most naked nakedness, the "defenceless" and "without resources" itself, the destitution and poverty of absence that constitutes the proximity of God—the trace.[85]

The face is an exceptional event, stripped and naked and without shame. The demand of the face is given to the oneself as a moral obligation,

---

82. Ibid., 187–93.

83. Ibid., 188.

84. Ibid.

85. This quotation is taken from an interview with Levinas published in *Autrement*, no. 102, November 1988, and subsequently appeared as chapter 4, "A Man-God?," in Levinas, *On Thinking-of-the-Other*, 57. While the translation has it as "Man-God," the original French work *Entre Nous* has it as "*un dieu-homme*."

revealed in the moment of *ekstasis* (the call of *eros* to consummate in action an inner drive which appears beyond propositional understanding) and always it remains a choice to be made, recalling that the human condition is beyond the instinctual and nonethical demanding-ness of other orders of life. As such, the gifting of the oneself is always a possible gift. Even in Derridean terms, it is the presentation of that which exceeds the categories of return, whether cyclical or as a closed moment of exchange. The other establishes gift, but cannot give its own self, nor incorporate itself into one's irreducibility.[86] The other gives the self to the self, and constitutes one's responsibility on behalf of the other. Its logic is always a self-kenosis. Such a gift is presence, and that presence is witnessed as the ethics of alterity: "Witness is humility and admission; it is made before all theology; it is kerygma and prayer, glorification and recognition."[87] In these terms, theology witnesses the gift after its reception.

This reorders the metaphysical basis for a natural law in terms of *privilege* and rejects any kind of democratic or egalitarian order. Indeed, Levinas reveals a horror at the egalitarian impulse; for him the self's relationship with the other is nonreciprocal.[88] His ethical structure cements a kind of aristocracy of the other. That is to say, Levinas' uncompromising movement (which can be described as the bowing of the self) in relation to the interruption of another subject (the other), is not merely the gifting of oneself as an expression of *caritas*. It is neither morally self-indulgent nor born from the order of obedience. It is rather an *erotic* movement of sacrificial self-giving, finding its demand in the metaphysical logic of a reality grounded in the ethical.[89] This explains Derrida's resistance to a complete acceptance of Levinas' phenomenology of the gifted other: the "primacy and priority of the other" requires an *absolute* response, beyond all liberal warrants for self-governance, self-expression, and human rights.[90] One might say that in Levinas, monarchy returns in a multiplicity of other persons.

---

86. Diprose, *Corporeal Generosity*, 141.

87. Levinas, *Otherwise Than Being*, 149.

88. It operates in the "inequality of terms, transcendent to one another . . ."; Levinas, *Totality and Infinity*, 251.

89. Ibid., 253: In thinking beyond the face, Levinas concludes that against the violence of tyranny we must indicate a plain presupposing and transcending the Other. This plain is both "love and fecundity."

90. Webb, *The Gifting God*, 77.

Pausing before the irreducible: The embodied gift according to John Paul II

Contemplating the embodied other

Before the mystery of human subjectivity, John Paul II wishes to "pause."[91] In an act of humility, he does not rush into a description of the human person in its subjectivity, but rather meditates upon the existential depths that lay hidden within the structures of human personhood.[92] This pause is one that interrupts the philosophical anthropological tradition just as much as it interrupts a chronological engagement with the other. Before the event of irreducibility, philosophy stands with head bowed, and in this way one can recognize a certain line of continuity between he and Levinas. Indeed, John Paul remarks that to resist such a pause is to risk putting aside exactly that in the *humanum* that makes a person human to begin with.[93] The inner subjectivity which experiences a moral conflict between good and evil is irreducible to the natural world, despite the positive objectivity accorded to its description in the Aristotelian tradition. Yet this pause before the mystery—this contemplative moment—does not mean the evasion of description, but rather a newness of the descriptive approach. It is given by way of phenomenology, in which objective values and their penetration in the conscience are identified with new perception, an observation Levinas makes of Wojtyla's work more generally.[94] John Paul's Thomist realism is enhanced by phenomenology's aptitude for the intuitive movement of objective realities, especially that of the human person.[95] It is important to view John Paul's contribution for its ingenuity here, but also for its profound continuity within the Western tradition.

In the "pause," what is in fact appearing to the observer of human subjectivity is something utterly transcendent to the simple operation of cognitive understanding. It is a fullness of meaning that incorporates descriptive language even as it exceeds the possibility of language. Despite this transcendence, it remains immersed in the event of human experience. As John Paul II explains:

---

91. John Paul II, *Person and Community*, 213.

92. Michael Purcell sees something like the "pause" in his phenomenological description of "hesitation" before the other. See Purcell, "On Hesitation before the Other."

93. John Paul II, *Person and Community*, 215.

94. Buttiglione, *Karol Wojtyla*, 276.

95. Lawler, *The Christian Personalism of Pope John Paul II*, 46.

The irreducible signifies that which is essentially incapable of reduction, that which cannot be reduced but can only be disclosed
or revealed. Lived experience essentially defies reduction. This
does not mean, however, that it eludes our knowledge; it only
means that we must arrive at the knowledge of it differently,
namely, by a method or means of analysis that merely reveals
and discloses its essence. The method of phenomenological
analysis allows us to pause at lived experience as the irreducible.[96]

It is an irreducibility that, according to its own inner structure, is *given*,
"disclosed," or "revealed." Two points are of importance in these words.

The first is that the irreducible in the human person is given as a quality of resistance, a dignity that cannot be compromised.[97] It refuses comprehensive explanation and cannot be bracketed out from its embodied
context. Its only interpretation is through an appreciation of its intuitive
content; intentionality itself is not sufficient.

The second point is that this disclosure of the irreducible is not given
in formal categories but according to its own order, which is phenomenological. Only the method of phenomenological analysis allows the possibility of such a disclosure. Even then, such a disclosure does not give itself
entirely to the receiver, but allows the receiver to pause (which is not the
same as passivity) in an active reception to the disclosure itself. In this way,
the irreducible reflects John Paul's personalism, which avoids falling into
subjectivism.[98]

The reference of John Paul II to that which can be "disclosed" or "revealed" places the power of discovery about other human persons primarily
in their own hands. That is to say, what may be discovered is only that which
can be disclosed or revealed by another. This is largely because the inner
self remains hidden within the structures of a human person. This means
something further in terms of ethics, for it forces the self to accept that before the irreducible other it remains but one other subject in the cosmos,
and nothing of the other's inner self is owed to the self's own knowledge or
understanding. No, the other's irreducibility extends even to the gaze of the
self, even if one's own self has nothing but an interest in the other's welfare.
What occurs in this phenomenological reading of the *humanum* is a dramatic ethics of irreducibility.

96. John Paul II, *Person and Community*, 215.

97. Lawler, *The Christian Personalism of Pope John Paul II*, 69.

98. Ibid., 22.

For John Paul II, this action allows a permeation of the "whole essence" of the experience of human subjectivity to be made manifest to the I.[99] That is not to say that it allows a comprehensive description of the human person, but rather the fullness of subjectivity is disclosed, leading to a phenomenological contribution of a "trans-phenomenal understanding . . . of the richness proper to human existence . . . ."[100] John Paul's pause is contemplative, and so belongs to all human experience. Its relationship to a phenomenology of human experience is certainly cognitive, but is fruitful in its capacity to be enacted as a contemplative moment before the mystery of the human person, which means it is not limited to any particular circumstance. Levinas understands responsibility for the other to be "awakened" by the call of the other's face, which is a precognitive, nonformal moment.[101] The consequences of this awakening are not dissimilar to John Paul's "pause," and so return to his treatment of the nuptial mystery, in which the pause is incarnated as a meditation on his principle paradigm of alterity.

Pondering the gift of married love: Embodying the "pause"

John Paul II considers married love to be more than a mere example of authentic love; it also acts as a paradigm through which other loves can be interpreted. As such, he describes the need for a "pause" before the gift of married love, so that its gravity can be better understood in a multilayered texture of meaning and symbol. A dramatic example is given in the many ways in which John Paul's characters are portrayed in his dramatic works, such as the play *The Jeweler's Shop*.[102] Until now, focus has been given to John Paul II's philosophical and theological works, but his more artistic and theatrical writings shed much light on how his scholarly considerations are animated in the characters and relationships described in such works. Specifically, in *The Jeweler's Shop*, three couples are presented in a simple narrative, each in a different stage of marital preparation or experience, and faced with a variety of questions concerning the nature of love.[103] The jeweler's shop itself is the primary social space of the play, in which wedding rings are bought, sold, and coveted. In the first act, newly engaged Teresa and Andrew, not yet having purchased a wedding band, pause before the glass window of a shoe shop, pondering past words and gestures by which they

99. John Paul II, *Person and Community*, 216.
100. Ibid.
101. Levinas, "The Awakening of the I," in *Is It Righteous to Be?*, 182.
102. John Paul II, *The Jeweler's Shop*.
103. This text is also explored in chapter 5.

may have signaled that they would be destined to marry each other, and no one else. In the previous dialogue, Teresa asks Andrew, "do you believe in signals?"[104] This takes him off guard and without a ready answer. Of course, he does believe in the power of social signals that are delivered without intention or words and this is evidenced by his interior reflections that follow. He is not surprised by the content of the statement, but the sudden appearance of truth in this way unnerves him subtly. He remembers her passing on an earlier occasion and thinks to himself:

> How close she passed by me then;
>
> She almost hemmed me in with her imagination and that discreet suffering,
>
> which at the time I did not want to know, and today am willing to regard as our common good.[105]

He continues to gain clarity about his sense of her importance to him, more by a reflection upon her personal impression in form and image than by a cognitive recognition. He continues:

> Teresa—Teresa—Teresa—
> like a strange focus of my way to maturity—
> no longer a prism of superficial rays,
> but a being of true light.
> And I know I cannot go further.
> I know I shall not seek anymore.
> I only tremble at the thought that
> I could so easily have lost her.[106]

In this moment, something very like the "pause" John Paul commends so strongly is witnessed in an embodied intersubjectivity. Indeed, Teresa "had just paused" before her nuptial "other," Andrew, who silently joins her presence with that of his own.[107] The two movements are in fact one. There is a poignancy made all the more apparent by Andrew's interior concerns at the possibility that he ever may have lost Teresa. There before the shop's wares, seated behind glass, the couple gaze at the dual reflection of themselves superimposed upon the items that are for sale. Andrew continues his interior dialogue in front of their imperfect reflection:

104. John Paul II, *The Jeweler's Shop*, 29.
105. Ibid., 30.
106. Ibid.
107. Ibid., 31.

So when we found ourselves all of a sudden on both sides of the
great mirror

—here alive and real, there reflected—

I—who knows why,

maybe to complete the picture, but more likely just in answer to
my heart's need—

asked, "What are you thinking about, Teresa?"

I asked this almost in a whisper,

for this is how those in love are wont to talk.[108]

The embodied other makes present an invisible mystery. It is, as it
were, clearly a mystery in terms of its subjective hiddenness in the human
self; not seen or understood for its full significance, yet known intuitively. As
a mystery, it is not grounded in an immediately obvious sense in anything
like divine transcendence. Rather, it is grounded in the enfleshed discourse
of human relationships, even amidst inner fears and nonarticulated anxiet-
ies. It is no accident that a recurring literary advice used by Wojtyla in *The
Jeweler's Shop* is the voicing of unanswered questions (either to themselves,
to another, or to no one in particular). Furthermore, they often lack receipt
of a response (this is seen continually, such as when Teresa imagines her
wedding and the questions her guests may have but never ask,[109] or Anna's
perplexing existential question, "[i]sn't what one feels most strongly the
truth?"[110] or her haunting recollection of the mysterious invitation from the
stranger who can afford a motor vehicle, "[w]on't you join me?"[111]). These
tell more about the mysteriousness of human relationships than if an answer
had been attempted. In the presence of the other, John Paul's pause involves
a question that is not necessarily answered. Even more appropriately, the
question itself is enough. Its very appearing confirms that the social context
of persons is the setting of the irreducible in the human condition.

This is no mystical overabundance that defies description, but rather a
bowing before the mystery of concrete lived experience, rejecting any trace
of reducibility. It owes much to a realism informed by the metaphysical
terrain explored by the Aristotelian tradition, without subsuming human
experience into that system. John Paul acknowledges the need to develop
and explain the relationship between these two ways of understanding the

108. Ibid., 32.
109. Ibid., 39.
110. Ibid., 56.
111. Ibid., 61.

human being, the cosmological (Aristotelian-Boethian anthropological objectivity) and the personalistic (the "pause" before the irreducibility of the human person described above). He sees in their relationship the space in which essential and burning questions concerning anthropology and ethics ought to be pursued and, by consequence, in which anthropological-ethical challenges might be faced.[112] In John Paul, the gift of the other is pondered in a contemplative posture; silence receives the gift and is aware of its non-reciprocal exchange with the giver.

The dimension of the gift in spousal perspective

In *Man and Woman He Created Them*, the relationship of bride to bridegroom becomes John Paul's principle paradigm of alterity.[113] Fifteen addresses are gathered under the title "Man in the Dimension of Gift," which follows the account of the human person in original solitude, nakedness, and unity.[114] Here, John Paul unfolds what he calls the spousal meaning of the body in two dimensions.

The first is the rootedness of his anthropology in a theology of the *imago Dei*. In "male and female," two diverse ways of being a body are the proper factors which coincide in the unity of the image of God.[115]

The second is what John Paul calls his "hermeneutics of the gift."[116] This criterion and interpretation is predicated on the above, confirmed in Christ's words, that God created the world in its totality, and the human person, who uniquely bears the divine reflection.[117] The dual creation of the world and of the rational human creature who bears the *imago Dei* confirms an act of giving which arrives through love, but is wrought from nothing. Existence itself is a nonreturnable gift. Further to this, the appearance of man in this gifted world is the point at which the gift finds a receiver with the capacity to receive. Only in the act of creating man does God locate a point at which the mutual givenness between world and an object within that world take place.[118]

---

112. In this way, Wojtyła's early essays in *Person and Community* and his dramatic productions such as *The Jeweler's Shop* interpret and illustrate one another and cannot be read apart from one another.

113. This is a key argument made in chapter 2.

114. John Paul II, *Man and Woman He Created Them*, 13-19.

115. Ibid., 13:2.

116. Ibid.

117. Ibid., 13:3.

118. Ibid., 13:4.

It is at this point that reciprocity—denied profoundly by Levinas—appears as a substratal feature of John Paul's anthropology.[119] The words of God in Gen 2:18, "[i]t is not good that the man should be alone," affirm the impossibility that man should "realize" his essence or find his "norm" without communion with others.[120] The actions by the Creator make possible the response of joy when, after the creation of woman, the man exclaims, "she is flesh from my flesh and bone from my bones" (Gen 2:23). According to John Paul's theology, reciprocity follows God's acknowledgement that the human person cannot fulfill its own destiny alone. It is not only an embodied other who appears in the text, but one whose body has the capacity for reciprocal and mutual union. Sexuality and personhood are intimately related here, for one cannot be thought of apart from the other. The gift is not given so that the self might find an isolated pleasure or happiness, but so that it might be revealed in the reciprocity of male and female.[121] The fullness of the two also reveals the absence borne in the presence of only one. As Angelo Scola puts it:

> Sexuality (man and woman, sexual difference) thus demonstrates its coessentiality with human nature, through that polarity which indicates reciprocity. I, who exist as a man of the male gender, do not exhaust the whole of being man. I always have before me, almost as a counterimage, the other way of being man, which is inaccessible to me.[122]

The one experiences absence if cut off from the other. The inaccessibility of the other's interiority is therefore related—via the somatic whole of the body—to the sexual nature of personal subjectivity. The discovery of this is a source of freedom for the human person, who is not reduced to a mere accord of bodily passions and desires.[123] This is a multilayered account of the gift. The body is a gift to the self that makes possible the personal gift of the self to the other. In this way, the body is the condition of the gift and indeed makes the gift of the self a consciously given act, thus allowing for the spousal meaning of the body to enact its drama within creation.[124] Love also makes its appearance at this point in John Paul's anthropology, in which the reciprocity of male and female, consciously imagined, is the "power to

119. This is in reference to Buber's insistence on reciprocity as the means by which the "thou" could be protected from reduction to an "it." See Buber, *I and Thou*.

120. John Paul II, *Man and Woman He Created Them*, 14:2.

121. Ibid., 14:5.

122. Scola, *The Nuptial Mystery*, 119.

123. John Paul II, *Man and Woman He Created Them*, 14:6.

124. Ibid., 15:1.

express love" to the other.[125] Just as the gift establishes the relationship, it serves as an unfolding revelation within the communion of the two, such that the gift is received more constantly and more deeply through time.

Carl Anderson interprets the structure of the gift in terms of a cognitive, preactive recognition of givenness that ends in blessing.[126] Recognizing the gift is to begin a process of receiving the gift prior to action. This preactive recognition is already a spiritual movement, even if it has not been concretized in bodily activity. It is a beatifying directionality of the spousal meaning of the body, achieved in the complementary relationship of reciprocity.[127] The embodied orientation towards the good is in part based on the mutual recognition of the *imago Dei* in the other, but is also based on the mysterious motivation of the divine in creating man. John Paul quotes "Gaudium et Spes" 24, which articulates that man is uniquely created for his own sake and may only find himself through the "gift of self."[128] By such a claim, the human person stands out in creation as both an object of God's love (as are all creatures) as well as a subject with a rational will. This is important because it views the human person as one who may learn and mature within a rational reflection on its own situation in the world. To be created for his own sake is to have been brought from nothing to something at the behest of a divine pleasure at seeing it develop and mature. In reflecting on this mystery, the human person is better able to see in the givenness of the other person the joy of a reciprocal gift of self. The joy of this encounter extends to the object of *communio* with God. As "Gaudium et Spes" suggests, the two cannot be separated, although the final objective of human yearning is of "God himself."[129] The human person has always before it the hope of this end, but remains in need of an immediate recognition of loving both God and the other within the materiality of creation.

Original innocence is the state that makes possible a mutual recognition of the gift in the spousal meaning of the body. In Gen 2:25, the man and the woman look upon each other and experience no shame. For John Paul, this is an overlooked text, in which "welcoming" and "accepting" the embodied beauty of the other in the nuptial relationship constitutes a recognition of what is inherently a gracious gift.[130] Because original innocence is the state in which the body was first intended, its unblemished consti-

---

125. Ibid.

126. Anderson, *Called to Love*, 67.

127. John Paul II, *Man and Woman He Created Them*, 15:5.

128. Ibid.

129. Catholic Church, "Gaudium Et Spes," 24.

130. John Paul II, *Man and Woman He Created Them*, 17:3.

tution is both something to look back to, as well as indicating the future tense of the resurrection, in which the body is called to participate. John Paul is providing a scriptural account of the state in which the body can be received positively and without shame. John Paul is drawing on this way of approaching the other to counter a lingering Manichaeism in contemporary Catholic theology, where the body is thought of negatively and devalued.[131] Instead of a diminished and negative view of the body, John Paul finds in it an occasion for accepting and caring for the other. Its refusal is not just a rejection of the gift, but its loss.[132]

The nature of receiving the gift within the nuptial mystery has a paradoxical interpretation in John Paul. As was outlined in chapter 2, it is indeed mutually reciprocal in that both persons recognize in each other the *imago Dei*. Nevertheless, the equality of persons that characterize this and other forms of human community is experienced in an ethically asymmetrical fashion. That is to say, from the perspective of one member of the spousal relationship, the other remains greater than the self. The self owes to the unique other a self-donation in constant need of renewal and deepening awareness. John Paul takes the text of Eph 5:21, that persons become "subject to one another," to mean that spouses realizes themselves by *serving* the other in a nuptial communion.[133] This is why for a commentator like Scola, the reciprocity of the two is fundamentally and mutually asymmetrical.[134] Certainly, a reciprocity of dignity is manifest in the intersubjectivity of the two. Yet, in an ethical sense, the relationship is a thoroughgoing asymmetry of self-donation. One discovers the truth of one's own dignity through an *ethos* of sacrifice for the other.[135] In turn, one finds that a new gift arises from the exchange: the gradual awareness of a "gift of self" in correlation to the consciousness of the original gift of the other.[136] While this reflection is centered on the original state of human existentiality, John Paul is concerned to ensure they orbit within the range of grace such that by the same, contemporary persons reimagine the body in their own historical situation. This "theological prehistory," as it were, constitutes the basis for a new

---

131. John Paul II is at pains to rebuke the Manichaen heresy, which derives from texts in the third century that taught a radical dualism between spirituality (the light) and materiality (the world). The body and sexuality were negated sorely. See ibid., 35:3, 41:4, 44:5–6, 45:1–5, 46:1, 4, 49:6, 55:3, 62:5, 77:6, 78:1, 82:6, 83:3, 85:5, 117B:2.

132. The "antithesis" of the gift. Ibid., 17:3.

133. Ibid., 89:6

134. Scola, *The Nuptial Mystery*, 120.

135. John Paul II, *Man and Woman He Created Them*, 17:4–6.

136. Ibid., 17:5.

theological aspect of the *"ethos of the body."*[137] Reciprocity has both a theological and an ethical dimension. Theologically, it is a strict term, denoting a rigorous reciprocal possibility in the mutual recognition and exchange of the *imago Dei* in a lived experience of the body. Ethically, reciprocity is experienced paradoxically in a radical asymmetry, in which the self finds itself through giving itself away for the other. John Paul II argues that "[o]riginal innocence manifests and at the same time constitutes the perfect ethos of the gift."[138] This innocence, which is being pure of heart, allows the imaging forth of the other, stripped of unworthy garments, and of the world itself.

In consciousness of the gift, the other is received as a free gift, and elicits a response of ethical hospitality. As this original *ethos* takes form, John Paul locates in marriage the "primordial sacrament," constituted upon the concrete presence of male and female in an embodied relationship of care and mutual regard.[139] What is, in effect, the sacrament of asymmetrical reciprocity, opens up a logic of the gift to others, not as a hidden or discrete exchange, but as one known consciously and enacted in a festal mood. Truth and love issue forth an extended exchange of the gift that, despite the horizon of death and sin, remains intact through the *imago Dei* in the integrated whole that is the human body.[140]

Moreover, for John Paul's anthropology, the other, if he or she is to be received in the full personalistic value to which the body is a witness, must be understood always as a sexual person. To think otherwise is to destabilize the human body. According to Scola, "[r]elation to the other is never constituted independently of sexuality."[141] In the paradigm of alterity, the nuptial mystery constitutes one flesh but two bodies. This mystery is made possible in the mutual gift of the entire body of each person, male and female. On this reading, the nuptial mystery acts as the guarantor of bodily otherness and of the integrity of the body in its reciprocity. The knowledge of this mystery allows for other aspects of the paschal mystery to unfold more clearly. For example, the eucharistic celebration, in which the bride and bridegroom relationship is dramatized in God's divine presence in the sacrament, relies on the typological significance of the almost mundane, domesticated, and recognizable experiences of marriage. Marc Ouellet calls the Eucharist the historical guarantee of the mutual "knowledge" and "recognition" of the

137. Ibid., 18:3.
138. Ibid., 18:5.
139. Ibid., 19:3–6.
140. Ibid., 19:6.
141. Scola, *The Nuptial Mystery*, 126.

divine bridegroom and earthly bride.[142] That is, the eucharistic celebration confirms the nuptial mystery at the heart of Christian faith between Christ and the church. By its continual recelebration, the Eucharist establishes the nuptial analogy repeatedly as an image before the church of the heavenly bride and bridegroom to be emulated.

The gift of this image is then celebrated and confirmed, as well as strengthening and clarifying the iconic nature of embodied relationships between spouses. Sexual reciprocity is not an end in itself, but a particular anthropological understanding of the gift. In spousal perspective, it is the recognition of an irreducible subjectivity that is intimately related to its own embodiment. John Paul's hermeneutics of the gift radicalizes the body in a movement of gift exchange, acting as a constant reference point that makes the gift possible. Furthermore, the use of the nuptial mystery necessitates a new coincidence of *eros* and *ethos*:

> It is necessary continually to rediscover the spousal meaning of the body and the true dignity of the gift in what is "erotic." This is the task of the human spirit, and it is by its nature an ethical task. If one does not assume this task, the very attraction of the senses and the passion of the body can stop at mere concupiscence, deprived of all ethical value, and man, male and female, does not experience that fullness of "eros," which implies the upward impulse of the human spirit toward what is true, good, and beautiful. It is, therefore, indispensable that ethos becomes the constitutive form of eros.[143]

This is a dense but crucial passage. John Paul explains the ethical task of rediscovering an aspect of theological anthropology that has been overlooked. He locates in the spousal meaning of the body a language of gift that is phenomenologically received in the presence of the body itself. *Eros* is invoked as the formal means in which *ethos* might be reappropriated. Desire is interpreted positively, allowing the possibility of gifting through the body. By this, John Paul indicates a regulative role of the nuptial mystery in a new development of the theology of the body. He calls for a phenomenological reading of the spousal meaning of the body. Further, he is seeking out the gift of the erotic (which is not bound to the language of sexuality). This "spiritual" task in itself is not limited to theology, but is a common "ethical" task, relying on a transcendent hope beyond the immediate sensations and passions of the body.[144]

142. Ouellet, *Divine Likeness*, 165.
143. John Paul II, *Man and Woman He Created Them*, 48:1.
144. Ibid.

The gift of the child

The spousal relationship grants a way of seeing the gift in terms of the body of the other. Moreover, for John Paul, a further gift arrives within the dimension of the nuptial mystery.[145] For him, the mutual self-gift in the nuptial mystery gives way to the gifting of the third, termed the "crown" of the married couple by the Second Vatican Council.[146] It is argued here that the child situates John Paul's theology of the body within a universal context in which every human person is received ethically as a gift. This approach endorses the notion that there is a greater logic of the gift at work through the work and self-donation of Christ and that the body is afforded a special place within that logic. The thought of Levinas, suspicious of embodiment and yet reliant on the body, also conceives of the other in terms of the gift. Yet, as has been argued, Levinas' approach is most fruitful in this regard when considered in light of his approach to the responsibility which arises by the gift of the other, rather than his strict polarity between the self and the absolute other. In looking upon the child as the *exemplar* and model of the gift, some attention ought to be paid to the possibility of interpreting it to dangerous effect. Specifically, rather than accepted in the movement of gratuity, the community of the couple could receive the child as a reward for their own self-donation. The notion of reward implies some accumulative value in the couple's capacity to give to each other, which results in a quantitative result. If the gift is understood in this problematic way, a person's value is already determined in the frailty of personal gift exchange between two persons, which is an unstable basis for which to accept the gift of responsibility that arises in the appearance of another person. As John Paul consistently argues, the human person must be received according to a personalist value and no other; each person is received at the level of the "communion of persons."[147] To inscribe the nascent human being with a value that relies on what is given by the couple would be to reduce the child to the quality of a product rather than a gift.

Against this dehumanizing tendency, John Paul's proposal is forged within a logic of the gift as patterned within the greater logic of divine self-donation. In *Familiaris Consortio*, the logic of the nuptial mystery affirms the child as gift, in the sense that parents participate in the broader fruitfulness of God, who is the origin of life.[148] The experience of embodied alterity

145. John Paul II, *Familiaris Consortio: Regarding the Role of the Christian Family in the Modern World*, 28.

146. Catholic Church, "Gaudium Et Spes," 48.

147. John Paul II, *Man and Woman He Created Them*, 117:6.

148. John Paul II, *Familiaris Consortio: Regarding the Role of the Christian Family*

allows a couple to open up further space within their interior capacity to welcome the stranger, who arrives naked and absolutely dependent. In this way, the child does not arrive as a reward for the couple, but as the *exemplar* of embodied gratuity. In making this case, John Paul insists that other fruits of marriage are not lessened by virtue of this being paramount (particularly the unitive dimension).[149] The gift of the child can be defended on the basis of the *communio* outlined by John Paul; that its logic is based on the higher logic of divine love and that it is to be received according to the irreducible nature of persons as persons, and not as a form of reward.

A further question spontaneously arises in the notion of child as fruit of love. That is, where in this approach is consideration of those concrete experiences in which children are conceived or born outside of any semblance of the kind of nuptial embrace John Paul II describes?[150] Is this model based on the enfleshed discourse of a marriage (natural or sacramental) or on the higher analogy of the nuptial mystery? If it is based solely upon the former, then it betrays the countless children who are not born in this model. One thinks of children born in contexts of violence and exploitation. If John Paul's approach is based on the latter, which in turn guides and makes possible the former, then there is a strong theological basis for interpreting the gift of the person within the nuptial mystery as a universal model or paradigm. First, within John Paul's notion of the gift the human person is created by divine agency and "inscribed" in the original sacrament of creation.[151] Because the person, the *imago Dei*, is a creation of God, the capacity of spouses to follow the logic of that divine gift is a moral one, which requires mutual assistance in the life of virtue.[152] This requires a recognition that sexuality is performed within the realm of free agency. Persons are free to make use of this gift in a reductionist, negative, or harmful way. Second, there remains a certain incompleteness in Wojtyla/John Paul II's theology of the body. He acknowledges this when he writes:

> These reflections do not include multiple problems which, with regard to their object, belong to the theology of the body (as, for example, the problem of suffering and death, so important in the biblical message).[153]

in the Modern World, 28.

149. Ibid.

150. For example, tragic instances such as rape, incest, environments of abuse and neglect, etc.

151. John Paul II, *Man and Woman He Created Them*, 102:7.

152. Ibid., 127:2.

153. Ibid., 129:1.

Here, the incomplete nature of the catechesis of the body is admitted. John Paul II recognizes that he does not include a developed reference to the problems of suffering and death, and leaves open the possibility that these themes might be developed by others. It is here argued that an incompleteness does not rob the theology of the body of its value, but that it does clarify an area in need of development. This situates the theology of the body within a broader need to recognize the complexities of suffering and death within human experience in the development of theological anthropology. This acknowledgement by John Paul is rarely commented upon, although the encyclical *Salvifici Doloris* goes some way to offering a clear exposition on the themes of suffering and death.[154] While that document deals with suffering within the broad scope of biblical witness and redemption, it does not place suffering clearly in relation to John Paul's theology of the body. For instance, how does the contemporary suffering body relate to the original states of solitude, unity, or nakedness? More concretely, how does the suffering body within the married relationship anticipate communion with its counterpart if the suffering itself is a result of some aspect of their shared life? In a significant essay on the topic, José Granados argues that the missing chapter in John Paul's theology of the body is an account of the "suffering body."[155] In fact, he argues that such an account would not be limited to the contemporary human person, but would require some handling of the intermediate period between fallen and redeemed man, with clear reference to the historical ministry of Christ.[156] To be sure, John Paul's catechesis on the body already makes reference to the fractious experience of the body in "historical man."[157] He refers to the "man of concupiscence," who must place himself in the "future-oriented perspective of conjugal consent" if present sufferings are not to rob the body of its significance.[158] And despite the fall, John Paul emphasizes that the passing from "error" to "truth" is a constant possibility for the historical human person.[159] Nevertheless, these themes are not developed as fully as they might be, and this is an area in which theologians ought to do further work.

It is precisely in the context of the intermediate state that John Paul II's reflections are situated, even if he offers no systematic account of that

---

154. This document was considered in the previous chapter. See John Paul II, *Salvifici Doloris: On the Christian Meaning of Human Suffering*.

155. Granados, "Toward a Theology of the Suffering Body," 540–41.

156. Ibid.

157. John Paul II, *Man and Woman He Created Them*, 106:5.

158. Ibid., 106:4–5.

159. Ibid., 107:3–4.

state in itself. For Granados, the period between the fall and redemption constitutes the state in which the contemporary human person experiences its imperfect and suffering body. Granados views Christ and his sufferings as a helpful lens through which to interpret the body. For Granados, Christ's sufferings inaugurate a dynamism of "compassion," which refashions the gift of suffering as a reawakening of love for the suffering person.[160] Only Christ is capable of perfect compassion and so a share in it perfects the limited occasions of love for the other. Christ is certainly an interpretive key in *Salvifici Doloris*, which interprets the Bible as linking bodily suffering to moral sufferings.[161] The suffering of the individual intersects with communal suffering, in which the body's privations and agonies open up the moral question of *why*—why is there suffering, and where is God when the innocent cry out to heaven? For John Paul, all suffering is an experience of evil within creation, and so is a reminder of Christ's confrontation with evil.[162] Christ does not rob suffering of its mystery, but instead endures it and confronts it with the affirmation of divine love, making it possible for all suffering to act as an opportunity to act in love. Indeed, it is for this reason that suffering becomes an occasion of reverence for the Christian *ecclesia*, which locates in it a meeting of the suffering Christ with those Christ suffers for.[163] This account offers some contextualization for John Paul's account of suffering generally, although it cannot fill completely what his theology of the body lacks. This makes it possible to view the theology of the body as a treatment of the body which is theologically fruitful, even if it requires further attention to the place of suffering and what is given in the moment of suffering.

This allows a return to the question of the nascent human person; the child. Rather than interpreting the child as a gift in such a way to burden marriage with the whole task of revealing the gift, a Christian approach to suffering recontextualizes the discussion. In human experience, many children arrive as suffering bodies, either in themselves or as members of families where a logic of love is not altogether obvious. The appearance of the child who suffers is cause for a mood of reflection on a phenomenality that halts and falters the reception of giftedness. The suffering of the child cannot be perceived as a good in itself, but rather as a "lack," "limitation," or "distortion of the good," as *Salvifici Doloris* acknowledges.[164] This

---

160. Granados, "Toward a Theology of the Suffering Body," 560.

161. John Paul II, *Salvifici Doloris: On the Christian Meaning of Human Suffering*, 6.

162. Ibid., 9, 13, 14–24.

163. Ibid., 24.

164. Ibid., 7.

suffering—both bodily and morally—is the distorting malevolence of evil. Nevertheless, the suffering of the other is also a beckoning experience that issues a demand upon others. It is a confrontation with the suffering other that halts the moral gaze and instructs the person to act in response. Granados argues that suffering, like that of shame in John Paul's thought, is a "boundary experience," opening up understanding of human limitations within the horizon of God's promise for the future.[165] In the agony of others, communion beckons, for perceived within their privations is the common boundary event of suffering, a constituent feature of human experience. Suffering confirms vulnerability, which is for John Paul also an aspect of human transcendence, opening up experience to what lies beyond.[166] Granados twice refers to Levinas' conception of suffering in light of John Paul's theology of the body, in which the suffering body awakens in the self the responsibility that is written into creation itself.[167] This responsibility is motivated by the fruit of the other's suffering: compassion. In compassion for the suffering other, the self recognizes the integral meaning of nuptial love in its widest application, which is of responsible love for another's body—to the glory not of each other, but of the origin of both.[168]

The body is indispensable for it is "the anthropological element that opens us up to the world and to our neighbors."[169] In this light, the question itself is altered. It is not whether a child can be interpreted as the "fruit of love," but how is it that one's own body ought to respond to the needs of the vulnerable other? Indeed, the vulnerability of the child calls for a level of responsibility that exceeds expectation and places all other acts of responsibility into a clear perspective; one is reminded that every other person is or was once a child and, in a biblical perspective, all people were given their life by God (Acts 17:25). Furthermore, the New Testament endorses the paradox that spiritual maturity lies in the movement from sin to new life as "children of God" (John 1:12–13). Fundamental to human experience is the complex development of childhood, which in its first appearing and its gradual progress remains the context in which a person is given to others. This embodied alterity is therefore a common experience and John Paul's approach situates it theologically and universally. His treatment of marriage and the nuptial mystery places the person as a gift to be ethically received and attended to responsibly. It is a gift that reveals a greater logic by way of

165. Granados, "Toward a Theology of the Suffering Body," 551.

166. John Paul II, *Salvifici Doloris: On the Christian Meaning of Human Suffering*, 2.

167. Granados, "Toward a Theology of the Suffering Body," 555, 556.

168. Ibid., 556.

169. Ibid., 559.

the suffering person. Compassion for the other is "reawakened" in response to the suffering other, precisely through the invitation of the first love, which is Christ.[170]

Now, this wider application of the nuptial mystery moves it beyond the limitations of sexuality, allowing the analogous form of marriage to operate in terms of creation. It answers the question concerning the child born outside of John Paul's ideal image of marriage by insisting on the irreducible nature of the gift of each person. In this perspective, the human person—the child—is not claimed as one's possession, but surpasses human expectation or capacity, as Granados also argues.[171] John Paul II addresses this wider application directly:

> Does it not embrace every human being and, in some sense, everything created, as the Pauline text on the "redemption of the body" in Romans indicates (see Rom 8:23)? In this sense, the *sacramentum magnum* is indeed a *new* sacrament of man in Christ and in the Church: *the sacrament "of man and of the world*," just as the creation of man, male and female, in the image of God was the original sacrament of man and of the world.[172]

For John Paul II, this mystery goes to the heart of both the sacramental life in Christ and the church as well as to the original creation. The notion of the nuptial mystery as a convergence of each human being and the world and of Christ and the church is therefore of universal applicability. It applies to every human person as a child who is given for the sake of responsible care, offered as a gift in light of the self-donation of Christ. In this sense, every person is a fruit of divine love, and the married communion of two persons provides the analogous relationship in which this is seen most clearly. In interpreting the child as the supreme gift in the erotic embrace of the couple, John Paul radicalizes the body within a logic of the gift. The embodied person bears the *imago Dei*, unique and yet common to all men, at once rupturing the communion of the two (the husband and wife) with the giving of flesh, blood, and tears in labor, and paradoxically further opening up their intimate capacity for the other. As such, the gift is not given in a sanitized ease of divine display. Rather, it is given within the fragile fabric of embodied relationships, where fecundity is the difficult "fruit and sign of conjugal love."[173] Grace is here witnessed in the mundane and the everyday experience of human life.

170. Ibid., 562.
171. Ibid., 547.
172. John Paul II, *Man and Woman He Created Them*, 102:7.
173. John Paul II, *Familiaris Consortio: Regarding the Role of the Christian Family*

Some have commented on the violence that appears in this love, for example Gerard Loughlin, who writes of the gift torn from the flesh of an other, "cut" from the body of its mother.[174] Separation and intimate responsibility are revealed in this dependency of one person (the child) for its parent. In this radicalized dependency, the child brings the gift of responsibility, which can be painful; it bestows parenthood upon the couple, granting them the authority to act uniquely on the child's behalf. The parent is urged by circumstance to give up personal sovereignty over time and energy and to give these things to the needs of another. In one sense, the child's life is utterly contingent upon the responsible acts of the parents and so is implicated in a self-interested gift exchange; yet the child lacks self-awareness, the absence of Jacques Derrida's posit that the gift hinges on a social deceit. In fact, the child undermines Derrida by gifting an authentic gift of responsibility in exactly that which he finds to be the only authentic gift: time.[175] Time is interrupted within the same and becomes the property of alterity. It is gifted to the other by way of a demand, and to an infinite degree. Levinas in turn has some notion of the result of what a true gift entails, even if he cannot see the body of the other as an authenticating presence of the person. He refers to the result of insomnia on behalf of the other, the disquieting "coring out" in the heart of that resting place within the same or the identical.[176] For Levinas, time belongs not to the self or relationships of the same, but to the other. Moreover, Levinas speaks of the other bursting forth within the confines of the subject itself, of a soul that is "ceaselessly woken up" in its *"state of soul."*[177] It can be seen that the arrival of the child is indeed the arrival of the other, but the responsibility it awakens is a cause for thankfulness and not simply ethical insomnia. For John Paul, the human subject, arriving as child, achieves also the dimension of "unrepeatability" within the intersubjectivity of the family.[178] The unique unrepeatability of each other person embodies forth the cause of responsibility and the mystery at the heart of the experience of the world. Every encounter with another person reawakens the gifted nature of the gift, providing an orientation towards both the theological mystery of Christ and the church as well as an ethical responsibility for others.

---

in the Modern World, 28.

174. Loughlin, *Alien Sex*, xii.

175. Derrida, *Given Time. 1, Counterfeit Money*.

176. Levinas, "In Praise of Insomnia," in *God, Death and Time*, 209.

177. Ibid., 210.

178. John Paul II, "The Family as a Community of Persons," in *Person and Community: Selected Essays*, 316.

The gift is the embodiment of an unrepeatable subjectivity, issuing the demand of an infinite ethics; an ethics that results in the kenosis of a lived insomnia. The visceral cry both extends the child's body to others in the logic of the gift, just as it harbors subjectivity within the interiority of the body. The contingency of child to parent is made strange in its authority to bestow such responsibility on the parent, even as categories like prayer and theology are also problematized. Jean-Jacque Rousseau comments:

> The first crying of children is a prayer. . . . They begin by asking our aid; then end by compelling us to serve them. Thus from their very weakness, whence comes, at first, their feeling of dependence, springs afterwards the idea of empire, and of commanding others.[179]

Rousseau theologizes the communicative dependence of the visceral cry. Within the weak flesh of the child is the seed of command over the other, but within a context of familial responsibility. In this regard, the child as the "fruit of love" clarifies further the nuptial mystery as the domestic home of alterity. The arrival of the child is also the arrival of the stranger. This can be extended further in that while biological parents have a natural claim to the titles of "mother" and "father," they in fact do not know their child in its labored arrival. In birth, parents *meet* their child "in the flesh," face to face for the first time, discovering a stranger who is an orphan, blinking, crying, desiring the care of parents. Even then, there is no quantifiable moment in which the face to face can be described. The period of gestation itself is a meeting of one person to the other within the flesh of the body, and knowledge of the child as a person is a gradation that can be witnessed from the first knowledge that conception has taken place. The flesh cannot be viewed as a silent, passive meeting of persons; and unborn children also kick out as one body pressing against another. As both "stranger" and "orphan," the child gifts its parents the motivation to receive both it and each other in the act of responsibility.[180] Marion calls the child the "third party," reproducing the visibility of the oath that is pledged in the erotic embrace.[181] In this way, the child gifts back to each parental other an original desire for the embodied alterity of the other. The child's own flesh incarnates a kind of mirror to their particularized relationship of *eros*, but refuses a reduction to mere mimicry or to an echo of an alternate subjectivity (such as that of

---

179. Rousseau, *Emile, or, on Education*, 66.

180. John Paul II, "Parenthood as a Community of Persons," in *Person and Community*, 333.

181. Marion, *The Erotic Phenomenon*, 196.

either parent).[182] The child's flesh is other to theirs (even despite a genetic continuity) and incarnates the distance between the "two fleshes" of its parents, the "distance" which was not overcome or abandoned in the oath and enjoyment of the union.[183]

One of the achievements of viewing the child in a logic of the gift is that it removes the possibility of viewing the theology of the body solely in terms of sexuality, a problem apparent in some interpretations.[184] Rather, fecundity is interpreted within a broader logic of self-donation. Levinas provides a helpful antidote to this temptation. For him, a phenomenology of *eros* shows itself in a "going beyond" the face.[185] It is oriented towards what remains "hidden" in the erotic other.[186] Furthermore, Levinas acknowledges the "total transcendence" in which the child is both perfectly other as well as extending one's "I" in the world: "[m]y child is a stranger (Isa 49), but a stranger who is not only mine, for he *is* me."[187] The child extends the self into the future, opening up a new horizon of temporal alterity. In the kenosis that is performed in the erotic embrace, the self gives the self over to the other, beyond the gleam of alterity that shines forth from the face, towards a hidden interiority. That interiority is for John Paul irreducible and unrepeatable, which is confirmed once again in the embodied presence of the child. Sexuality is thus ordered towards an insatiate logic of desire that both goes beyond, and is always revealed, by the body.[188] The oneself and the union of the two gives way to a third, in which *communio* and separation are confirmed in the flesh. In Levinas, the union of the two cannot be complementary. That is to say, "voluptuosity" moves the relationship beyond every possible project towards the engendering of the child; the third interrupts

---

182. The adopted child is no less a confirmation of this phenomenon of alterity; perhaps they incarnate a responsibility of otherness even more so, cutting across the enclosure of familial communities and appealing to the openness of the other. In this way, the parents of adopted children have freely embraced the paradigm of alterity defended by John Paul II, and embark on a certain adventure of self-sacrifice that ought to be better respected, supported, and honored by the present culture.

183. Marion, *The Erotic Phenomenon*, 197.

184. For example, the works of popular theology of the body interpreter Christopher West have been criticized because of an emphasis on sexuality as a realized locus of ecstasy, instead of its wider implications for both the child as gift or indeed, God as the first giver. See for example Dawn Eden's work, "Towards A 'Climate of Chastity,'" 23; Alice von Hildebrand, "Dietrich Von Hildebrand, Catholic Philosopher, and Christopher West, Modern Enthusiast."

185. Levinas, *Totality and Infinity*, 263–64.

186. Ibid., 264.

187. Ibid., 267.

188. Ibid., 272.

reciprocity.[189] The body's responsibility is interrupted and magnified as the third appears in the social context. The body is reduced neither to the sexual embrace nor to the fleshly pleasures of the other in a self-enclosed union, but rather in the order of another who results from this meeting of bodies, a multiplicity engendered by the two.[190] Yet this is not limited to the embodied meeting of a particular familial unit, but has a wide applicability that can be called universal.

Interpreting the child as gift offers a universal aspect upon the body, because each person finds within his or her experience the event of childhood. In affirming a logic of the gift by way of the child, the gift becomes an embodied presence able to be received universally. The reason for this is the universal quality of the familial basis for the human subject.[191] Through the intersubjective community of the family, the gifting of responsibility is inscribed within the *esse* of each human subject, whether or not the local incarnations of the family live according to the order of love.[192]

This is why the family is a "rational *communio*"; self-donation, the adequate response to the gifting of the other, must be predicated upon the free agency of one who chooses self-donation, or what John Paul II calls the "disinterested gift."[193] Aware of both the freedom and limitations existent in the body, the person gives without self-interest or the desire of satiation. One is motivated by the desire for the other and not *of* the other. In this way, a logic of the gift touches on each nascent person, each childhood experience, each familial context, confirming that the child is given as a gift properly when it is also given as a "task."[194] Crucially, John Paul argues that this gift is a "gradual" gift.[195] Maturation of the gift in the embodied person is an indivisible whole, not confined to a moment or to a static presence but to the order of persons before the horizon of personal self-donation across a spectrum of lived experience. Elsewhere for Levinas, this theme is confirmed towards the end of *Totality and Infinity*, in a section on filiality and fraternity that precedes the topic of infinity. Levinas writes of the role of the

189. Ibid., 266.

190. Ibid., 273.

191. John Paul II, "The Family as a Community of Persons," in *Person and Community*, 316.

192. Ibid., 319.

193. Ibid.

194. John Paul II, "Parenthood as a Community of Persons," in *Person and Community*, 333.

195. In this way, the gift of the person confirms the necessity of time. Mature persons, recognized within a logic of the gift, come about through time given over to prayer and education. See Ibid., 333–34.

face in constituting sociality, the arrival of the third, in which signifyingness and decency encompass the structure of the family:

> The erotic and the family which articulates it ensure to this life, in which the I does not disappear but is promised and called to goodness, the infinite time of triumph without which goodness would be subjectivity and folly.[196]

Conclusion: The gift between communio and alterity

This analysis of the gift in Levinas and John Paul II seeks to circumvent the Derridean insistence on the impossibility of the authentic gift exchange, with the purposes of rethinking the gift economy. In Derrida, an austere insistence on an impossible purity of the gift closes itself off from a life lived in goodness or happiness. Indeed, to accept Derrida's analysis would be to insist that the child, upon receiving the wrapped gift under the Christmas tree, ought to be implored not to offer any word of "thanks" upon reception of that same gift.[197] No gesture of thankfulness could be expressed, for to do so would be to enter a cycle of endless exchange in which the original item—whether asked for or not, expected or unexpected, whether desired and enjoyed or neither—becomes an economic imposition upon the receiver, causing an obligation upon the giver which would be impossible to break and entirely without warrant; furthermore, "thanks" nullifies the gift.[198] To be sure, Derrida has highlighted an important feature of the social economy in trying to locate an ethical place for the gift.[199] He looks to the giving of gifts in order to describe a logic that guides and informs human activity. Yet, he fails in his account. Levinas also lacks a full account of the gift's possibility, but his emphasis on giving and receiving and of what alterity makes possible can be interpreted positively. Levinas rightly identifies the disturbing urgency of the suffering other, and how the gift of the other invokes the gift of responsibility. For John Paul, the greater gift of Christ creates a logic of the gift in which the intersubjective experience of embodied

---

196. Levinas, *Totality and Infinity*, 280.

197. Thanks is offered to Michael Purcell for generously sharing his thoughts on this Derridean example, and pressing the logic of the gift further.

198. Derrida, *Memoires*, 149.

199. In every social exchange is the spectre of ethics, which raises the question of justice. "Justice demands a 'gift without exchange.' . . . In this aporia, justice takes on a quasi-messianic tone." Caputo, *Against Ethics*, 105.

persons can recognize an authentic gift; that of the human person presence of the child.

In light of the incarnation, thinking about the human person is al tered. No longer can the other be easily equated with the categories of alien and outsider, but the other is interpreted as gift, one of flesh that carries the misfortune of a shared fallen nature, but in deference to a redemptive possibility offered by its Creator. In looking to the first Christmas, an original inversion of cultural misunderstanding about the gift can be witnessed: in Bethlehem, a gift is given who is naked and entirely dependent on the self-donation of two parental figures, aliens in a foreign city and subject to the bureaucracy of a power greater than their own (See Matt 1:18–25; Luke 2:1–21). In receiving the child, the persons of Joseph and Mary do not so much unwrap glitter and tinsel, but instead wrap *a person*, swaddling his body against the elements, bundling him in tired arms, and responding with the body's own gift of emotion, cries of exhaustion and joy, tears perhaps, and possibly irregular smiles and the intake of breath. The very lack of detail about the birth of Jesus of Nazareth protects the intimate domesticity of his arrival, of his homeliness in the arms of two parents far from home and without recourse to wealth, power, or status. The gift is given, yet it must be attended to, held gently, severed from its mother, fed and eventually bathed in patterns of domestic ritual and habit; and so a logic of the gift begins in a moment which will repeat itself as the years progress and the child grows into maturity. In the face of this child, all further social and cultural traditions regarding its religious memory—meals, carols, visits, gift-giving, decorations for the home, and the like—begin and find their meaning. Because of the logic of the gift wrought in this most domestic of all encounters, so all human faces bear the trace of the gift, naturally given perhaps, but made all the more possible because of the supernatural narrative of incarnation.

The face of the other is a divine reflection and gives itself to the self, making of itself a gift in the realm of sociality that demands something sacrificial, without the torture of an exacting cycle of economic exchange. Rather, the gift is given in both festive posture and sacrificial deference and in this way remains an excess. As Stephen Webb argues, "the Christian conception of generosity connects gifting to an antieconomy of surplus, not scarcity, displacing strife and competition with sharing and mutuality."[200] It exceeds Derrida's nullification of the gift, precisely because it affirms the gracious freedom in which thanks is offered. John Paul and Levinas furnish a constructive approach to the gift that is both ethical and contemplative; in

---

200. Webb, *The Gifting God*, 157.

which the person is the center. Being itself is inscribed within the reciprocity of personal kenosis.[201]

In fact, the cycle of uninterruptable exchange foisted upon the self in an economic model is not so much interrupted, as preceded by the body. It is at this juncture that Levinas and John Paul II accent different aspects of alterity in its embodied perspective. In Levinas, the form of ethics is illustrated as a deferential posture of self-kenosis before the epiphany of the face.[202] The other carries an infinity of meaning and possibility, transcendent in its capacity for otherness and its directionality, a centering upon the human "before all system."[203] Indeed, by this, "God comes to mind."[204] The kind of sociality that follows Levinas' logic requires a radical asymmetry in intersubjectivity. What matters is that the gift of the other is not besmirched by one's own body in its appetites or desire. The "pure gift" of the other is always a gift beyond, towards a "not yet" of responsibility which is foreshadowed in the ethical.[205] Levinas and John Paul II agree profoundly in the asymmetry of this relation with the embodied other, and both confirm such an account of reciprocity. But for John Paul, a crucial integrity is maintained by affirming the relationship between sexuality, erotic desire, and ethics in the human body. Michael Waldstein observes the correlation in the teaching of John Paul between the "common good" and the "gift of self."[206] The gift of self is predicated on what is called the "spousal meaning of the body," and it has consequences for *communio* across different social contexts, such as the family, the state, the church and so forth.[207]

Contrary to Levinas, John Paul's theology of the body insists that in the particularities of the other—not just the gleam of the face, but its unrepeatable configuration of features and expression—an authentic self-donation is possible.[208] This is predicated upon the operation of the nuptial mystery in

201. Schindler, "The Embodied Person as Gift and the Cultural Task in America: Status Quaestionis," 404.

202. Levinas, *Totality and Infinity*, 199.

203. Levinas, "Discussion Following 'Transcendence and Intelligibility,'" in *Is It Righteous to Be?*, 270.

204. Ibid.

205. Kearney, "Desire of God," in Caputo and Scanlon (eds.), *God, the Gift, and Postmodernism*, 118.

206. Waldstein, "John Paul II and St. Thomas on Love and the Trinity (First Part)," 574.

207. John Paul II, *Man and Woman He Created Them*, 15.

208. As discussed in chapter 4 concerning the iconic body, John Paul II offers an alternate reading of Matt 5:27–28. When Christ teaches that to look with desire upon a woman is already to have committed adultery in one's heart, John Paul departs from the intuitive interpretation we might normally find. He places his teaching in the context

John Paul's thought. As the regulating analogy and principle paradigm of alterity (constantly relating the nuptial union of Christ and the church, of God and the world), it constitutes *ethos* on the basis of the foundational union of human spouses.[209] This is a theological mystery of the embodied plenitude of Christ, which is explained and interpreted in light of the self-gifting that is continually repeated and never exhausted in the married relationship.[210] The spousal meaning is a signification of the body in excess of itself. Levinas confirms the ethical end of fecundity and *eros*, but finds himself in the realm of contradiction by refusing the incarnational avatar.[211] He is bound to the body as a gift to the self who gives the self also as an authentic "I" [*moi*], yet refuses the integration of the body theologized by John Paul. In the end, the reflection of the divine gives itself especially in the suffering other and theological language, as long as it remains a decentered device, serves the humility of the other within a measure of anticipated glory. It is the gift that gives itself most perfectly in the coincidence of *eros* with *ethos*, as Levinas cannot avoid: "In *Desire* are conjoined the movements unto the Height and unto the Humility of the Other."[212] The gift of the other is seen profoundly in the arrival of the third, the child, whose interruption of the same—even when the "same" is already an alterity of spousal meaning—irrupts as an embodied alterity who is intimately a stranger. The self also discovers itself as gift in this result of *eros* and *ethos* as John Paul discovers phenomenologically: "the *other*, after all, is also an *I* for whom I can be an *other*."[213] In this way, thanks and responsibility are made possible in the gift of the body and the gift of the other.

---

of the heart, in which a purified desire for the other in terms of their "personal dignity" makes it possible to look upon the other, overcoming the limitations of concupiscence. In effect, John Paul teaches not that we avert our eyes in such a circumstance, but that we *look more deeply* into the face of the other. Rather than stop our gaze at the concupiscent limitation of sexual desire, we are invited to honor the irreducible and unrepeatable subjectivity of the other person. In other words, do not look away but look *more closely*. For John Paul, it is a lingering Manichaeism that makes us interpret this text with an antibody and antimaterialistic bias. See ibid., 42:7.

209. Ibid., 91:2.

210. Ibid., 89:1.

211. It is the "destitution" and "height" of the epiphany of infinity that calls me outside of myself for the other, yet expression cannot be avoided. See Levinas, *Totality and Infinity*, 200.

212. Ibid.

213. John Paul II, "Participation or Alienation?," in *Person and Community*, 201.

Conclusion
Towards a Theology of Embodied Alterity

The place of the body

THREE CONCLUDING JUDGMENTS CAN be made based on the study of the place of the body in Karol Wojtyla/John Paul II and Levinas. First, that the fruitful dialogue between John Paul and Levinas has been largely overlooked. Second, John Paul and Levinas' approaches to the body are discordant (more on this below). Third, John Paul's account of the body is a positive theological development that is made clearer and enhanced by reading Levinas. In consideration of these three judgments, a way is opened up that indicates how a theological approach to the body can be fruitfully developed. In fact, John Paul's approach provides a corrective to the limitations of the body in Levinas, and fosters a constructive relationship between theology and phenomenology. Having said that, by John Paul's own admission, his theology is not complete, and requires further development.

From the outset, the question of the body was framed here in terms of theological anthropology, the study of the human person in relation to God. The words of Matt 6:25 serve to articulate a context in which to theologize about the body: "Therefore I tell you, do not worry about your life, what you will eat or drink; or about your body, what you will wear. Is not life more than food, and the body more than clothes?" In one sense, this text indicates the limits of a body theology; that the body is not an object for which great mental expenditure is to be exerted and that to worry about the body or its clothing is to misrepresent the gospel, which is of greater importance. Nevertheless, the comparison of the body to life itself, insofar as food, like clothing, is of little importance in light of the good news rendered in Christ, opens a way to speak of the body. For in this comparison lies an argument

not for the insignificance of the body as such, but rather for its contextualization in light of revelation, as was articulated especially in chapter 1 of this
book. In such light, which would include reflection on topics such as divine
incarnation, the sacrifice upon the cross, and the resurrection, a broader
significance of the body can be given account. It is not that the body lacks
significance, but that its significance is proportional to the gospel. In this
scriptural point of departure, the present study has attempted to analyze
the treatment of the body in John Paul II and Levinas without undermin-
ing the role of the body nor in overextending its importance. A generous
mean has been the object. In this way, the full breadth of the significance
of John Paul's development of a contemporary theology of the body can be
seen more clearly, precisely on the basis that he limits his theology to what
Scripture might clarify about the body, in a critical relationship with the
possibilities that phenomenology opens up on the same topic. John Paul is
not expending energy on a speculative theology. The dialogue with Levinas
about the body can bear fruit only if his thought is weighed carefully in
terms of his references to incarnate existence. The denial of a signification
of incarnate presence beyond simply acting as a moment on the way to the
ethical demands of alterity is constant and effusive (see especially the description of the disincarnate body in chapter 3).

It has been argued in this book that the dialogue between John Paul and
Levinas is fruitful. Such fruitfulness is not diminished by their differences
but enhanced. For example, their shared phenomenological approaches are
indelibly related to religious interests that together provide structure and
coherence to their thought. This was seen clearly in chapter 2, where John
Paul's theological framework can be seen to be christocentric, Trinitarian,
eucharistic, and Marian, and always in dialogue with human experience.
On the other hand, Levinas' thought is rich in promise and subtlety, as John
Paul describes in his papal texts such as *Crossing the Threshold of Hope* and
Memory and Identity.[1] Levinas' Talmudic commentaries reveal a fundamen-
tal interest in interpreting the Hebrew Scriptures with an ethical awareness
concerning alterity, and in turn this broadens the appeal of his philosophy.[2]
It was seen in chapter 1 that John Paul could say positively of Levinas that his
thought, "showed us the truth about man and the world from new angles."[3]
He found in Levinas a fruitful engagement with the I-other problem and

1. John Paul II, *Crossing the Threshold of Hope* and *Memory and Identity*.

2. See Levinas' works: *In the Time of the Nations*; *New Talmudic Readings*; *Beyond the Verse*; *Nine Talmudic Readings*.

3. John Paul II, *Crossing the Threshold of Hope*, 35.

a personalist account of dialogue that could enrich contemporary ethics.[4] Levinas appreciated John Paul's approach in the field of philosophical argument and methodology. For example, careful attention was paid to the article about John Paul that Levinas published in 1980.[5] This was developed from a paper presented at a conference on the theme of the philosophy of John Paul II. It is telling that despite the conference theme, Levinas insists on referring to the "phenomenological cardinal" or to "Cardinal Wojtyla," calling to mind the developed thought of a man who had published in philosophy and theology before he became pope.[6]

For Levinas, Wojtyla was a fellow phenomenologist whose reflections begin with human experience, closing the gap between religion and ethics.[7] The correlation of ethical action and the experience of God is viewed positively, although it relies on different presuppositions to Levinas. It is for this reason that Levinas can find in John Paul some appeal in the way that the unique subjectivity of the individual is not pitted against the unique experience of a community. He sees in John Paul an account of human experience that is based in a concrete transcendence open to description, and therefore of a nonreduced subjectivity.[8] Such a subjectivity refuses every paradigm in which its irreducible nature is diminished, including all forms of totalitarianism. This demonstrates some convergence between John Paul's position in *The Acting Person* and *Love and Responsibility* with Levinas' account of the subjective experience of the other in transcendence in *Totality and Infinity*: "To think the infinite, the transcendent, the Stranger, is hence not to think an object."[9] The young Wojtyla's study of Max Scheler led him to a similar, if not identical, position concerning human subjectivity. He argues that Scheler's system cannot provide an adequate basis for Christian ethics, but takes from him the significance of "values" as an objective category.[10] As such, John Paul locates in human affectivity a way of ensuring the emotions are not disconnected from other characteristics (such as cognitive awareness or bodily sensations), and are a means of refusing the reduction of the human person to a mere object.[11] These convergences help to explain

4. Ibid., 210–11.

5. Levinas, "Notes Sur La Pensée Philosophique Du Cardinal Wojtyla."

6. Ibid., 89.

7. Ibid., 87.

8. Ibid.

9. Levinas, *Totality and Infinity*, 49.

10. See especially John Paul II, *Ocena Mozliwosci Zbudowania Etyki Chrzescijanskiej Przy Zaozeniach Systemu Maksa Schelera*. Also, see the incorporation of this perspective in *The Acting Person*, 139–233.

11. This was central to Wojtyla's account of sexual ethics. See John Paul II, *Love and*

the mutual recognition of the need to explain human dignity in terms of a recognizable presence that transcends juridical and legalistic frameworks, such as that of the face. For John Paul and Levinas, the face is an ethical revelation, although it is developed by the former theologically and the latter philosophically.[12] There is more than a mutual appreciation of each other's work in evidence here. Indeed, thematic interests in both thinkers indicate a fundamental openness and interest in the success of each other's projects.

Nevertheless, close inspection reveals a mutual incompatibility between the approaches of John Paul and Levinas to the body. They certainly share an interest in describing human dignity in its subjective dimension, but ultimately offer differing accounts of how that might be achieved. In fact, it seems that John Paul could not recognize the limitations of Levinas' thought, especially in regard to the significance of the body. That is to say, John Paul's reflections on Levinas lack an interrogation of the consequences of the latter's logic on the theme of the body. Such an interrogation, which has been executed in this book, shows how dramatic Levinas' hesitation before incarnate presence is. His commitment to alterity abolishes any valuable content in incarnate presence, and so produces an account of the body that is disincarnate.

An inconsistency arises periodically in Levinas, where he takes up metaphorical language of the body to argue his account of alterity, but this in turn only accentuates the absence of investment in the lived body. Despite his references to the language of embodiment, his ethics of responsibility is ultimately for another who remains, as it were, disincarnate. This is why it was argued in chapter 3 that the face, for Levinas, reveals not the meeting of an authentic human body with the world, but only what Levinas calls the "principle of phenomenality."[13] Phenomenality is experienced, but is a mode of operation that points the oneself towards the objective of an ethical responsibility, and not the presence of a human person with a body of signification as such. The glory of the other so exceeds the body that the language of signification itself dissolves, denying "anything that shows itself."[14] No authentic experience of somatic presence is possible, but is always deferred and ultimately dissolved in this manner. Such a "glory" in alterity exceeds categories of description and experience such that it is "without noematic

---

Responsibility.

12. Examples include: John Paul II, *Crossing the Threshold of Hope*, 210–11; also Levinas, *Totality and Infinity*, 81.

13. Levinas, *Totality and Infinity*, 92.

14. Levinas, *Otherwise Than Being*, 145.

correlation" of any kind.[15] If such a glory is excessive to the point of denying a signification in the body, it can be described as disincarnate; it is not
bound to the body, nor does it disclose the body, and merely passes through
and beyond the body. Or, as it was put in chapter 3, the body passes on the
way to alterity. John Paul recognized the attempt of Levinas to envisage an
I-thou relationship of coexistence in ethical terms, but made no comment
on Levinas' departure from, for example, the thought of Martin Buber in his
work *I and Thou*.[16] Buber's I-thou relationship relies on the possibility of a
fundamental reciprocity with a symmetry of dignity and equality, by which
the beauty of eternity might be glimpsed in time.[17]

Strictly speaking, Martin Buber's I-thou is symmetrical, whereas
Levinas' I-thou is asymmetrical. Could John Paul see the radical difference
between Levinas and Buber? It is not clear. If he did, he remained committed to promoting both of their projects, albeit subtly. If he did not, it falls
into a pattern of John Paul's approach to Levinas, in that he did not critically
evaluate the full logic of Levinas' position. What can be said for certain is
that John Paul's scriptural descriptions of a theology of the body and its
critical relationship with phenomenology is discordant with Levinas' approach to the body. It must be remembered that, for John Paul, the somatic
whole of the human person is of fundamental goodness within the created
order and that the actions of the body constitute the embodiment of the human person as a whole. For him, "action is what most fully and profoundly
reveals the human being as an *I*."[18] The constitution of the human person
reveals itself in action as a free agent, and as one whose body manifests a
desire and need for communion with others.

It was described how John Paul's anthropology finds in concrete action
the externalization of the self and the means by which the body becomes
an object of free action.[19] This is crucial for his account of *communio* as the
dimension in which human bodies offer an ethical self-donation in community with others. For him, the *imago* of the nuptial mystery serves as
both a key theological image, as well as a means of understanding the space
of difference between the I and the thou. In this way, it is a paradigm that
serves as John Paul's principle means of conceiving alterity in an ethical
light. Each other person, in this light, is one who is loved first by Christ
and signals the authoritative description of how he or she is to be loved by

15. Ibid., 145.
16. John Paul II, *Crossing the Threshold of Hope*, 36.
17. Buber, *I and Thou*, 31, 82.
18. John Paul II, *Person and Community*, 198.
19. John Paul II, *The Acting Person*.

others; completely, irreducibly, and respectfully.[20] The body is the place and the event of this opportunity to be both loved and to love. Each other person, named by John Paul as "neighbor," reveals in his or her bodily presence the "humanness of every man."[21] For John Paul, the body offers this nuptial promise, not limited to the concrete experiences of human marriage in all its complexity and diversity, but in its capacity for interpreting and fulfilling the paradigm of the Christ-church or God-world relationship. Significantly, John Paul defends the position that sexual differentiation is an important factor in experiencing the human body. As was also shown in chapter 2, he was far more reticent than theologians like Karl Barth or Hans Urs von Balthasar in detailing the characteristics that constitute male or female bodies in a complementary symmetry. John Paul views it as sufficient to insist upon a strong basis of coequality between the sexes in both the nuptial and generally social dimensions.

This clarifies the nature of discordance between John Paul and Levinas, but also sheds light on the limitations of Levinas in his account of the body. In respect to John Paul's work and its contrast with Levinas, this book argues that his contribution to a theology of the body is a positive development. It is positive for at least two reasons:

First, John Paul contributes a theology of the body that is invested in the realities of human experience. While he begins most catechesis on the body with reference to biblical texts, his theological reading of those texts attends to the experience of what he calls "historical man."[22] That is, the experience of the human person subject to history, transcending every age by virtue of belonging to every age. The historical human person is not only subject to the vexing instabilities of every age—including that of postmodernity—but is also subject to the body's conflicting desires, so that John Paul's "historical man" is also the "man of concupiscence."[23] The redemption of the body is an aspect of the redemption of the whole person, including the redemptive re-ordering of human action. This is not confined to an eschatological hope, but enacted as a concrete ethics for the sake of others in the present moment. This confirms the present state of the body (despite its complex imperfection) and grants a promise of self-authentication for the sake of others, in which "the body expresses the person."[24] In this way,

---

20. This relies on the "personalistic norm," which is described as an irreducible value in the human person. See, John Paul II, *The Acting Person*, 266.

21. Ibid., 294.

22. John Paul II, *Man and Woman He Created Them*, 87:2.

23. Ibid., 26–33.

24. Ibid., 7:2.

John Paul defends two meanings of the term "body": the "metaphorical" (for example the church as the *body* of Christ) and its "concrete meaning" (the experienced human body in its masculinity or femininity).[25]

By holding these in tension, John Paul conserves a signification of the human body in its historical or concrete meaning, while holding that signification in a proportional relationship with the theology of the nuptial mystery. In both, alterity offers not the ethical promise of Levinas, but an ethical-sacramental promise of redemption. That is to say, it grants participation in the promise of the redemption for the whole person as well as a concrete ethics to be practiced in historical and local circumstances. For John Paul, the redemptive promise of the body cannot be separated from the sacramentality of the church or the "most ancient sacrament" of marriage.[26] In each of these bodily relationships (either church-Christ or bride-bridegroom), John Paul coincides the desire for the other in its authentic beauty with a desire for the good of the other, thus enacting a "restless" desire.[27] It is restless because in desiring the good of the other, it desires that which cannot be fulfilled in the world, but acts in hope. This is not an idealization of either the body or marriage, but a carefully structured theology of the body that situates Scripture and human experience in close proximity. *Communio* is not then merely an objective or a promise, but a redemptive work which begins in the historical experience of intersubjectivity. It is an activity or a work in which one is involved as a participant.

Second, John Paul's account develops an approach that is aware of contemporary problems of *eros* and giftedness. This was shown in chapters 4 and 5, which engaged John Paul and Levinas' approaches to the body with themes of *eros* and the gift. It was argued that the close association of erotic desire with sexual desire in postmodern thought misconstrues the former as limited to the latter, thus destroying what is truly given in the body. The work of Jean-Luc Marion highlights this problem and shows a way forward. Specifically, the phenomenological description of the idol and the icon describes the ethical distinction between two types of object. The idol receives a gaze and reproduces a mimicked reconstruction of the subject who offers that gaze, thus replicating a reduced version of human experience.[28] The icon is the embodiment of that which withdraws from infinity and discloses itself in the world, achieving the impossible.[29]

25. Ibid., 87:3.

26. Ibid., 93:7.

27. Ibid., 92:4.

28. Marion, *The Idol and Distance*, 4–7.

29. Ibid., 155.

This schema was applied to the problem of the body, by which the interpenetrating spheres of sexuality and spirituality could be seen more clearly. In a context in which sexuality and spirituality can be convoluted or in which they draw on similar language, the icon-idol distinction clarifies how a body can be received or given in either ethical or unethical terms. In this light, the body can of course be treated either idolatrously or iconically. For Marion, the movement of the body towards an iconic interpretation cannot avoid the presence of the idols, but must move through them in an *ethos* of abandonment to the other. This is not the dissolution of idolatrous forms of the body, but a description of the kind of movement that John Paul indicates when he calls for a theology of the body that transforms the "fear of Christ" into the habit of *pietas*.[30] In other words, a movement that begins with a well-formed awareness of the iconic gaze of the risen Christ and habituates this awareness in beliefs and practices that conform to the iconic gaze. The body is the mediation of either the iconic or the idolatrous gaze and it is the person who, in line with John Paul's concerns illustrated in chapters 1 and 2, makes a decision and acts. These themes were brought to bear in the contemporary debate concerning the gift. The contribution of John Paul is that a gift is possible, but that it must be interpreted in light of a greater logic of the gift that is given in Christ. Christ's self-donation crafts a divine logic in which an authentic human gift can be exemplified. In John Paul, that gift is the child, who is not a reward or the instrumentalization of the relationship of the parents, but the presence of a body who is gratuitous in its authentication of others. Despite the problematic nature of Levinas' approach to the body, his emphasis on responsibility lends itself to John Paul's logic of the gift because of what the child gives; he or she presents an excess of responsibility to its carers that cannot be adequately explained or understood.

Action on behalf of the child's interest makes present an adequate ethics. For Levinas, a true gift is that which awakens the self for the interest of another.[31] Also for him, need and desire must be distinguished and it is in the later that a care for the other is best described. The arrival of a child creates an environment in which desire for its good is the only adequate ethical response; any needfulness in relation to the child must be understood in light of such a desire. While Levinas describes this ethics of responsibility for the other as absolute, John Paul argues for a "pause" before the irreducibility of the other.[32] A moment of contemplation is necessitated by the pres-

---

30. John Paul II, *Man and Woman He Created Them*, 92:4.

31. Levinas, *God, Death and Time*, 102.

32. John Paul II, *Person and Community*, 213.

ence of the gift, and only by receiving the gift in this moment can an ethics of responsibility follow. As was argued in chapter 5, the essential character of John Paul's pause is not action but the contemplative moment in the presence of the gift, which, as a human person, is irreducible.

The pause before the gift of the other makes possible the action upon which John Paul's case then insists. The mystery of the human person both resists tyranny and positively affirms the dignity that is present. This account of the body not only affirms bodily presence, but preserves the infinity of an interior dimension in such a way that it is not primarily an ethics of parental responsibility, but a sacramental ethic of care for *each* person. Expressly, the logic of the gift makes a demand on behalf of each human person in its irreducibility. In other words, in affirming the bodily presence of the child, every person is ethically present as one who requires responsible care in light of the greater logic of the gift.

Towards a theology of embodied alterity

What vision of the body emerges from this study? Primarily, a theological vision of the body dawns that is committed to the person as gift, without diminishing the irreducibility of the other. To aid this vision, the judgments above provide an important point from which the dialogue of Levinas and John Paul can be fruitfully taken. The account given in this book of the key documents and topics in this overlooked dialogue is a useful study for any full account of either thinker. It bears witness to a dialogue not simply between two prolific writers, but to the interstices of theology and philosophy in an age in which both are under increased suspicion. The work of interpreting and critically evaluating Levinas is an important aspect of the present study, especially as his turn to ethics in French phenomenology comes under increased scrutiny and interest. Theology can find in Levinas a thinker who is not only influential, but, for a continental philosopher, uncharacteristically hospitable to theological language. Meanwhile, the work of interpreting and evaluating the contribution of Karol Wojtyla, now known widely as St. John Paul II, is a crucial task. Given the length of time John Paul II's papacy ran for and the voluminous quantity of published texts he produced during, and before, that time, the task of understanding his legacy will go on long into the future. It is interesting that his immediate successor as Bishop of Rome committed himself to progressing John Paul II's written legacy rather than producing many new documents of his own. The work of Pope Francis incorporates the work of Benedict and John Paul within a new idiom for the church, in which intellect and humility are seen in fusion and unity.

Now, the mutual divergence of John Paul and Levinas on the place of the body is an important moment of dialogue. Because dissimilarities between them are significant, an account of the body that is both phenomenological and theological should not rely on an easy alliance between their projects, nor assume that differing accounts are not important. The complex arrangement of multiple voices, such as John of the Cross, Thomas Aquinas, and Max Scheler, or on the other hand, Edmund Husserl, Martin Heidegger, and Monsieur Chouchani (to name a few), result in diverging conclusions on how to protect human subjectivity and the dignity of persons. Furthermore, the positive nature of John Paul's catechesis on the body places theology in a new position regarding the body. This is not to say that his contribution is a radical departure, but rather a positive development that has the capacity to open and sustain a conversation on the theological significance of the body. For John Paul, the body has a theology. With the insights of Levinas in mind it is argued that a theology of embodied alterity can be pursued fruitfully into the future.

The task of theology is enriched by constantly returning to the intersection between faith and experience. Indeed, the participation of the body in a logic of the gift is a case in point. It was seen in chapter 5 that John Paul's notion of the gift, and the event of the other person in Levinas, comes into particular focus in the arrival of the child. This *exemplar* of the gift fulfills Levinas' criteria of an alterity whose transcendence is "total" and whose otherness is not reducible to the sexual embrace nor to the fleshly pleasures of the other.[33] Yet the child also resists the Levinasian account of the ethics of alterity, in that its incarnate expression is a constituent aspect of its bodily call for communion with others. The "destitution" and the "height" that Levinas locates in the other can indeed be seen; not in the denial of incarnation, as he argues, but its affirmation.[34] In John Paul, who spends much time articulating a sexual ethic that avoids any trace of Manichean negativity towards the body, the logic of the gift ultimately engenders an appeal written in the face of the child. In the constellation of features and expression in the face, authentic self-donation is possible.[35] The other seeks the oneself out with a gaze that interrupts self-interest and seeks out the good of self-abnegation. To return to a theme in chapter 2, participation in Christ's kingship is made apparent in such deferral to the otherness of the

33. Levinas, *Totality and Infinity*, 267 and 273.

34. Ibid., 200.

35. John Paul II, *Man and Woman He Created Them*, 42:7.

other. As John Paul argues: "Man's obedience to his conscience is the key to his moral grandeur and the basis of his 'kingliness,' his 'dominion'; and this—ethically speaking—is also a dominion over himself."[36]

To act for the other, in defiance of one's own personal need and desire, is to act in accordance with Christ's kingship. In this sense, John Paul II also defends a notion that is absent from Levinas, that there is some account of kingly glory rendered in the one who acts for the sake of the other. By no means is it self-referential nor sought after as an object to be obtained. But between the two—the one who self-abnegates in an act of ethical responsibility and the one whose otherness calls for such care—is the event of *communio*. The participation by persons in a body that is not contingent on one's own acts of mercy (the body of Christ) provides a means by which inter subjectivity is not limited simply to authentic community building (whether in the family, politics, the nation, etc.) but to a transnational and transpolitical body that overcomes the limitations of each individual member. In other words, an *ecclesia*, whose logic looks to the face of the innocent, the most in need, the most restless, and the most hungry, and fosters an embodied ethic of care in that place, without diminishing a responsibility for others who suffer out of reach. What can be witnessed in this account of the body and its call for ethical action is the epiphany of a communion that is both concentrated locally and mediated universally.

The person who receives the gaze of one whose body speaks of a reliance on the service of others is also faced by the call of a personal conscience within such a communion and it is indispensable that the incomplete nature of John Paul's project be kept in mind. As was discussed at numerous points in this book, and especially in chapter 5, John Paul acknowledges that "numerous problems" are not dealt with in his catechesis on the body, including the problems of "suffering and death."[37] In other documents he deals with these themes, but *Man and Woman He Created Them* does not explicitly relate them to the fundamental stages of original solitude, unity, or nakedness.[38] Of course, the suffering of the other is a pivotal point of Levinas' philosophy, but his problematic description of the body makes a direct theological appropriation tendentious. Rather, there remains work to be done in accounting for the significance of suffering and death in terms of the body's theology. This is especially so in an era in which suffering of any kind is denied any positive significance, let alone an ethical call that

36. John Paul II, *Sign of Contradiction*, 141.

37. John Paul II, *Man and Woman He Created Them*, 129:1.

38. See especially: John Paul II, *Salvifici Doloris: On the Christian Meaning of Human Suffering*; and *Evangelium Vitae: The Gospel of Life*.

demands immediate attention, and in which death is either a project to complete or a topic to be avoided. Moreover, awareness of how a significant twentieth-century voice such as Levinas places the body provides a way of thinking through weaknesses in other contemporary and postmodern accounts of the body. Specifically, light has been cast on the limitations that arise in giving an account of the body that denies its signification. The body is present in a way that, in relation to the irreducibility of the person identified by John Paul, refuses diminishment.

A theology of embodied alterity is oriented and informed by the content of revelation. The greater logic of Christ's self-donation is the gift by which all other gifts are interpreted. The innocence of the other, and the guilt of each acting human subject, are afforded the possibility of radical reconfiguration in the forgiveness afforded in Christ. A theology of the body can proceed with confidence from the foundational work of John Paul, but its fragility consists in a delicate reliance on these biblical themes. This is more than a conceptual framework; rather it is a biblical orientation that becomes enfleshed in the multilayered experience of Christian discipleship in a context of suffering bodily existence and new ethical quandaries. Such a theology is therefore profoundly in touch with human experience. In John Paul's words, the work of building such a theology, "can be correctly carried out from the moment when the light of revelation touches the reality of the human body."[39] The conviction that the nuptial mystery is both a phenomenality and, analogously, a theological paradigm places the body in an ethical-sacramental context. In this book, it is argued that such a paradigm is a fruitful means of conceptualizing the body and its *telos* of *communio*. It is by no means the only paradigm, nor is it restricted to its scriptural, patristic, and medieval roots. In John Paul, it is developed in close dialogue with a phenomenological description of the irreducibility of the human person, which remains unique and unrepeatable. This development shows how a theology of embodied alterity touches not only on moments of extreme suffering—hunger, homelessness, torture, war—but that it radicalizes a logic of the gift in those places most intimate to human existence; domesticity, the home and the least public of social endeavors. Habits of care and responsibility are fostered in domesticity as an *ethos* ordered to love.

Finally, a theology of embodied alterity deepens the significance of human domesticity in this way, enlivening it with an ethics that must be enacted immediately and immanently in intersubjectivity. Such a theology displaces the temptation to prescribe the body as a commodity or a project, and insists that *ethos* becomes the constitutive form of *eros*. In other words,

---

39. John Paul II, *Man and Woman He Created Them*, 129:1.

a Christian *ethos* fosters an intimate desire for the good of the other. This begins in the extant, pressing moment, but is developed over the arduous challenges of time and habit. It cannot look to itself for strength to maintain a commitment to the good of the other, but to the invisible one who became visible, instituting divine presence in an iconic form. Otherwise, the meaning of the body is fostered idolatrously. The event of incarnation, of God's body received and disclosed to the world, arriving in the womb and dwelling "among us" (John 1:14), indicates a theological point of departure. A theology of embodied alterity proceeds fruitfully, and with a creative philosophical awareness it may serve the body of the other, and receive it joyfully as a gift.

Bibliography

Abraham, William J., Jason E. Vickers, and Natalie B. Van Kirk. *Canonical Theism: A Proposal for Theology and the Church*. Grand Rapids: Eerdmans, 2008.

Ajzenstat, Oona. *Driven Back to the Text: The Premodern Sources of Levinas's Postmodernism*. Pittsburgh: Duquesne University Press, 2001.

Alcoff, Linda, and Eduardo Mendieta. *Thinking from the Underside of History: Enrique Dussel's Philosophy of Liberation*. Lanham, MD: Rowman & Littlefield, 2000.

Allen, Sarah. *The Philosophical Sense of Transcendence: Levinas and Plato on Loving Beyond Being*. Pittsburgh: Duquesne University Press, 2009.

Ambrose. *Exposition of the Holy Gospel according to Saint Luke; with, Fragments on the Prophecy of Isaias*. Translated by Theodosia Tomkinson. Etna, CA: Center for Traditionalist Orthodox Studies, 1998.

Ammicht-Quinn, Regina. "Cult, Culture and Ambivalence: Images and Imaginations of the Body in Christian Traditions and Contemporary Lifestyles." In *Fluid Flesh: The Body, Religion, and the Visual Arts*, edited by Barbara Baert, 67–81. Leuven, BE: Leuven University Press, 2009.

———. *Von Lissabon Bis Auschwitz: Zum Paradigmawechsel in Der Theodizeefrage*. Studien Zur Theologischen Ethik: Etudes D'éthique Chrétienne. Freiburg, DE: Herder, 1992.

———. "Whose Dignity is Inviolable?: Human Beings, Machines and the Discourse of Dignity," in *Concilium* 2003/2, edited by Ammicht-Quinn et al. London: SCM, 2010.

Ammicht-Quinn, Regina, Maureen Junker-Kenny, and Elsa Tamez, eds. *The Discourse of Human Dignity*. London: SCM, 2003.

Ammicht-Quinn, Regina, and Elsa Tamez. *The Body and Religion*. Concilium 2002/2. London: SCM, 2002.

Ammicht-Quinn, Regina, Marie-Theres Wacker, Diego Irarrázabal, and Felix Wilfred. *Evil Today and Struggles to Be Human*. Concilium 2009/1. London: SCM, 2009.

Anderson, Carl A., and José Granados. *Called to Love: Approaching John Paul II's Theology of the Body*. New York: Doubleday, 2009.

Aristotle. *The Nicomachean Ethics*. Translated by W. D. Ross and Lesley Brown. Oxford: Oxford University Press, 2009.

Atkins, Kim. *Self and Subjectivity*. Oxford: Blackwell, 2005.

Augustine. *The Confessions*. Translated by Maria Boulding and John E. Rotelle. New York: New City, 1997.

———. *On Christian Doctrine*. Translated by J. J. Shaw. Mineola, NY: Dover, 2009.

———. *St. Augustine on the Spirit and the Letter.* Translated by W. J. Sparrow Simpson. London: SPCK, 1925.

———. *The Trinity.* Translated by Edmund Hill. Edited by John E. Rotelle. New York: New City, 1991.

Azevedo, Marcello de Carvalho. *Basic Ecclesial Communities in Brazil: The Challenge of a New Way of Being Church.* Washington, DC: Georgetown University Press, 1987.

Badiou, Alain. *Ethics: An Essay on the Understanding of Evil.* London: Verso, 2002.

Baert, Barbara. *Fluid Flesh: The Body, Religion and the Visual Arts.* Lieven Gevaert. Leuven, BE: Leuven University Press, 2009.

Balthasar, Hans Urs von. *The Glory of the Lord: A Theological Aesthetics.* Translated by Joseph Fessio and John Kenneth Riches. Edinburgh: T & T Clark, 1982.

———. *Love Alone.* Translated by Johannes Verlag. New York: Herder and Herder, 1969.

———. *Martin Buber and Christianity.* Translated by Einsame Zwiesprache. London: Harvill, 1960.

———. *Theo-Drama: Theological Dramatic Theory.* Translated by Graham Harrison. 5 vols. San Francisco: Ignatius, 1988.

———. *A Theological Anthropology.* Eugene, OR: Wipf & Stock, 2010.

Barth, Karl. *Church Dogmatics. Vol. 3, the Doctrine of Creation.* Translated by Geoffrey William Bromiley and Thomas Forsyth Torrance. 4 vols. Edinburgh: T & T Clark, 1958.

Beattie, Tina. *New Catholic Feminism: Theology and Theory.* London/New York: Routledge, 2006.

Beavers, Anthony. "Emmanuel Levinas and the Prophetic Voice of Postmodernity." In *"Andiron" Lecture at the University of Evansville,* 1993. Published by the author. Online: http://faculty.evansville.edu/tb2/PDFs/PropheticVoice.pdf

Bell, Vikki. "On Ethics and Feminism: Reflecting on Levinas' Ethics of Non-(in) Difference." *Feminist Theory* 2.2 (2009) 159–71.

Benedict XVI. *Caritas in Veritate: On Integral Human Development in Charity and Truth.* San Francisco: Ignatius, 2009.

———. *Deus Caritas Est: Encyclical Letter on Christian Love.* San Francisco: Ignatius, 2006.

———. *Values in a Time of Upheaval.* New York: Ignatius, 2006.

Benhabib, Seyla. *Situating the Self: Gender, Community and Postmodernism in Contemporary Ethics.* Cambridge: Polity, 1992.

Benson, Bruce Ellis, and Norman Wirzba. *Words of Life: New Theological Turns in French Phenomenology.* New York: Fordham University Press, 2010.

Bernasconi, Robert. "The Truth That Accuses: Conscience, Shame, and Guilt in Levinas and Augustine." In *The Ethics of Postmodernity: Current Trends in Continental Thought,* edited by Gary Brent Madison and Marty Fairbairn, 24–34. Evanston, IL: Northwestern University Press, 1999.

Bernasconi, Robert, and Simon Critchley, eds. *Re-Reading Levinas.* Studies in Continental Thought. London: Athlone, 1991.

Bernasconi, Robert, and David Wood. *The Provocation of Levinas: Rethinking the Other.* London: Routledge, 1988.

Bernstein, Richard J. *The New Constellation: The Ethical-Political Horizons of Modernity/ Postmodernity.* Cambridge: Polity, 1991.

Bertens, Johannes Willem, and Joseph P. Natoli. *Postmodernism: The Key Figures.* Oxford: Blackwell, 2002.

Bevis, Kathryn. "'Better Than Metaphors'? Dwelling and the Maternal Body in Emmanuel Levinas." *Literature & Theology* 21.3 (2007) 317–29.

Bloechl, Jeffrey, ed. *The Face of the Other and the Trace of God: Essays on the Philosophy of Emmanuel Levinas.* New York: Fordham University Press, 2000.

Blond, Phillip. *Post-Secular Philosophy: Between Philosophy and Theology.* London: Routledge, 1998.

Braybrooke, Marcus, and Tony Bayfield. *Christian-Jewish Dialogue: The Next Steps.* London: SCM, 2000.

Buber, Martin. *Between Man and Man.* Translated by Ronald Gregor Smith and Maurice Friedman. New York: Collier, 1965.

———. *I and Thou.* Translated by Ronald Gregor Smith. London: Continuum, 2004.

Bulgakov, Sergei Nikolaevich. *The Burning Bush: On the Orthodox Veneration of the Mother of God.* Translated by T. Allan Smith. Grand Rapids: Eerdmans, 2009.

Burggraeve, Roger. *The Awakening to the Other: A Provocative Dialogue with Emmanuel Levinas.* Leuven, BE: Peeters, 2008.

Buttiglione, Rocco. *Karol Wojtyla: The Thought of the Man Who Became Pope John Paul II.* Grand Rapids: Eerdmans, 1997.

Calin, Rodolphe, and François-David Sebbah. *Le Vocabulaire De Lévinas.* Vocabulaire De. Paris: Ellipses, 2002.

Candler, Peter M., and Conor Cunningham, eds. *Transcendence and Phenomenology.* London: SCM, 2007.

Caputo, John D. *Against Ethics: Contributions to a Poetics of Obligation with Constant Reference to Deconstruction.* Bloomington, IN: Indiana University Press, 1993.

———. *Heidegger and Aquinas: An Essay on Overcoming Metaphysics.* New York: Fordham University Press, 1982.

Caputo, John D., and Michael J. Scanlon, eds. *God, the Gift, and Postmodernism.* Bloomington, IN: Indiana University Press, 1999.

Catholic Church. *Catechism of the Catholic Church.* Vatican City: Libreria Editrice Vaticana, 1997.

———. *Compendium of the Catechism of the Catholic Church.* London: Catholic Truth Society, 2006.

———. "The Final Report of the 1985 Extraordinary Synod." Vatican City, 1985.

———. "Gaudium Et Spes: Pastoral Constitution on the Church in the Modern World." Vatican City 1965.

———. "Lumen Gentium: Dogmatic Constitution on the Church." Vatican City 1964.

———. "Sacrosanctum Concilium." In *Second Vatican Council.* Vatican City, 1963.

Chanter, Tina. *Feminist Interpretations of Emmanuel Levinas.* University Park, PA: Pennsylvania State University Press, 2001.

Chauvet, Louis-Marie. "Editorial: Liturgy and the Body." *Concilium, Liturgy and the Body* 1995.3 (1995) vii–x.

———. *The Sacraments: The Word of God at the Mercy of the Body.* Translated by Thomas Shanahan. Collegeville, MN: Liturgical, 2001.

———. *Symbol and Sacrament: A Sacramental Reinterpretation of Christian Existence.* Translated by Patrick and Beaumont Madigan, Madeleine. Collegeville. MN: Liturgical, 1995.

Chesterton, G. K. *The Everlasting Man.* London: Hodder & Stoughton, 1925.

Ciocan, Cristian, and Georges Hansel. *Levinas Concordance*. Dordrecht, NL: Springer, 2005.

Coakley, Sarah. "Religion and the Body." In *Religion and the Body*, edited by Sarah Coakley, 1–13. Cambridge: Cambridge University Press, 1997.

———. "Rethinking the Sex Crises in Catholicism and Anglicanism." *ABC Religion and Ethics* (2010). Online: http://www.abc.net.au/religion/articles/2010/07/14/2953473.htm.

———. "Why Gift? Gift, Gender and Trinitarian Relations in Milbank and Tanner." *Scottish Journal of Theology* 61.2 (2008) 224–35.

Cohen, Richard A. *Elevations: The Height of the Good in Rosenzweig and Levinas*. Chicago: University of Chicago Press, 1994.

———. *Face to Face with Levinas*. Albany, NY: State University of New York Press, 1986.

Congar, Yves. *A History of Theology*. Translated by Hunter Guthric. Garden City, NY: Doubleday, 1968.

Cornwell, John. *Hitler's Pope: The Secret History of Pius XII*. New York: Viking, 1999.

———. *The Pontiff in Winter: Triumph and Conflict in the Reign of John Paul II*. New York: Doubleday, 2004.

Cortez, Marc. *Embodied Souls, Ensouled Bodies: An Exercise in Christological Anthropology and Its Significance for the Mind/Body Debate*. London: T & T Clark, 2008.

Critchley, Simon. "Five Problems in Levinas's View of Politics and the Sketch of a Solution to Them." *Political Theory* 32.2 (2004) 172–85.

Critchley, Simon, and Robert Bernasconi, eds. *The Cambridge Companion to Levinas*. Cambridge: Cambridge University Press, 2002.

Curran, Charles E. *The Moral Theology of Pope John Paul II*. London: T & T Clark, 2006.

D'Costa, Gavin. *Resurrection Reconsidered*. Oxford: Oneworld, 1996.

———. *Sexing the Trinity: Gender, Culture and the Divine*. London: SCM, 2000.

Dalin, David G. *The Myth of Hitler's Pope: How Pope Pius XII Rescued Jews from the Nazis*. Washington, DC: Regnery, 2005.

Dalton, Drew M. *Longing for the Other: Levinas and Metaphysical Desire*. Pittsburgh: Duquesne University Press, 2009.

Davies, Norman. *God's Playground: A History of Poland in Two Volumes*. 2 vols. Oxford: Oxford University Press, 2005.

Davis, Stephen T., Daniel Kendall, and Gerald O'Collins, eds. *The Resurrection: An Interdisciplinary Symposium on the Resurrection of Jesus*. Oxford: Oxford University Press, 1998.

de Paulo, C. J. N. "The Augustinian Constitution of Heidegger's Being and Time." *American Catholic Philosophical Quarterly* 77.4 (2003) 549–68.

Derrida, Jacques. *Adieu to Emmanuel Levinas*. Translated by Pascale-Anne Brault and Michael Naas. Stanford: Stanford University Press, 1999.

———. *The Gift of Death*. Translated by David Wills. Chicago: University of Chicago Press, 2008.

———. *Given Time. 1, Counterfeit Money*. Translated by Peggy Kamuf. Chicago: University of Chicago Press, 1992.

———. *La Voix Et Le Phénomène: Introduction Au Problème Du Signe Dans La Phénoménologie De Husserl*. Paris: Presses Universitaires de France, 1976.

————. *Memoires: For Paul De Man*. Rev. ed. New York: Columbia University Press, 1989.

————. *Of Grammatology*. Translated by Gayatri Chakravorty Spivak. Baltimore: Johns Hopkins University Press, 1997.

————. *On Cosmopolitanism and Forgiveness*. London: Routledge, 2001.

————. *Speech and Phenomena, and Other Essays on Husserl's Theory of Signs*. Evanston, IL: Northwestern University Press, 1973.

————. *Writing and Difference*. Translated by Alan Bass. Routledge Classics. London: Routledge, 2001.

Desmond, William. *Desire, Dialectic, and Otherness: An Essay on Origins*. New Haven: Yale University Press, 1987.

————. *Ethics and the Between*. Albany, NY: State University of New York Press, 2001.

Diprose, Rosalyn. *Corporeal Generosity: On Giving with Nietzsche, Merleau-Ponty, and Levinas*. Albany, NY: State University of New York Press, 2002.

Dulles, Avery Robert. *The Splendor of Faith: The Theological Vision of Pope John Paul II*. New York: Crossroad, 1999.

Duncan, Roger. "Emmanuel Levinas in the Light of Fides Et Ratio." *Communio: International Catholic Review* 29 (2002) 107–32.

Duns, S. J., and G. Ryan. "Being in the Face of Nameless Mystery: Levinas and the Trace of Doctrine." *Heythrop Journal* 49 (2008) 97–109.

Eden, Dawn. "Towards A 'Climate of Chastity': Bringing Catechesis on the Theology of the Body into the Hermeneutic of Continuity." Washington, DC: Pontifical Faculty of the Immaculate Conception at Dominican House of Studies, 2010.

Elshtain, Jean Bethke. *Who Are We?: Critical Reflections and Hopeful Possibilities*. Grand Rapids: Eerdmans, 2000.

Emery, Gilles. *The Trinitarian Theology of Saint Thomas Aquinas*. Oxford: Oxford University Press, 2007.

"Essential Articles and Resources." In *Pope Pius XII and the Jews*, 2011. Online: http://popepiusxiiandthejews.blogspot.com.au/

Fagan, Madeleine. "The Inseparability of Ethics and Politics: Rethinking the Third in Emmanuel Levinas." *Contemporary Political Theory* 8.1 (2009) 5–22.

Ferrone, Rita. *Liturgy: Sacrosanctum Concilium*. New York: Paulist, 2007.

Feuerbach, Ludwig. *Principles of the Philosophy of the Future*. Indianapolis: Hackett, 1986.

Ford, David. *Self and Salvation: Being Transformed*. Cambridge Studies in Christian Doctrine. Cambridge: Cambridge University Press, 1999.

Foucault, Michel. *Discipline and Punish: The Birth of the Prison*. Translated by Alan Sheridan. New York: Random House, 1995.

————. *The History of Sexuality, Vol II: The Use of Pleasure*. Translated by Robert Hurley. London: Penguin, 1992.

————. *The Order of Things: An Archaeology of the Human Sciences*. London: Routledge, 2005.

Ghislain, de Barmon. *Jean-Paul II Professeur D'amour: Lecture D'amour Et Responsabilité De Karol Wojtyla*. Paris: François-Xavier de Guibert, 2004.

Gibbs, Robert. *Correlations in Rosenzweig and Levinas*. Princeton: Princeton University Press, 1992.

Gillis, Chester. *The Political Papacy: John Paul II, Benedict XVI, and Their Influence*. London: Paradigm, 2006.

Glendinning, Simon. *In the Name of Phenomenology*. London: Routledge, 2007.

Graef, Hilda C. *Mary: A History of Doctrine and Devotion*. Translated by Thomas A. Thompson. Notre Dame, IN: Christian Classics, 2009.

Granados, José. "Toward a Theology of the Suffering Body." *Communio* 33 (2006) 540–63.

Gregg, Samuel. *Challenging the Modern World: Karol Wojtya/John Paul II and the Development of Catholic Social Teaching*. Lanham, MD: Lexington, 1998.

Gregory. *On God and Christ: The Five Theological Orations and Two Letters to Cledonius*. Translated by Frederick Williams and Lionel R. Wickham. Crestwood, NY: St. Vladimir's Seminary Press, 2002.

Grignon de Montfort, Louis Marie. *A Treatise on the True Devotion to the Blessed Virgin*. Translated by Frederick William Faber. London: Robson, Levey, and Franklyn, 1863.

Grondelski, John M. "Sources for the Study of Karol Wojtyła's Thought, Appendix." In *At the Centre of the Human Drama*, written by Kenneth L. Schmitz. Washington, DC: Catholic University of America Press, 1993.

Gutiérrez, Gustavo. *A Theology of Liberation: History, Politics, and Salvation*. Translated by John Eagleson and Caridad Inda. London: SCM, 1988.

Hannaford, Robert, and J'annine Jobling, eds. *Theology and the Body: Gender, Text and Ideology*. Leominster, UK: Gracewing, 1999.

Hart, David Bentley. *The Beauty of the Infinite: The Aesthetics of Christian Truth*. Grand Rapids: Eerdmans, 2003.

Hart, Kevin, ed. *Counter-Experiences: Reading Jean-Luc Marion*. Notre Dame, IN: University of Notre Dame Press, 2007.

Hart, Kevin. *The Trespass of the Sign: Deconstruction, Theology and Philosophy*. Cambridge: Cambridge University Press, 1989.

Hart, Kevin, and Michael Alan Signer, eds. *The Exorbitant: Emmanuel Levinas between Jews and Christians*. New York: Fordham University Press, 2010.

Harvey, David. *The Condition of Postmodernity: An Enquiry into the Origins of Cultural Change*. Oxford: Blackwell, 1989.

Hayes, Michael A., and Gerald O'Collins, eds. *The Legacy of John Paul II*. London: Burns & Oates, 2008.

Heidegger, Martin. *Being and Time*. Translated by John Macquarrie and Edward Robinson. London: SCM, 1962.

Hemming, Laurence Paul. "A Transcendental Hangover: Lévinas, Heidegger and the Ethics of Alterity." *Studies in Christian Ethics* 18.2 (2005) 45–65.

Hildebrand, Alice von. "Dietrich Von Hildebrand, Catholic Philosopher, and Christopher West, Modern Enthusiast: Two Very Different Approaches to Love, Marriage and Sex." *Catholic News Agency*, 2010. Online: http://www.catholiceducation.org/en/marriage-and-family/sexuality/dietrich-von-hildebrand-catholic-philosopher-and-christopher-west-modern-enthusiast-two-very-dif.html

Holloway, Carson. *The Way of Life: John Paul II and the Challenge of Liberal Modernity*. Waco, TX: Baylor University Press, 2008.

Holy See. "Fundamental Agreement between the Holy See and the State of Israel." Israel Ministry of Foreign Affairs, 1993.

Horace. *The Odes*. Translated by Robert Bly and J. D. McClatchy. Princeton: Princeton University Press, 2002.

Husserl, Edmund. *Cartesian Meditations: An Introduction to Phenomenology*. Translated by Dorion Cairns. The Hague: Nijhoff, 1993.

———. *Logical Investigations*. Translated by J. N. Findlay. London: Routledge, 1970.

Hutchens, B. C. *Levinas: A Guide for the Perplexed*. New York: Continuum, 2004.

Irenaeus. *Against the Heresies*. Translated by John J. Dillon and Dominic J. Unger. New York: Paulist, 1992.

Janicaud, Dominique. *Phenomenology and The "Theological Turn": The French Debate*. New York: Fordham University Press, 2000.

Jeal, Roy R. *Human Sexuality and the Nuptial Mystery*. Eugene, OR: Cascade, 2010.

Jeanrond, Werner G. *A Theology of Love*. London: T & T Clark, 2010.

Jeeves, Malcolm A., ed. *Rethinking Human Nature: A Multidisciplinary Approach*. Grand Rapids: Eerdmans, 2010.

John of the Cross. *John of the Cross: Selected Writings*. Edited by Kieran Kavanaugh. New York: Paulist, 1987.

John Paul II. *The Acting Person*. Translated by Anna-Teresa Tymieniecka. Analecta Husserliana. Dordrecht, NL: D. Reidel, 1979.

———. "Address of John Paul II to the Representatives of Jewish Organizations." *Apostolic Journey to the United States of American and Canada* (1987). Online: http://w2.vatican.va/content/john-paul-ii/en/speeches/1979/march/documents/hf_jp-ii_spe_19790312_org-ebraiche.html

———. *Crossing the Threshold of Hope*. Translated by Vittorio Messori. London: Cape, 1994.

———. *Dies Domine: Apostolic Letter on Keeping the Lord's Day Holy*. Vatican City: Catholic Truth Society, 1998.

———. *Dives in Misericordia: Rich in Mercy*. London: Catholic Truth Society, 1980.

———. *Dominicae Cenae: Apostolic Letter on the Mystery and Worship of the Eucharist*. Boston: St. Paul Editions, 1980.

———. *Dominum Et Vivificantem: The Giver of Life*. London: Catholic Media Office, 1986.

———. *Ecclesia De Eucharistia: Encyclical Letter on the Eucharist in Its Relationship to the Church*. London: Catholic Truth Society, 2003.

———. *Evangelium Vitae: The Gospel of Life*. New York: Random House, 1995.

———. *Faith According to St. John of the Cross*. Translated by Jordan Aumann. San Francisco: Ignatius, 1981.

———. *Familiaris Consortio: Regarding the Role of the Christian Family in the Modern World*. Vatican City: Vatican Polyglot, 1981.

———. *Fides Et Ratio: Encyclical Letter on the Relationship between Faith and Reason*. London: Catholic Truth Society, 1998.

———. *The Jeweler's Shop: A Meditation on the Sacrament of Matrimony, Passing on Occasion into a Drama*. Translated by Boleslaw Taborski. San Francisco: Ignatius, 1992.

———. *Love and Responsibility*. Translated by H. T. Willetts. London: Collins, 1981.

———. *Man and Woman He Created Them: A Theology of the Body*. Translated by Michael Waldstein. Boston: Pauline, 2006.

———. *Man in the Field of Responsibility*. Translated by Kenneth W. Kemp and Zuzanna Maślanka. South Bend, IN: St. Augustine's Press, 2011.

———. *Mane Nobiscum Domine: Apostolic Letter for the Year of the Eucharist October 2004–October 2005*. Dublin: Veritas, 2004.

———. "Mary Leads Us to Eucharist: Message to 19th International Marian Congress Czestochowa, Poland." Castel Gandolfo, 1996. Online: http://www.ewtn.com/library/PAPALDOC/JP96-815.HTM

———. *Memory and Identity: Conversations at the Dawn of a Millennium*. New York: Rizzoli, 2005.

———. "Message of His Holiness John Paul II on the 50th Anniversary of the Warsaw Ghetto Uprising." Vatican City, 1993.

———. *Ocena Mozliwosci Zbudowania Etyki Chrzescijanskiej Przy Zaozeniach Systemu Maksa Schelera*. Lublin, PL: Tow. Naukowe Katolickiego Uniwersytetu Lubelskiego, 1950.

———. *Pastores Dabo Vobis: Post-Synodal Apostolic Exhortation*. Washington, DC: United States Catholic Conference, 1992.

———. *Person and Community: Selected Essays*. Translated by Theresa Sandok. New York: Lang, 1993.

———. *Personne Et Acte*. Translated by Gwendoline Jarczyk. Saint-Maur (Val-de-Marne), FR: Parole et silence, 2011.

———. *Redemptor Hominis: The Redeemer of Man*. Washington, DC: United States Catholic Conference, 1979.

———. *Redemptoris Mater: On the Blessed Virgin Mary in the Life of the Pilgrim Church*. London: Catholic Truth Society, 2003.

———. *Rise, Let Us Be on Our Way*. Translated by Walter Ziemba. New York: Warner, 2004.

———. *Rosarium Virginis Mariae: Apostolic Letter on the Most Holy Rosary*. London: Catholic Truth Society, 2002.

———. *Salvifici Doloris: On the Christian Meaning of Human Suffering*. Washington, DC: United States Catholic Conference, 1984.

———. *Sign of Contradiction*. Translated by Mary Smith. London: Chapman, 1979.

———. "Speech to the Jewish Community of Rome." Rome: The Vatican, 1986.

———. *The Theology of the Body: Human Love in the Divine Plan*. Reprinted from the English edition of *L'Osservatore Romano*. Boston: Pauline, 1997.

———. *The Trinity's Embrace, God's Saving Plan: A Catechesis on Salvation History*. Boston: Pauline, 2002.

———. *Veritatis Splendor: The Splendor of Truth*. Boston: St. Paul, 1993.

Kamionkowski, S. Tamar, and Wonil Kim. *Bodies, Embodiment, and Theology of the Hebrew Bible*. London: T & T Clark, 2010.

Kant, Immanuel. *Critique of Practical Reason*. Translated by Werner S. Pluhar. Indianapolis: Hackett, 2002.

———. *Critique of the Power of Judgment*. Translated by Paul Guyer. Cambridge: Cambridge University Press, 2001.

———. *Groundwork for the Metaphysics of Morals*. Translated by Thomas E. Hill and Arnulf Zweig. Oxford: Oxford University Press, 2002.

Katz, Claire Elise. *Levinas, Judaism, and the Feminine: The Silent Footsteps of Rebecca*. Bloomington, IN: Indiana University Press, 2003.

Kemp-Welch, A. *Poland under Communism: A Cold War History*. Cambridge: Cambridge University Press, 2008.

Kerr, Fergus. *Twentieth-Century Catholic Theologians: From Neoscholasticism to Nuptial Mysticism*. Oxford: Blackwell, 2007.

Kosky, Jeffrey L. *Levinas and the Philosophy of Religion*. Bloomington, IN: Indiana University Press, 2001.

Kupczak, Jaroslaw. "The Meaning of Theological Anthropology in the Teaching of John Paul II." John Paul II Cultural Center, 2002. Online: http://jp2forum.org/articles_about_pope/god_and_man/kupczak_on_wojtyla.pdf

Lacoste, Jean-Yves. *Experience and the Absolute: Disputed Questions on the Humanity of Man*. Translated by Mark Raftery-Skehan. New York: Fordham University Press, 2004.

Lakeland, Paul. *Postmodernity: Christian Identity in a Fragmented Age*. Guides to Theological Inquiry. Minneapolis: Fortress, 1997.

Lawler, Ronald David. *The Christian Personalism of Pope John Paul II*. Chicago: Franciscan Herald, 1982.

Levinas, Emmanuel. *Altérité Et Transcendance*. Saint-Clément-la-Rivière, FR: Fata Morgana, 1995.

———. *Autrement Qu'etre Ou Au-Dela De L'essence*. Paris: Nijhoff, 1974.

———. *Beyond the Verse: Talmudic Readings and Lectures*. Translated by Gary D. Mole. Bloomington, IN: Indiana University Press, 1994.

———. *Collected Philosophical Papers*. Translated by Alphonso Lingis, Phaenomenologica. Dordrecht: Nijhoff, 1987.

———. *De L'existence Ý L'existant*. Paris: Vrin, 1990.

———. *Difficile Liberté: Essais Sur Le Judaïsme*. Paris: Michel, 1976.

———. *Difficult Freedom: Essays on Judaism*. Translated by Seán Hand. Baltimore: Johns Hopkins University Press, 1990.

———. *Discovering Existence with Husserl*. Translated by Richard A. Cohen and Michael B. Smith. Evanston, IL: Northwestern University Press, 1998.

———. *Emmanuel Levinas: Basic Philosophical Writings*. Translated by Adriaan Theodoor Peperzak, Simon Critchley, and Robert Bernasconi. Bloomington, IN: Indiana University Press, 1996.

———. *Existence and Existents*. Translated by Alphonso Lingis. The Hague: Nijhoff, 1978.

———. *God, Death and Time*. Translated by Bettina Bergo. Stanford: Stanford University Press, 2000.

———. *In the Time of the Nations*. Translated by Michael B. Smith. London: Athlone, 1994.

———. *Is It Righteous to Be?: Interviews with Emmanuel Levinas*. Translated by Jill Robbins. Stanford: Stanford University Press, 2001.

———. *Le Temps Et L'autre*. Paris: Presses universitaires de France, 1983.

———. *New Talmudic Readings*. Pittsburgh: Duquesne University Press, 1999.

———. *Nine Talmudic Readings*. Translated by Annette Aronowicz. Bloomington, IN: Indiana University Press, 1990.

———. *Noms Propres: Agnon, Buber, Celan, Delhomme, Derrida, Jabès, Kierkegaard, Lacroix, Laporte, Picard, Proust, Van Breda, Wahl*. Montpellier, FR: Fata Morgana, 1976.

———. "Notes Sur La Pensée Philosophique Du Cardinal Wojtyla." *Communio* 4 (1980) 87–90.

———. *Of God Who Comes to Mind*. Translated by Bettina Bergo. Stanford: Stanford University Press, 1998.

————. *On Thinking-of-the-Other*. Translated by Barbara Harshav and Michael B. Smith. London: Athlone, 1998.

————. *Otherwise Than Being, Or, Beyond Essence*. Translated by Alphonso Lingis. Pittsburgh: Duquesne University Press, 1998.

————. *Proper Names*. Translated by Michael B. Smith. Stanford: Stanford University Press, 1996.

————. *Théorie De L'intuition Dans La Phénoménologie De Husserl*. Paris: Vrin, 1963.

————. *The Theory of Intuition in Husserl's Phenomenology*. Translated by Andre Orianne. Evanston, IL: Northwestern University Press, 1995.

————. *Time and the Other and Additional Essays*. Translated by Richard A. Cohen. Pittsburgh: Duquesne University Press, 1987.

————. *Totalité Et Infini; Essai Sur L'extériorité*. La Haye [The Hague]: Nijhoff, 1961.

————. *Totality and Infinity: An Essay on Exteriority*. Translated by Alphonso Lingis. Pittsburgh: Duquesne University Press, 1969.

Lipari, Lisbeth. "Listening for the Other: Ethical Implications of the Buber-Levinas Encounter." *Communication Theory* 14.2 (2004) 122–41.

Loughlin, Gerard. *Alien Sex: The Body and Desire in Cinema and Theology*. Oxford: Blackwell, 2004.

Loumanksy, Amanda. "Reply to Fagan. Hanging God at Auschwitz: The Necessity of a Solitary Encounter with the Other as the Genesis of Levinasian Ethics." *Contemporary Political Theory* 8.1 (2009) 23–43.

Lubac, Henri de. *At the Service of the Church: Henri De Lubac Reflects on the Circumstances That Occasioned His Writings*. Translated by Anne Elizabeth Englund. San Francisco: Ignatius, 1993.

Ludwig, Paul W. *Eros and Polis: Desire and Community in Greek Political Theory*. Cambridge: Cambridge University Press, 2002.

Luxmoore, Jonathan, and Janusz A. Ihnatowicz. "How an Unknown Text Could Throw New Light on John Paul II's Views on Economics." *Houston Catholic Worker*, 1 June 2007.

Lyotard, Jean-François. *The Postmodern Condition: A Report on Knowledge*. Translated by Geoffrey Bennington and Brian Massumi. Manchester: Manchester University Press, 1984.

Malka, Salomon. *Emmanuel Levinas: His Life and Legacy*. Pittsburgh: Duquesne University Press, 2006.

Mannion, Gerard. *The Vision of John Paul II: Assessing His Thought and Influence*. Collegeville, MN: Liturgical, 2008.

Mansfield, Nick. *The God Who Deconstructs Himself: Sovereignty and Subjectivity between Freud, Bataille, and Derrida*. New York: Fordham University Press, 2010.

Marion, Jean-Luc. *Being Given: Toward a Phenomenology of Givenness*. Translated by Jeffrey L. Kosky. Stanford: Stanford University Press, 2002.

————. *The Erotic Phenomenon*. Translated by Stephen E. Lewis. Chicago: University of Chicago Press, 2007.

————. *God without Being: Hors-Texte*. Translated by Thomas A. Carlson. Religion and Postmodernism. Chicago: University of Chicago Press, 1991.

————. *The Idol and Distance: Five Studies*. Translated by Thomas A. Carlson. New York: Fordham University Press, 2001.

————. *In Excess: Studies of Saturated Phenomena*. Translated by Robyn Horner and Vincent Berraud. New York: Fordham University Press, 2002.

———. "They Recognized Him; and He Became Invisible to Them." *Modern Theology* 18.2 (2002) 145–52.

Marx, Karl, and Friedrich Engels. *The Communist Manifesto*. Translated by L. M. Findlay. Peterborough, UK: Broadview, 2004.

Mauss, Marcel. *The Gift: Forms and Functions of Exchange in Archaic Societies*. Translated by Ian Cunnison. London: Cohen & West, 1969.

May, Todd. *Reconsidering Difference: Nancy, Derrida, Levinas, and Deleuze*. University Park, PA: Pennsylvania State University Press, 1997.

Mayama, Alain. *Emmanuel Levinas' Conceptual Affinities with Liberation Theology*. New York: Lang, 2010.

McAleer, G. J. *Ecstatic Morality and Sexual Politics: A Catholic and Antitotalitarian Theory of the Body*. New York: Fordham University Press, 2005.

McNerney, John. *John Paul II: Poet and Philosopher*. New York: Continuum, 2004.

Meir, Ephraim. *Levinas's Jewish Thought: Between Jerusalem and Athens*. Jerusalem: Hebrew University Magnes Press, 2008.

Mensch, James R. *Hiddenness and Alterity: Philosophical and Literary Sightings of the Unseen*. Pittsburgh: Duquesne University Press, 2005.

Merleau-Ponty, Maurice. *Phenomenology of Perception*. Translated by Donald A. Landes. London: Routledge, 2004.

———. *Le visible et l'invisible: suivi de notes de travail*. Tel 36. Paris: Éditions Gallimard, 1964.

Mettepenningen, Jürgen. *Nouvelle Théologie, New Theology: Inheritor of Modernism, Precursor of Vatican II*. London: T & T Clark, 2010.

Milbank, John. "Can a Gift Be Given?" *Modern Theology* 11 (1995) 119–61.

———. "The Ethics of Self Sacrifice." *First Things* 91 (1999) 33–38.

———. "Socialism of the Gift, Socialism by Grace." *New Blackfriars* 77.910 (2007) 532–48.

———. *The Word Made Strange: Theology, Language, Culture*. Oxford: Blackwell, 1997.

Modras, Ronald. "The Moral Philosophy of Pope John Paul II." *Theological Studies* 41.4 (1980) 683–97.

Moltmann, Jürgen. "The Resurrection of Nature: An Aspect of Cosmic Christology." *Concilium* 5 (2006) 81–89.

Moran, Dermot. *Introduction to Phenomenology*. London: Routledge, 2000.

Morgan, Michael L. *The Cambridge Introduction to Emmanuel Levinas*. Cambridge: Cambridge University Press, 2011.

———. *Discovering Levinas*. Cambridge: Cambridge University Press, 2007.

Morrison, Glenn. "Levinas, Von Balthasar and Trinitarian Praxis." PhD thesis, Australian Catholic University, 2004.

Mulligan, Kevin. "How Not to Read: Derrida on Husserl." *Topos: Continental Philosophy Analysed* 10 (1991) 199–208.

Nachef, Antoine. *The Mystery of the Trinity in the Theological Thought of Pope John Paul II*. New York: Lang, 1999.

Nichols, Aidan. *Scattering the Seed: A Guide through Balthasar's Early Writings on Philosophy and the Arts*. Washington, DC: Catholic University of America Press, 2006.

———. *Yves Congar*. London: Chapman, 1989.

Nietzsche, Friedrich. *Beyond Good and Evil: Prelude to a Philosophy of the Future*. Translated by Friedrich Wilhelm and R. J. Hollingdale. London: Penguin, 2003.

Nikulin, D. V. *On Dialogue*. Lanham, MD: Lexington, 2006.

O'Collins, Gerald. *Easter Faith: Believing in the Risen Jesus*. London: Darton Longman & Todd, 2003.

———. *The Tripersonal God: Understanding and Interpreting the Trinity*. London: Chapman, 1999.

O'Donovan, Oliver. "Pope John-Paul II." *Fulcrum* (2005) 1–5. Online: http://www.fulcrum-anglican.org.uk/articles/pope-john-paul-ii/

———. *Resurrection and Moral Order: An Outline for Evangelical Ethics*. Leicester, UK: IVP, 1986.

Osteen, Mark. *The Question of the Gift: Essays across Disciplines*. London: Routledge, 2002.

Ouellet, Marc. *Divine Likeness: Toward a Trinitarian Anthropology of the Family*. Grand Rapids: Eerdmans, 2006.

Panoff, Michel. "Marcel Mauss's 'The Gift' Revisited." *Man* 5.1 (1970) 60–70.

Pascal, Blaise. *Pensées*. Translated by Roger Ariew. Indianapolis: Hackett, 2005.

Paul VI. *Humanae Vitae, on the Regulation of Birth*. Vatican City, 1968.

Peddicord, Richard. *The Sacred Monster of Thomism: An Introduction to the Life and Legacy of Reginald Garrigou-Lagrange*. South Bend, IN: St. Augustine's Press, 2005.

"Phenomenology Represents an "Intellectual Charity," Says John Paul II." *Zenit* 24 March 2003.

Pickstock, Catherine. *After Writing: On the Liturgical Consummation of Philosophy*. Oxford: Blackwell, 1997.

———. "Liturgy and the Senses." *South Atlantic Quarterly* 109.4 (2010) 719–39.

Plato. *Phaedrus*. Translated by Robin Waterfield. Oxford: Oxford University Press, 2009.

———. *The Republic*. Translated by G. R. F. Ferrari and Tom Griffith. Cambridge: Cambridge University Press, 2000.

———. *Symposium*. Translated by K. J. Dover. Cambridge: Cambridge University Press, 1980.

Prażmowska, Anita. *Poland: A Modern History*. London: Palgrave Macmillan, 2010.

Purcell, Michael. "Christ the Stranger: The Ethical Originality of Homelessness." *Concilium* 5 (2008) 562–74.

———. "Glimpsing Grace Phenomenologically: Prevenience and Posteriority." *Irish Theological Quarterly* 73.1–2 (2008) 73–86.

———. *Levinas and Theology*. Cambridge: Cambridge University Press, 2006.

———. "'Levinas and Theology'? The Scope and Limits of Doing Theology with Levinas." *Heythrop Journal* XLIV.4 (2003) 468–79.

———. *Mystery and Method: The Other in Rahner and Levinas*. Milwaukee: Marquette, 1998.

———. "Nec Tamen Consumebatur. Exodus 3 and the Non-Consumable Other in the Philosophy of Emmanuel Levinas." *Scottish Journal of Theology* 48.1 (1995) 79–96.

———. "On Hesitation before the Other." *International Journal of Philosophy & Religion* 60 (2006) 9–19.

Putnam, Hilary. *Jewish Philosophy as a Guide to Life: Rosenzweig, Buber, Lévinas, Wittgenstein*. Bloomington, IN: Indiana University Press, 2008.

Ravaisson, Félix. *Of Habit*. Translated by Clare Carlisle and Mark Sinclair. London: Continuum, 2008.

Renaud-Chamska, Isabelle. "The Liturgy as Citation." *Concilium: Liturgy and the Body* 1995.3 (1995) 79–86.

Ricœur, Paul. *Figuring the Sacred: Religion, Narrative, and Imagination.* Translated by David Pellauer. Minneapolis: Fortress, 1995.

———. *Le Conflit Des Interprétations: Essais D'herméneutique.* L'ordre Philosophie. Paris: Editions du Seuil, 1969.

———. *Oneself as Another.* Chicago: University of Chicago Press, 1992.

Rogers, Eugene F. *Sexuality and the Christian Body: Their Way into the Triune God.* Challenges in Contemporary Theology. Oxford: Blackwell, 1999.

Rosenzweig, Franz. *The Star of Redemption.* Translated by Barbara E. Galli. Madison, WI: University of Wisconsin Press, 2005.

Rousseau, Jean-Jacques. *Emile, or, on Education.* New York: Basic, 1979.

Rowland, Tracey. *Culture and the Thomist Tradition: After Vatican II.* London: Routledge, 2003.

———. "In Search of Real Freedom." *The Tablet* 265.8893 (2011) 6–7.

———. "Natural Law: From Neo-Thomism to Nuptial Mysticism." *Communio: International Catholic Review* 35 (2008) 374–96.

Salzman, Todd A., and Michael G. Lawler. *The Sexual Person: Toward a Renewed Catholic Anthropology.* Washington, DC: Georgetown University Press, 2008.

Saward, John. *Christ Is the Answer: The Christ-Centred Teaching of Pope John Paul II.* Edinburgh: T & T Clark, 1995.

Schall, James V. "The Greatest of Men." *Ignatius Insight* (2010). Online: http://www.ignatiusinsight.com/features2010/schall_gweigeljp2_nov2010.asp

Schärtl, Thomas. "Metaphysical Aspects of the Concept of Resurrection." *Concilium* 5 (2006) 65–77.

Scheler, Max. *Formalism in Ethics and Non-Formal Ethics of Values: A New Attempt toward the Foundation of an Ethical Personalism.* Translated by Manfred S. Frings. Evanston, IL: Northwestern University Press, 1973.

———. *On the Eternal in Man.* Translated by Bernard Noble. London: SCM, 1960.

Schindler, David L. "The Embodied Person as Gift and the Cultural Task in America: Status Quaestionis." *Communio* 35 (2008) 397–431.

Schmitz, Kenneth L. *At the Center of the Human Drama: The Philosophical Anthropology of Karol Wojtyla/Pope John Paul II.* Washington, DC: Catholic University of America Press, 1993.

Schroeder, Brian, and Silvia Benso, eds. *Levinas and the Ancients.* Bloomington, IN: Indiana University Press, 2008.

Schumacher, Michele M. "The Unity of the Two: Toward a New Feminist Sacramentality of the Body." In *Women in Christ: Toward a New Feminism,* edited by Michele Schumacher, 201–31. Grand Rapids: Eerdmans, 2004.

Scola, Angelo. "Gli Interventi Di Karol Wojtyła Al Concilio Ecumenico Vaticano II: Esposizione Ed Interpretazione Teologica." In *Karol Wojtyła: Filosofo, Teologo, Poeta,* edited by Rocco Buttiglione et al., 129–34. Vatican City: Libreria Editrice Vaticana, 1984.

———. *The Nuptial Mystery.* Translated by Michelle K. Borras. Grand Rapids: Eerdmans, 2005.

———. "The Nuptial Mystery: A Perspective for Systematic Theology?" *Communio* 30.2 (2003) 209–33.

Scola, Angelo, and Margaret Harper McCarthy. "Jesus Christ, Our Resurrection and Life: On the Question of Eschatology." *Communio* 24 (1997) 311–25.

Séguin, Michel. "The Biblical Foundations of the Thought of John Paul II on Human Sexuality." *Communio* 20.2 (1993) 266–89.

Simmons, J. Aaron, and David Wood, eds. *Kierkegaard and Levinas: Ethics, Politics, and Religion.* Bloomington, IN: Indiana University Press, 2008.

Simpson, Peter. *On Karol Wojtyla.* Belmont, CA: Wadsworth, 2001.

Sipe, A. W. Richard. *Celibacy in Crisis: A Secret World Revisited.* New York: Brunner-Routledge, 2003.

Smith, A. D. *Routledge Philosophy Guidebook to Husserl and the Cartesian Meditations.* Routledge Philosophy Guidebooks. London: Routledge, 2003.

Sobrino, Jon. *The True Church and the Poor.* London: SCM, 1985.

Staehler, Tanja. *Plato and Levinas: The Ambiguous Out-Side of Ethics.* New York: Routledge, 2010.

Steeves, James B. *Imagining Bodies: Merleau-Ponty's Philosophy of Imagination.* Pittsburgh: Duquesne University Press, 2004.

Stuart, Elizabeth, and Adrian Thatcher. *Christian Perspectives on Sexuality and Gender.* Leominster, UK: Gracewing, 1996.

Sutton, Agneta. "The Complementarity and Symbolism of the Two Sexes: Karl Barth, Hans Urs Von Balthasar and John Paul II." *New Blackfriars* 87.1010 (2006) 418–33.

Tan, Matthew. "Bodies of Christ in Seas of Change: The Relationship between Ecclesiology, Politics and Practice in the Conditioning of Twentieth Century Roman Catholic Responses to Violence." PhD thesis, Australian Catholic University, 2009.

Tanner, Kathryn. "Economy of Grace." *Word & World* 2 (2010) 174–81.

Taylor, Mark C., ed. *Deconstruction in Context: Literature and Philosophy.* Chicago: University of Chicago Press, 1986.

Teresa, and David Lewis. *The Life of S. Teresa of Jesus, of the Order of Our Lady of Carmel.* London: Burns, Oates, & Co., 1870.

Thomas Aquinas. *Quaestiones Disputatae De Potentia.* Translated by English Dominican Fathers. Westminster, London: Newman, 1952.

———. *Summa Theologiae.* Translated by Thomas Gilby. 61 vols, Latin Text and English Translation, Introductions, Notes, Appendices, and Glossaries. London: Blackfriars & Eyre & Spottiswoode, 1964.

Torevell, David. *Losing the Sacred: Ritual, Modernity, and Liturgical Reform.* London: T & T Clark, 2004.

"Uniting Theology of the Body with Theology of Love." *Vatican Information Service,* 13 May 2011.

Unknown author. "Havamal, A Poem of the Scandanavian Edda." Translated in *The Theory of Social Economy,* vol. 2, by Gustav Cassel. London: Benn, 1932.

Vanhoozer, Kevin J. *The Cambridge Companion to Postmodern Theology.* Cambridge: Cambridge University Press, 2003.

Veling, Terry A. "In the Name of Who? Levinas and the Other Side of Theology." *Pacifica* 12 (1999) 275–92.

Villemot, Matthieu. *Dieu et la chair au 17ème siècle.* Parole et Silence/ Collège des Bernardins (Cours, colloques, conférences). Paris: Parole et Silence, 2010.

Vries, Hent de. *Minimal Theologies: Critiques of Secular Reason in Adorno and Levinas.* Baltimore: Johns Hopkins University Press, 2005.

Waldstein, Michael. "John Paul II and St. Thomas on Love and the Trinity (First Part)." *Anthropotes* 18.1 (2002) 113–38.

———. "John Paul II and St. Thomas on Love and the Trinity (Second Part)." *Anthropotes* 18.2 (2002) 269–86.

Wardley, Kenneth Jason. "'A Desire unto Death': The Deconstructive Thanatology of Jean-Luc Marion." *Heythrop Journal* 49 (2008) 79–96.

Webb, Mary-Ann. "Eros and Ethics: Levinas's Reading of Plato's 'Good Beyond Being.'" *Studies in Christian Ethics* 19.2 (2006) 205–22.

Webb, Stephen H. *The Gifting God: A Trinitarian Ethics of Excess.* New York: Oxford University Press, 1996.

———. "The Rhetoric of Ethics as Excess: A Christian Theological Response to Emmanuel Levinas." *Modern Theology* 15.1 (1999) 1–16.

Weigel, George. *Witness to Hope: The Biography of Pope John Paul II.* New York: Harper Collins, 2005.

Welton, Donn, ed. *The Body: Classic and Contemporary Readings.* Oxford: Blackwell, 1999.

West, Christopher. *Theology of the Body Explained: A Commentary on John Paul II's "Gospel of the Body."* Boston: Pauline Books & Media, 2003.

West, David. *Reason and Sexuality in Western Thought.* Cambridge: Polity, 2005.

Williams, George Huntston. *The Mind of John Paul II: Origins of His Thought and Action.* New York: Seabury, 1981.

Willis, Megan. "Language as the Sanctuary of Being: A Theological Exploration with Louis-Marie Chauvet." *Heythrop Journal* 51.5 (2010) 872–80.

Wirzba, Norman, and Bruce Ellis Benson, eds. *Transforming Philosophy and Religion: Love's Wisdom.* Bloomington, IN: Indiana University Press, 2008.

Wright, Tamra. *The Twilight of Jewish Philosophy: Emmanuel Levinas' Ethical Hermeneutics.* Amsterdam: Harwood Academic, 1999.

Wyschogrod, Edith. *Emmanuel Levinas: The Problem of Ethical Metaphysics.* New York: Fordham University Press, 2000.

Yeago, David S. "The Presence of Mary in the Mystery of the Church." *Nova et Vetera* 2.1 (2004) 147–68.

Žižek, Slavoj, Eric L. Santner, and Kenneth Reinhard. *The Neighbor: Three Inquiries in Political Theology.* Chicago: University of Chicago Press, 2005.

Scripture Index

Names Index

Subject *Index*

32960209R00211

Printed in Great Britain
by Amazon